The Firebird in Russian folklore is a fiery, illuminated bird; magical, iconic, coveted. Its feathers continue to glow when removed, and a single feather, it is said, can light up a room. Some who claim to have seen the Firebird say it even has glowing eyes. The Firebird is often the object of a quest. In one famous tale, the Firebird needs to be captured to prevent it from stealing the king's golden apples, a fruit bestowing youth and strength on those who partake of the fruit. But in other stories, the Firebird has another mission: it is always flying over the earth providing hope to any who may need it. In modern times and in the West, the Firebird has become part of world culture. In Igor Stravinsky's ballet *The Firebird,* it is a creature half-woman and half-bird, and the ballerina's role is considered by many to be the most demanding in the history of ballet.

The Overlook Press in the U.S. and Gerald Duckworth in the UK, in adopting the Firebird as the logo for its expanding Ardis publishing program, consider that this magical, glowing creature—in legend come to Russia from a faraway land—will play a role in bringing Russia and its literature closer to readers everywhere.

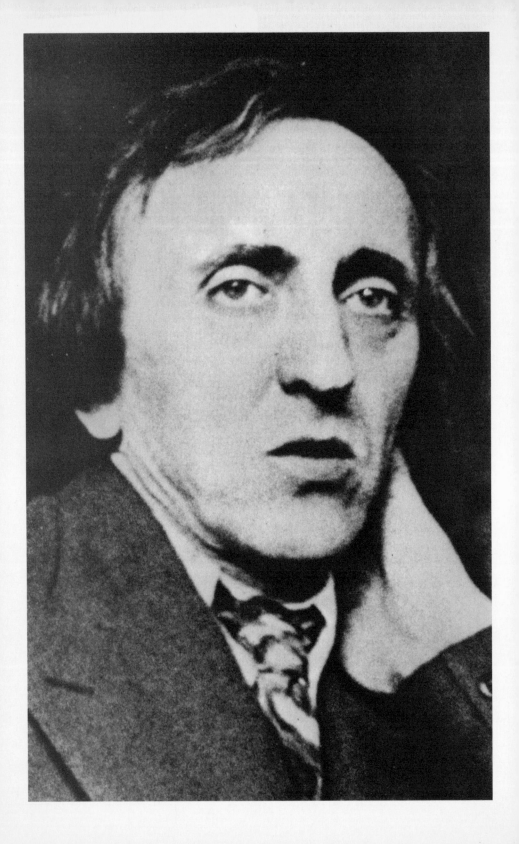

Theater as Life

Five Modern Plays

Nikolai Evreinov

Translated from the Russian and edited by
Christopher Collins

ARDIS PUBLISHERS
NEW YORK, NY

This edition published in the United States and the United Kingdom in 2012 by
Ardis Publishers, an imprint of Peter Mayer Publishers, Inc.

NEW YORK:
The Overlook Press
Peter Mayer Publishers, Inc.
141 Wooster Street
New York, NY 10012
www.overlookpress.com
For bulk and special sales, please contact sales@overlookny.com

LONDON:
Gerald Duckworth Publishers Ltd.
90-93 Cowcross Street
London EC1M 6BF
www.ducknet.co.uk
info@duckworth-publishers.co.uk

Printed in the United States of America
ISBN: 978-1-59020-900-4

2   4   6   8   10   9   7   5   3   1

Go to **www.ardisbooks.com** to read or download the latest Ardis catalog.

TABLE OF CONTENTS

ACKNOWLEDGEMENTS

In my work on Evreinov I am deeply grateful to:

—Anna Alexandrovna Evreinov, for her support and friendship, for the great help she gave me on my research in Paris on her late husband;

—The National Translation Center, for its encouragement and financial support for the translation of the plays in this collection;

—The taxpayers of the United States, for the fellowship (Fulbright-Hayes) I received for the study of Evreinov;

—Theater Wagon, a group of talented and warm people, for fine productions of three Evreinov plays;

—A few dear friends who have helped and shared.

FOREWORD

The modern plays of Nikolai Evreinov (1879-1953) have been produced in English in drama schools and little theaters in recent years with increasing frequency. His master of theater, his irony, his wild theatrical humor, his cheerfully cynical views of life, love, and society rarely fail to earn an enthusiastic reception—as this writer has seen many times—by audiences, performers, and critics. Yet texts of Evreinov plays in English translation have been almost non-existent—never done, poorly done, or merely long out of print.

With this collection I hope to make this master of the theater available to a larger audience, especially to actors, directors, producers. As a translator it has been my aim to be faithful to the original text, and as an actor, to give my fellow actors lines that speak well and play well. Three of the translations here have been refined through successful productions, and all have been read aloud again and again in hopes of producing the best possible lines for the stage—Evreinov's lines, not mine.

Those interested in producing Evreinov's plays should contact me for the scores of the zonky music Evreinov wrote for *A Merry Death* and *The Ship of the Righteous*. For information on recent productions of Evreinov by a Virginia group, and for the text of Evreinov's delightful one-act play for two actors, *Styopik and Manya*, I refer the reader to the anthology *Theater Wagon; Plays of Place and Any Place*, University of Virginia Press, 1973.

C. C.
Whitehall, Virginia 22987
September 3, 1973

Christopher Collins

NIKOLAI EVREINOV AS A PLAYWRIGHT

Noting the fine directors and actors in post-Revolutionary theater, many critics have lamented a seeming anomaly, the absence of equally fine playwrights. There was, however, one Russian whose plays were critical and box-office successes in pre-Revolutionary Russia, plays that were produced in leading European theaters by such lights as Luigi Pirandello, Jacques Copeau, and Charles Dullin. Had the party not chosen to proscribe[1] these by no means anti-regime plays and to drive into exile their still productive author, the history of the Soviet theater might look rather different today. The plays of Nikolai Evreinov are masterpieces of theater, broadly philosophical works with a modern—at times absurdist—point of view. Commenting on the success of these plays on the French stage, former Imperial Theater Director Serge Volkonsky argued that Evreinov must be considered Russia's only modern playwright.

Evreinov has been better known up to now as one of the three, four, or five greatest Russian regisseurs. He staged medieval plays at his Theater of Antiquity (*Starinny teatr*), replaced Meyerhold at Vera Komissarzhevsky's theater, was head regisseur at the Crooked Mirror Theater (*Krivoe zerkalo*) during its seven greatest years, directed the greatest mass spectacle in Russian history[2] and some of the grandest productions of Russian opera ever seen in Western Europe. He was also an aggressive, prolific writer on his theories of theatricality on the stage and in life, and an erudite and provocative writer on everything from the origins of drama to the art of Beardsley. His *History of the Russian Theater*[3] is regarded as one of the best in its field. A talented composer, he studied at the Conservatory with Rimsky-Korsakov. At social gatherings, such as the famed Repin Wednesdays, he charmed and fascinated everyone with his ability to improvise theatrical spectacles, juggle wine glasses, and play music on everything from the piano to combs and spoons.

Despite—or perhaps because of—his intimidating range of talents Evreinov is yet to be the subject of a comprehensive study. But several books on him are now underway in the West. There are also significant indications that some of his writings and plays—proscribed for forty years—will appear soon in his native Russia. Still, Evreinov the playwright is often unjustly overshadowed by Evreinov the regisseur or Evreinov the theorist. The present article seeks to draw attention to what I believe is Evreinov's most relevant talent today, his plays.

Before proceeding to a discussion of his plays, a few words on his biography are in order. Nikolai Nikolaevich Evreinov (of old Boyar, not Jewish stock) was born in 1879 and almost immediately displayed a passionate love of theater. His childhood and youth were filled with writing, directing, and acting in amateur productions, and he once ran away to join a circus. Graduated from the Imperial Law School in 1901, he was obliged to serve ten years in the government. Still he found time to study composing, attack Stanislavsky's naturalism and Meyerhold's abstractions, assault the world with his theories of theatricality, and write and direct plays at leading capitol theaters. In 1910 he was able to resign his post, join the Crooked Mirror as head regisseur and to devote the rest of his life to directing, writing, and research, in Russia until 1925 and in France from then until his death in 1953.

Early Plays

His first success on the professional stage was *The Foundation of Happiness (Fundament schast'ia)*, written in 1902, performed in 1905. The cast includes a cheerful *samodur*-undertaker and oppressed members of his household. Macabre humor, a long dream sequence (the beginning of Evreinov's monodrama) and a surprise ending all indicate much of Evreinov's future development. The same year his one-act *Stepik and Maniurochka* opened at the Alexandrinsky and played for several seasons. The play's only two characters, an old couple, face a series of revelations about their and their daughter's adulterous affairs. Evreinov—as he was to do in many later plays—emphasizes that people are at once foolish and heroic, ridiculous and noble. The play has been done in the West and is known by Russian actors even today. If amateur productions are considered, it is probably Evreinov's most frequently performed play. In *The Beautiful Despot (Krasivyi despot)*, written 1905, performed 1906, the protagonist decides to give up being an "ugly liberal" and be a "beautiful despot" instead. He retires to a remote estate, and plays the role of a barin of 1808, complete with servants, costumes, and journals of the day for news of the outside world. Not only a few peasants but even a leading feminist welcome the chance to submit to illusion and to his colorful brand of despotism. Nonetheless, like Evreinov himself, and like the related hero of Pirandello's *Enrico IV* (1922), the "despot" very clearly understands the difference between reality and theater.

Next was what Evreinov regarded as his greatest one-act play, *A Merry Death (Veselaia smert')*, written 1908, performed 1909. It was done in the United States as early as 1916, in France by Jacques Copeau, and in Italy by Pirandello. It continues to be performed today. It was recently (1969) featured at the Festival du Marais in Paris. The plot is simple—Harlequin is dying. But he mocks the Doctor and accepts Death. He enjoys a last meal with his friends Pierrot and Columbine. Pierrot's discovery that his wife Columbine has been Harlequin's lover is the focus of a lot of Evreinovian paradox and humor on one of his favorite themes. In Pierrot's lengthy, humorous addresses to the audience at the beginning, middle, and end of the play, Evrelnov uses a theatrical device he employed more sparingly but to great effect in later plays.

Monodrama

Influenced by morality plays, by Przybyszewski's *The Eternal Fairy Tale* (Russian production 1906) and by subjectivist trends in philosophy, psychology, and the arts, Evreinov developed a theory of monodrama. In a 1909 lecture "An Introduction to Monodrama" (later published as *Vvedenie v monodramu*) he calls it the most perfect form of drama. It is defined[4] as a dramatic representation in which there is one central figure, and in which the central figure himself, the other characters, the set, the action are not to be considered as representing some objective reality, but as representing the central figure's varying subjective perceptions of himself and the world around him. The spectator is asked to identify, to *fuse* with the central figure, to experience reality as he does.

Evreinov's first "experiment in monodrama" was *The Theater of Love (Predstavlenie liubvi)*. It was published in the summer of 1910 in the almanac *Studiia Impressionistov*, but Evreinov was unable to get the play produced.

The protagonist is simply "I." There is also "My Inner Voice," a heroine "She! She!," and a villain, "My Rival," an enormous, brutal, swarthy officer whose sword clanks constantly. The exquisite Impressionist color plates by Bashchenko, Schmidt-Ryzhovy, and Kulbin illustrate Evreinov's concept of a "constantly changing set." As "I's" mood and feelings toward "She! She!" vary, not only the color and intensity of stage lighting must vary, but the scenery itself. As Evreinov emphasizes in an introduction to the play, gestures, movement, scenery, costumes are of crucial importance in presenting the inner world of the monodrama's protagonist. The inner world is, after all, organized on a theatrical basis.

Evreinov was never regisseur at any theater suitable for *The Theater of Love* and other producers shied away from it. There are perhaps two difficulties—the monodrama as a form seems to wear thin over three acts, and the "constantly changing set"—at least until the advent of modern projection techniques—is financially and even technically beyond the capabilities of the theater. The monodrama did offer more possibilities in motion pictures and "monodramatic effects" were soon being employed by Russian and European film directors.

The monodrama's true stage potential was realized not in the lyric, full-length play, but in the one-act, satirical, tragifarcical monodrama. Whereas Evreinov's attempt at the former must be accounted a failure, his next attempt, *The Theater of the Soul (V kulisakh dushi)* proved a great critical and box-office success and has—along with *A Merry Death*—become one of the world's classic one-act plays.

The Theater of the Soul may be regarded as a monodrama in the Crooked Mirror style, the style prevailing at that theater from its birth in 1908 and highly developed during the years when Evreinov was head regisseur (1910-1917).

A brief review of the history of the Crooked Mirror is appropriate before going on to discuss the plays Evreinov wrote for it. Following the successful examples set earlier in the year by The Bat *(Letuchaia mysh')* in Moscow, and similar cabaret theaters earlier in France and Germany, two "intimate theaters" were established in St. Petersburg in December 1908. Meyerhold's Lukomor'e (Seashore)—quickly dubbed Mukomor'e (Sea of Torments)—folded after a week. Zinaida Kholmsky's and A. R. Kugel's Crooked Mirror, on the same premises, ran short parodies, generally with music, from midnight to 2:30 a.m. Kholmsky put up the money and developed into a fine actress, while journalist Kugel contributed his managerial talent and a generally unerring sense of what would appeal to the public. The two were also publisher and leading writer, respectively, of one of Russia's most successful and longest lasting weeklies, *Theater and Art (Teatr i iskusstvo)*.

The Crooked Mirror aimed successfully at creating a cheerful, intimate setting for merriment and humor on its small stage. By 1910 Evreinov was hired as head regisseur and the Crooked Mirror moved to a larger theater. As opposed to the grand and heavily subsidized productions at the Imperial Theaters of Moscow and St. Petersburg, the Crooked Mirror was entirely self-supporting. Casts had to be comparatively small and production costs low. Nevertheless gross box office receipts often exceeded those of the lavish productions at the much larger Imperial Theaters, especially those by the rival Meyerhold.

The Crooked Mirror's first production was a parody bouffe with music and some skits. V. G. Erenberg and B. F. Geyer emerged as artistic mainstays before their early deaths. Erenberg was a genius at composing parodies on music, especially opera. His *Vampukha, The African Bride*, was a hilarious parody—especially under Evreinov's later direction—on the excesses of the Italian opera and went through over a thousand performances at the Crooked Mirror over the years. Geyer loved tragifarce and parody and found monodrama an excellent vehicle for both.

The roots of the Crooked Mirror go back to Prutkov, and its genius lay in parodying not individual works or characters, but entire tendencies, ideas, styles. In such parodies, it is as much the regisseur's imagination as the author's that is crucial, and here the incredibly fertile brain of Evreinov (even his detractors testify to this) was to serve the theater well.

Considering the Crooked Mirror's style and reputation it is hardly surprising that the first monodrama that Evreinov wrote for production there was not only a parody on modern psychological theories, but one on Evreinov's own form, the monodrama itself. If the fantasies of a disappointed lover are not fit for a three-act lyrical drama, perhaps they would do better in a one-act tragifarce. The success of Geyer's *The Water of Life, A Monodrama in Four Decanters* (1911) indicated some of the possibilities of the satirical monodrama. If the spectator won't identify, won't *fuse* with the protagonist and share his subjective perceptions, then perhaps the spectator may be more easily persuaded to laugh at the protagonist's distorted views of reality, his naive, laughable assumption that he is experiencing reality.

The Theater of the Soul begins with a prologue by "The Professor" in front of a closed curtain. In a parody on the pretentious scholar the Professor proceeds to comment on the play that is to be presented, "a strictly scientific work based on the latest developments in the field of psychophysiology." With the aid of blackboard, colored chalk and elaborate diagrams and formulae he describes the characteristics of the various selves and the stage on which they act, the interior of a man's chest. The professor then retires and the curtain rises revealing a scene quite similar to the Professor's drawings. Right and left are two bright green, spotted lungs, center is an enormous red heart. The scenery is of cloth and is connected to ropes backstage which keep the lungs and heart in constant motion, varying as the action and the music require. In front of the heart and lungs, representing nerves, are long, slanting, tightly drawn musical strings, which resound when struck. The soul is soon revealed to be that of a middle-aged clerk in love with the bottle and an aging cafe singer. On stage are the three "Selves." Mr. Rational Self is arguing restraint and a return to wife and baby, while Mr. Emotional Self sweeps about, banging the nerves, full of passion for a cafe singer. Mr. Eternal Self is asleep at stage right. To support their arguments Rational Self and Emotional Self bring on stage their respective concepts of wife and cafe singer. The Rational Concept of Wife is a lovely, devoted wife and mother, while the Emotional Concept is a coffee-stained, sharp-tongued harpie. The Rational Concept of Cafe Singer is a forty-year-old whore with false teeth, bust, and hair, while the Emotional Concept is a beautiful young temptress. The Selves and Concepts come quickly into violent conflict culminating in the strangling of the Rational Self, demands over the "telephone" that the clerk shoot himself, and finally a loud shot. A sea of red ribbons shoots out of a large hole in the heart as the stage goes dark. A conductor enters and rouses the Eternal Self, telling him it's time to change trains.

Evreinov was applauded madly at the premiere in 1912 and the play remained in the Crooked Mirror's repertory until its end in 1931. By the 1930's *The Theater of the Soul* was well known in the western world.

Critics give Evreinov credit for his concept of monodrama and for writing two such plays. But Evreinov has often been wrongly praised or attacked for insisting that "every play must be the drama or comedy of a single person." In fact, most of his plays and productions were not monodramas at all and his major theoretical works do not even mention the concept.

Polydrama

A variation on the monodrama and one that provided many of the Crooked Mirror's plays was what we ought to call—for want of any term by Evreinov or others—the polydrama. It may be considered as consisting of several scenes representing different subjective perceptions of the same reality. The subjective views may be those of several different persons, or—the technique and the impact are the same—of several schools of thought, nations, or ages. As in the case of the simple monodrama the possibilities for satire and regisseurial imagination are endless. If one person's exaggeratedly subjective perceptions strike us as absurd and amusing, how much more absurd and amusing are several contradictory, exaggeratedly subjective views of the same reality.

There are a number of polydramas that Evreinov directed and that he and Geyer wrote in collaboration. Assigning the precise share of authorship for some of them is impossible today, but some would appear to be the work of one man. Geyer was apparently the main author of *Reminiscences (Vospominaniia)*, in which the same shotgun wedding is presented as recalled by the groom, the bride's mother, an optimist guest and a pessimist guest. Geyer also seems to have written *The Evolution of the Theater (Evoliutsiia teatra)*, in which the same love story is presented as it might have been done by Gogol, Ostrovsky, Chekhov and Andreev, but Evreinov's original idea for the play and later direction and revisions resulted in a work that Evreinov and his partisans claimed as his.

Despite Kugel's sour-grapes assertion years later that *Revizor; A Regisseurial Bouffonade in Five Versions (Revizor; rezhisserskaia buffonada v piati postreniiakh)* was not written by Evreinov at all, but by himself, Kholmsky, and others, it would appear the play was Evreinov's. Unlike the plays whose authorship he shared, this one was advertised before (and after) its premiere and reviewed as solely Evreinov's and was included in Evreinov's collected works without provoking any controversy. *Revizor* consists of the same brief bits from Gogol's play as Evreinov imagines different directors would do it. The play is introduced by a scholarly prologue by "The Regisseur" who explains how the theater, through modern interpretations, now has the possibility of solving its repertory problem by multiplying the number of classic plays available by at least five. To illustrate his thesis, the curtain opens and bits from Gogol's play are done in satires on productions by a provincial theater, the Moscow Art Theater, Gordon Craig, Max Reinhardt, and the silent movies.

Fall 1912 was a banner season for monodrama and polydrama. Evreinov's production (and script?) of *Napoleon in the Crooked Mirror* opened in September, *The Theater of the Soul*, in October, Sologub's *Hanky Panky through the Ages (Vsegdashni shashni)* in November, and *Revizor* in December. Wild applause for *Revizor* brought Evreinov repeatedly to the stage. The play remained in the Crooked Mirror's repertory, even after Evreinov left the Soviet Union in 1925.

The Trilogy on Theater in Life

In addition to writing and directing for the Crooked Mirror, Evreinov became increasingly occupied in the 1910's with historical and theoretical research and writing. To his *The Theater as Such (Teatr kak takovoi)* (1913) he added another (three-volume) work on his theories of theater in life, of "the will to theater," *The Theater for Oneself (Teatr dlia sebia)* (1915-1917).[5]

Not until the Civil War years while in the Caucasus did he turn to writing another full-length play. He brought the script of *The Main Thing (Samoe glavnoe)* with him when he returned to Petrograd in the summer of 1920. In November he showed it to Nikolai Petrov of the newly formed Free Comedy Theater *(Vol' naia komediia)*. The theater had just been established by Gorky's wife, M. F. Andreev, with the support of the Political Administration of the Baltic Fleet. The theater limited itself to new, contemporary plays, and preferred political satire. Mme Andreev predicted failure if the play were produced, others objected to the absence of any Bolshevik message, but—at Petrov's insistence—the play was accepted.

Evreinov's assitants in *The Taking of the Winter Palace (Vziatie zimnego dvortsa*, November 7, 1920), director Petrov and decorator Yury Annenkov, agreed to handle the direction and decorations for *The Main Thing*. Rehearsals in January and February 1921 were hectic—the Kronshtadt sailors were getting restive, the theater was freezing, the actors half-starved. Yet the premiere in February was greeted with great enthusiasm.

The Main Thing resembles no other play in the theater. It is a philosophy of theater and an attack on the formal stage, yet it is a masterpiece of stage technique. The protagonist is Paraclete, a man of many guises. As a lady fortune-teller he gains the confidence of some of the members of an acting troupe and some of the lodgers in a boarding house. He resolves to go in the guise of a philanthropical Dr. Fregoli to the actors' theater and employ some of them to go with him to the boarding house and play whatever roles are necessary to save the lodgers from despair and suicide. Act II consists of a "rehearsal" of a Nero feast scene in *Quo Vadis* at the troupe's third-rate provincial theater. The "rehearsal" is in the best Crooked Mirror satirical tradition—the Regisseur is pretentious, the costumes are tacky, the in-fighting among the actors riotously vicious, and everything that could possibly go wrong in a rehearsal does so. The rehearsal is of course, not simply an entertaining diversion, but serves to develop the play's theme of the absurdity of the formal stage. Fregoli enters, makes a (rather windy) speech on the futility of the stage and the importance of theater in real life, and persuades three of the actors to go with him to the boarding house on his soul-saving mission. In Act III the actors do their good work and the lodgers seem to be saved, but by Act IV conflicts arise among the actors and the whole play-within-a-play is in danger of being exposed during a Carnival. Many critics miss the point in taking Fregoli's good natured pleas for theater and illusion for the unfortunate too literally. In fact, the trigamist Fregoli is more than faintly ridiculous, and his schemes become so botched and fraught with disaster that he must finally, in the guise of Harlequin, step altogether out of the play and the play-within -a-play and appeal to the audience for help. Neither Paraclete nor Evreinov is capable of coming up with a convincingly happy ending in the theater of life, so Paraclete must simply stop the play and offer the audience several possible endings. The "Regisseur" and the "Theater Director" from the *Quo Vadis* scene, invited by their old actor friends to help celebrate Carnival, do not even attempt a solution to the problems of life. Instead the Director tells Paraclete that the *main thing* is to finish the play quickly, get the audience home while the trolleys are still running, while the Regisseur argues the *main thing* is to have a smash ending. He starts waving roman candles about and leads the entire cast in dancing and general merriment as the play ends on that confusing note.

The Main Thing was an instant success, played over a hundred times the first season, more on tour and in later seasons and far outpaced the crudely tendentious plays that made up most of the rest of the Free Comedy's repertory.

Plays by Soviet authors were rarely seen on the Polish stage in the twenties and thirties, but *The Main Thing* enjoyed major productions in Krakow in 1922 and Warsaw in 1923. Through a Polish friend the Italian dramatist Luigi Pirandello soon learned of Evreinov's works and recognized a kindred spirit. The Italian was delighted to find a Russian who shared his conviction that the modern theater's most valid concerns should be those of reality and illusion, self and mask, life as theater. It is an interesting coincidence that Pirandello's *Six Charac-*

ters in Search of an Author had premiered the same year as Evreinov's *The Main Thing*. When Pirandello succeeded in launching his own theater in Rome in 1924, Evreinov's *Cio che piu importa* was the only non-Italian play chosen for the first season.

Americans who had seen Pirandello's production took news of the play back to the United States. It was produced at the Pasadena Community Playhouse and at Harvard. When the Theater Guild discovered in early 1926 that Evreinov was visiting the United States he was signed on to assist in the production of "The Chief Thing." The Theater Guild was known for excellent acting and productions, especially of modern European plays that were, as one critic put it, "involved, obscure, and indefinite." The play ran for seven weeks, but Broadway economics and the expense of a large cast forced an end. Some reviewers took Fregoli's "message" literally and found it unconvincing and sentimental, others were confused. Still, many noted a "cheerful cynicism," and that the play avoided sentimentality by "a sardonic tinge, by the clear-eyed, pensive consciousness that its message of happiness may be false," Hard-to-please Alexander Woolcott called it "all told, a goodish evening in the theater." The *New Leader* termed it "one of the most searching and theoretically true plays" in the Guild's history. Brooks Atkinson found the play refreshingly modern, and Stark Young was delighted by "life blowing where it listeth . . . It has no beginning and no end, and leaves off finally with telling us that we may end it any way we choose, if we insist on ends."[7]

Modernism and relativism are not necessarily welcomed by all audiences. *Footlight and Lamplight* was shrewd enough to observe that "the inherent strength of the Chief Thing is at the same time its weakness . . . In America we would do this thing either with a lot of false sentimentality or as an uproarious and incredible farce or in deadly realistic earnest. Not so the Russians. The Russian mind prefers to treat a fantastic theme like this with a strange blend of fantasy, burlesque, and seriousness. Your pleasure consists of wondering which of these three moods is uppermost at the moment. When the author deliberately cuts his play short by telling you in so many words that you could finish the story according to your own taste, he accomplished at one stroke the winning of an enthusiastic audience in Europe and the losing of all save a few dramatic connoisseurs in this country."[8]

The Main Thing also reached Paris by way of Rome. Charles Dullin, a great actor and the director of the Theater de l'Atelier, and an admirer of Pirandello, learned of Evreinov and *The Main Thing* when Pirandello visited Paris in mid-1925. Despite warnings that the play was over the heads of Parisians and would not survive a week, Dullin staged the French premiere of *La Comedie du bonheur* (as it is called in French) in late 1926. The Atelier was in desperate financial condition and had no money to spend on the elaborate production that Evreinov plays invite. Except for Dullin himself, none of the actors were then (or since) regarded as very good. But the play was an instant success, put Dullin's theater on a sound financial basis for the first time, and ran over two hundred times the first two seasons. It was later revived successfully several times, even during the Depression.

The play has appeared all over Europe and in many other countries in some twenty-five languages in the past fifty years. A French-Italian film company made a movie of it in 1941-1942 and despite wartime production difficulties and the loss of portions of the film in a fire, it managed to run for some twenty years. The entire play has also been done several times on French radio and television.

Evreinov was delighted with the Russian success of his play and with the receptivity to his ideas of theater in life by some influential writers on the left. But increasing censorship and poor material conditions made him complain that it was "hard indeed living in a half-ruined country that you love more than it loves you." In the West, on the other hand, Russian musicians, painters and actors seemed to be making reputations and fortunes. Evreinov began thinking of travelling abroad again (he had travelled a great deal in Europe before the war), but did not want to leave his aged mother. When she died in 1923 Evreinov and his young actress wife began thinking seriously about tours in Europe. But she had to go to southern Russia for tuberculosis in 1924, while Evreinov remained in the north. There he wrote and dedicated to her *The Ship of the Righteous (Korabl' pravednykh)*. As he said later, the play was an attempt to deal with the problem of good unopposed by evil; to examine the likely fate of a society of righteous people cut off from their native land, from the "sinful" world; to write a thoroughly theatrical piece integrating word, gesture, movement, music, and dance, all in a structure akin to Chinese boxes, one within another. The play was written, the music composed, and the work was accepted by a publisher. But the Soviet censor rejected the play, even though the emigres were depicted as foolish and the one Bolshevik as an attractive young man, and even though Evreinov had tacked on a fourth act (later removed) showing the utopian protagonist eventually returning from the high seas to Russia again.

With censorship and party control tightening, Evreinov saw chances dimming for future productions of his plays on the Russian stage. Hence when Kugel suggested that Evreinov rejoin the Crooked Mirror and lend his prestige for a tour to Poland in 1925, Evreinov accepted.

Evreinov arrived in Warsaw and was received as a celebrity—his *The Main Thing* was well-known, and the secretary of the National Theater had just published a book about him. His hopes for real success abroad were nearly demolished by the Crooked Mirror's tour. Other than lending his name Evreinov had little to do with the tour, but its poor management, poor financing and uncharacteristically poor productions were blamed on him. Russian emigres and anti-Soviet Poles denounced Evreinov as a Bolshevik agent, while Soviet critics back home were moved to a storm of protest when some of the Crooked Mirror's works were (incorrectly) advertised in the Polish press as satires on Soviet society.

Yet despite the bad press and the recriminations, Warsaw's *Teatr Polski* (which had done *The Main Thing*) decided to do *The Ship of the Righteous*. The poet Juljan Tuwim was engaged to translate the play. A first-rate director, decorator, and cast were enlisted. The premiere of *Okret sprawiedliwych* in April 1925 drew the most wildly enthusiastic audience of Evreinov's career as a playwright.

Act I is set in a pension on the Black Sea, Acts II and III take place aboard the Anchorite, a ship placed at the disposal of the Community of the Righteous by an anonymous philanthropist. In Act I we learn that the Madman musician and his dancer wife Anna ("Dream") have become exhausted with the struggle against evil on land and, together with the Madman's old friend, a mysterious, unsmiling Captain, have decided to leave "the human herd that tramples on high ideals" to find salvation on the high seas with a community of others who share their ideals.

The other idealists gathered at the pension on the eve of the ship's departure include a selfless physician, his unhappy wife, a middle-aged nurse who adores the physician, "The Walking Joke"—who wears his arm in a sling "to avoid shaking hands with scoundrels"—and a Professor. Act I ends with the community, divided into male and female choirs, joyfully singing their "Anthem of the Community of the Righteous." It is a compendium of utopian cliches put to some conventionally "inspirational" melodies. The anthem, like the innocent faith of the utopians, simultaneously inspires laughter and deep sympathy in the audience.

Act II finds the Anchorite at sea, with the citizens all enjoying the peaceful life of the "righteous." As part of the celebration of the birth of the first child aboard, the Madman presents a play within a play, his tragicomedy with music, "Ham versus Noah." The audience consists of the community—all masked for the occasion as animals on Noah's ark. The young Ham (played by the Madman) denounces the sinful world the ark is returning to and proposes to defy his father, defy "that evil jester Jehovah" and slay everyone on the ark, leaving the world cleansed for him and his beloved, childless Second Wife (played by Dream). Dream pleads with him to believe in the eventual triumph of good and not to counter repression with repression. Ham apparently yields as the play ends. The play, the ceremony of baptism, and a party leave the community members in apparently high spirits, but the future is all but secure: the Captain's heart is on the verge of failing, there are frustrations among the increasingly bored passengers, and Vitalius—an aggressive young stowaway previously involved with two of the women in the community—turns up. Before Act III can begin, Dream rushes out in front of the curtain and makes an impassioned speech. She begs the stagehands to leave the curtain down and the audience to go home:

> Leave this theater with a light heart before it is disturbed by the author, the actors, the director, all ready to raise the treacherous curtain! Oh yes, treacherous! Because that curtain conceals the betrayal of dream to desecration, to ridicule, to disgrace! . . . I protest! I call upon you to revolt! The destruction of ideals has no place in the theater, where illusion, greater than truth, is inspired by dream! Revenge yourselves on the author who has betrayed the very essence of theater! Leave this place as if the play had ended!

Her desperate appeal is cut off when the curtain rises, revealing a stormy day in the Black Sea. The ship is on its way to port to put ashore the stowaway and a growing number of dissident members of the community. The stowaway has served as a catalyst for intrigues, political arguments, and fights. Madman, Dream, and the Captain see their society collapsing before their eyes. A series of dramatic revelations as to the true motives and identities of the members and as to the true ownership of the vessel destroys illusion after illusion. When the ship reaches shore everyone except the Madman, Dream, and the Captain abandon it to return to land, to the real world. As the play ends, the Captain dies laughing at his own absurd ambitions and Madman and Dream resolve to take the ship back to sea alone.

As in the case of *The Main Thing*, many critics were led astray by reading the play too literally. Noting that the stowaway Bolshevik was presented in a favorable light and that the "emigre" Madman and his consort and friends were made to appear like a "Ship of Idiots," some critics denounced Evreinov as a Soviet propagandist. In this case, however, we must credit the Soviet censor with a keener appreciation of the play's paradoxes and ambiguities. Are the utopians emigres leaving an imperfect socialist society, or socialists leaving the imperfect world? Are Ham's arguments for bloody revolution convincing or ridiculous? Whatever the "righteous" are leaving, whoever they are, are they heroes, martyrs, or fools?

The Ship of the Righteous has—over the years—been the least performed of Evreinov's major plays. The only other productions were Jacob Ben-Ami's in Yiddish at the Irving Place Jewish Art Theater in New York in 1926 and Virginia Theater Wagon's in English in 1970. The productions have always inspired good reviews, but there are several factors inhibiting a greater number of productions so far. The play has never been published or performed in the Soviet Union, and there are no published translations in foreign languages. In its Warsaw production the play attracted enthusiastic audiences, but also managed to offend both pro-Soviet and anti-Soviet theater-goers. And although the critics may be delighted by the modern mixture of parody, sentiment, farce, and tragedy, audiences lacking proper preparation may feel confused.

In the preface to his last major play, *The Theater of Eternal War (Teatr vechnoi voiny)* Evreinov declared it to be the final work in a trilogy which began with *The Main Thing* and *The Ship of the Righteous*. He called the trilogy *The Dual Theater*, and insisted its subject was "the theater in real life." By dual he referred to such antimonies as reality and illusion, truth and falsehood, self and mask. The first play, as he saw it, presented the phenomenon of theater in life from the religious-moral point of view, the second from the politico-social, and the third from what we might translate in this case as the existential *(zhiteiski-filosofskaia)*.

By any account the latest play presented his least cheerful view of life and theater in life. The first two had been written in better days. *The Main Thing* had been written at the dawn of what seemed a better world. And his convictions in the saving power of illusion had just been confirmed by a personal experience: his devoted ward had died peacefully rather than in terror because of his repeated false assurances she would recover. *The Ship of the Righteous* had been his wedding present to his bride. But by the time of his trip to the United States in 1926, life and theater seemed to be going sour. Despite the excellent Broadway production of *The Main Thing*, the publishing of two books in English, and some well-received public lectures, solid success in America eluded him. He had appendicitis on the ship back to Europe, nearly died on the operating table six months later, and his marriage was on the verge of breaking up. He turned to writing for relief. His bitterest, even if colorful and witty play was completed in the fall of 1927, published in 1928, and it was produced by the Tatiana Pavlova troupe in Milan in 1929.

As the curtain rises on *The Theater of Eternal War* a posh reception is being held at Sofya Daryal's and Yu-Gen-Li's "Theatrical Institute" in New York. Soon we learn that some of the guests are patsies and that others are playing various social roles as part of an examination in the arts of deception and hypocrisy. Sofya Daryal's institution has been organized to teach these arts, so that her pupils would learn to survive in life, in "the theater of eternal war." Act II takes place in a summer house near Atlantic City, where one of the pupils is posing as a widow ("grief inspires trust") forced to sell her priceless antique furniture—actually clever, mass-produced reproductions. Other intrigues and deceptions in business and love abound.

As a graduation party the pupils decide to hold an "Unmasked Ball" (in the final act) where—for a refreshing change—everyone is to be ruthlessly frank. The natural result is shattered love affairs, attempted rape, fights, and hilariously vicious dialogue. Sofya Daryal is freed of her illusions that her pupils and daughter love her for her work. Her daughter discovers that the "innocent, sincere" musician she loves has been playing a role. The heroine, Sofya Daryal's half-sister Yu-Gen-Li loses her lover and turns to opium as the play ends. She explains to a protesting friend that her lover, even if only in the world of illusion, is still with her:

> Over there . . . far from the roar of our eternal war! . . . far from this endless war of the sexes, with its betrayals, victims, and endless grief! . . Over there, where sweet butterflies flutter around the dragon's maw! . . in the world of long desired and certain truth.

Italian critics wrote extensive reviews, noted the dazzlingly witty and devastating dialogue, the intricate structure, and Evreinov's convincingly bitter view of life. The excellent decorations by Leon Zach drew special mention—bright, but garish and bitter colors "that seemed to have been painted with poison."

Reversing the direction of *The Main Thing's* voyage, *The Theater of Eternal War* travelled from Italy to Poland. Stanislawa Wysocka directed the play (the only Russian play she ever did) and played Sofya Daryal in Poznan and Wilno in 1930 and 1931. Her production was so successful that the magazine *Swiat kulis* devoted an entire issue to articles by and about Evreinov.

Conclusion

The Evreinov style, as we have seen, consists of full, unashamed exploitation of a multitude of the theater's traditional resources: music, dance, gesture, color, plays-within-plays, addresses to the audience, exaggerated characters, stock characters, masks, disguises, witty repartee, complicated plots, and surprise endings. Although some complain that it is all *de trop*, Evreinov's theatrical style is precisely that necessary for his theme of theater in life.

Pirandello's not so theatrical dramas show man estranged from life and enslaved by the mask and the role, but Evreinov, like Nietzsche and Oscar Wilde (two of his early favorites) found raw life unbearable. Similar to Nietzsche's thinking on power and Wilde's on art, Evreinov sought to transcend life through theater. If there are no certainties, no God, in the post-Nietzschean world, then we ought to be consciously, deliberately elaborating our illusions, creating theater in life, rather than leaving man naked in the name of murderous truth.

Applying this principle in life, however, is not so easy, and Evreinov—as we have seen—tried many approaches. One of his most appealing qualities too is his talent for challenging and mocking his own various raisonneurs. They are often ridiculously single-minded and their theories are refuted by the events they set in motion. *The Main Thing's* raisonneur argues that illusion and theater can bring happiness to suffering humanity. But as his experiment in a boarding house approaches disaster he must break the realistic structure of the play and appeal to a higher principle of theater. In *The Ship of the Righteous* the Madman musician and his young consort Anna (plainly recognizable as parodies of Evreinov and his young wife Anna) try to found an ideal community based on altruism and theater, but it fails. Anna appeals to a higher principle of theater and tries unsuccessfully to stop the action. In the last major play, *The Theater of Eternal War*, the regisseur-figure has given up on altruism, accepts the world as a dog-eat-dog proposition, and makes no attempt to stop the play and appeal to higher principles. Sofya Daryal seems somewhat successful in teaching her pupils how to use theater in the pursuit of their own selfish interests, but neither she nor any one else finds true happiness in a selfish life built on deceit.

Accompanying Evreinov on his explorations into the ironies of theater in life was the spirit of the immortal Harlequin as he understood him: no matter how grim life is, one must look for and appreciate good theater because that's all there is, and the abyss must be faced with laughter that derives from a recongition of absurdity because there is no other response.

Notes

1. Mayakovsky's dictum, still important enough in 1960 to grace the dust cover of a book by the important director Nikolai Petrov:

    Don't befoul

    > *the theater with slobbering psychologism!*

    Theater,

    > *serve Communist propaganda!*

2. *The Taking of the Winter Palace*, November 7, 1920, featured 8,000 actors, 500 musicians, and 150,000 spectators.

3. *Histoire du théâtre russe* (Paris, 1947) and *Istorlia russkogo teatra s drevneishikh vremen do 1917 goda* (New York, 1955; London, 1971).

4. "Monodrama" has been used in a more limited sense for at least two centuries to denote simply a play with only one performer.

5. Evreinov summed up the arguments presented in these two and other works in a work in English: *The Theater in Life* (New York-London, 1927; New York, 1970).

6. In 1913 Evreinov was the first to recognize the young painter's potential in the theater and hired him for a production at the Crooked Mirror. Annenkov was soon doing most of the sets there as well as work for The Bat and many other leading theaters.

7. Stark Young, "The Chief Thing," *The New Republic*, April 7, 1926.

8. New York, June 3, 1926.

above—*Evreinov as a student at the Imperial Law Institute (c. 1900).*

right—*Evreinov after trip to Africa (1913).*

Portrait by Savely Sorin (1914). (Chalk, 47 × 32 cm.)

right—*Portrait by Mayakovsky at Repin's home in Kuokalla (1915).*

below—*Evreinov in Sukhumi with friends (1919). Kamensky, the futurist writer and biographer of Evreinov; N. I. Butkovskaya, Evreinov's publisher and collaborator at the Theater of Antiquity.*

above—*Evreinov and his wife in Warsaw (1925). Anna Kashina-Evreinova was an author, publisher and actress.*

below—*Evreinov in Sukhumi (1923).*

Evreinov at home on rue d'Alboni, Paris (1928).
Butkovskaya, Evreinov, his wife, her sister, Iraida.

Portrait by Grigory Shiltyan (c. 1932).

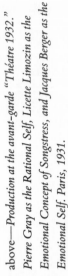

above—*Production at the avant-garde "Théatre 1932." Pierre Gray as the Rational Self, Licette Limozin as the Emotional Concept of Songstress, and Jacques Berger as the Emotional Self. Paris, 1931.*

Left—*Decorator Ivan Bilibin and régisseur Evreinov at their lavish production of Rimsky-Korsakov's Tsar Saltan. Prague's National Theater (1935).*

The Main Thing

above—*The Barefoot Dancer. Sketch by decorator
Sergei Sudeikin for the Theatre Guild production, New
York, 1926.*

right—*Paraclete as the Fortune Teller.
Same production.*

The Theater of the Soul

right—*Paraclete in the guise of Fortune Teller (McKay Morris). Photograph of the Theatre Guild production, New York, 1926.*

below—*Evreinov's own sketch of the set, for the benefit of the stage designer M. P. Bobyshev, for the premiere at Evreinov's Crooked Mirror Theater, 1912.*

The Main Thing
Theater Guild production, New York, 1926
above—*Alice Cliff as the Boardinghouse Landlady, Henry Travers as the Retired Civil Servant, and Ernest Cossart as the Comic in the guise of the Retired Army Doctor.*

below—*"Rehearsal of Quo Vadis." Edward G. Robinson as the Regisseur (center left with cane), Harold Clurman as Nero (center right, white costume), and McKay Morris as Paraclete in the guise of Dr. Frégoli (center right with top hat in hand).*

The Main Thing. The "*Quo Vadis*" scene of Charles Dullin's production at his Atelier theater, Paris, 1928. Dullin (left center with cane) as Paraclete in the guise of Dr. Fregoli.

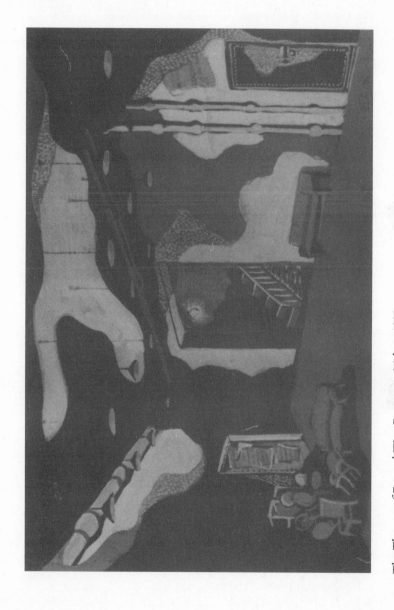

The Theater of Eternal War. Premiere. Milan, 1929.
Poison–colored (brown and gold) sketch by decorator Leon Zack. Warehouse. Scene of the "Unmasked Ball" that ends the play.

The Theater of Eternal War. Milan production.
above—*classroom at Sofya Daryal's "Theatrical Institute."*
below—*Summer house near Atlantic City.*

Ball ending the play The Main Thing *Theatre Guild New York production, 1926.*
Decorations by Sergey Sudeikin.

below—*from* The Ship of the Righteous. *Premiere, Warsaw, 1925.*
"Ham vs. Noah," the play-within-a-play on board the "Anchorite." Staunton, Virginia, 1970.

The Main Thing. *Sketch by decorator Konstantin Popov of the boardinghouse
for the Carnival Théatre de la Potinière, Paris, 1935.*

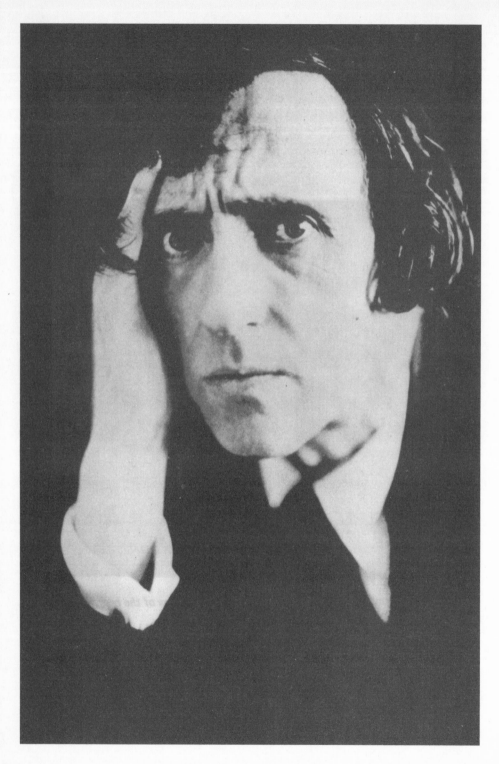

Evreinov's "American Portrait" (1926).

A MERRY DEATH

A harlequinade in one act with a brief, although extremely amusing, prologue and a few concluding words on behalf of the author, N. Evreinov.

CHARACTERS

Harlequin

Columbine

Pierrot

The Doctor

Death

Doors to the right and left. Center stage is a bed; a large clock over it shows eight o'clock. Below and stage left of the clock is a large indoor thermometer, to the right is a lute. Two stools and a small table with a lamp on it are downstage left. Downstage right is a glass-doored cupboard with bottles, wine glasses, bread, and fruit. If the third stool by the bed were mentioned, then one would have to acknowledge the stage description as complete. As the curtain rises, Harlequin is asleep with his head facing upward and his arms straight at his sides. His hair is gray, and as for the rest of him, Harlequin looks like Harlequin. Flies are heard buzzing. Pierrot shoos them off Harlequin's face—with the cuffs of his long sleeves, of course—and brushes the sleeper's nose in the process—of course. Then he walks over to the audience and waves his hands at it.

PIERROT. Shh . . . Quiet! Take your seats as noiselessly as possible and try to keep any talking and shifting in your chairs to a minimum, because if any of you were dragged along by one of your uncultured friends, and you're too serious to take any interest in some harlequinade, then there's no point in your bringing it to the attention of the rest of the audience, who, after all, are not concerned with your personal tastes. Furthermore, Harlequin is asleep . . . You see! Shh . . . I'll explain everything later! In the meantime, don't wake him up, please! And when Columbine shows up, don't applaud like mad, just to show your friends that you had an affair with her and know how to appreciate real talent! I implore you! This is no laughing matter—Harlequin is gravely ill! Just think, he's delirious over Columbine, although he hasn't the slightest in common with her, since Columbine is my wife, and that, naturally, settles it. I strongly suspect Harlequin will not survive the night; a fortune-teller once predicted that the day he slept more than he drank, he would die at the stroke of midnight. You can see it is now eight o'clock in the evening and he's still sleeping. I can even say more—I know, perhaps for certain, that Harlequin will soon die, but what decent actor would tell his audience the end of the play before it begins! I'm not one to let the management down, and I understand quite well that an audience comes to the theater not because of some meaning or other or for the masterful dialogue, but simply to find out how it all turns out in the end; and nevertheless I find myself unable to hold back a sigh and to say, crying on my long sleeve *(does so)*: "Poor, poor Harlequin, who would have supposed." I loved him very much! He was my first friend, which, by the way, never hindered me from envying him a little, because as everyone knows, if I am Pierrot, it is only because I am a harlequin who has not succeeded like the madly popular Harlequin. No matter what you might think, I'm not so simple as my costume, and, I assure you, I've already run for the doctor, useless as it may be, since Harlequin will die perfectly well without the doctor, but . . . that's the way decent people handle these things, and I'm not one to be unconventional; after all, If I didn't behave like everybody else then I'd be the bold, merry Harlequin, for whom laws don't exist, but I . . . I'm merely the stupid, cowardly Pierrot, whose character, incidentally, will become quite clear to you during the subsequent development of the play, if you will only stay till the end of the performance and don't clear out right away because of all my babbling. So I'll stop, informing you only of the following plan which came to mind without any outside assistance whatsoever: if Harlequin is fated to die at the stroke of twelve by this clock, then wouldn't it be a nice gesture on my part to set the hands back, even if only by two hours! I've always enjoyed swindling people and so when it comes to swindling death and Harlequin into the bargain, to the disadvantage of the former and the advantage of the latter—I would say that you can't call the plan anything other than sheer genius. And so, to work! The play begins! *(Climbs up on a stool and, balancing precariously over the bed, sets the clock back exactly two hours.)* Poor, poor Harle . . . *(Falls with a crash on the floor.)* Poor Pierrot! *(On his knees, he rubs his back with a tearful expression on his face.)*

HARLEQUIN *(He awakes, smiles, pulls Pierrot by the chin toward him and kisses him tenderly.)*

PIERROT *(innocently)*. It seems I woke you up?

HARLEQUIN. Why didn't you do it sooner?

PIERROT. What for?

HARLEQUIN. My hours are numbered

PIERROT. Oh, stop it!

HARLEQUIN. I want to live them.

PIERROT. You will.

HARLEQUIN. And you almost let me sleep right through them.

PIERROT. I thought . . .

HARLEQUIN. What time is it?

PIERROT. Six.

HARLEQUIN. Is that all?

PIERROT. Yes. How do you feel?

HARLEQUIN. Like I'm dying.

PIERROT. The way you worry about your health makes me laugh. *(He cries.)*

HARLEQUIN. Stop it! I *am* alive. What have you been doing? The clock isn't lying?

PIERROT. I went for the doctor. Try to rest! I've got to take your temperature. *(Takes the thermometer from the wall.)*

ACT ONE

HARLEQUIN. You went for the doctor? *(Laughs loudly.)* Well, after all, he might amuse me . . .

PIERROT. Move your arm! Like that. *(Places the thermometer in Harlequin's armpit.)* Sounds like someone coming. *(He runs off right and immediately returns. The thermometer has burst into flames.)* What happened to the thermometer?

HARLEQUIN. It shows the exact temperature. *(Pierrot hastily removes the thermometer, puts out the fire, and hangs the thermometer back in its place. Harlequin leaps up and twirls around, snapping his fingers.)* Oh ho! Harlequin's not dead yet!

PIERROT *(sounding dissatisfied)*. Only you wrecked the thermometer!

HARLEQUIN *(approaching the lute)*. It's true, I haven't long to live, but . . . *(Takes down the lute.)* Just look how many strings are broken, and the rest are worn! But is that anything to keep me from playing a serenade? *(He plays.★ Steps are heard right.)*

PIERROT. Do you hear that? The doctor. Stop playing and lie down quick. It's him. I can recognize people instantly by their footsteps. Only people hurrying to the aid of those near and dear sound like that.

HARLEQUIN *(stops playing and hangs up the lute)*. Hurrying after the money. *(A knock at the door; Harlequin lies down.)*

PIERROT. Come in!

THE DOCTOR *(in an enormous pair of glasses, bald, with a large red nose, with a syringe under his arm, enters right, stops, and sings to the audience)*.

> The minute that they call for me
> The sick to see, the sick to see,
> I'm off to patients day and night
> And strive to heal with all my might.
>> Millionaires and proletarians
>> I come flying to care for 'em
>> And yet all the pink pills 'n mess
>> Never cure any illnesses.
> And soak a ragged invalid?
> Why, God forbid, God forbid!
> When the patient's poor, what can you ask?
> You ask a kopeck, his very last.
>> Millionaires and proletarians, etc.

★The harlequinade music must be a plainly simple arrangement, sounding pleasantly child-like, to remind the old folks of some poor *balagan*. N.E.

How do you do, my dear Harlequin! What seems to be the problem?

HARLEQUIN. That's for you to say.

THE DOCTOR. You're quite right. *(Turns to Pierrot. In his ear.)* You should never contradict a sick person *(to Harlequin)*. Did you take your temperature? *(Sits on a stool near the bed; Pierrot is to his right.)*

PIERROT *(after waving his hand)*. Don't ask!

THE DOCTOR *(To Harlequin)*. Do you feel something coming on?

HARLEQUIN. An attack.

THE DOCTOR. Of coughing?

HARLEQUIN. Laughing.

THE DOCTOR. What's so funny?

HARLEQUIN. You are! *(Laughs merrily.)*

THE DOCTOR *(to Pierrot)*. Doesn't he believe in medicine?

PIERROT. No, only in you, it seems.

THE DOCTOR. Strange patient, all right. *(To Harlequin.)* Let me take your pulse. *(With his right hand takes out his watch, with the left grabs the foot presented by Harlequin.)* Oh ho! Never count that! *(Releases the foot.)* Stick out your tongue.

HARLEQUIN. At who?

THE DOCTOR. Me!

HARLEQUIN. Oh, you? With great pleasure! *(Sticks out his tongue and makes a face at the Doctor.)*

THE DOCTOR. Thank you.

HARLEQUIN. You're welcome! *(Sticks out his tongue again.)*

THE DOCTOR. That's enough now!

HARLEQUIN. For God's sake, don't be shy! *(Sticks it out again.)*

THE DOCTOR. I already saw it.

HARLEQUIN. All right then! *(Pulls his tongue back in his mouth.)*

THE DOCTOR. Now I've got to listen to you.

HARLEQUIN. What should I talk about?

THE DOCTOR. You don't understand me.

HARLEQUIN. Don't understand *you*? The hell I don't! People like me see right through people like you, but people like you—you can bet your life on it—will never understand people like me.

THE DOCTOR *(to Pierrot)*. Delirious. *(To Harlequin.)* All right! But allow me to put my head on your chest! I have to do that, so . . .

HARLEQUIN. You wife isn't jealous?

THE DOCTOR *(listens to all sides of the patient, to Pierrot)*. He has quite a fever. It'll be a miracle if my ear and cheek don't burn up. *(To Harlequin.)* Yes, yes, you're a sick man, all right, but let's hope you'll recover shortly. *(To Pierrot.)* Hopeless, the mechanism's completely broken down. *(To Harlequin, as he listens once more.)* You'll live a long time yet. *(To Pierrot.)* He'll die any time now. *(To Harlequin.)* You did the right thing to send for me. *(To Pierrot.)* You'd have done better to send for the undertaker. *(To Harlequin.)* You've got a healthy organism. *(To Pierrot.)* But it won't live. *(To Harlequin.)* Proper care is all you need. *(To Pierrot.)* It's no use.

HARLEQUIN. What do you advise?

THE DOCTOR. You must go to bed early. No excitement. Absolutely no drinking. No spicy, salty, greasy, sweet, sour, or rich foods, nothing too hot, too cold, or too filling. Move around very gently; don't get emotional over anything. Constantly guard against drafts. Stay well clear of any commotion.

HARLEQUIN. So that's it! But is such a life worth the living?

THE DOCTOR. That, sir, is for you to say.

HARLEQUIN. What's your diagnosis?

THE DOCTOR. Old age.

HARLEQUIN. But I could be your son.

THE DOCTOR. You're much too rude for that. Goodbye. *(Takes his leave and goes over to Pierrot. Softly.)* And who's paying for the call? *(Pierrot nods in Harlequin's direction. The Doctor again takes his leave of Harlequin.)* Goodbye.

HARLEQUIN. Goodbye. *(The Doctor walks off indecisively, then stops.)* Did you forget something?

THE DOCTOR. Didn't you forget something?

HARLEQUIN. Nope, not a thing; I remember all your instructions perfectly. Don't worry!

THE DOCTOR. No, no, that's not the problem.

HARLEQUIN. What is then?

THE DOCTOR. Hm . . . Between the two of us—you forgot to pay me for the call.

HARLEQUIN. Odd! How could that have happened?

THE DOCTOR. I do hope you won't be angry at me!

HARLEQUIN. Of course not, for goodness' sake!

THE DOCTOR *(once more taking his leave)*. Well, goodbye.

HARLEQUIN *(touches his hand with feeling)*. Goodbye, doctor, goodbye!

THE DOCTOR. Hm . . . You've again lapsed into forgetfulness.

HARLEQUIN. Yes, yes! So I did! You're so right! It'd be rude of me to deny it.

THE DOCTOR. And so I'm reminding you.

HARLEQUIN. I'm so grateful.

THE DOCTOR. It was nothing, really.

HARLEQUIN. Oh no, it wasn't! For goodness' sake!

THE DOCTOR. And so . . . the money?

HARLEQUIN. You'll get it as soon as I recover, as soon as you cure me.

THE DOCTOR. Yes, but . . . I should warn you that I endeavor to cure all diseases except incurable ones; and yours . . .

HARLEQUIN. Well, when I get a little better, when your advice starts to work. But who knows? Maybe you lied to me; why should I pay, then?

THE DOCTOR. In that case I must inform you, that . . . that, judging by the condition of your organism, you won't survive the night.

HARLEQUIN *(leaping from his bed)*. What?! In that case why the hell should I pay you anything?

THE DOCTOR. But when you're dead, who's going to pay me then?

HARLEQUIN. Pay for what, if I may ask?

THE DOCTOR. What do you mean, for what?

HARLEQUIN. If I really die today, what is your art worth if it can't save me from death! And if I live, then it's not worth anything either, if it can't do any better than illiterate fortune-tellers!

THE DOCTOR. I didn't come here to philosophize.

HARLEQUIN. I know why you came.

THE DOCTOR. Without the innuendoes, if you please.

HARLEQUIN *(to Pierrot with a laugh)*. He calls that an innuendo. *(Takes some money from under his pillow.)* Here's why you came! *(Goes over to the door left and offers him the money.)*

THE DOCTOR *(reaches for the money)*. Thank you! *(Harlequin disappears with a loud laugh behind the door and instantly appears in another; the Doctor rushes over to him. Pierrot doubles up with laughter, and Harlequin has already run out the opposite door and whirled around the Doctor. He whirls, disappears right, reappears left, and repeats the whole performance again, then stops in front of the Doctor and gives him the money.)* Pretty frisky, wouldn't you say? *(A hammering sound, similar to a heartbeat, is heard.)*

THE DOCTOR. You know, sir, may the Good Lord bring you fortune in the next world—the first time I've seen a dying man like this. But what's that noise?

HARLEQUIN. That's my heart beating. *(A locomotive's puffing is heard.)*

THE DOCTOR. And that?

HARLEQUIN. That's my breathing.

THE DOCTOR. And you're still on your feet?

HARLEQUIN. Yes indeed; and I've preserved enough good spirits to welcome death.

THE DOCTOR. How do you mean, welcome?

HARLEQUIN. Oh, it happens to be coming right on time. The man who has lived wisely will always welcome death.

THE DOCTOR. You speak in riddles.

HARLEQUIN. But for people like you . . . *(He laughs.)*

THE DOCTOR. How do you know?

HARLEQUIN. Would you like me to show you how you're going to die?

THE DOCTOR. Might be interesting.

HARLEQUIN *(lies down on the bed, trembles all over, then moans)*. Ah! Oh! Oo! I'm still so young . . . I haven't really lived yet . . . Why have I been so virtuous all my life? . . I'm still full of all sorts of desires . . . Turn me toward the window . . . I'm not tired of looking at this world yet . . . Save me! . . I haven't done half what I wanted . . . I was in no rush to live, because I kept forgetting about death. Save me! Save me! . . I haven't had any fun yet, I was always preserving my health, my strength, my money, for the morrow, I loaded it down with the most wonderful hopes and rolled it along like a snowball getting bigger all the time! That morrow has rolled clear off the edge of the possible! Right off the cliff of my worldly wisdom! . . Ah! Oh! Oo! *(Stretches one last time, trembles, and goes limp. The Doctor cries. Harlequin gets up with a loud laugh and claps his hands.)* No! That's not how Harlequin will die.

THE DOCTOR *(tearfully)*. What must I do?

HARLEQUIN *(extends his hand)*. Something for the advice!

THE DOCTOR. How much?

HARLEQUIN. Same as you.

THE DOCTOR *(returns the money)*. Well then?

HARLEQUIN *(with an air of importance)*. Go and live. That's all.

THE DOCTOR. What does that mean?

HARLEQUIN. Well, if you don't understand, you are incurable. I say to you: "Go and live, but live, not as if you were immortal, but as if you might die tomorrow."

THE DOCTOR *(nods his head distrustfully)*. Hm . . . I'll try. *(Wipes his eyes.)* Farewell, Mr. Harlequin.

HARLEQUIN. Farewell, Mr. Doctor. *(The Doctor puts a finger to his forehead and, swaying meditatively in time with the same music that was heard at his entrance, goes off right.)*

HARLEQUIN *(to Pierrot)*. What would you say about a man like that?

PIERROT. Nothing good. *(He grows somber.)*

HARLEQUIN. The old fool supposes I can't sense death coming! As if a man who spent more time sleeping than drinking could still doubt the approach of death. By the way, what time is it? *(The clock shows eight.)* My clock isn't slow?! It was always right in step with me, but now . . .

PIERROT. You're too suspicious.

HARLEQUIN. Not everybody ought to be like you.

PIERROT. Like what, then?

HARLEQUIN. You'll soon see. Help me set the table for supper.

PIERROT *(running toward the cupboard)*. With great pleasure.

HARLEQUIN. We'll need to set three places.

PIERROT. Three?

HARLEQUIN. Yes.

PIERROT. Who's the third for?

HARLEQUIN. For Death.

PIERROT. It'll sit at the table with us?

HARLEQUIN. If you don't go and frighten it away . . .

PIERROT. Two glasses should be enough; I won't be eating with you.

HARLEQUIN. Come, come! I was joking! Death will be feasting on me. That will be enough for it. But set three places anyway. *(Lights an oil lamp.)*

PIERROT. But who's the third place for?

COLUMBINE'S VOICE *(singing offstage right)*.

> My wifely honor disregarding
> When nights I hear a distant lute
> By moon I run to meet my darling
> My doubly sweet forbidden fruit.
>
> Heart thumpin', ears ringin'
> And fearing perdition
> Just what if my husb'n
> Were hiding and listenin'.

PIERROT. What's this? The voice of Columbine . . . The voice of my wife! . .

HARLEQUIN. Now you know who the third place is for . . .

PIERROT *(tragically)*. Ahhh! Treachery! . . Ahh! Perfidy! So that's your idea of friendship! . .

HARLEQUIN. Calm down, nothing's happened yet!

PIERROT. That's all I need!

HARLEQUIN. And it's exactly what I need!

PIERROT. And I'm supposed to be your friend!

HARLEQUIN. You're both my friends. But you want to be the only one, so you're jealous?

PIERROT. You know very well why I'm jealous and who's to blame.

HARLEQUIN. Be sensible. If you really love me and love Columbine, you ought to be very happy for both of us. What's more, you know both of us love you. So why complain? Set the third place!

PIERROT. No, I'm not that simple. Nice people don't behave that way and the only thing for me to do is to avenge my honor.

HARLEQUIN. By?

PIERROT. Killing you.

HARLEQUIN. But I'm going to die very shortly anyway; my hours are numbered. What's to stop you from telling everybody you did it?

PIERROT. You're right . . .

HARLEQUIN. Then there's nothing to talk about! Set the third place.

PIERROT *(meditatively)*. How can I?

HARLEQUIN. Come on! We're wasting time. *(Pierrot hesitates for another second, then goes for the third place setting, but on the way back stumbles and drops the plate.)* Clumsy! Going around destroying the dishes!

PIERROT *(with pathos)*. A fine one to talk! You destroyed my happiness.

HARLEQUIN *(setting the third place)*. Skip the rhetoric, thank you! You lost interest in Columbine a long time ago, and the only reason you're acting jealous is because it's the conventional thing to do . . . But shh . . .

COLUMBINE'S VOICE *(singing again offstage)*.

> Behind a mask we find our Columbine
> And dressed so fine from head to toe
> She has to see her darling Harlequin
> She dreads to meet her spouse Pierrot.
>> Heart thumpin', ears ringin'
>> And fearing perdition
>> Just what if my husb'n
>> Were hiding and listenin'.

HARLEQUIN. I'll meet Columbine, and you fix the lamp. *(He runs off right. Pierrot stands lost in thought.)*

PIERROT. Hm . . . Fix the lamp! . . *(Suddenly claps himself on the forehead.)* I'd do better to fix the clock! *(Leaps on the bed and takes hold of the clock hand.)* If Harlequin's death must be my doing, so be it! Ladies and gentlemen, you are my witnesses! Such things cannot go unavenged: I'll set the hands ahead two hours! . . *(Does so.)* Ah! Harlequin, it's plain no one can escape his fate. *(Leaps from the bed.)* Now my mind's at ease, I have been avenged. *(Paces around the room rubbing his hands. The Columbine Theme is heard offstage right.)* I wonder how she'll react. *(Stands near the door, feet wide apart, body leaning forward and hands on hips.)* Come right in, Mrs. Unfaithful! . .

HARLEQUIN'S VOICE *(offstage right).* Don't worry, Columbine! Walk right in. I talked to him and, honest to God, he agreed with me.

COLUMBINE *(enters, eyes flashing, pounces on Pierrot).* You agreed?! So that's it! Agreed! . . So, you good-for-nothing, you value your wife so little! Her betrayal doesn't mean a thing! Nothing? Answer me! *(Beats Pierrot.)*

PIERROT *(distraught).* But listen, Columbine . . .

COLUMBINE. What? I have to listen to you! Listen to the most worthless husband of all worthless husbands . . .

PIERROT. But Columbine . . .

COLUMBINE. You blockhead . . .

PIERROT. You won't let me get a word in . . .

COLUMBINE *(beats Pierrot).* No excuses! . . And I, unhappy woman, married a scoundrel like you! Gave him the best years of my life! And he won't even stand up for his wife's honor! *(Beats him.)* Take that! And that! And that, you fathead!

PIERROT. You're going too far! Harlequin, defend me!

HARLEQUIN *(backing off).* But it's strictly a family affair.

PIERROT. But dear friend . . .

HARLEQUIN. I wasn't brought up to interfere in the married lives of other people.

COLUMBINE *(to Pierrot).* So that's how you love me! That's how jealous you are! What about your vows, you atheist?

PIERROT *(recovering).* God damn it, this is unheard of! You brazen hussy, you're the one who came here for a tryst and you still have the gall to accuse . . .

COLUMBINE. Enough! Shut up! I know very well how scoundrels like you weasel out of things: when they're guilty, then they try to defend themselves by attacking the innocent. But you won't fool me, you good-for-nothing.

HARLEQUIN *(stepping between them).* My friends, let's not waste precious time! When the supper is on the table, why spoil the appetite!

COLUMBINE and PIERROT. But this is outrageous!

HARLEQUIN. I don't care for long drawn out quarrels.

PIERROT and COLUMBINE. It's not my fault.

HARLEQUIN. It's time to make up! The course of true love never did run smooth.

PIERROT and COLUMBINE. Not for anything!

HARLEQUIN. Stubborn.

PIERROT and COLUMBINE. My deepest feelings have been outraged!

HARLEQUIN. That's enough!

PIERROT and COLUMBINE. No.

COLUMBINE. First, he's got to be punished.

HARLEQUIN. How?

COLUMBINE. Kiss me, Harlequin! My dear, sweet Harlequin!

HARLEQUIN. So as not to give offense by refusing . . . *(Kisses her.)* I always was a kind lover. *(Kisses her.)* Besides that, I have a tender heart. *(Kisses her.)* Even children know about it. *(Kisses her.)* What's more, as master of the house *(kisses her)*, I must be polite to the guests *(kisses her)*, especially if it's one *(kisses her)* of the fair sex *(kisses her)*.

PIERROT *(to the audience).* Poor people! They haven't the faintest suspicion that I've already avenged myself and so my mind's completely at ease.

COLUMBINE *(to Harlequin).* Kiss me harder. Passionately. Make it hurt. Bite me. Don't hold back! *(They kiss as she desires.)*

PIERROT *(coolly, even sneering a little, to the audience).* They imagine they've mortally wounded me.

COLUMBINE *(to Harlequin).* More! More! *(To Pierrot.)* Oh, you insensitive clod.

PIERROT *(to Columbine).* Go right ahead, help yourself! *(To the audience.)* My conscience is clear, I stood up for my honor and there's nothing for me to get excited about.

COLUMBINE *(to Harlequin).* Kiss my eyes, my forehead, cheeks, chin, temples! *(Harlequin doesn't have to be asked twice.)*

PIERROT *(to the audience).* Ladies and gentlemen, you are my witnesses, I have been avenged.

COLUMBINE. Kiss me on the back of my neck, where it makes me tremble. *(Harlequin is as kind as ever.)*

PIERROT. It's all the same to me. They can do anything they please. I have done my duty as an outraged husband and I feel great.

COLUMBINE *(stamping her foot at Pierrot).* So, you scoundrel! It doesn't mean a thing to you!

PIERROT *(to the audience; smiling blissfully).* I'll drive them crazy with my utter calm.

COLUMBINE *(to Harlequin).* Well, let's treat him to our Dance of Love!

HARLEQUIN. I wouldn't think of refusing you, but . . .

COLUMBINE. But what?

HARLEQUIN. But suppose Pierrot isn't enough of a choreography lover to appreciate it properly?

PIERROT *(to Columbine and Harlequin).* Go ahead, don't be shy! *(To the audience.)* I've avenged myself in advance for everything and there's no reason to get upset about the past.

HARLEQUIN *(handing Pierrot the lute).* Perhaps you'd like to do the accompaniment?

COLUMBINE. Of course! He ought to be doing something during the dance!

PIERROT *(takes the lute and sits down).* With the greatest pleasure, if that is what you desire. *(To the audience.)* I hope you do understand, how indifferent a husband can be once he has properly avenged his outraged honor.

COLUMBINE. Play!

PIERROT *(to the audience).* My God, how easy is the heart after one has avenged oneself, and so no one has any right to laugh. *(Plays with feeling as Harlequin and Columbine enthusiastically do the Dance of Love. Suddenly Harlequin stops, staggers, and—hardly breathing—flops on the bed. Pierrot breaks off the music.)*

COLUMBINE. What's the matter? What's happened?

HARLEQUIN *(clutching at his heart).* No . . . nothing, nothing at all. *(Again a heart is heard beating, like cannons going off, and the furious puffing of a locomotive is heard.)*

COLUMBINE *(horrified).* Your heartbeat is deafening! Such terrible wheezing!

PIERROT *(to the audience, joyfully).* Harlequin's giving in! Harlequin's getting weaker! Rejoice with me, you poor husbands! You, whose wives are in danger!

COLUMBINE *(to Harlequin).* Nothing like this has ever happened to you before.

PIERROT *(to the audience).* On the other hand, don't! Grieve with me, because when all is said and done, Harlequin is my friend and that's all there is to it. Don't quarrel with him over some slut! And if Columbine does find him more to her taste than me, don't blame him, but Columbine, who's always had such abominable taste. But that's not fair of me. *(Becomes quite meditative.)*

HARLEQUIN *(gets up and laughs).* Did I scare you? *(Kisses Columbine.)* Forgive me! *(Looks at the clock, which shows twelve o'clock.)* Soon you'll know the real reason.

COLUMBINE. What's the matter?

HARLEQUIN. Let's have some supper. The Dance has given me an appetite and I feel wonderful. *(They sit down, drink, and eat.)*

COLUMBINE. What are you keeping from me!

HARLEQUIN. Drink, Columbine, drink! When there's good wine on the table, there's nothing to worry about. *(They drink, kiss each other, laugh softly.)*

PIERROT *(to the audience).* Oh God, what unbelievable pangs of conscience I'm experiencing. Think of what I've done to Harlequin! And for what? For what? I can't eat a bite and I can't look Harlequin in the face. I'd be only too happy to confess my evil deed to them! But alas! I can't do that, because then what would become of my vengeance! And not to avenge is impossible:

I am the deceived husband and had to avenge myself, because that's the way decent people handle these thing. Ah, how awful I feel, how I want to cry! *(Waves his fist at the audience.)* Nasty evil people! You're the ones that dreamed up these stupid rules! It's because of you I had to shorten the life of my best friend. *(Turns his back on the audience.)*

HARLEQUIN *(to Columbine)*. Why were you late today?

COLUMBINE. The Doctor held me up—I met him not far from here. *(The Doctor Theme is heard in the distance.)* He was limping along, drunk, and stopping all the girls.

HARLEQUIN. And so?

COLUMBINE. He begged me to make him happy. He assured me he was full of strength and had been very handsome thirty years ago. By the time I convinced him I wasn't a historian fascinated by the past, I was late.

HARLEQUIN *(to the audience)*. The poor Doctor! Why oh why didn't he come to me for advice sooner!

COLUMBINE. I felt very sorry for him.

HARLEQUIN *(to the aoudience)*. So near and yet so far.

COLUMBINE. He cried and kept asking "why the hell was I so virtuous!" And I answered "Your wrinkles inspire in me respect, but not passion."

HARLEQUIN. But you know, Columbine, he's younger than I am, even though he's twice my age in years.

COLUMBINE. I don't understand.

HARLEQUIN. Because you haven't given any thought to true old age. *(Claps Pierrot on the shoulder.)* But, my friend, you're not drinking anything, or eating, or participating in the conversation?

COLUMBINE. He's trying to depress us, but a good-for-nothing never succeeds.

PIERROT (crying).Unhappy woman, it would never occur to you that Harlequin is dying.

COLUMBINE. What do you mean "is dying?" Or did you slip some poison in the wine? No, no *(disdainfully)*, people like you are incapable of that.

PIERROT *(still crying)*. Poor Harlequin, your minutes are numbered.

COLUMBINE. What's he talking about?! What rubbish is this?

HARLEQUIN *(turning to the clock)*. Yes, Columbine, it's true. It's time you knew . . . I feel certain I'm going to die soon.

COLUMBINE *(mournfully)*. Harlequin! . . My love! *(She cries.)*

HARLEQUIN. Don't cry, Columbine! I'm leaving with a smile on my lips. I want to die, the way I want to sleep when it's late and time to rest. I've sung all my songs! I've danced up all my joy! I've used up all my laughter! . . I've joyfully squandered my strength and my health along with my money. I was never stingy and so I was eternally happy and carefree. I, Harlequin, will die as Harlequin. Don't weep, Columbine! Rather rejoice that I am dying, not like the others, but surfeited with pleasure, happy with my fate and the life I've lived. Or would you rather see me desperately hanging on to life, with a prayer on my lips! No, that's not Harlequin. He has fulfilled his destiny and dies happy! And that's the truth! Didn't I give my kisses to whoever needed them! Didn't I lavish my soul on the good of others! And how much I comforted the wives of ugly husbands! And how many times I fooled people who thought they were smart! How many people I aroused with a passionate song or a nasty crack! How many did I set a good example for! And now I've lived up my life! And all Death gets is the shell! Seize the moment—that's my motto! And I wasn't lazy about seizing it! I seized so many I don't need any more. Well, one more kiss, a swallow of wine, a burst of merry laughter and that'll do it!

COLUMBINE. How can you not be afraid?

HARLEQUIN. Being born was scarier! Now I'm going back!

COLUMBINE. To sink into non-being, into nothing!

HARLEQUIN. And if it's *nothing*, then how can I be afraid of it?

COLUMBINE. Well, I'm afraid!

HARLEQUIN. Your cup is not yet empty, you're afraid you won't finish it.

COLUMBINE. But just imagine . . .

HARLEQUIN. Death will take care of the imagining for us.

COLUMBINE. And us?

HARLEQUIN. Let's talk about the way the clock moves! . . How swiftly the hands go around! Abandon yourself, Columbine! Press the grapes of life! Turn them into wine! Don't be slow with pleasure, be sure to get enough before Death arrives! *(Takes the lute in hand.)* And you abandon yourself, too, friend Pierrot, if you're capable of it. *(Pierrot sobs violently in reply. Harlequin laughs loudly.)* No, no! Not that way, you don't understand!

PIERROT. The lamp's going out . . .

HARLEQUIN *(sadly)*. And there's no oil in the house.

COLUMBINE. But it's still burning! Look!

HARLEQUIN *(joyfully)*. It's burning, Columbine! It's burning! *(Plays on the lute and sings.)*

> Oh, listen to this song of mine!
> My many friends, Pierrot, and sweet Columbine,
> All my life I've sung this song of mine,
> And so now I'll sing this song of love,
> I'll sing this song of love . . .

(The strings break off as does the song.)

COLUMBINE *(sadly)*. The strings broke!

HARLEQUIN *(laughs)*. My song is sung . . . *(A knock at the door.)* Who's there? *(Again a knock right.)* Pierrot, go see who it is! *(Pierrot takes the lamp and opens the door. Death enters, a bright, white skeleton dressed in a billowy transparent dress similar to Columbine's; there's some sort of triangle on the skull. Death majestically extends a hand in Harlequin's direction. Pierrot trembles, causing the lamp to flicker agonizingly. Columbine remains motionless on a stool, with her arms hanging weakly at her sides and with her eyes closed. Pierrot's eyes are also closed. Harlequin rises to meet Death. Harlequin is very gracious.)* Welcome, madam, you're right on time. We were just talking about you. So good of you not to keep us waiting. But why so tragic? Look around, madam! You're in the house of Harlequin, where they know how to laugh at the tragical, even at you. *(Death melodramatically approaches the clock and extends her hand to it.)* Enough, madam, enough! If I weren't already all laughed out, I'd die laughing—literally. What?! You want to stop the clock? There's still time, madam. As far as I know, my time's not up yet. Or do you expect a fight from me? No, no, I'm not one of those stupid, vulgar bourgeoisie. I know how to treat a charming lady. I wouldn't contradict her, I haven't even the strength, I've used it all up. But the traditional dance? The dance like they had in the good old days when people still knew how to die, not like today. And Death herself was a source of amusement. I beg you! Ah, you're surprised at the request? Oh yes, Harlequin these days is nearly extinct! *(Pleasant violin music is heard, appetizingly mingled with the sharp sounds of a xylophone and castanets. Death dances . . .)*

HARLEQUIN. Columbine! Pierrot! Open your eyes, now! See how merry it is! *(He claps his hands to the music and then tenderly takes Columbine by the waist and sits on the bed with her. The Dance is over. Death stops in front of Harlequin and puts her hand on his shoulder. Pierrot, trembling all over, creeps over to the door left.)*

HARLEQUIN *(to Death)*. One moment, my dear, one moment. Allow me to part from the world in worldly fashion. One more, just one more kiss, Columbine! Pierrot, where are you going, you coward? . . *(Gets up.)* So you're not up to lighting the way for me . . . *(Takes the lamp and hands it to Death.)* Hold the lamp, Death, there's still a drop of oil left. *(He returns to Columbine; Death stands in front of the embracing couple. Kisses and languorous sighs are heard. Somewhere far off the Harlequin Theme is heard.)*

COLUMBINE *(as if in a dream)*. Harlequin, my beloved! . . *(The lamp goes out; the music dies with the last kiss. Several seconds of silence and darkness . . . Then the stage is illuminated with beautiful, deathly pale moonlight. The clock shows twelve. Columbine is kneeling by Harlequin's death bed. Pierrot appears left.)*

PIERROT *(to the audience)*. That's the situation! I haven't the slightest idea what I ought to mourn first: the loss of Harlequin, the loss of Columbine, my own bitter fate, or yours, dear audience, subjected to a work so lacking in seriousness? And what is the author of the play trying to say? . . . I don't understand. However, I'm the stupid, cowardly Pierrot, and it's not up to me to judge the play in which I played an unenviable role. But you're going to be really surprised when you hear what the culprit guilty of perpetrating this strange—just between you and me—mockery has commissioned me to say by way of conclusion. Shh . . . Listen! "When the great Rabelais lay dying, the monks all clustered about his bed and tried everything to get him to repent his sins. Rabelais merely replied with a smile, and when his last moment had come, said merrily—lower the curtain, the farce is over . . . He said it, then died." Now why the unscrupulous playwright had to stick somebody else's words in the mouth of one of the cast, I can't imagine—I'm not a free agent—but, being a conscientious actor, I shall remain loyal to the end, and so, implicitly subjecting myself to the author's will, I merrily shout: Lower the curtain! The farce is over! *(The curtain descends. Pierrot remains in front of it.)* Ladies and gentlemen, I forgot to tell you that neither your applause nor your hisses will be taken seriously by an author who proclaims that nothing in life is worth taking seriously. And I might add that if he's right, then I fail to see why anyone should take that author's play seriously, especially since Harlequin has no doubt already risen from his death bed and is now preening himself for the curtain call. Because, say what you will, actors aren't responsible for the playwright's wild ideas. *(He turns and walks off.)*

CURTAIN.

THE THEATER OF THE SOUL

A One-Act Monodrama with Prologue

CHARACTERS

Professor

S_1 (The rational aspect of the Soul)

S_2 (The emotional aspect of the Soul)

S_3 (The subconscious aspect of the Soul)

Wife Image No. 1

Wife Image No. 2

Songstress Image No. 1

Songstress Image No. 2.

Conductor

The action takes place in the Soul
within the space of thirty seconds.

A blackboard and chalk have been set up in front of the lowered curtain.

PROFESSOR *(enters from the side, moves to the board, bows, and takes a piece of chalk in his hand).* Fellow citizens! The other day the author of the work being presented today came to me. I'm a specialist, you understand. I must confess I at first took a very dim view of this work, supposing it to be—as so often happens in the theater these days—some useless vaudeville, devoid of any deeper meaning or moral significance. So I was all the more pleased to find in The Theater of the Soul a strictly scientific work based on the latest developments in psychophysiology. The researches of Wundt, Freud, Theodule Ribot and others demonstrate that the human soul is not something indivisible, but consists of several *Selves*. Is that clear so far? *(Writes on the board: $S_1 + S_2 + S_3 = S_n$.)* Now Fichte argues that if the Self is the Self, then the world is not the Self. Perfectly clear, isn't it? Fine. But, according to the most recent data, although the world is not the Self, neither is the Self the Self. Perfectly clear? The Self is not the Self, because the Self consists of several Selves. In fact, the Self consists of three Selves. *(He writes on the board: $S = x/3$.)* Therefore, the true Self, the basic Self—what we used to call the Soul—may be broken down to Self sub one, the rational self, the thinking self—what we used to call Reason; Self sub two, the emotional Self, the romantic Self—what we used to call Feeling; and Self sub three, the subconscious Self, the psychical Self—what we used to call the Eternal. That's all clear now, isn't it? These three Selves together make up a larger entity, the Self. *(Writes on the board: $s + s + s = S$.)* Now, the ancients supposed that the Self was located in the liver. Descartes held that it was to be found in the brain, but the author of the present work believes—with no small justification—that the soul happens to be located in our body near the very spot on our chest that we strike instinctively when we wish to emphasize our good faith or when we say things like "my soul is filled with joy . . . My heart bleeds for you . . . My soul burns with indignation!" and so forth. And so, taking the above into account, the theater of the soul may be diagrammed as follows. *(With multicolored chalk draws a picture which he then explains.)* Here, above the diaphragm, we see a large heart suspended by the aorta and the superior vena cava, beating from 55 to 125 times per minute, surrounded right and left by the lungs, contracting and expanding at the rate of 14 to 18 times per minute. In the back, representing the spine and its attached ribs, is a small, garish, yellow colored telephone. Some pale threads, nerves, stretch upward from the diaphragm. We have then, so to say, a model of the stage for the Self to perform on. Now science, my fellow citizens, not only explains, but also gives a certain measure of consolation—for example, it is not sufficient to say that the Self has done something stupid! One has to determine which Self was the stupid one. If the emotional Self was stupid, it doesn't mean a thing. You don't have to

25

worry about the subconscious either. But if the rational Self has been stupid, then it is time to be alarmed! But, my respected fellow citizens, whose Self clearly expresses itself in this insane day and time? . . At this point, I should like to conclude my speech and yield to the author, to the actors, and to you, a most worthy audience for this unusual presentation.

(The Professor retires. The blackboard is taken away. The curtain rises revealing a picture of the soul very much like that the Professor drew on the blackboard. On stage, that is, on the diaphragm, are all three Selves. They are quite similar, all are dressed in black, but in different kinds of clothes. S1 wears a frock coat, S2 wears an artist's smock, and a bright red bow, S3 wears a travelling coat. They are further distinguishable in that S1 has graying, neatly combed hair, he wears glasses, thin lips grace his pale face, and he is rather reserved. S2 seems quite young, is dishevelled, has crimson lips and makes extravagant gestures. S3, wearing a black half-mask, is sleeping downstage with one arm around his suitcase like some exhausted traveller on a train.)

S_2 *(on the telephone).* What? Hello! You can't hear me? But I'm speaking loud enough . . . There's a loud hum? That's because your nerves are stretched extremely tight . . . Well, all right . . . A drink! . . I tell you, another drink! . .

S_1 Don't forget you're the one that's forcing him to drink the third bottle for your own selfish pleasure. The poor heart! . . Look at it beat! . .*

S_2 And so it's your opinion that it ought to be snoozing away all day like Subconscious over there? . . A fine way indeed to spend one's life . . .

S_1 If the heart keeps on beating like that, it won't go on much longer.

S_2 So, it'll stop sooner or later anyway.

S_1 You're using my very words.

S_2 Ah well, you don't talk nonsense all the time.

S_1 Don't pluck on the nerves! . . You've been told many times . . . *(The nerves resound each time they're plucked.)*

S_2 *(flaring up).* By who? Who was told? . . What am I around here, a lackey or something? I'm a poet! . . I'm love! . . I'm fire! . . If it weren't for me this place would be full of mold and cobwebs . . . a classroom, a cemetery! Because where there's no passion, there's a cemetery . . .

S_1 Pure rubbish . . .

S_2 I'm speaking the honest truth . . . Whose fault is it he drinks, do you suppose?

*Translator's note: In Evreinov's own production of the play at the Crooked Mirror Theater, the heart, lungs, the entire set moved rhythmically throughout the play, varying according to the mood and keeping time with the music.

S₁ You're the one demanding he drink more!

S₂ Sure, I demand it, so you and your boredom won't drive him to hang himself.

S₁ Pure rubbish . . . I think it's just the other way around, all his unhappiness and misfortunes are because you, the emotional Self, are such a debauched, lost soul! Don't you ever have the faintest interest, well, let's say, in intellectual pursuits, in the noble work of the mind, aren't you ever visited by any higher, moral considerations?

S₂ You make me sick! You and your damned morality, you and your miserable catechism!

S₁ I despise you, emotional Self! . .

S₂ And I despise you, rational Self! *(With his extravagant gestures he accidentally brushes the nerves.)*

S₁ You scoundrel! Don't pluck on my nerves! . .

S₂ Shut up! . . Allow me to observe, Mr. Rational Self, that we have our nerves in common, and that when I pluck on your nerves, I'm also plucking on my own, and when, thanks to you, my nerves get numb, then I get stupid as a log, that is, like you. I'll pluck on the nerves any time I damn well feel like it. In fact, I'm quite happy they're strained so tightly, that gives me a chance to play a hymn of love and freedom on them! . . *(Plays his hymn, after which the heart commences beating still faster. On the telephone.)* Another drink! . .

S₁ *(tearing the receiver from S₂).* Valerian drops!

S₂ *(tears it back).* Another drink!

S₁ *(tears it back and holds off S₂).* Valerian drops! . . You hear? . . None left? Go to the medicine cabinet . . . Valerian drops! . . Thirty in a glass of water. *(Leaves the telephone . . . Both pace around the stage. They meet face to face.)* Have you calmed down now?

S₂ Have you?

S₁ What do you think? *(Goes over to S₃. Pause.)*

S₂ How's Subconscious doing?

S₁ Same as ever . . . Perfectly tranquil . . . Don't disturb him! . . It'll be worse for you if you do . . . *(On the telephone.)* Did you take the drops? Fine, I'll try one more time to talk some sense into him. *(Takes S₂ by the arm and walks around with him.)* The truth of the matter is I don't understand the basic problem. Well, all right, this woman has captivated you with, so to say, the originality of her talent, if we can call it talent at all, but for a man on that account to desert his wife and children—forgive me for saying so—is not exactly a solution to the problem . . . at least not unless we're polygamists, that is, wild savages for whom soft thighs or round hips are of greater importance than a temple like this, that is, the soul . . .

S₂ Oh, you and your damned logic! . . What is it all to me?!. She's beautiful! . . What's there to reason about?

S₁ Animals don't reason, sure enough, but man, in whom a certain logical approach should obtain . . . *(Into the telephone as he walks past it.)* Light up a cigarette!

S₂ God, but you're boring! . . It's perfectly awful to be eternally connected with anything so boring as all this sweetness and light of yours.

S₁ You didn't use to talk that way.

S₂ Sure, I even used to like you a lot, when you and I used to go arm in arm. I'll never forget, for instance, the service you rendered me when I was aflame with love for Anna. Convincing a distrustful girl and lulling the vigilance of her parents . . . When you put your mind to it you're a real clever rascal! But since then you've not only failed to get any sharper, but you've gotten quite dull, my good friend, like a rusty razor . . .

S₁ Much obliged for the compliment . . . But I'm not going to be offended. You're just all worked up at the moment.

S₂ Ah, but she's beautiful! . . Ye Gods! . . You've forgotten how beautiful she actually is, how unusual she is, so dainty, so piquant! . . Sure, she's a cafe singer, what does that prove? . . . You've forgotten what she looks like . . . You've forgotten! I'll call her. *(He leads out from stage left an image of the cafe singer, an extraordinarily seductive one. To her.)* Sing, sing, like you sang yesterday, the day before, last week, on that Sunday. *Chantez, je vous prie!* I beg you! . . *(To S₁, who turns away from the image.)* Try to pick up a little French, will you, I really need it.

SONGSTRESS IMAGE NO. 1 *(singing and dancing in time to the joyfully beating heart).*

> *Est-ce vous le p'tit jeun' homme*
> *Qu'était l'autre jour tantot*
> *Pres d'moi dans l'metro?*
> *A la station*
> *De l'Odeon?*
> *Je n'ai pas pu vous voir*
> *Car il faisait trop noir*
> *Mais j'voudrais savoir*
> *Est—c'vous? est-c'vous?*
> *Dont mon baiser si doux*
> *M'a rendu amoureux fou?*

> *L'autre jour j'étais dans le metro*
> *Un monsieur s'assied pres de moi.*
> *Je le regarde aussitot.*
> *Mais la lumiere juste a ce moment*
> *S'eteignit subitement.*
> *Mon voisin effraye s'jette dans mes bras!*
> *Affolee je l'embrasse et depuis c'jour la*
> *Je le cherchais en vain et plein d'emoi.*
> *J'dis a chaque homme, que j'apprecois:*
> *Est-c'vous le petit bon homme etc.*

S₂ *(ecstatic)*. Enchanting! . . This joy is worth more than the whole world! . . And those feet! . . My God, can there by anywhere in this world a carpet worthy of being trod upon by those feet, so tiny they make you want to cry . . . Dance on me! . . Dance in me! . . Oh, fragrant incense! . . *(Kisses her feet, then her hands and lips.)*

S₁ Oh, delusion! . . Leave her alone! . . Leave her . . . it's only your imagination! . . She's not like that at all! You're kissing her makeup, you're caressing her wig . . . She's forty years old . . . Leave her . . . It's all fake . . . Here's the reality. *(As his speech began Songstress Image No. 1 drifted off left, whence S₁ then leads in Songstress Image No. 2, a grotesque caricature.)* Look, if you want to know the truth . . . In-grown toenails on those divine feet and those "beloved" corns . . . Calf's head *au nature!*—without wig or makeup. *(Lifts off her wig revealing a bald head underneath.)* Let's take off the bust now! *(She removes her falsies.)* Let's take out the teeth now! *(She removes her false teeth.)* Now sing! *(She sings off-key, gumming the words and prancing around, with all the grace of some old nag sent off to the glue factory.)*

S₂ *(shouting)*. It's not true, it's not true! . . She's not like that at all! *(To her.)* Get out of here!!! *(chases her off.)*

S₁ "You are angry, Jupiter, ergo you must be wrong."

S₂ Rubbish.

S₁ Oh, you know perfectly well that this grand passion of yours is not worthy to tie the shoelaces of the one you're prepared to betray . . . And for what? For what? *(Leads out from right a magnificent image of a wife, rocking a baby in her arms.)* For always being so dutiful, for caressing you, nursing your children? . . Oh, she can't sing, to be sure, like your cafe singer, but just listen to the way she sings a lullaby, if you still have ears for such pure sounds. True, she doesn't sing very well, but she's been singing without sleep the last three nights . . . She's been waiting for you . . .

WIFE IMAGE NO. 1*(singing softly)*.

Sleep, oh darling baby boy,
Sweetly dream, my little joy . . .
Mommy's here so don't you cry,
Lullaby, lullaby . . .

Sleep, little baby, go to sleep . . . Does 'a baby hurt? It'll go away, darling . . .
You'll see, you precious . . . What? . . Dada? . . Where's Dada? Dada'll be here
soon. Dada's working now and pretty soon he'll bring you a nice new toy. You
want a horsie? Gallopy, gallopy . . . Want a horsie? . . Dada's so good . . .

S₂ *(rudely).* Enough of this comedy! . . That's not it at all . . . It's a crude ideal-
ization . . . *(Chases her off.)* Get out of here! . . Imagine what a heroine! . .
All exaggerated . . . She's not like that at all . . . I know her . . . She's poisoned my entire life . . . Not a drop of poetry or joy, bores me to tears and
acts like some damned heroine . . . A scullery maid! . . Here she is . . .
*(Brings in Wife Image No. 2 and replaces Wife Image No. 1 with her. Wife Image
No. 2 is a sharp-tongued petty bourgeoise with a slovenly chignon and dressed in a
shabby dressing gown covered with coffee stains.)*

WIFE IMAGE NO. 2 *(shrilly).* Imagine, such happiness, a bookkeeper! . . If my
mother and father only knew how I suffer with this wretched bastard . . .
It's a pure wonder he hasn't been fired by now! . . The drunken sot! . . His
stupid brain won't even operate without alcohol . . . Gave me all these kids
and now la-de-da . . . I'm in love, he says, with art, with the theater . . .
This cafe singer a theater? I wouldn't let painted sluts like that come anywhere near me! He'll infect all the kids yet! Good-for-nothing idiot . . .
Some breadwinner! . . If it hadn't been for me he'd have hocked the kids'
diapers long ago . . . Won't cross himself either, the atheist . . . Stupid as a
log, but he loves to philosophize . . . Freedom, he says, a citizen's duty . . .
Freedom to guzzle vodka? . . I'll freedom you, you wretch! . .

S₂ There she is, your heroine . . . That's the one I dare not leave for *(leads in
from left Songstress Image No. 1)* this one, who, like some magic nectar into-
xicates me, justifies my existence on earth . . . *(The Songstress sings and
does the can-can, forcing Wife Image No. 2 right and into the shadows, but then
backs up, stops singing as Wife Image No. 1, noble, majestic, aggrieved, advances on
her.)*

WIFE IMAGE NO. 1. Go away, I beg you, there is no place for you here.

S₁ Right.

WIFE IMAGE NO. 1. You don't love him anyway . . . You wouldn't sacrifice a
thing for him. You've had dozens just like him before . . . Don't get him all
excited if you have the slightest shred of decency left. I need his presence,

his support . . . Don't take him away . . . Don't take him away from his family! . .

SONGSTRESS IMAGE NO. 1 *(laughing gaily)*. Ha, ha, ha, ha! *(Speaking deep in her throat with a French accent.)* Such big words! . .

WIFE IMAGE NO. 1. Go away, I repeat, don't drive me too far . . .

SONGSTRESS IMAGE NO. 1. Are you threatening me? And why, pray tell? Because my legs are beautiful, my breasts are firm, and happy words fly from my mouth like doves, like champagne corks! . .

S_2 *(applauding)*. Bravo, bravo . . .

WIFE IMAGE NO. 1 *(to her)*. All you need is money, you floozie for sale! . .

SONGSTRESS IMAGE NO. 1. What? I'm a floozie for sale, am I? . . You take that back . . . *(Approaches threateningly.)*

WIFE IMAGE NO. 1. Get out! . . *(They rush at each other and battle furiously, while the quivering heart thumps loudly, seemingly in agony. We also hear curses and bitter threats: "shameless hussy . . . floozie . . . parasite . . . idiot . . . whore . . . slut . . . damn you to hell." They disappear into a dark corner, then come out again even more furious, but now in the form of Images No. 2. The wife has her teeth in the songstress' wig, the songstress has a firm grip on the wife's tresses. They switch back again to their positive images and reveal the songstress' victory over the wife. The wife is held flat on the floor by the songstress' powerful knee. The unfortunate wife then runs off right with a wail amid the songstress' loud laughter and S_2's applause. Meanwhile an enraged S_1 slaps the songstress loudly in the face, she shrieks pitifully as she backs off upstage like a wounded puppy. S_2 is not going to stand for that! He hurls himself at S_1 and strangles him. The heart stops for an instant, two or three overstrained nerves burst. S_2, satisfying himself his enemy is dead, throws himself at the Songstress' feet.)*

S_2 You are now the ruler here! . . My queen! . .

SONGSTRESS IMAGE NO. 1. Oh no, sweetheart, no indeed . . . I was just teasing . . . First the money, then the love . . . And you don't smell much like money to me . . . Where are you going to get any? . . No, no, I'm not yours . . . I was just teasing. *(She disappears left. S_2 is paralyzed with despair. The Songstress' teasing singing drifts in from the left, far away. The infinitely sorrowful Wife Image No. 1 clutches her sick baby at right and fixes her enormous eyes on S_2. She seems to be rocking her baby a little, or is it nodding her head reproachfully in S_2's direction?)*

S_2 *(unable to bear it any longer, rushes to the telephone)*. Oh please . . . quick . . . It's all over now . . . I'm exhausted . . . The pistol's in the right back pocket . . . Hurry! . . Hurry! . . I can't bear it any longer . . . Don't miss! . . Between the third and fourth ribs! . . Go on, go on! . . What are you afraid of? . . It's just an instant. Quick! . . *(A pause. S_3 awakes and uneasily looks around as if* *sensing impending disaster. A shot rings out, very loud, as if from a cannon, and the roar reverberates through the soul. An enormous, gaping hole appears in the heart, out of which roll red ribbons. Darkness descends. S_2 falls convulsively to the floor beneath the heart, drowning in a sea of red ribbons. The heart stops. The lungs cease breathing. A pause. S_3 trembles and stretches nervously a few times. The Conductor enters with a lighted lantern.)*

CONDUCTOR. Newville . . . Who's getting off here? . . Mr. Subconscious, hey, Mr. Subconscious! . . Here's where you change . . . Newville . . .

S_3 Newville? All right . . . let's go! Newville! . . *(Puts on his hat, picks up his suitcase and yawns as he follows the Conductor.)*

CURTAIN.

THE MAIN THING

*A Comedy for Some and a Drama
for Others, in Four Acts*

*Dedicated to the fond memory of
Julia Ivanovna Davydova (nee Gravel)
who taught me the Good.*

N. Evreinov

CHARACTERS

Paraclete—meaning counselor, helper, consoler

Lady Fortune-Teller
Doctor Fregoli
Schmidt   —Various guises of Paraclete
Monk
Harlequin

Provincial Theater Director

Regisseur

Prompter

Electrician

Romantic Lead
Barefoot Dancer, his wife
Comic   —Actors and
Actor Playing the Role of Nero
Actor Playing the Role of Petronius   Actresses
Actor Playing the Role of Tigellinus
Actor Playing the Role of Lucan   of the
Actress Playing the Role of Poppaea Sabina
Actress Playing the Role of Lygia   —Provincial Theater
Actress Playing the Role of Calvia Crispinilla
Actress Playing the Role of Nigidia

Boardinghouse Landlady
Typist, her daughter
Retired Civil Servant   —Resident of the
                                     Boardinghouse

Student, his son
Aglaya Karpovna, deportment mistress
at a Gimnaziya

Lady with the Small Dog
Deaf-mute   —Wives of a Trigamist
Fallen Woman

*The action takes place in a provincial city in Central Russia
at the very beginning of the twentieth century.*

ACT ONE

The Lady Fortune-Teller's room. It is small and poorly furnished. Three stuffed animals attract instant attention: an owl with shiny eyes on a perch, a large bat suspended from the ceiling, and an emaciated black cat which doesn't help the looks of the Fortune-Teller's table very much. The table stands at stage right by the only window. A faded Oriental shawl serves as a curtain on the window. There are two doors: the one stage left leads into a reception room and the one center leads into a bedroom. A vanity with a muslin canopy occupies a prominent position in the bedroom. Right of the center door is a large wardrobe; left is a low screen. On the walls hang ancient charts of the starry heavens and of "The Oracle" as well as signs of the zodiac, horoscopes, photographs of seances, ghosts, etc. On the table there are—besides the cat—a jar with coffee grounds, a small mirror, a crystal ball, three small yellow wax candles and one large black candle—all four in antique candleholders, very old books with metal hasps, soiled playing cards, a stack of newspapers and magazines, a metal box with a slot for money, several small jars with green and violet liquids, a sprig of mistletoe in a wide bottle, and a skull. All in all the furnishings seem quite capable of producing the effect desired by the Fortune-Teller on a superstitious client. Natural daylight illuminates the room, not too dim, but none too bright either. The Fortune-Teller is sitting at the table with her back to the window in a black leather armchair as old as she is. Her clients are obliged to take a chair at the table opposite her. They are thus comparatively well illuminated by the light spilling in the window. As the curtain rises we find ourselves at the Fortune-Teller's, it so happens, during her morning "reception." She is sitting at the table and her slightly trembling hands are laying out the cards in some elaborate pattern. She is wearing an old gray house dress covered with coffee stains. It fits her hunchbacked figure very poorly. The hump in her nose supports a pair of huge tortoise-shell glasses, above which—like a mask covering her eyes, eyebrows, and forehead—there is a faded green visor, held on by an elastic band, the very kind oculists prescribe to preserve one's eyesight. The old woman's gray, dishevelled hair is covered with a lace cap. Her upper lip—which does a poor job of hiding her rotten teeth—seems to be stained with snuff. Two large, hairy warts on the chin and the right cheekbone make the teller of human fates even more ugly. Around her neck is a necklace of some bizarre talismans. On her arms are jangly silver bracelets, some with jade, some with the defending "hands of Fatima," etc. Rings with turquoise and moonstones flash on her fingers. Her voice is hoarse and her speech is somewhat guttural, firm, the kind Caucasians often have. In front of her sits a stout lady—one might say far nicer things about her finery than her beauty. Blinking her eyes she is paying careful attention to the old woman's predictions, while also not

neglecting to keep an eye on the small dog she brought along with an elegant leash, a
lovely sweater, and a beautiful, shiny collar.

FORTUNE-TELLER. . . . money . . . a lot of activity there, a package—a letter . . . success in business . . . financial problems . . . Forgive me, madam,
you do play the stock market? . .

LADY WITH THE SMALL DOG *(holding back, unwilling to show her hand)*. A
little, why? . . *(Purses her lip and makes sounds to call her dog to her, then pats it.)*

FORTUNE-TELLER. Well, I thought so—your cards have a lot to say about
money matters . . . not much happiness . . .

LADY WITH THE SMALL DOG. Of course! Ever since the day he left me . . .

FORTUNE-TELLER. Who?

LADY WITH THE SMALL DOG *(in a half-offended tone)*. My husband! . . I
certainly wouldn't be carrying on like *that* with anybody else . . . Ever
since that day I see happiness only in my dreams . . .

FORTUNE-TELLER. Was he a good man?

LADY WITH THE SMALL DOG. I wouldn't have loved a bad one . . .

FORTUNE-TELLER. Well of course not! But just why did he leave you?

LADY WITH THE SMALL DOG. Who knows! *(Pulls out a gold cigarette case
and lights up a cigarette.)* He married me when I was a poor orphan girl, living with a strict old stingy aunt, impossible to live with . . . He gave me all
the happiness of love, he set my wildest fantasies free . . . But when my
aunt died and left me a fortune, he . . . left me and all my money . . . *(Puts
her lace handkerchief to her eyes.)*

FORTUNE-TELLER. Ve-ry unusual man!

LADY WITH THE SMALL DOG. Is it possible then after something like that
to speak of the "enigma of a woman's heart"? What would you know about
a man's heart? . .

FORTUNE-TELLER. What I would say is of no importance. What the cards
say is something else.

LADY WITH THE SMALL DOG. But there's not a peep out of your cards! . .
Won't say a word about the most interesting part.

FORTUNE-TELLER. That means his fate is not tied in with yours.

LADY WITH THE SMALL DOG. Thank you so much! That hardly makes it
any easier for me! Seeing a handsome man riding by in a carriage, knowing
that he's been listed in his passport as my husband for the last ten years,
and . . . and . . . if he would only nod!

FORTUNE-TELLER. And you're sure it's really him?

LADY WITH THE SMALL DOG. Well of course! . . Shaving your beard off
doesn't make you unrecognizable, especially to a wife . . . I already spoke

to a lawyer about it—it's a 24-carat crime and carried the death penalty in England until just recently! . .

FORTUNE-TELLER. What crime? . .

LADY WITH THE SMALL DOG. Trigamy. There was a similar case some seventy years back. They take a very dim view of things like that in England.

FORTUNE-TELLER. But pardon me, in the first place this is Russia, and in the second, can your husband really by a trigamist?

LADY WITH THE SMALL DOG. Can he ever! . . . What do you suppose I'm so upset about? Last year I had to go to Willdungen—my kidneys, you understand, aren't working too well . . . What can one do—I'm so fond of good cognac—there's so little joy in life! . . And imagine! I meet this deaf-mute who has a lovely picture of my husband in her photo album. I get to be friends with her; I don't care, you understand, for these vacation spot chatterboxes! Deaf-mutes are something else—jot down something in her notebook and she'll answer you, quietly, calmly, won't blast your ears off, and people like her won't deny what they said either. "That's my husband," I write her and "No, it's mine," she answers and underlines it three times. "What do you mean!" . . . "How can it be!" "Bigamist," I write to her. "We've been deceived." "Maybe even a trigamist?" she answers and gives me an account right then of how she once caught him with some street girl, and then he ran off with her, God knows where. But she wasn't any dumbbell and you have to suppose that—just as we did—she too dragged that servant of the Lord off to the altar to prove his love.

FORTUNE-TELLER. A very interesting story! . .

LADY WITH THE SMALL DOG. Well, of course! The whole detective profession has gotten interested in it. By the way—just between the two of us—what a detective they assigned me . . . *(kisses her finger tips)* charming! . . Even works in the theater just to study makeup, facial expression, and stuff like that . . . Svetozarov . . . You've heard of him? . . Fascinating! . . His manners . . . His eyes . . . I promised him a fortune if he finds my Don Juan . . . Oh! . . Don't suppose I'm going to get him arrested for trigamy! . . What for? . . Wouldn't help me a bit! No, I'll simply demand the gendarmes and him step forth, I'll demand a divorce and then—out of my sight . . . Really! So what's he! I'm still young, I could marry again, but now—with no divorce—it's not such a good idea to be running around! . . Thank you so much . . . Forms mean a great deal to me!

FORTUNE-TELLER. Oh, so there's someone else. Well, at least that's a comfort.

LADY WITH THE SMALL DOG *(laughs and puts the dog on her lap)*. I have two friends: this one—his name is Mimi, and the other—his name is . . . however, it doesn't make any difference what his name is! Isn't that right,

Mimi? . . *(She kisses the dog.)* Where did you get so dirty? *(Brushes the dust off the dog's sweater. To the Fortune-Teller.)* Tell me please, would you be able to tell my Mimi's fortune?

FORTUNE-TELLER. Your dog's?

LADY WITH THE SMALL DOG. Yes, he's been so melancholy over something lately! Sits on the window-sill for hours and sadly looks out at the street, ever so sadly . . .

FORTUNE-TELLER. Yes, but, madam, I don't have any dog cards. How could I tell his fortune?

LADY WITH THE SMALL DOG. Why dog cards? He understands everything, just like a human being.

FORTUNE-TELLER. But who is then to cut the cards?

LADY WITH THE SMALL DOG. I could do it for him, and he could touch the deck with his paw . . . to confirm it, so to say . . . *(She cuts the deck and pokes it with the dog's paw.)*

FORTUNE-TELLER *(sighs)*. Ohhhh . . . first time I ever told a dog's fortune . . . *(She lays out the cards.)*

RETIRED CIVIL SERVANT *(an old man with a large gray beard over his trembling jaws, wearing a worn formal coat, with a military cap with a metal emblem in one hand and a rubber-tipped cane in the other, pathetic, with teary eyes and a reddish nose, enters limping from the door left and says, mumbling through his old, sparsely toothed gums)*. Excuse me, benefactress . . . I have some urgent business . . . I'm too old to wait . . . I just barely stumbled over here . . . be so kind! . .

FORTUNE-TELLER. We'll be through in a minute . . . I'll be at your disposal right away . . .

RETIRED CIVIL SERVANT. Yes m'am . . . thank you . . . I beg your humble pardon . . . *(Goes off)*.

LADY WITH THE SMALL DOG *(in the direction he went off)*. Bad manners! . . Sneaking in like that without asking! And at the most fatal moment at that. Isn't that right, Mimi? *(She kisses the dog.)*. Look how scared he is! . . Well then, what good fortune have you to tell us?

FORTUNE-TELLER *(looking at the cards)*. Very little good fortune . . . In the first place, illness . . .

LADY WITH THE SMALL DOG. My Mimi fall ill?

FORTUNE-TELLER. Certainly . . . in the first place, from gluttony, and in the second, from the sedentary life he leads.

LADY WITH THE SMALL DOG. Really! You mean you can tell all that from the cards? And will it be serious?

FORTUNE-TELLER. If you would donate to sick children all the milk and candy your dog uses up, then the illness, perhaps, won't be too serious . . .

LADY WITH THE SMALL DOG *(to the dog)*. You hear that, Mimi, you have to go on a diet, unhappy creature! *(To the Fortune-Teller.)* Well, and then what?

FORTUNE-TELLER. The queen of clubs . . . a great love . . . longing for the queen of clubs . . .

LADY WITH THE SMALL DOG. I know—that's that black Zhúchka that lives across the street . . . Ai, ai, ai, Mimi, I didn't expect this . . .

FORTUNE-TELLER. And here's the queen of hearts . . . also . . . a gr-eat liking for . . .

LADY WITH THE SMALL DOG. You worthless Mimi! Answer me now this instant, who's this queen of hearts? This is the first time I've heard anything about it, well, speak up! . .

FORTUNE-TELLER *(scratching behind her ear)*. Perhaps, madam, you'd do better to talk it over with him at home, especially since if my clients have to wait for a dog to speak up, they might lose their patience! Don't you think so?

LADY WITH THE SMALL DOG *(hurt)*. Heavens, I had so many things to ask you about. But you're always in such a rush . . . *(Stands up and puts the dog on the floor.)* Am I all paid up? *(Points to the money she has left on the table.)*

FORTUNE-TELLER. Thank you. Only you forgot to make a donation. *(Presents her the collection box.)* For the poor.

LADY WITH THE SMALL DOG *(takes out her money and puts a coin in the collection box)*. Heavens, there's just no getting by these poor . . . A beggar or a collection jar at every step . . . Isn't that right, Mimi? Aren't those beggars insufferable? . . Oh how he barks at them, you should hear him! But, oh well, this one's from me, and this one's from Mimi! We won't go broke! Goodbye! *(She leaves. The Fortune-Teller puts the money in the table drawer and picks up the cards.)*

RETIRED CIVIL SERVANT *(entering)*. May I?

FORTUNE-TELLER. Please.

RETIRED CIVIL SERVANT. Here's what, benefactress . . . it'll only take a minute . . . I won't keep you, my word of honor! . . Marya Yakovlevna sent me, our landlady . . . the landlady with the boardinghouse where my son and I are living . . .

FORTUNE-TELLER. Please sit down. *(He sits down opposite her.)* Marya Yakovlevna was planning to drop in on me today . . .

RETIRED CIVIL SERVANT. Yes, yes! That's exactly why I'm here. She's coming with her daughter today . . . But that's her business . . . I came on account of my son . . . Fedya, he's a student . . . Marya Yakovlevna persuaded him to accompany them here . . . He considers your fortune-telling—now don't be angry, my dear—to be pure superstition . . . and I, the sinner, don't actually believe in it either . . . But I've heard from Marya Yakovlevna that you're the kindest of souls and won't refuse your advice to your neighbors in their moments of sorrow . . . And it's a major sorrow all right! . . Just imagine—a young man in the flower of life, so to say, and suddenly . . . lays hands on himself . . . disgusted with life . . .

FORTUNE-TELLER. But . . . thank God, it seems it all came out all right? Marya Yakovlevna told me that . . .

RETIRED CIVIL SERVANT. Marya Yakovlevna was the one that saved him . . . I was at church . . . True enough, the hook couldn't stand the weight, "the hand of the Almighty," so to speak, but the rope, the damned rope cut into his neck . . . Ah yes, they saved the boy! But God only knows what he'll do next . . . So that's why I'm here, benefactress, dropped in ahead of time . . . He won't listen to an old man like me! He just might listen to you—they say you're a wonderful hypnotist—at least try to persuade him, the madman, to have pity on an old man like me! . . Why punish me! Even without things like this life is hard enough . . . Unjustly forced to retire . . . A pitifully small pension . . . ravaged by illness . . . One might expect a little support from the younger generation! But, oh no! One son, Volodya, joined the Navy, off sailing the high seas, and the other—sad to say—has brought down such shame on my gray head . . . *(Blows his nose tearfully and wipes his eyes.)*

FORTUNE-TELLER. I'd be happy to help you if I had any idea how! . . it's not so simple you know!—you have to crawl into a man's soul, and not everybody lets you! . .

RETIRED CIVIL SERVANT. Change his way of thinking, my dear! . . Tell him whatever's necessary to turn him around, the heartless boy! . . You know him . . . it's not up to me to teach you! . . Here! . . *(Thrusts some money at her with trembling hands.)* Forgive me, don't refuse me, benefactress . . .

FORTUNE-TELLER *(pushing the money aside)*. No, no! . . I don't take money in advance . . .

RETIRED CIVIL SERVANT *(gets up and backs toward the door)*. Oh no, don't refuse me, benefactress! . . Only help me, please! . . I'll pray to God for you if you'll help me. Forgive me. I don't dare bother you another minute . . .

FORTUNE-TELLER. But I don't need your money! Take it! . .

RETIRED CIVIL SERVANT *(in the doorway)*. It's not mine, ma'am, but yours, yours, ma'am . . . don't offend an old man . . . be so kind! *(He bows.)* I have the honor to bid you good day. *(The Fortune-Teller shakes her head and puts the money in the collection box "for the poor.")*

BAREFOOT DANCER *(enters, modestly dressed and wearing a thick veil)*. How do you do! *(Warmly shakes the old woman's hand.)* I came a little early, since there's a 12 o'clock rehearsal at the theater, and I'm afraid to be late . . .

FORTUNE-TELLER. Sit down. You got my letter?

BAREFOOT DANCER *(sits down and raises her veil, revealing a beautiful and thoughtful face).* I hardly know how to thank you . . . You're so considerate . . . With neither a father nor a mother I could come to . . . And your attitude to me the whole time we've known each other . . .

FORTUNE-TELLER *(interrupting).* Fine, fine! Only let's dispense with the sentiment. I have some news for you, I was at your theater the other day . . .

BAREFOOT DANCER *(astonished).* You!? At our theater!? Impossible! Well, of course, you were horrified by that cheap show? My God, to realize that I first entered the theater as if it were a temple, seeing my own art as some act of transcendance, and then to wind up in some sleazy hole in the wall, it's really horrible . . .

FORTUNE-TELLER. I saw your husband on the stage . . .

BAREFOOT DANCER. Svetozarov? . .

FORTUNE-TELLER. He's a good actor, but his makeup wasn't done very well . . .

BAREFOOT DANCER. I've told him a dozen times! The disillusioned Pierrot—the same old face every time.

FORTUNE-TELLER. It was precisely on your account that I dropped in to have a look at the fellow.

BAREFOOT DANCER. Really!

FORTUNE-TELLER. You've assigned me a most difficult mission. After all, trying to decide—when you haven't seen the man or even heard his voice—whether his love may cool or not . . .

BAREFOOT DANCER. Well, and so what do you say now! . . Go ahead, don't torture me, you know how much I adore him . . .

FORTUNE TELLER *(after a pause).* Hm . . . Your problem is not so serious . . .

BAREFOOT DANCER. Really? . .

FORTUNE-TELLER. Yes . . . I looked at the cards again . . . When you see a man it's much easier to make sense of his cards . . .

BAREFOOT DANCER. And so? . .

FORTUNE-TELLER. Just as I wrote you before: you love him too much, but . . . don't let him be too sure of you.

BAREFOOT DANCER. But how, I don't understand?!

FORTUNE-TELLER. Make him jealous . . .

BAREFOOT DANCER. Yes, but he's paid me so little attention lately . . .

FORTUNE-TELLER. Doesn't mean a thing! Stock up on the patience and calculation of an engineer, then build a bridge of jealousy and your husband's locomotive heart will come roaring back full steam over that bridge! *(An abrupt double ring is heard on the bell.)*

BAREFOOT DANCER *(startled).* Good heavens, that's strange! . .

FORTUNE-TELLER. What's strange?

BAREFOOT DANCER. The bell . . . That's the way my husband usually rings . . . Well, I must go! *(Bids goodbye to the Fortune-Teller.)* Goodbye! . .

FORTUNE-TELLER. Good luck!

BAREFOOT DANCER *(smiling gratefully)*. I'll do my best! . . Oh yes! Excuse me, I almost forgot! In your letter you foretell something's going to happen at the theater! . . Seems we're in for some sort of surprise today . . .

FORTUNE-TELLER. In any event an interesting proposal that shouldn't be rejected.

BAREFOOT DANCER. Who'll get it? Me? My husband? Or the whole company?

FORTUNE-TELLER. I only told *your* fortune . . .

BAREFOOT DANCER. Oh, of course! . . Thank you . . . *(The bell rings.)* Well, I'm off! I won't keep others from trying their fortune. Goodbye! *(She leaves. Pause.)*

FORTUNE-TELLER *(gets up impatiently with the intention of going to the door)*. Who is it? . . Who's next? . . Come in! . .

ROMANTIC LEAD *(with a small beard and pince nez with dark lenses, enters with a newspaper in his hands)*. How do you do! Is this . . . is this you? *(Reads an advertisement in the paper.)* "Oriental Fortune-Teller, physiognomist, handwriting analysis, reads palms, cures secret ailments, and gives advice in matters of the heart?"

FORTUNE-TELLER *(who sat down again on his appearance)*. At your service.

ROMANTIC LEAD. I've come to ask you to tell . . .

FORTUNE-TELLER. To tell? . . And I thought you wanted a shave! . .

ROMANTIC LEAD. But how, I don't understand.

FORTUNE-TELLER. Tell what? Sit down!

ROMANTIC LEAD *(pulling up a chair and sitting down)*. About a certain disappearance.

FORTUNE-TELLER. Of a needle?

ROMANTIC LEAD. No, a little larger.

FORTUNE-TELLER. Something of yours disappeared?

ROMANTIC LEAD. Doesn't make any difference whose.

FORTUNE-TELLER. Are you really you?

ROMANTIC LEAD. What do you mean?

FORTUNE-TELLER *(stands up and bends over across the table to him)*. Is this beard yours? *(With a swift movement she tears off the false beard and moustache.)*

ROMANTIC LEAD *(amazed, defensive)*. I'm sorry . . . but listen . . .

FORTUNE-TELLER. The Fortune-Teller sees all! . . Sees right through any man . . . sees even better than you do without the glasses!

ROMANTIC LEAD *(taking off his pince nez and putting his beard in his pocket).* It's . . . it's . . . simply amazing . . . I'm speechless.

FORTUNE-TELLER. Why have you come? Come clean! You won't hide anything from me.

ROMANTIC LEAD. Give me a minute to recover!

FORTUNE-TELLER. Only make it fast! Otherwise you'll be late for your rehearsal!

ROMANTIC LEAD. What! You even know I'm an actor? You saw me on stage?

FORTUNE-TELLER. Whether I did or didn't is *my* business. But what's *your* business, that brought you here?

ROMANTIC LEAD. Hm . . . you see . . .

FORTUNE-TELLER. I see everything, so don't lie!

ROMANTIC LEAD *(recovering from his surprise and now even a little ironical).* Well, if you're so clairvoyant, you perhaps are aware that I've been shadowing a certain gentleman, who, if he doesn't actually live here, then at least visits often . . . here's his picture! . . *(Takes a snapshot out of his pocket.)* He has a beard on here *(laughs in embarrassment)* like I used to . . . But he's apparently shaved it off . . . Looks a lot like this picture in any case.

FORTUNE-TELLER. So?

ROMANTIC LEAD. They're looking for him . . . He's deceived three woman already! A criminal type. Marries, takes the dowry and vanishes . . .

FORTUNE-TELLER. Very bad . . .

ROMANTIC LEAD. And so I wanted you to help the law . . .

FORTUNE-TELLER. You're a detective?

ROMANTIC LEAD *(hesitating).* Hm . . . theater work doesn't pay very well . . .

FORTUNE-TELLER *(finishing).* . . . so you became a detective?

ROMANTIC LEAD. Is that so reprehensible? We risk our lives sometimes y'know for the sake of our fellow man . . . well, for law, for justice . . .

FORTUNE-TELLER *(lays out the cards).* So that's it! . . *(Tells his fortune.)* Oho! . . You're in luck! . . you'll have some news shortly . . . maybe even today, in your business . . . we have to suppose that means the theater or . . .

ROMANTIC LEAD *(interrupting).* My wife told me already; she's been writing you, hasn't she? For God's sake, not a whisper to her about me being a detective. She's such an idealist that God only knows what she'd think of me if she knew.

FORTUNE-TELLER. She was just here a moment ago.

ROMANTIC LEAD. Of course, I saw her, but she didn't recognize me.

FORTUNE-TELLER. As to your "disappearance," that is, as to this trigamist you're looking for, I can't say a thing . . . The cards are keeping quiet and won't give him away . . . But I'll give it a try . . . every week. Leave me your address—if I see anything I'll write you. *(He writes his address on a calling card and hands it to her.)* You'll soon be moving to a new apartment—be sure and let me know your new address then.

ROMANTIC LEAD. I'm . . . moving, you say?

FORTUNE-TELLER. That's what the cards say. *(Hands him back the snapshot.)* Here, take it! *(She laughs.)* Quite a coincidence! . . Really looks a lot like . . . very much so . . .

ROMANTIC LEAD *(excited)*. Looks like him, you say?

FORTUNE-TELLER. Absolutely . . . Moreover, he's my "admirer," as you would put it. Rich—that's true, but not from stealing dowries! . .

ROMANTIC LEAD. Are you sure of that?

FORTUNE-TELLER. Just as sure as I am that he might be a lot of help to you . . .

ROMANTIC LEAD. To me?!

FORTUNE-TELLER. Yes! He's also in the theater! Not a producer exactly, but something like that.

ROMANTIC LEAD. My God! And I, the idiot, was going to arrest him!

FORTUNE-TELLER. That would've made for some great vaudeville!

ROMANTIC LEAD. Damn it all, that's coincidence for you! *(Puts the snapshot in his pocket.)* But tell me, please, couldn't you tell from the cards where my Don Juan's third wife lives?

FORTUNE-TELLER. Of this man you're trying to track down?

ROMANTIC LEAD. Yes! We already have the address of the second one . . .

FORTUNE-TELLER *(with a big, stupid grin)*. Hm . . . cards won't help a bit . . . but I have this powder from India . . . I'll take it before I go to bed, maybe I'll dream something!

ROMANTIC LEAD *(leaps up gleefully, takes out some money and thrusts it in her hand)*. I'm prepared to pay you 25% of my fee, 30%! 40% even! Only you must tell me . . . This is my debut in the role of detective! I'm so excited, more than I ever was on stage! You, of course, understand, that if you fall flat on the stage nobody's going to suffer over it! But here! . . . it would mean losing the whole case, leaving the law, justice, society powerless to deal with some unpunished Bluebeard. *(A knock at the door.)*

FORTUNE-TELLER *(yells)*. Who's there? Come in! *(The Boardinghouse Landlady, the Typist, and the Student all walk in. The first is a sweet old lady, the second—her daughter—plain, likable but rather pathetic aesthetically, especially in view of the bandage she's wearing for her toothache. The third visitor—the Student—has a skimpy beard, shaggy hair, looks a little pimpled and wears glasses. Behind the lenses his small reddish eyes squint near-sightedly.)*

FORTUNE-TELLER. Marya Yakovlevna?

BOARDINGHOUSE LANDLADY. Yes, and not only me, but . . .

FORTUNE-TELLER *(going to meet her)*. Welcome . . .

ROMANTIC LEAD. Well, I'm off! Time for the rehearsal. Goodbye! So I should keep my hopes up?

FORTUNE-TELLER. Yes, yes! *(The Romantic Lead leaves.)*

BOARDINGHOUSE LANDLADY. I thought you were busy, perhaps . . . *(Shakes hands.)*

FORTUNE-TELLER. Oh come now! I was expecting you. I'm so glad you're not late, I'm winding up my reception hour early today . . . *(opens the door and yells)*. Dunya! Don't take anybody else today, except for the gentleman I told you about . . . You hear?

BOARDINGHOUSE LANDLADY. Forgive me, I forgot to introduce my daughter . . . Lidochka . . .

FORTUNE-TELLER. Pleased to meet you. *(Shakes hands with the Typist.)*

BOARDINGHOUSE LANDLADY. The best typist in town . . . If you need anything typed, you won't find a better one anywhere . . .

FORTUNE-TELLER *(not letting go of the Typist's hand)*. Ai, ai, ai, what a thin little hand! I nearly crushed it! . . *(To all of them.)* Please be seated.

BOARDINGHOUSE LANDLADY. Won't eat anything, coughs all the time, won't listen to the doctors! I plead with her to send in a sputum sample— "I don't feel like it," she says, "why bother"—Keep it up and something awful is going to happen . . . I know very well what it is! My husband died of consumption!

FORTUNE-TELLER. And her teeth hurt?

BOARDINGHOUSE LANDLADY *(settle down in a chair)*. Gums are all swollen up! . . always catching cold, won't take care of herself for anything! . .

TYPIST. Mama told me you can charm away toothaches. Is that true?

FORTUNE-TELLER. Yes, it is.

TYPIST. Well, go ahead and try then, I'm rather skeptical though somehow . . .

FORTUNE-TELLER. I will! You won't be skeptical long! . . And this young man . . . one of your tenants no doubt? . . *(Takes the Student's hand.)*

BOARDINGHOUSE LANDLADY. Yes . . . hm . . . also a distant relative of ours . . . I told you about him.

FORTUNE-TELLER *(not letting go his hand, to him)*. Come to have your fortune told?

STUDENT *(speaks, stammering here and there)*. No . . . don't bother . . . I just came to accompany them to your chamber of curiosities! . . That's quite enough for me.

BOARDINGHOUSE LANDLADY *(to him)*. Fedya, why not? It's no effort on your part.

FORTUNE-TELLER *(still holding him by the hand)*. Wait a moment, Marya Yakovlevna, I'll divine what he's thinking now, even without the cards.

STUDENT *(ironically)*. What am I thinking then?

FORTUNE-TELLER. You're thinking: you lie, you old witch, you'll never guess what I'm thinking! You won't catch me!

STUDENT *(grinning)*. Well, that's no trick . . . anybody could've guessed that! . .

FORTUNE-TELLER *(letting go his hand)*. I don't do tricks, my dear, but if you'd like to call the whole thing a trick—go right ahead! Just because you called this room a chamber of curiosities doesn't make it one, although, to be sure, some real *monsters* show up in it on occasion . . .

TYPIST. Aha, Fedya, touché! Right through the heart! *(She tries to laugh, but her toothache prevents her; she puts her hand to her cheek and coughs painfully, using a handkerchief to catch her sputum.)*

STUDENT *(in a pleasant, mocking tone)*. Well now, maybe I'm a *monster* and maybe not, but you're hardly one to talk with a face all swollen up like that.

FORTUNE-TELLER. You might add—and not around anyone as beautiful as the lady of the house. Let's go into the other room, young lady! I'll charm your toothache away in no time at all! And you two be so good as to sit tight for a few moments! If you don't have anything else to do, you can say nasty things about me! *(She and the Typist go into the bedroom. The Student paces around the room. A pause.)*

BOARDINGHOUSE LANDLADY. You're a good man, Fedya, but learning hasn't helped you a bit.

STUDENT. What do you mean, hasn't helped?

BOARDINGHOUSE LANDLADY. I mean your mind's all fogged up. That's why your life seems so empty.

STUDENT. Marya Yakovlevna, I beseech you: don't talk about things you don't understand!

BOARDINGHOUSE LANDLADY. What's there not to understand? Ask anybody you want, anybody'll tell you.

STUDENT. Tell me what?

BOARDINGHOUSE LANDLADY. That you at least ought to take pity on your father. Do you suppose he enjoys realizing that any moment you might get some . . . crazy idea!

STUDENT. Let's talk about something else! You'll never understand me! You'd have to be a psychologist.

BOARDINGHOUSE LANDLADY. And this fortune-teller doesn't understand you either, I suppose?

STUDENT. Who? *(The Boardinghouse Landlady nods in the direction of the room where the Fortune-Teller is.)* That Pythia?

BOARDINGHOUSE LANDLADY. Shh . . . don't be so sarcastic, please!

STUDENT *(with a grin)*. What does she have to say?

BOARDINGHOUSE LANDLADY. She says only egotists are any good at that.

STUDENT. Egotists?! How so?

BOARDINGHOUSE LANDLADY. Because the man who overcomes his fear of death will fear nothing in the struggle for justice. And if there were enough of them, then the powers that be would be done for! But as it is they know everybody's a coward, so they laugh at us, like they do at your father! Why was the man fired, I ask you? Because he took a stand against bribes? Is that justice?! And no one avenges him! Even his own son would rather kill himself than lay a finger on the one responsible.

STUDENT. Some argument! And what's egotism go to do with it?

BOARDINGHOUSE LANDLADY. This—that if you're tired of life and it's become some unwanted thing, then sacrifice it for others, and don't kill yourself just for the fun of it. Only egotists do that.

STUDENT (thoughtfully, but still somewhat ironically). That's an amusing way to look at it . . .

FORTUNE-TELLER (appears in the bedroom doorway). Young man, please don't be angry, but step out for five minutes, we have something to talk about in private.

STUDENT. Step out? . . . Certainly! Then also allow me to bid you good day altogether, my head aches and I'd like a little fresh air.

BOARDINGHOUSE LANDLADY. But the fortune-telling? Fedya, you promised? . .

STUDENT. I only promised to come here with you. As for the rest—that would be sheer repression. Goodbye. (He leaves.)

BOARDINGHOUSE LANDLADY. Now do you see? . . What can you do with anybody like that?

FORTUNE-TELLER. Not a thing . . . don't worry about it! It'll work out! . . I know these philosophers . . . Oh, by the way!—you asked me to recommend a maid, so I . . .

BOARDINGHOUSE LANDLADY. Yes, thank the Lord, our Fekla is a real trial; old, steals things . . .

FORTUNE-TELLER. I happen to know of one. Good worker, nice looking, and such a flirt it'll cure anybody's melancholy on the spot.

BOARDINGHOUSE LANDLADY (laughs, embarrassed). Do you suppose it might help?

FORTUNE-TELLER. It'll save him! I know the age. Now you just pretend not to notice anything and I'll tell her it's a matter of saving a person's life. And now . . . (Goes over to the screen, makes a small nook with it by the footlights and sets a chair there.) . . . have no fear! (Sotto voce.) I . . . hypnotized your daughter . . .

BOARDINGHOUSE LANDLADY. What do you mean?

FORTUNE-TELLER. Shh . . . I hypnotized her.

BOARDINGHOUSE LANDLADY *(softly)*. What on earth for?

FORTUNE-TELLER *(also softly)*. So that she'd tell us the whole truth about herself! It wasn't because of her teeth you brought her here, was it?

BOARDINGHOUSE LANDLADY. Well, of course, that was just an excuse . . .

FORTUNE-TELLER. Well, now we'll find out what the real problem is; people speak the truth only in their sleep. Over here if you please! *(Indicates the chair behind the screen.)* Now we'll see if her toothache isn't really here. *(Points to her heart.)*

BOARDINGHOUSE LANDLADY. You suspect . . .

FORTUNE-TELLER. We'll see . . . Sit down and keep calm. *(The Boardinghouse Landlady obediently, although with some agitation, does what she is told. The Fortune-Teller goes off to the bedroom. Loudly.)* Come here, Lidochka! . . don't be afraid, my child, there's no one here but me . . . your friend! Open your eyes a little! . . *(The hypnotized Typist appears in the doorway with her eyes half open. The Fortune-Teller takes her by the hand and leads her to the armchair now turned facing the audience.)* Sit here! . . That's right . . . Feel all right? Your teeth don't hurt? *(Strokes her cheek.)*

TYPIST *(shakes her head and answers, just barely audible)*. No.

FORTUNE-TELLER. And they're not going to hurt! Only smear a little camphor oil on your cheek and then see a dentist . . . do you hear?

TYPIST *(softly, almost inaudibly)*. All right.

FORTUNE-TELLER. Speak up!

TYPIST *(loudly)*. All right.

FORTUNE-TELLER. Tell me quite frankly now what you think of yourself, of your life, what your greatest desire is? Be truthful, as if you were standing before God, there's no one else here . . . Now then! What do you think about most? . . .

TYPIST *(after a pause, excruciatingly)*. I think . . . I think . . . *(A convulsion of sobbing seizes her throat.)*

FORTUNE-TELLER. Calm yourself! . . no need to cry! . . Speak calmly, don't be upset! . .

TYPIST *(having repressed her sobs)*. I think . . . the years are going by . . . nobody loves me but Mama . . . but I do know . . . there are other caresses . . . not maternal ones . . . burning caresses, just the thought of which makes your head whirl and your heart pound so hard and so painfully . . . I don't even need to get married! I really don't! . . But . . . my God, am I going to die, never knowing the love I scarcely dare dream about! Pathetic, ugly, it makes me cry just to look in the mirror . . . not knowing why I was deprived of the simplest, the most natural of joys . . . *(The Boardinghouse*

*Landlady, who has been tensely following the confession, unable to bear the terrible
simplicity of her hypnotized daughter's words, begins to cry.)*

FORTUNE-TELLER *(to the Typist).* Close your eyes! *(She puts her hands over the
girl's ears and addresses her mother.)* Marya Yakovlevna . . . *(The latter pokes out
from behind the screen and, shaking her head in grief, wipes her tears.)* Did you
hear? . . Do you understand the true reason . . .

BOARDINGHOUSE LANDLADY *(weeping).* Lord in heaven! . . My beloved
Lidochka! . . My poor darling! . . and why did I bring you into this world,
poor miserable thing! . .

FORTUNE-TELLER. Calm yourself! . . I'm going to wake her up in a minute . . . Wipe your eyes and pretend you don't know a thing . . . You now
know what's the matter and you ought to know what's the cure . . . As for
the rest, rely on the Lord . . . *(Removes her hands from the Typist's ears and says
to her.)* Open your eyes! . . Go in that room, sit on the bed and awake! . .
Hurry! . .

*The Typist hurries back—with a sleepwalker's gait—to the bedroom. As soon as she leaves,
the Fortune-Teller puts the screen back in place and follows her. The Boardinghouse
Landlady blows her nose and wipes her eyes dry. An energetic ringing of the bell in the
reception room is heard; a door is heard opening.*

TYPIST *(appears with the Fortune-Teller, rubs her eyes, blinks, and smiles wanly).* I
must have dozed off? . .

FORTUNE-TELLER. That's all right! . . Toothache all gone?

TYPIST. Gone . . . thank you . . . did Fedya leave! . . *(To her mother.)* Why are
your eyes so red? . . have you been crying? . .

FORTUNE-TELLER. It's nothing . . . pay no attention . . . *(A knock at the door.)*

FORTUNE-TELLER *(going to the door, but not opening it).* Coming, coming . . .

BOARDINGHOUSE LANDLADY. Well, we won't keep you! . . We've
stayed too long already. *(Leaving.)* Thanks for everything! *Thrusts some
money in her hand.)* Thank you so much.

FORTUNE-TELLER. You're welcome . . . Don't mention it! . .

BOARDINGHOUSE LADY. Goodbye. *(Handshakes, after which the Boardinghouse Landlady and the Typist go out, nearly colliding at the door with a fat, exotic-
looking theater Director whom the Fortune-Teller is welcoming in.)*

DIRECTOR *(walks in wearing an overcoat and gloves and carrying a top hat).* Is
Doctor Fregoli in?

FORTUNE-TELLER. Oh yes indeed!

DIRECTOR. Tell him that the Director of the local theater is here to see him.
(Puts his top hat on one of the chairs and unbuttons his overcoat.)

FORTUNE-TELLER. I'll tell him right away. In the meantime have a chair
and help yourself to the magazines. *(Takes some magazines and newspapers*

from the table, thrusts them into the Director's hands and disappears for two or three seconds into the bedroom.)

DIRECTOR. *(Looks around the room wide-eyed, shrugs his shoulders, takes off his gloves, throws them in his top hat and looks at his watch. To the Fortune-Teller, who has now returned.)* You'd do well to add that I'm in quite a hurry . . . *(Sits down and looks through the magazines.)*

FORTUNE-TELLER. Very well. *(Yells into the bedroom.)* The Director is in quite a hurry! *(In a different voice, low, masculine, jaunty.)* Right away! *(Takes off her glasses, the green visor, and the wig and cap, unbuttons the gown and opens the clothes closet. The Director turns at the squeak of the closet door. Dr. Fregoli removes his Fortune-Teller's outfit and, to the Director's great amazement, reveals his shirt front, trousers and vest. He hangs the gown in the closet, takes out a jacket, swiftly puts it on, goes into the next room, goes over to the vanity, takes a towel from the wall, removes the old woman makeup, powders himself and combs his hair.)*

DIRECTOR *(flabbergasted, gets up and whistles in amazement).* I'll be damned! Can you beat that! . . And an old theater rat like me couldn't see through the make up! Damn it all to hell, then you're the famous fortuneteller that everybody in our theater's buzzing about?

DR. FREGOLI. *(Comes out of the bedroom. He is an elegant, handsome, fifty-year-old gentleman, with slightly gray, short hair. He holds himself erect, confident, but not defiant. He has an inspired face. Clever, kind, penetrating eyes. A trace of irony wanders over his fine, lips. His chin is thrust slightly forward—the typical mark of a strong will. His whole body seems overflowing with irresistible charm.)* You are not mistaken, sir. *(Shakes the Director's hand.)* How do you do again!

DIRECTOR. And you're not afraid I might give you away?

DR. FREGOLI. Not a bit! Because, in the first place, no one would believe you, in the second place I'm finishing my engagement in this town tomorrow, in the third place I rely on your integrity, and in the fourth place on that part of our agreement which specifies that failure to honor confidences shall be considered a breach of contract. Do you have the contract with you?

DIRECTOR. I do. *(Takes some formal documents out of his side pocket.)*

DR. FREGOLI. Wonderful.

DIRECTOR. But if it's not a secret, tell me, my dear doctor, what inspires you to practice a strange profession like this?

DR. FREGOLI. Fortune-telling? . . But I've made a great deal of money on it.

DIRECTOR. Excuse me for being such an old skeptic, but isn't this profession based entirely on deceit?

DR. FREGOLI. All of mankind, if one may believe the psychologists, instinctively prefers a pleasant deception to an unpleasant truth. Remember what the poet said:

More dear than darkness' lower truths,
Illusion soars with us on high.

DIRECTOR. You're a strange one, Dr. Fregoli! And listening to you, I'm completely baffled as to whether you're in earnest or just joking. In any case I hope you don't exploit your victim's ignorance too much!

DR. FREGOLI *(smiling)*. Special price for poor people! On the other hand I'm merciless with rich people. However, I made my fortune not out of greed, as you might suppose from this contract! *(Reaches toward the papers held by the Director.)* May I?

DIRECTOR. Certainly! *(Hands him one of the sheets.)* This one's a copy. *(Keeps the other sheet.)*

DR. FREGOLI. Please sit down! *(He sits in the "Fortune-Teller's" chair and looks through the contract.)*

DIRECTOR *(sitting opposite him)*. All the same you're a strange, an inscrutable person, Dr. Fregoli!

DR. FREGOLI *(looking at his watch)*. We won't be late for your rehearsal?

DIRECTOR *(checking the time on his watch)*. Yes, it's getting late. You really want to go to the theater *today*?

DR. FREGOLI. Why, we already agreed on it!

DIRECTOR. No, no, please don't be angry. I already warned the appropriate people . . . hinted at the purely American flavor of your enterprise. In short—they're all intrigued, and anxiously awaiting you. There's only one more thing we have to take care of . . . *(Hesitates.)*

DR. FREGOLI *(understands the nature of the problem)*. Aha. *(Hands him a bundle of money.)* There you are. Count it if you'd like. *(The Director counts the money; Dr. Fregoli dips his pen in the ink, is ready to sign the contract, and then examines it one more time.)* Paragraph eight . . . breach of contract . . . Hm . . . So, right . . . And the time—until Lent.

DIRECTOR. The last day of Shrovetide.

DR. FREGOLI. Yes sir.

DIRECTOR *(suddenly roars with roguish laughter)*. Ha, ha, ha, ha, ha . . . yes sir, I'll tell you.

DR. FREGOLI *(astounded)*. What are you laughing at?

DIRECTOR. It just occured to me that if someone were to overhear us, then . . . *(laughs loudly)*.

DR. FREGOLI. Then . . . go ahead.

DIRECTOR *(laughing)*. Then if it were wise old Solomon himself, he'd never guess what you've cooked up here and what sort of contract this is.

DR. FREGOLI. Yes . . . For the most part people don't have much imagination. *(Signs the contract and hands it to the Director.)* Please . . . *(Director signs the copy and passes it in turn to Dr. Fregoli.)* Thank you . . . So—let's go! . .

DIRECTOR. Let's go! . . *(Dr. Fregoli puts on his overcoat.)* Damn it all to hell, this is the first time I've dealt with a real fanatic.

DR. FREGOLI. Here's your hat. *(Hands it to him.)*

DIRECTOR. Thank you. *(Puts on his gloves.)* But tell me quite frankly, are you really convinced you've found a way to *save* the world?

DR. FREGOLI *(his face clear, his eyes looking upward with inspiration).* Perhaps that's why I was brought into this world, to serve as a witness to the truth. Those who seek truth will heed my voice.

DIRECTOR *(mockingly).* But what is truth? *(He looks searchingly at Dr. Fregoli, like Pilate at Christ. After a pause in which Dr. Fregoli endures with fond indulgence the Director's steady stare, the latter exclaims "Let's go!" with the intonation of a Monte Carlo croupier "rien ne va plus." They leave.)*

CURTAIN.

ACT TWO

The second act follows the first without an intermission. Hardly has the curtain fallen when a bell is heard ringing continuously, nervously, backstage. The Regisseur's voice is heard: "Places, ladies and gentlemen, places! . . When are you going to finish that ramp? I told you to have it done yesterday! . . Not now, sweetheart! I'm not going to hold up the rehearsal on your account . . . Everyone here? . . What? . . Svetozarov still isn't ready! . . That's all we need!" A roar of voices drowns out the Regisseur's words. Two stage carpenters with the ramp come out from behind the curtain left. Some Oriental dance with modernistic harmonizing is being played on a piano. The carpenters lazily set up the ramp down to the orchestra floor. The Regisseur appears from the right accompanied by the Electrician. The Regisseur's clothes and general appearance reveal an extreme attempt "to be different from everybody else,"—a lot of pretension in the shaggy, gray-flecked hair, in the black tie knotted with deliberate carelessness, in the way he smokes his cigarette. The Electrician, on the other hand, is obviously "a common man," with moustache, freckles, and a pink nose revealing a partiality to alcohol.

REGISSEUR *(to the Carpenters)*. Hurry, hurry! . . and stronger too, please, I don't intend to break my neck on your account! . . *(Leaning over the footlights to the Electrician.)* Now just stand there and admire what a great job you did on the lights! . . Dust, dirt, the blues burned out, broken, and it didn't occur to you to change them! . . I suppose you'd like me to take care of them? Then why have an electrician? . . Why keep you around? . . I can't run around watching you like a nursemaid! A regisseur has his own responsibilities, more complex than yours! *(The abashed Electrician wipes the dust off the lights. To the Carpenters.)* You can go eat later! Only leave one man here! And we won't need a runner, because the set won't be ready till this evening! And before you go, push the piano over to the wings and raise the curtain! *(The Carpenters remain long enough to set up the ramp, then depart. Not pausing, the Regisseur turns again to the Electrician.)* Well, are you convinced now we can't rely on you? Dust, dirt, cobwebs. It wouldn't be very ingenious to have the stage be pitch dark. *(Squats, runs his finger over the lights the Electrician hasn't wiped yet and thrusts the finger reproachfully under the Electrician's nose.)* Look at that! And in a play like *Quo Vadis*, where the brightness of the noonday sun is required! *(Wipes the dust off his finger with his handkerchief and stands up.)* What in the hell've you been doing? And they expect a work of art from me. But how in the hell am I to produce anything when everybody from the electrician on up is out to sabotage me! . . *(The Electrician suddenly plunges into his work, then shakes out his dust rag, causing the Regisseur to sneeze.)* Achoo . . . you could get asphyxiated around here. Bear in mind that this isn't going to be any ordinary production, but an *artistic* one! And therefore the lighting's got to be first-rate—you understand? I want *Quo Vadis* to be a chef d'oeuvre, a real chef d'oeuvre! Do you understand?

ELECTRICIAN. What's a "shiduver," Aristarchus Petrovich?

REGISSEUR. "Chef d'oeuvre" means ideal. Wipe it cleaner please! . .

ELECTRICIAN. You deal? . . How many cards do you deal in Kwovadiss?

REGISSEUR. Not a deal, *the ideal.*

ELECTRICIAN. Listen, you're a very learned man, Aristarchus Petrovich! But I haven't the faintest idea who this Kwovadiss is—a general, a tsar, or maybe some crook?

REGISSEUR. *Quo Vadis* means "Where art thou going?"

ELECTRICIAN. Oh, so that's it! . . And where is it, Aristarchus Petrovich?

REGISSEUR. Where's what?

ELECTRICIAN. Where "thou art going"! Is it very far?

REGISSEUR *(at a loss).* Hm . . . well, it all depends! . . I'll say this—we won't be going very far with you if you keep this up!

ELECTRICIAN. I'm sorry, Aristarchus Petrovich!

REGISSEUR. You forget how important your assignment is! . . . If the playwright manages to *enlighten* the public with his play, then it is solely because the electrician has *lighted* the play on the stage! . . Without *lighting* there can be no *enlightening.* And so you must always *dedicate* all your efforts to *lighting* the play properly! Do you understand?

ELECTRICIAN. I understand, Aristarchus Petrovich. And whose play is it, this Kwovadiss?

REGISSEUR. Mine. That is, it's Sienkiewicz's novel, but it's my adaptation. But that doesn't change a thing! Sienkiewicz or me, either way you've got to do an equally good job of lighting.

ELECTRICIAN. The Good Lord gives some people talent! "Where art thou going?" all right! You're going a long way, Aristarchus Petrovich, honest to God! You write plays and you spot every speck of dust on the lights! The Good Lord knew what he was doing when he made you! *(The Romantic Lead enters right carrying a Roman tunic embroidered in gold. By the time he appears the Carpenters have finished with the ramp and are going behind the curtain left. The Regisseur and the Electrician, passing the footlights from right to left, are by now at the Prompter's box.)*

ROMANTIC LEAD. Aristarchus Petrovich, I'm not putting on this costume.

REGISSEUR. What? . . You know very well this is a dress rehearsal?

ROMANTIC LEAD. Yes, but it's not right!

REGISSEUR. What's not right?

ROMANTIC LEAD. My costume.

REGISSEUR. Genuine Roman? What kind do you need anyway?

ROMANTIC LEAD. One that fits.

REGISSEUR. Weren't you at the fitting?

ROMANTIC LEAD. I was. But then Stepanov got fitted after me . . .

REGISSEUR. Stepanov is playing Nero!

ROMANTIC LEAD. Fine, but he told the tailor he was playing Marcus Vinicius, alternating with me.

REGISSEUR. Well, so?

ROMANTIC LEAD. So the tailor sewed it half for me, half for Stepanov.

REGISSEUR. So it fits like a glove?

ROMANTIC LEAD. Fitting like a glove isn't the point! A shroud might fit like a glove, but that's no reason I should wear one.

REGISSEUR. Why not?

ROMANTIC LEAD. Because I'm not ready to die yet.

REGISSEUR. We're not talking about a shroud, we're talking about your costume.

ROMANTIC LEAD. It's a shroud. Sending an actor out on the stage in a poorly tailored costume is like giving him a first-class funeral.

REGISSEUR. Excuses, excuses, excuses! One minute your costume's not right, then the prompter's messed you up, then your foot hurts, then something else! . . You don't learn your part, you're late to rehearsals, you get to performances with only five minutes to spare, and in general go about your work lately in such a way that you're forcing me to look for an understudy.

ROMANTIC LEAD *(indolently)*. Skip the reprimands! I haven't any use for them. You'd do better to tell me whether you've spoken to the Theater Director about my raise? With the high prices these days, I am absolutely not . . .

REGISSEUR *(interrupting)*. My God, but you're a strange one, Pyotr Petrovich! Haven't you heard how the Director's hooked up with some American, who's picking up actors from various theaters to make up his own company, and so why should the Director have anything to do with pay raises for actors that might be turned over tomorrow to the American, damn him and his whole project.

ROMANTIC LEAD. What kind of project is it?

REGISSEUR. Damned if I know.

The curtain rises. There is no scenery. The stage looks the way it does at rehearsals in provincial theaters. Upstage, about eight paces from the footlights, are some saw horses with boards on them representing Nero's feast table; behind them are some benches with brightly colored pillows for "reclining." A similar, rather primitive "table" and "couch," only half the size, are placed right. To the left, at approximately the same distance as the table is to the right, is a raised platform with two tall, fantastic harps. A pan's flute also lies on the platform. The set thus forms roughly a squat letter U with space between the sides and bottom. A piano is stage left. Its body and music stand conceal the piano-player except for his feet on the pedals. The actors and actresses are dressed in fancy, tasteless costumes trying to suggest Neronian Rome. Among them are three dressed as Assyrian musicians. The Barefoot Dancer is wearing slippers and a light robe partly covering her rather scanty Assyrian costume. As the curtain rises some are sitting on the tables and the platform, others on benches, others are milling around in couples, and still others are standing, carrying on lively conversations and smoking cigarettes.

ELECTRICIAN *(gets to the left end of the footlights with his dust rag, shows a bulb he has removed to the Regisseur).* This one's not my fault. *(The general hum of the actor's voices makes it difficult to hear him.)*

REGISSEUR. Burned out? . . Apparently you've been putting in used bulbs . . .

ELECTRICIAN. Oh God forbid! . .

REGISSEUR. Why didn't the other one burn out then?

ELECTRICIAN. Am I some kind of mind-reader?

REGISSEUR. Are you some kind of spendthrift?

ELECTRICIAN. You're not a God-fearing man, Aristarchus Petrovich.

REGISSEUR. And you're not a wasted-money fearing man. *(To the actors.)* Let's go people! *(Claps his hands.)* Let's go! . . Places, please, places! *(The actors take their places as follows: Nero and Poppaea are center behind the center table. Tigellinus is to the left of Nero, and Petronius to the right of Poppaea. The fat, flabby, carelessly made-up Comic playing Vitelius and Calvia Crispinilla—only slightly resembling the dissolute courtesan she's trying to portray—are both half-sitting, half-lying, imitating the reclining of the Romans, at the left (narrow) end of the table. At the right end of the table, facing Vitelius and Crispinilla, are Nigidia and Lucan. Lygia, portrayed by a rather plump actress—in distinction to Poppaea—and the Romantic Lead—not in costume or made up, playing the role of Marcus Vinicius— arrange themselves behind a separate table. The "feasters" all wear wreaths of paper roses on their heads, producing a rather pathetic impression. The female Assyrian musicians—two harpists and a flutist—are on the platform stage left. The Barefoot Dancer stands in front of them with her robe off. A single hairy-armed, clumsy "slave" is serving everyone sandwiches from a rather limited quantity on a simple white plate. The creaking old Prompter, with a copy of the play in hand, finishes a cigarette as he minces rapidly in out of the left portal. He hastily, but not without difficulty and silent curses, takes his place in his box. Since everyone is still chattering away, the Regisseur claps his hands once more.)* Quiet . . . Shh . . . *(Yells upward in the direction of the cat walk.)* Is the property man up there?

VOICE FROM ABOVE. I'm taking his place.

REGISSEUR. Who?

VOICE FROM ABOVE. Me! Me! Don't worry, Aristarchus Petrovich!

PROMPTER *(poking out of the box, to the Regisseur).* It's his assistant! The property man couldn't make it today.

REGISSEUR *(upward).* Ah, so it's you, Ivan Ivanych? What happened to your boss?

VOICE FROM ABOVE. His wife's having a baby today. *(Excitement among the cast.)*

REGISSEUR. Ah, so that's it . . . The flowers ready?

VOICE FROM ABOVE. Ready.

REGISSEUR. Roses?

VOICE FROM ABOVE. Yes.

REGISSEUR. A lot?

VOICE FROM ABOVE. Fair number.

REGISSEUR. You know when to let them go?

VOICE FROM ABOVE. You can count on me.

REGISSEUR *(claps his hands).* Let's go . . . Music! . . The first piece . . . *(The nuptial song from A. G. Rubinstein's opera* Nero *is heard. The actors do their best to appear to be drinking, eating, and "living on the stage." The Regisseur brings in a chair from offstage left and seats himself at the edge of the stage.)* More life, people! . . And don't forget the voluptuousness! . . Smooth, continuous flow of movement! Drunkenness, languour, debauchery, but all with the most aristocratic manners! . . Petronius, set the tone! . . Nero, your emerald! . . Sneer at them all through your lorgnette! . .*(Nero does so.)* More bestiality in that look! . . Don't forget they considered Nero the anti-Christ . . . Bloodthirsty manners, bearing, and so forth . . . Laughter! . . Everybody roar with laughter! *(The cast all laughs simultaneously and with absurd artificiality.)* More merriment! More life! A little more fire and a little more satiety! . . Petronius, more irony! Vinicius, more passion! . . Poppaea, more depravity! . . Lygia, more Christian martyrdom! . . *(The music stops. Awkward pause.)* Now then . . . whose line is it? . . Dialog! Begin! . .

PROMPTER *(whispering intensely).* So this is the hostage that . . .

NERO *(catching on).* Oh yes, my fault! *(Pompously.)* So this is the hostage our Vinicius has fallen in love with? *(Peers through his emerald at Lygia.)*

PETRONIUS *(foppishly).* Yes, Caesar, it is she.

NERO. What is her name.

PETRONIUS. Lygia.

NERO. Does Vinicius think she's beautiful?

PETRONIUS. Yes, but I've already seen her sentence on your face, oh connois-seur of connoisseurs . . . You needn't pronounce the sentence, I know what it is—"Too narrow in the hips." I was ready to bet that in the midst of a feast, with everybody lying down, no one could judge, but you've already told yourself—"Too narrow in the hips."

NERO. Right! Too narrow in the hips.

POPPAEA *(with a demonstrative sneer)*. Some narrow hips!

NERO. Sorry, is that your line?

POPPAEA. No, it's my opinion.

REGISSEUR *(gets up)*. What's this? What's going on?

POPPAEA. Nothing special! I'm just paying the necessary tribute of amaze-ment to Madame Arkadevna's "narrow" hips.

LYGIA. Kindly leave my hips out of this!

POPPAEA. Oh, I'm sorry! Your hips don't concern me in the least! But your part, which rightfully belongs to me, now that, young lady, concerns me very much.

REGISSEUR *(caustically)*. Pardon me, but for the role of Lygia, we need not only the proper hips, but the proper talent too.

POPPAEA. Quite right. Only it's funny that you didn't manage to notice the actress' talent until you had dinner with her. But then not everybody finds your company so pleasant . . .

NERO *(getting a little nervous)*. Let's go on, people! *(Saying his lines.)* Too narrow in the hips.

POPPAEA. Just look at her. How appropriate for a work of art! Ha, ha, ha!

REGISSEUR. Shh . . . That's enough, or I'll fine you. *(Sits down.)* Go on!

COMIC *(playing Vitelius very broadly, apparently already intoxicated even before the libations at Nero's feast)*. You're wrong, Petronius. I agree with Ceasar's opinion.

PETRONIUS. Fine. I was just arguing that you had a great mind, but Ceasar said you were a jackass. *(He laughs loudly along with the other "feasters.")*

REGISSEUR *(to Petronius)*. Who's laughing like that? . . Would Petronius, the *arbiter elegantiarum*, laugh like that? You have to laugh elegantly—something like this—ha, ha, ha . . . *(Demonstrates "elegant" laughter.)* Try it like that. Go ahead. *(Several people snicker.)*

PETRONIUS *(imitating, almost parodying the Regisseur)*. Ha, ha, ha . . . *(Everybody roars with sincere laughter this time.)*

REGISSEUR *(at the end of his rope)*. Ladies and gentlemen, if this ha, ha, ha, and hee, hee, hee doesn't stop right away I'm calling off the rehearsal and fining the laughers.

CAST. Yes, but according to the script we're supposed to laugh.

REGISSEUR. Then laugh according to the script and not at me, thank you. I'm not a child. Go on.

LUCAN. But I believe in dreams—I was talking to Seneca the other day and she told me . . .

REGISSEUR. Seneca was a man! "He" not "she"!

LUCAN. Prompter! Louder with the lines!

PROMPTER. You ought to learn them.

LUCAN. You ought to learn them.

REGISSEUR. Don't be funny.

LUCAN. I'm just repeating the line the prompter gave me.

REGISSEUR. Save your wit for a comedy. But the way you do comedy makes the audience yawn, and when it's drama they all die laughing.

LUCAN. Well, naturally, if instead of the moon coming up, you see some chamber pot rising up over the horizon.

REGISSEUR. Enough. Go on!

LUCAN. He told me the other day . . . *(To the "slave" who has butted in again with the sandwiches.)* Leave me alone, for God's sake! . . This is the tenth time you've come butting in with that idiotic platter—give me a chance to act a little.

REGISSEUR *(to the "slave")*. Don't overdo it . . . Off the stage for a little while. *(The slave retires.)*

LUCAN. Seneca told me the other day that he believes in dreams too.

NERO. How about fortune-telling? . . I once heard a prophecy that Rome would fall but I'd be Emperor of the entire Orient.

PETRONIUS. Fortune-telling and dreams have a lot in common . . . *(To the Regisseur.)* I think we ought to make a few cuts here. The monologue drags a little.

REGISSEUR. Another cut? . . I've already cut everything possible. We've got to give the audience a play, not some mish-mash. *(Approaches the Prompter, to him.)* Let me have your script. *(Takes the Prompter's script over and compares it with Petronius' script, crossing out and arguing here and there.)* "Fortune-telling and dreams" . . . Hm . . . "Fortune-telling" . . .

ROMANTIC LEAD *(to Lygia)*. Oh yes, fortune-telling . . . I finally did go see the famous fortune-teller.

LYGIA. And what did she say to you?

ROMANTIC LEAD. A real wonder. Sees everything like the palm of her hand. We're going to get such an offer she says . . . *(Kisses his finger tips.)*

LUCAN *(approaching them)*. What's this about? The new producer? They say he's fantastically wealthy, and not exactly crazy, but more like a fanatic . . . he has some kind of great idea, in other words, an apostle.

BAREFOOT DANCER. Where did you hear that?

LUCAN. The Director was talking about it at dinner yesterday . . . True, I didn't get it all—I was pretty smashed on some strong sherry then—but I was amazed anyway. How could I not be! Have you ever heard of a producer giving another producer, a competitor, the pick of his own company! Give him complete freedom to lure away his actors? Either there's some dirty deal going on here or else . . .

REGISSEUR *(winding up the discussion of the excisions and expurgations)*. That does it. *(Claps his hands.)* Ladies and gentlemen, be so good as to. .

NERO *(who has been looking over the excisions with Petronius)*. Sorry, but now what's my line? It doesn't make any sense now!

REGISSEUR. Oh, Lord in Heaven . . . three trees and you're lost in the forest! Look! *(Points to the page in the script.)* Vitelius laughs . . . and then right away it's your line. *(The Comic comes over, attracted by the mention of his part. The Regisseur nervously finishes his explanation.)*

LUCAN *(not leaving the couple he just joined)*. What time is it?

ROMANTIC LEAD *(looks at his watch)*. Twelve thirty. What of it?

LUCAN. I'm a little nervous . . . He might show up any minute. The Director said today was the day . . .

BAREFOOT DANCER *(peering out into the house)*. Some people are out there again . . . Ump, it's dark out there . . . Can't tell who it is. What do they let them in at rehearsals for?

LUCAN. They're all people we know . . I have terrific vision . . . *(Looks off into the house.)* The property man's kids . . . the box office girl's sisters . . . the electrician's brother . . .

BAREFOOT DANCER. And further back . . . all the way back?

LUCAN. What are you worried about?

BAREFOOT DANCER. What do you mean "what?" Suppose this "American" . . .

LUCAN. Does what?

BAREFOOT DANCER. . . . sits down in back without anybody noticing and starts looking over all of us, criticizing everything.

LUCAN. What a wild idea! The Director said he'd bring him right on stage . . . was even going to go get him . . .

REGISSEUR *(returning the Prompter's script to him)*. Quiet! . . Places! *(They all take their previous places.)* So—we've made a cut here! . . *(To Comic.)* Petronius says "fortune-telling and dreams have a lot in common," then you laugh. Go ahead.

COMIC. All right. *(Very solemnly pencils in the change in his script and then breaks into hilarious laughter.)*

REGISSEUR. Nero! Your line!

NERO. What is that tub of lard laughing at?

PETRONIUS. Laughter is what distinguishes people from beasts, and he doesn't have any other way to show he's not a pig.

COMIC *(tramping down hard on his "comical pedal")*. I just dropped the patriarchal ring my father left me.

NERO. Who was a shoemaker!.. *(Comic laughs in reply and begins looking for his ring among the folds of Calvia Crispinilla's peplos.)*

NIGIDIA. Looking for something he never had!

LUCAN. And which he wouldn't know what to do with, if he found it . . . Ha, ha, ha . . .

CRISPINILLA *(indignantly, to the Comic)*. Now listen, Semyon Arkadevich, behave yourself!

COMIC. It says here in the stage directions: *(reading from the script)* "Looks for his ring in the folds of Crispinilla's dress" . . . I beg your pardon, but are you playing Crispinilla?

CRISPINILLA. I am.

COMIC. Well then, that's why I'm searching you. What are you crabbing about?

CRISPINILLA. You're supposed to be pretending, and not . . . You scoundrel! You know perfectly well what I'm talking about, if you're not too drunk.

COMIC. "Pretend?" For God's sake, please get it into your head, darling. Twenty years on the stage and as for "pretending" to look for something, we artists of the Naturalist school—God in heaven—simply aren't equipped . . .

CRISPINILLA. I suppose then that if the script says "he chops off her head," you'd really chop my head off?

COMIC. Where did you ever see a script like that?

CRISPINILLA. In any event, I demand you behave yourself. I'm not just any old woman. The script doesn't say a word about you ravishing me.

COMIC. Ravishing?.. Were you ever ravished, sweetheart?.. If we lived in Nero's day and you were my slave, why I'd ravish you every day, like Petronius and Eunice, and I'd tell you not to protest, but have some respect for an actor who has served art for twenty years. And you may rest assured that it wouldn't be any "just pretend" ravishing either, but the real thing.

CRISPINILLA. If we lived in Nero's Rome I would toss anybody as depraved as you to the lions, and cheer like mad, too.

REGISSEUR. Enough! Enough! At least we can be thankful we're not living in Nero's day! So don't waste time fantasizing . . . Let's go on.

BAREFOOT DANCER. Now we come to my *Dance of the Assyrian Bondswoman*. Only couldn't they let the curtains down? . . There're some strange people out there . . .

REGISSEUR. And so?

BAREFOOT DANCER. This isn't the final dress rehearsal after all.

REGISSEUR. Makes no difference—I need to get a general impression. I'll be watching from the house myself. Also we've got to check the effect of the roses falling down on the stage. *(Yells upward.)* You remember the rain of flowers comes here?

VOICE FROM ABOVE. I remember.

REGISSEUR *(steps down the ramp to the orchestra floor, speaking as he goes).* Don't forget, ladies and gentlemen, this is a work of art! Every detail is of the utmost importance . . . Music! The prelude! *(The piano is heard playing some languid Oriental dance.)*

BAREFOOT DANCER *(kicks off her shoes and is assuming a pose when she steps on a nail).* Nails on the stage again. *(Picks up the nail.)* Is this part of the *work of art* too?

REGISSEUR *(standing up in the center aisle, yells in a mighty voice).* Sweep up the stage! Ivan!

ROMANTIC LEAD *(yelling off stage right).* Ivan! Hurry up and sweep up the stage!

BAREFOOT DANCER *(in the direction of the piano).* Hold on, Maestro! . . *(The music stops. A worker with a broom walks on.)*

POPPAEA. He's going to stir up a lot of dust again! You know very well what awful asthma I get! *(Paper roses descend from above on the actors, the worker with the broom, and the table.)*

ACTORS. A-ah . . . the rain of flowers. *(They all look up.)*

BAREFOOT DANCER *(to the worker, who is about to commence sweeping).* You should have done it earlier. Nothing at the right time! It destroys the whole mood.

NERO *(squeals).* Ow! . . Goddamnit, you could lose an eye around here. *(Examining the paper rose that hit him in the eye.)* And it's got a wire in it, the damned . . . *(Yells at the house.)* For Christ's sake, Aristarchus Petrovich, we'll all go blind at this rate.

REGISSEUR. What are you doing staring at the ceiling . . . Why all the curiosity! Remember, you're Roman aristocrats, who wouldn't be amazed by anything.

COMIC *(throwing a paper rose at the worker with the broom)*. What? Not even your *work of art?* Oh, come now, they'd be amazed all right! *(General laughter.)*

BAREFOOT DANCER *(to the worker)*. We haven't the time now! You should have done it earlier. *(In the direction of the piano.)* Play, Maestro! *(Oriental dance music is heard. The Assyrian Musicians pluck the harp strings. The Regisseur standing in the orchestra keeps time with one hand and sometimes by clapping. The Barefoot Dancer dances assiduously. Paper roses rustle down onto the stage. The worker with the broom, puzzled, scratches the back of his head and walks off.)*

LYGIA *(during the Barefoot Dancer's dance)*. Ah, Marcus, that bondswoman is so supple and beautiful! But then look at Poppaea, how beautiful she is, our divine Augusta!

ROMANTIC LEAD *(passionately)*. Oh yes, she's beautiful, but you're a hundred times more beautiful . . . Put your lips on this goblet of wine so that I may then press mine to the same spot . . . *(She drinks from the goblet, then he does.)* I saw you at the pool at Aulus' house and I fell in love with you . . . And now you seem the same beautiful woman again, even though you've got your clothes on this time. Take them off, like Crispinilla. Men and gods all crave love.

COMIC *(to Crispinilla)*. I beg your pardon, but are you playing Crispinilla?

CRISPINILLA. What of it?

COMIC. According to the script you're supposed to be undressed.

CRISPINILLA. Another invention!

COMIC. Didn't you hear what Marcus Vinicius said? "Take them off, like Crispinilla." Are you playing Crispinilla?

CRISPINILLA. Stop it, Semyon Arkadevich! I really mean it, leave me alone.

COMIC. Only first you've got to take your clothes off, because that's what this *work of art* requires. *(To the Regisseur.)* Isn't that right? *(Prepares to rip off her peplos.)*

CRISPINILLA. You want me to slap your face, you drunken slob! . . Let go! . . *(Leaps from behind the table. The Regisseur rushes on stage.)*

REGISSEUR. What's this? What's going on? *(The dance stops.)*

CRISPINILLA. Order this idiot to behave himself or I won't be responsible for myself.

REGISSEUR. Ye Gods! We can't even get through one rehearsal without a fracas!

BAREFOOT DANCER *(to the Regisseur)*. I told you you should have let the curtain down . . . Who wants to be a laughing stock for strangers! . . . One has to have some sense of self-respect! . .

COMIC *(approaching the footlights)*. But why all the strangers? . . Who let them in? . . *(Yells at the audience.)* Ladies and gentlemen, you're not wanted here! . . Leave! . . Well, hurry up then! Get a move on! . . Yech, look at 'em all! . . and who let you in?

REGISSEUR *(to the audience).* Be so kind, ladies and gentlemen, as to vacate the theater, or I shall be obliged to be unpleasant.

ROMANTIC LEAD *(to the audience).* Ladies and gentlemen, nothing instructive, beautiful, or sublime will you see in our theater. I hope you are already convinced. Please leave! This is a dreadful show. We ourselves recognize how pitiful and laughable our attempts are at portraying heroes when we haven't a trace of the heroic in our own souls. Don't shame us with your presence . . . What can be amusing in seeing people make fools of themselves over a crust of bread, people incapable of real, creative work? Make fools of themselves, imagining that they serve art, humanity, the lofty ideal of ennobling the human soul. Now you see how Melpomene's modern priests set about ennobling souls. I hope it is enough to drive you from the theater forever. Leave then, please, and don't shame us with your presence.

REGISSEUR *(to the Romantic Lead).* What a thing to say!

COMIC *(slapping the Romantic Lead on the shoulder).* Really got steamed up!

REGISSEUR. Off the deep end. *(To the audience.)* Once more, ladies and gentlemen, I beseech you to remove yourselves. Please.

DR. FREGOLI *(appearing on the orchestra floor near the stage accompanied by the somewhat embarrassed Provincial Theater Director).* Perhaps you'd make an exception in my case? *(The cast is somewhat baffled; several leave their places and with great curiosity rush over in the direction of the new arrival.)*

DIRECTOR *(steps on the stage along with Dr. Fregoli).* Ladies and gentleman, allow me to introduce Dr. Fregoli, who has been kind enough to come here in his capacity as a producer in need of some good actors. Out of professional courtesy I have given him permission to negotiate with you, all of which is to say that Dr. Fregoli is our guest and I ask you to receive him with the utmost kindness and affection.

DR. FREGOLI *(bowing).* I am most grateful to the Director for the lovely recommendation, but I should warn you right away that the theater of which I am the producer is one that—from the purely professional point of view—has nothing theatrical in it—no sets, no curtain, no footlights, and not a trace of a prompter. But all jokes aside, it's a wonderful theater. And I regret very much that it's only partly mine, since the greater half belongs to the producer . . . you probably know him—hmm . . . I don't seem to be able to recall his real name—some people call him Brahma, others Allah, others Adonai, still others something else. But that's not important. My associate, even though he sometimes interferes with my affairs, gives me enough leeway for initiative, and I will fully justify your confidence in me if you would like to join the theater under the conditions I propose. *(To the Director.)* The Director here has—in all probability—already acquainted you with these conditions?

DIRECTOR *(somewhat embarrassed)*. No, I merely sketched in the broad outlines. And I didn't actually talk to everybody . . . I don't know whether they passed it on to the rest of you or . . .

SEVERAL VOICES. We didn't hear a thing . . . What's this all about? . . What conditions? We don't know anything . . .

DIRECTOR *(to Dr. Fregoli)*. I thought that you would describe the project . . . I just hinted a little . . .

DR. FREGOLI. That's too bad. I supposed that the audience was already prepared . . . Ladies and gentlemen, I imagine you have already guessed what theater I'm talking about. It's called Life, that wonderful theater. And if it enjoys a certain superiority, it also is no stranger to certain deficiencies. First of all, it's a very old-fashioned theater, with outmoded traditions, with a cast as yet unrehearsed, a theater where the most talentless directors have held forth for years, where some actors starve and others make fabulous salaries . . . However, this problem seems to be near a solution, since the overwhelming majority now absolutely insists on the appointment of a new director . . . you've heard of him, of course! The sweetest person, his illegal origin notwithstanding. I'm speaking of Socialism . . . But there are millions of people on this earth not only deprived of material needs, but also of personal joys, owing to impoverishment of the body or spirit, millions of our fellow men for whom the equality of Socialism isn't enough. I hope, ladies and gentlemen, it's now clear to you what I'm driving at and what experimental reforms I have in mind for the near future?

DIRECTOR *(smoothly)*. Excuse me, Dr. Fregoli, but . . . very few of the cast have had the advantage of a high school education, and I'm afraid not all of them understand what you . . .

SEVERAL VOICES. Listen to that! . . What's a high school education got to do with it . . . What's so tough to understand?

DR. FREGOLI *(seriously)*. Keep in mind, ladies and gentlemen, that I have gone into theater "not to break the law, but to fulfill it." Along with the official theater, a sort of laboratory of illusion, I argue we need an unofficial theater, a sort of marketplace for illusions, a theater in even greater need of reform, for it is Life itself! Life, where illusion is no less necessary than on these boards, and where, if we are unable to give the deprived happiness, we must at least give them the illusion of happiness. That is the main thing. I'm an actor myself! But my field is not the theater stage, but the stage of

Life, to which I now summon you, masters in the art of salvation through illusion! With all my heart I believe in the actor's calling, the actor who steps off these boards into the pitch darkness of Life armed only with his art! For it is my sincere belief that the world will be transformed through the actor, through the actor's magic art.

BAREFOOT DANCER *(excited)*. I'm starting to understand! Only I'm not sure whether . . .

DIRECTOR *(to Dr. Fregoli)*. Excuse me, I'd like to explain your idea in more simple terms, to use a few examples.

DR. FREGOLI *(smiling)*. Please do!

DIRECTOR. Let me use some of your examples . . . Ladies and gentlemen . . . Dr. Fregoli has come up with something like this. There exist certain unfortunates who lack things much more important than material needs—talent, beauty, spiritual strength, health, youth, and so forth. There lives—let us suppose—an old man, lonely, pathetic, unneeded by anyone. Doesn't feel like going to an old people's home, "depositing himself in the archives," as it were. And yet how is he to lead a happy life with neither friends nor relatives? So that's why Dr. Fregoli has invited you, as experienced actors, to get acquainted with some unfortunate like that, pretend to be his friend and with your friendship brighten up his few remaining days. *(To Dr. Fregoli.)* Have I understood you correctly?

DR. FREGOLI. A fine example.

DIRECTOR *(to the Actors)*. Or, for instance, make yourself pretend to be in love with some homely girl, who, as the saying goes, "doesn't tempt any-body." *(Light laughter among the actors.)*

DR. FREGOLI. Forgive me, friends, but is it really so difficult or so comical for you young professionals who make passionate love every day on stage to both beautiful and not so beautiful actresses?

DIRECTOR. Anyone who finds it too difficult can dedicate himself to another art! Sick children, for instance, abandoned by their healthy playmates. "Dress up," says Dr. Fregoli, "like clowns, buffoons, Punchinellos, and put yourselves in the hands of poor people, like living toys!" *(Perplexity, snorts of laughter, whispering, among the actors.)*

COMIC. Pardon me, Doctor Fregoli, are you . . . are you proposing this as a joke or in all seriousness?

DR. FREGOLI. You may take it anyway you please!

COMIC. Aha . . . Hm . . . Very well . . . We understand you, Dr. Fregoli. A very touching idea! It really is! Philanthropical, one might say. But allow me—meaning no criticism—to inquire what sort of pay you have in mind for performing on the stage of life as you call it? *(Restrained laughter among the actors.)*

DR. FREGOLI. I will answer you in Socrates' terms, that virtue is the knowledge one acquires through practical experience. The part played creates a man's character at times, just as the man, in performing, creates the part's character. *Transformation* through *transfiguration*. Changing for the better—isn't that sufficient reward?

COMIC. Well now, for twenty years on the stage I wouldn't mind something a little more substantial! *(Laughter among the actors.)*

DR. FREGOLI. I'm not surprised by your laughter, ladies and gentlemen, since I know very well that not all are capable of great deeds purely in the name of charity. Everybody knows that if society didn't pay its Sisters of Mercy, there'd be a lot fewer than what's needed. Some day that same society or the state itself will assume the responsibility of paying "actors and actresses of mercy," as I call them, for their labor, but in the meantime . . . in the meantime private enterprise is needed, and that's why I have come to you, both as producer, and as playwright of a play which I'm planning to present on the stage of Life under my personal direction.

DIRECTOR. Basically Dr. Fregoli requires only three actors at present—two men and one woman. Types—one lover, one comic, one soubrette. Terms: same salary as you get from me, plus 25 per cent; from tomorrow until Lent.

DR. FREGOLI. This is my first experience in producing *a play in life* using professional actors. I therefore urge you to accept the challenge, ladies and gentlemen, especially since the play I'm doing is not a difficult one.

BAREFOOT DANCER *(stepping forward, enthusiastic)*. I agree . . . Will I do for the soubrette?

DR. FREGOLI *(shakes her hand once)*. So glad to have you!

COMIC. The Director's accepted also. That makes two already!

DIRECTOR. What do you mean? What are you driving at?

COMIC. At your role in the play's prologue.

DIRECTOR. What role?

COMIC. "The honest broker" . . . the only thing I'm not clear about is the commission you're making. *(Laughter among the actors.)* However, please pardon me, that's a private matter.

DIRECTOR *(cut to the quick)*. Now listen! There's a limit to everything! Even to your wit. You've become absolutely unbearable lately. I'll say this in all seriousness: if Dr. Fregoli is kind enough to take you off our hands I doubt if anyone in the cast will cry over it.

CRISPINILLA. That's right, don't expect any tears from me.

COMIC. Well, I won't cry either, since in Dr. Fregoli's company I'll find more respect for a talent that has faithfully served art for twenty years.

DR. FREGOLI. In any case, you'll be no less respected. *(Restrained laughter among the actors.)*

COMIC. That's good enough for me! . . Will I do?

DR. FREGOLI. Glad to have you.

DIRECTOR *(to the Barefoot Dancer).* But as for you, my dear, I can't bear losing you! You know very well that in *Quo Vadis*, for instance, you . . .

REGISSEUR *(leaping over to the Barefoot Dancer).* Listen, are you joking? . . I don't understand a thing . . . is this in earnest? . . . Without you, how are we going to . . But no, you've purposely, apparently . . . There's no one else to put in your place—you yourself know that.

BAREFOOT DANCER. Nonsense! Get some cafe singer! The audience doesn't know a thing about the finer points of art! . . All you need is a cute face and some pretty legs. There're lots of them around.

DIRECTOR. And how about your husband? You'd be separated in that case . . . Would he allow that?

ROMANTIC LEAD. I allow it, don't worry! . . I give my permission and my blessing!

BAREFOOT DANCER *(cut to the quick).* I obviously don't mean a thing to him! Apparently you don't know what kind of man he really is!

ROMANTIC LEAD. Apparently the Director knows me better. In fact everyone here, except you, understands under what conditions I give my permission!

DIRECTOR. What . . . and so you're leaving me too? . . *(Grabs his head with exaggerated despair, not without, however, a little deliberate comic shading.)*

ROMANTIC LEAD. If only Dr. Fregoli thinks I'll do—what argument could there be! . .

DR. FREGOLI *(shakes his hand once).* Oh, I was counting on you! . . I was just waiting for you to respond . . .

ROMANTIC LEAD *(to him).* With all my heart, my dear doctor! You've thoroughly intrigued me . . . I can't resist anything unusual, and *Don Quixote's* my favorite book . . . Ask my wife.

BAREFOOT DANCER. It's true. *(Fondly takes him by the arm.)*

DIRECTOR *(to Dr. Fregoli).* You're a real predator, sir! Yes, that's it! An evil old bird dragging my favorite fledglings from the nest . . . *(The Comic bows low to him.)* Not referring to you . . . *(Laughter among those present.)*

DR. FREGOLI *(smiling).* But this bird has flown here on wings of love and with your consent.

DIRECTOR. I was hypnotized. Honest to God, I was literally hypnotized to give my consent to a monster like you.

REGISSEUR. What's done is done. We'd do better to think about who's going to play the parts now . . . Could I speak to you for a moment? . . *(Leads the Director off by the arm upstage right.)*

NERO *(walking after them)*. As for the role of Vinicius, you may rest assured, Mr. Director . . .

NIGIDIA *(also goes off after the Regisseur and the Director, along with the other Actors, all somewhat agitated over recent as well as forthcoming reassignment of parts.)* Keep in mind, that the Assyrian Bondswoman's role . . . *(Her words are lost in the general hubbub as the actors surround the Regisseur and the Director as they—vainly seeking a little solitude—try to shoo off the Actors like some persistent flies. Only Dr. Fregoli, the Romantic Lead, the Barefoot Dancer and the Comic remain downstage).*

BAREFOOT DANCER *(against a background of a somewhat subdued roar of voices, to Dr. Fregoli)*. Whom should I report to? Tell us what our responsibilities are, our roles! Am I a maid, a cook, a dishwasher?

DR. FREGOLI. You'll be simply the "merry servant girl." *(To all of them.)* This is a very gloomy house, my friends, where I'm sending you as lodgers . . . and your first assignment is to do something about it, make it into something else.

ROMANTIC LEAD. What kind of place is it?

DR. FREGOLI. I'm speaking of the boardinghouse of a certain Petrova, Marya Yakovlevna, where some "theatrical first aid," so to say, is required. One of the lodgers has already tried to hang himself. Marya's daughter is steadily wasting away. The other lodgers are in a similar fix, that is, "they don't spoil the ensemble," as the reviewers put it.

COMIC. And what roles are we to assume?

DR. FREGOLI. I suggest you play a doctor! Laughter, as everybody knows, is the best medicine, and you're a slapstick comedian by trade, aren't you? Besides, the Director told me you were educated as an Army surgeon's assistant.

COMIC. What sort of doctor am I to be—military, civilian, a neurologist, or a gynecologist?

DR. FREGOLI. I think you would be best as a retired Army doctor. No practice, you can say, a small pension. In general, pretend to be oppressed by your fate but not despondent. One anecdote at the dinner table every day! All right? We'll even put it in the contract. I'll give you all the details later. *(To the Romantic Lead.)* You are to assume the role of Don Juan, or better yet, a tender Romeo, in the form of a humble insurance agent. Poor, humble, immensely appealing and seductive to the feminine heart . . .

COMIC *(to the Romantic Lead, ironically).* Just play yourself and that'll be plenty.

DR. FREGOLI *(continuing to address the Romantic Lead).* You've got to create the illusion of someone madly in love with this Marya's daughter and also make friends with Marya's student lodger, who needs moral support. *(Taking the Barefoot Dancer and her husband by the hand.)* The coquettish chatter of a nice-looking servant girl and the cordiality of a friend he won't be afraid to confide in when he's depressed will certainly cure this "potential suicide" once and for all. As you see, the roles are not too difficult, but responsible ones . . . As for myself, I'm going to play the author's spokesman, a kindly *raisonneur*, but in the form of a record salesman. From now on my name is Schmidt, don't forget! *(All smile.)*

BAREFOOT DANCER. Tell me, Mr. Schmidt . . .

DR. FREGOLI. Call me Karl.

BAREFOOT DANCER *(smiling).* Karl . . . but why have you picked your actors from some shabby provincial theater for such important parts and not from St. Petersburg, or . . .

DR. FREGOLI. The apostles of the Great Teacher didn't ask Him why He sought them in Galilee and not in Jerusalem.

ROMANTIC LEAD. You know, Doctor, from this day on I've decided to believe in fortune-tellers. Honest to God! . . How about you? . .

DR. FREGOLI. Depends on the fortune-teller . . . *(The rest of the cast and the Director and the Regisseur come back onto the stage.)*

DIRECTOR *(to Dr. Fregoli).* Well then? All set? No changes in the cast?

DR. FREGOLI. All we have to do is sign the contract.

DIRECTOR. In that case come on over to my office.

DR. FREGOLI *(to the Comic, the Romantic Lead, and the Barefoot Dancer).* Let's go. *(The Director, Dr. Fregoli, the Comic, the Romantic Lead, and the Barefoot Dancer walk off left.)*

REGISSEUR *(clapping his hands).* Places! The rehearsal will continue. I'll be Lucan, Genetsky will be Nero, Stepanov—Vinicius, Gorsky—Vitelius, and Miss Shatrova—the Assyrian Bondswoman. Music! Begin! *(A. G. Rubenstein's nuptial song is heard. The actors take their places as follows: the actor who had played Lucan takes Nero's place, the one who had played Nero reclines in Vinicius' place, the one who had played Tigellinus replaces Vitelius, the former Nigidia takes over the Barefoot Dancer's role, and the Regisseur himself now sits in Lucan's place. The slave with the platter of sandwiches appears once more and shoves them every now and then under the noses of Nero and his fellow feasters.)*

NERO *(the former Lucan, reading the script).* So this is the hostage our Vinicius has fallen in love with?

PETRONIUS. Yes, Caesar, it is she.

NERO, THE FORMER LUCAN. What is her name?

PETRONIUS. Lygia.

NERO, THE FORMER LUCAN. Does Vinicius think she's beautiful?

PETRONIUS. Yes, but I've already seen her sentence on your face, oh connoisseur of connoisseurs: "Too narrow in the hips."

LYGIA *(to the Regisseur, motioning toward the house)*. There're some more people out there again. Couldn't we drop the curtain?

REGISSEUR *(rises and looks out into the house)*. Yes, I've had enough public scandals for one day already. Fed to the teeth. *(Yells off backstage.)* Lower the curtain. *(He sits in Lucan's place.)*

POPPAEA *(hissing in Lygia's direction)*. The kitten knows who ate the goldfish, that's why she's worried.

REGISSEUR: Let's go on! . .

NERO, THE FORMER LUCAN *(looking in the script)*. It's your line, Aristarchus Petrovich.

REGISSEUR. Mine . . . So it is . . . Give me the cue!

NERO, THE FORMER LUCAN. Too narrow in the hips.

CURTAIN.

FLOOR PLAN FOR ACTS THREE AND FOUR

(1) Door to entryway, (2) door to hallway, (3) door to the Landlady and Typist's room, (4) door to Aglaya Karpovna's room, (5) door to Dr. Fregoli's room, (6) door to the Comic's room, (7) door to the kitchen, (8) door to the Romantic Lead's room, (9) door to the Civil Servant and Student's room, (10) stove, (11) buffet, (12) small table with record player, (13) an ottoman, (14) the dining table, (15) small table with typewriter, (16), (17), etc.—chairs.

ACT THREE

Marya Yakovlevna's boardinghouse. A large dining room with a large extensible table in the middle covered with an oilcloth. Eight chairs surround the table. At right the walls of one room jut into the dining room. A cozy ottoman stands in front of it. Downstage left is a small table with a covered typewriter. A chair is placed by it. The door left (No. 1 on the Floor plan) leads to the entryway, the door center (No. 2) to the hallway, ending in the door to the kitchen (No. 7). Doors 5, 6, 8, and 9 lead from the hallway into rooms occupied by Schmidt (No. 5), the Comic (No. 6), the Romantic Lead (No. 8) and the Civil Servant and his son (No. 9). The door upstage right leads to the room (No. 3) occupied by Marya Yakovlevna and her daughter. The door downstage left (No. 4) leads to the room occupied by Aglaya Karpovna. In the left corner there is a tile stove. To the left of the center doors is an electric bell button, then a buffet. A pitcher of water, a glass, a fruit bowl, and so forth are visible in the open part of the buffet. To the right of the center doors is a high table with shelves and graced by a well-made gramophone. Several pictures of naive content and execution hang on the walls, a lamp with a large shade hangs from the ceiling, and finally some brightly colored curtains on the doors complete the dining room's furnishings. As the curtain rises the Barefoot Dancer and the Student are on stage. She is scrubbing the floor. Her hairdo and dress are appropriate for a servant girl. Her dress is tucked up enough to reveal her seductive bare legs. The Student has a book and is standing leaning with his elbow against the jamb of the doors leading to the hallway, and isn't taking his eyes off the supple figure of the coquettish floor-scrubber.

STUDENT *(after a long pause in which he apparently was trying to think up something to talk about).* How are you doing, Aniuta, you're not getting a backache?

BAREFOOT DANCER *(in a faintly lower class accent).* 'S all right, we're used to it.

STUDENT. Just the same I imagine work like that must make you ache all over.

BAREFOOT DANCER. 'S not work . . . back on the farm now, you really . . . 'specially during the mowing . . . Get up three in the mornin', workin' in the fields till sundown with ary a moment's rest . . .

STUDENT *(silent for a moment).* Did you have a reading room anywhere nearby?

BAREFOOT DANCER. Couldn't rightly say, maybe there is now . . . wasn't when I was there.

STUDENT. Do you like books?

BAREFOOT DANCER. All depends on what kind . . . Our pappy now had mighty fine books, his niece showed 'em to me—religious books, with ever'thin writ so purty, I couldn't begin to tell you . . .

STUDENT. But religion is just superstition, Aniuta. That actress you used to work for, she probably wasn't too fond of religious books?

BAREFOOT DANCER *(wiping the sweat off her face with her sleeve and smiling slyly.)* And who told you I used to work for an actress?

STUDENT. Marya Yakovlevna . . . the landlady . . .

BAREFOOT DANCER *(laughs).* You have to know everything, don't you? I didn't notice any religious books at her place, that's for sure . . . Wasn't any time, prob'ly, or maybe she'd read 'em all . . . What's that book you've got there?

STUDENT. Roman law.

BAREFOOT DANCER. A religious book?

STUDENT. Juridical. *(Pours himself a glass of water and drinks it.)*

BAREFOOT DANCER. You mean it's not in Russian?

STUDENT. Hm . . . Half Russian, half Latin.

BAREFOOT DANCER. Think o' that! What'll they think of next! . . And what's a latin?

STUDENT. It's been dead for centuries.

BAREFOOT DANCER. Dead . . . Ooh, how awful! I hope I don't have any bad dreams, God forbid!

STUDENT *(laughing).* You don't understand, there's nothing so awful here. "Dead" means nobody speaks Latin any more . . . And anyway, being afraid of dead things is just superstition . . . I, for instance, am not at all afraid of death, not the slightest bit.

BAREFOOT DANCER. You're afraid of life instead.

STUDENT. Life? . . What makes you think I'm afraid of life? . .

BAREFOOT DANCER. The landlady told me you almost hung yourself one time . . . Life must have seemed pretty awful! Wasn't that it?

STUDENT. Not awful, just hard.

BAREFOOT DANCER. How so?

STUDENT. Hm . . . how so? . . . Can't explain things like that in one sentence.

BAREFOOT DANCER *(half-offended).* Well o' course, us country girls aren't educated . . . prob'ly wouldn't understand . . .

STUDENT. For God's sake, don't be offended . . . I wasn't trying to say that at all. You see, I have this brother Vladimir . . . Volodya . . . that is actually, I used to, because . . . *(Breathes heavily and blows his nose.)* But no, I'd better not say! It's a secret . . . it's a deep secret. *(A long ring on the bell is heard.)*

BAREFOOT DANCER. It's your business . . . all up to you, sir . . . *(The Landlady has walked out of the kitchen and now appears in the hallway. She is wearing an apron and is stirring something in a small saucepan.)*

BOARDINGHOUSE LANDLADY *(going over to door No. 2 which leads to the dining room.)* Aniuta! The bell's ringing, can't you hear? Number four. *(She walks away and stops in the hall by room No. 8 and listens to what's going on behind the door.)*

AGLAYA KARPOVNA *(a skinny, elderly lady—with her hair slicked down and with the sort of face that does not inspire warm feelings—comes out of room No. 4 right in a rage and, as the saying goes, "jumps on the servant girl")* Have you gone deaf, my dear?

BAREFOOT DANCER. But I have to finish scrubbing the floor!

AGLAYA KARPOVNA. It ought to be done at six o'clock in the morning, not at eleven.

BAREFOOT DANCER. So as to wake everybody up?

AGLAYA KARPOVNA. . . . And not on Sunday either, but yesterday, because floors are to be scrubbed on Saturdays . . .

BAREFOOT DANCER. I *wanted* to do 'em yesterday, but you sent me to the drugstore to get you some, what's it . . .

AGLAYA KARPOVNA *(interrupts, embarrassed, envenomed)*. On top of that you have to shout all over the place what kind of medicine you got—everybody has to know that? Stupid wench! Hurry up and do my room. *(The Barefoot Dancer picks up her pail and rag and goes off to room No. 4.)*

STUDENT *(pours himself some water out of the pitcher)*. You ought, you know, to be a little calmer, otherwise, with your temperament we won't be able to keep a decent maid around here. *(Drinks.)*

AGLAYA KARPOVNA. "Decent"? That, in your opinion, is a decent maid?

BOARDINGHOUSE LANDLADY *(appearing in the No. 2 doorway, still stirring something in a saucepan)*. What's going on?

AGLAYA KARPOVNA *(to the Student)*. Just because you've got a crush on her doesn't make her decent. And you're hardly one to talk about decency anyway.

STUDENT *(flaring up)*. What do you mean? Why not?

AGLAYA KARPOVNA. Because decent people don't violate the laws of God and man. But you were all set to end your life, kill yourself, in somebody else's house at that, where it would upset everyone, so your decency *c'est une chose bien doutable!*

STUDENT. I suppose then, that the philosopher Hartmann who killed himself was not a decent man, in your opinion?

AGLAYA KARPOVNA. That was Hartmann!

STUDENT. Well then, the mystic Novalis, who preached that "suicide is a truly philosophical deed?"

AGLAYA KARPOVNA. That was Novalis! Look whom he's comparing himself to!

STUDENT. So, Otto Weininger can deprive himself of life because he's Otto Weininger, but I don't dare even consider such a thing . . . *(Meanwhile the Barefoot Dancer carries her pail from room No. 4 to the kitchen.)*

AGLAYA KARPOVNA *(to the Servant Girl)*. Tuck up your skirt a little higher why don't you! . . Country bumpkin! . .

STUDENT. You mean she ought to wear a petticoat and a train to scrub floors?

AGLAYA KARPOVNA. I'm not talking to you! *Vous êtes ridicule, mon cher*, in your role as defender.

TYPIST *(entering right from door No. 3 with a business folder in her hands, in a very modest but lovely dress, her hair becomingly done, a little lipstick and powder on, in other words, a great improvement over her previous appearances)*. What's going on? *(Passes over to the table left and takes the cover off the typewriter.)* You're always raising the roof, Aglaya Karpovna, over some trivia. *(She sits down at the typewriter.)*

AGLAYA KARPOVNA. Oh, it's my fault! . . Well, of course . . .

BOARDINGHOUSE LANDLADY. Stop it, all of you! Why do you have to keep on . . . *(The Student waves his hand once, apparently in anger, goes off into the hallway and then to room No. 9.)*

TYPIST *(interrupting her mother)*. Aniuta, a poor working girl, good-natured, keeps the place neat as a pin, and here you are . . .

AGLAYA KARPOVNA. A perfectly marvelous servant girl to be sure! Why wouldn't you stick up for her, when she taught you to curl your hair, put on powder, paint your lips, and . . . I don't want to say it, but I see everything, my dear, everything!

TYPIST *(cheerful, perky)*. Congratulations on your terrific talent for espionage. I rejoice with all my heart, especially since I'm in such a great mood that, honest to God, I spit on all your carping. *(Starts typing.)*

AGLAYA KARPOVNA. "Spit?". . Very elegant . . . Did you learn that from Aniuta too? *(To the Boardinghouse Landlady.)* I must say she's a great influence on your daughter. *(The Barefoot Dancer has returned by now from the kitchen with her skirt no longer tucked up, with shoes on, carrying a dust rag and a scrub brush.)*

BOARDINGHOUSE LANDLADY. Pardon me, Aglaya Karpovna, but you're getting yourself all excited over nothing . . . Aniuta's a perfectly wonderful girl, and I'll even say more: she brings happiness . . . laugh if you want to, but the month she's been living here, it's like the sun's shining on us . . .

AGLAYA KARPOVNA *(with malicious irony)*. Only not on me, Marya Yakovlevna! Only not on me. *Je vous demande mille pardons*, but I don't care for any sunshine like that. I was raised under different rays and I value only the rays of enlightenment, and not ignorance. And I'm not superstitious either: I don't consult fortune-tellers, I don't believe them, and I wouldn't give a kopeck for all this nonsense about anybody "bringing happiness," "shining like the sun," and all that stuff.

BOARDINGHOUSE LANDLADY. However, if you'll pardon me for saying so—everything the fortune-teller predicted has come true, word for word.

AGLAYA KARPOVNA. Your imagination.

BOARDINGHOUSE LANDLADY. "Imagination!" She predicted some good lodgers and they appeared, predicted Lidochka would get better *(indicates her daughter)* and sure enough; she doesn't cough at night any more, her appetite's come back, her eyes are bright and I believe she's even gained a little weight! Predicted Fedya would get over his depression and sure enough . . .

AGLAYA KARPOVNA *(finishing the sentence)*. . . . he got over his depression and started having an affair with the maid . . . wonderful, just wonderful!

TYPIST. Mama! Why argue! . . There's just one thing I don't understand: if Aglaya Karpovna doesn't like it around here why doesn't she leave? After all, we're not forcing her to stay here. *(A bell ringing in the entryway is heard.)*

AGLAYA KARPOVNA. Well then, you should know, miss, that when your mother was in need of money to pay for your treatment, I—without thinking what I was doing—I paid for my room five months in advance. And in as much as *j'y suis, j'y reste. (Turns sharply and with haughty dignity heads off for her room No. 4, but collides—in the funniest way—with the Servant Girl.)* Have you gone blind, my dear? You almost knocked me off my feet! Clumsy oaf! Like they've all ganged up on me at once! But we'll just see who comes out on top! *(She goes off, slams the door behind her at the same instant the Barefoot Dancer runs into the entryway, suppressing her laughter with her apron.)*

BOARDINGHOUSE LANDLADY. What a temper, merciful heavens! And why they hired a lady like that to teach young ladies deportment, God only knows. *(Glances at the entryway.)*

TYPIST. At school they call her "The Mean Old Witch."

BOARDINGHOUSE LANDLADY *(in the direction of the entryway)*. Ah . . . Nikolai Savelich and Semyon Arkadevich! Back from mass? . . All tired out . . . lots of people there? I wanted to go over and pray a little myself, but I was so busy . . .

RETIRED CIVIL SERVANT *(meanwhile enters from the entryway—that is, from door No. 1—with the Comic and greets the Boardinghouse Landlady. The Comic has a gray bristle on his upper lip, wears a pince nez with light blue lenses on a black cord, and has on a short military-style jacket. He supports the old clerk's elbows slightly as they enter. The Comic greets the ladies after the Retired Civil Servant does.)* Good afternoon . . . good afternoon. How are you . . . the priest said a prayer for your health . . . *(Hands the Boardinghouse Landlady a prosvira.)*

BOARDINGHOUSE LANDLADY *(bows and kisses the prosvira)*. Thank you so much . . .

RETIRED CIVIL SERVANT. Och, I'm so tired. *(Sits down.)* No letters from Volodya?

BOARDINGHOUSE LANDLADY *(sympathizing)*. No.

RETIRED CIVIL SERVANT *(shaking his head in despair)*. Out on the high seas he's forgotten an old man. Try to prattle about filial love now . . .

COMIC *(to the Barefoot Dancer, who has appeared in the entryway door)*. Aniuta, my dear, do a good job on my boots, the mud's just awful. *(The Barefoot Dancer returns to the entryway. The Comic stands behind the Typist and watches her type.)*

RETIRED CIVIL SERVANT. Is Fedya up already?

BOARDINGHOUSE LANDLADY. Oh yes, he's up . . .

RETIRED CIVIL SERVANT. Cramming Roman law all night . . . makes you feel sorry for him . . . *(Gets up.)* I'll go see him. *(Goes off through the hall to door No. 9, and the Boardinghouse Landlady then goes immediately into the Kitchen.)*

COMIC. Is Schmidt home?

TYPIST. Went to the store.

COMIC. But today's a holiday?

TYPIST. Got in a new shipment of records yesterday . . .

COMIC. Oh yes, he told me: he didn't have time to unpack them yet . . .

TYPIST. That's right! And he promised to play all the new ones for me today . . .

COMIC. A concert, you mean? Isn't he nice? . .

TYPIST. We can't praise him enough . . . God himself must have sent us a lodger like him. Full of fun, kindhearted, and the minute he sees me feeling sad he puts on just the right record and like magic . . .

COMIC. A magic record-player, you mean?

TYPIST. It really is magic.

COMIC. Is Viktor Antonych up yet?

TYPIST. Not yet . . .

COMIC. He's really sleeping in!

TYPIST. He came in very late last night . . . they had a meeting at the insurance company.

COMIC. A likely story! Out on the town probably. *(Adding hastily.)* That is, not getting smashed exactly, but . . .

TYPIST *(flaring up)*. He drinks? . . Semyon Arkadevich, dear, tell me, does he drink a lot?

COMIC. Who?

TYPIST. Viktor Antonych.

COMIC. Why are you so concerned about him?

TYPIST. It'd be bad for his health. He's so pale . . .

COMIC *(smiling slyly)*. I had no idea you were so concerned over his health . . .

TYPIST *(blushing quite noticeably)*. I wasn't . . . I was just . . . it's only the human thing to . . .

COMIC. I'm sure it's not the animal thing.

TYPIST. No, you don't understand.

COMIC. Don't understand you?! I understand you all too well. *(Conspiratorially, insolently.)* Better confess.

TYPIST *(mustering up her courage)*. Well, if you know then, tell me—you're a man of experience—what does it mean when a man holds on to your hand when he shakes it? . .

COMIC. Everyone knows what that means! The very first symptom that the man's fallen in love.

TYPIST *(hardly daring to believe her ears)*. You're . . . joking.

COMIC. Not at all. Show me how he holds your hand. *(Takes her right hand.)* Like this? *(Demonstrates a prolonged handshake.)*

TYPIST. Yes . . . yes . . . like that . . .

COMIC *(peremptorily)*. In love. I'd bet my head on it, he's in love.

TYPIST. It can't be . . . It must be some mistake . . . some misunderstanding . . .

BOARDINGHOUSE LANDLADY *(appearing in the hall with the same old saucepan)*. Lida, dear, come help me in the kitchen! My arm's gone numb stirring . . . *(To the Comic.)* You're getting a dinner tonight that'll make your eyes pop out.

COMIC. A little vodka, too?

BOARDINGHOUSE LANDLADY. Look where your mind is!

COMIC *(whining)*. Marya Yakovlevna, our benefactor!

BOARDINGHOUSE LANDLADY *(laughs)*. We'll see . . . Come on, Lida! *(The instant Lida gets up to go to the kitchen, the Romantic Lead appears in the hall dressed rather simply but a little foppishly, his hair done differently, and displaying the beginnings of a moustache.)* Ah! Viktor Antonovich! . . At last! And here we were thinking you'd never get up . . . *(The Romantic Lead kisses the Boardinghouse Landlady's hand and holds the daughter's hand an extra moment as he shakes it.)*

ROMANTIC LEAD *(greeting her)*. Good morning!

COMIC. Some "morning!" It's past noon, time for dinner!

ROMANTIC LEAD *(to the daughter)*. Why are your hands so cold?

COMIC. Warm heart, heh, heh, heh. *(The Boardinghouse Landlady and her daughter go off to the kitchen. The Comic and the Romantic Lead watch them go out, then*

*the Comic pokes his finger in the Romantic Lead's stomach with a hackneyed farcical
motion and they both laugh.)*

BAREFOOT DANCER *(appearing from the entryway).* Quiet, you idiots! You
want to get everybody all suspicious?

COMIC. Suspicious? Listen to that! Simpletons like them get suspicious! You
could wrap them right around your finger and they'd never notice it.

BAREFOOT DANCER. In any case we've got to be careful . . . *(looks around.)*
There's another little matter I wanted to discuss, my friend *(turning to the
Comic),* that is, if you keep on taking advantage of my position to force me
to clean your boots, shoes, and so on twice a day, I'm . . .

ROMANTIC LEAD *(to the Comic).* Now that, brother, is just not a comradely
thing to do.

COMIC. What's not comradely? And who's going to clean them then? Me?

ROMANTIC LEAD. I clean my own shoes.

COMIC. That's the way, my dear boy, to get everybody suspicious of you! And
not so much of you, as of her. "A regular princess." they'll say, "an aristocrat! Why is it they don't ask her to clean their shoes?"

BAREFOOT DANCER. You know very well what I'm talking about . . .

COMIC. What about, my jewel?

BAREFOOT DANCER. About how you, on purpose, yes, quite frequently
on purpose, load me down with work for no good reason. I know good
and well what a scoundrel you are.

COMIC. But after all, my dear girl, I thought you took to your part like melted
butter. Why, I thought it was all pure pleasure.

BAREFOOT DANCER. I won't deny that I'm fond of a part where I can do
real—not ephemeral—good for others. I've always been an idealist at
heart. But it's petty, my friend, petty and crude what you force me to do
some of the time.

ROMANTIC LEAD. Yes, yes, my friend, you sometimes forget *what she means*
to me. You're getting carried away a little too much with your part . . .
You're overjoyed there isn't a prompter, so you make the most dreadful ad
libs. You've got to have a sense of proportion . . .

COMIC. It's bad enough around here without you jumping on me too . . . *(To
the Romantic Lead.)* You're a fine one to talk, living here like a lord, your
wife close by *(indicates the Barefoot Dancer),* eat, drink, be merry and carry
on with the daughter. Not bad work. But mine! Pretending to be some
half-buffoon, half-parasite, playing nursemaid to this witless, senile old
codger, wandering around with him from church to church and monastery
to monastery, playing chess with him, trying to lose just to cheer him up a
little. Court that old witch *(turns to door No. 4),* pacifying her with jokes, in

which even the word "garter" is forbidden, on grounds of indecency! *Parlez francais*, and there's hell to pay!

BAREFOOT DANCER. I suppose that if you didn't know the old miser had piled up a little nest egg, you wouldn't work so hard.

ROMANTIC LEAD *(to the Comic)*. Besides, you make almost twice what we do.

COMIC. Twice as much! It'd take mountains of gold to even it up.

BAREFOOT DANCER. You're always griping at everything. If anybody should complain, it ought to be me: living in the kitchen, toting scrub buckets around, ruining my hands washing floors and dishes, being required to flirt with that boring student, all so he won't—God forbid—go and hang himself, and on top of all that take a lot of garbage from that old witch *(indicates door No. 4)*.

COMIC. But you're the idealist! You admitted yourself you're an idealist!

BAREFOOT DANCER. I'm not complaining! I'm just saying you're not the only one with a hard job.

COMIC. But I'm not an idealist. Do you understand? *(Patting himself on his fat belly.)* I am not an idealist.

ROMANTIC LEAD *(laughing)*. That is obvious.

COMIC. . . . and if this raving Dr. Fregoli feels like philanthropizing a bunch of morons at the expense of poverty-stricken *(strikes himself on the chest)*, honest actors who have served sacred art for twenty years, then he ought to be paying not kopecks, but . . .

ROMANTIC LEAD *(laughing)*. Some kopecks!

BAREFOOT DANCER. You're insatiable.

COMIC. What do you know about it? Try being in my shoes. Hire a clown, then pay him royally. Why, I've read how in the olden days the tsars kept clowns— in the first place, food fit for a tsar, not the slop around here that's making me waste away to nothing *(the Romantic Lead and the Barefoot Dancer laugh)* and what's more . . .

ROMANTIC LEAD. Well, go to a restaurant then! Who's keeping you?

COMIC *(interrupting)*. I can't: according to the contract I'm supposed to get slopped here. *(Takes the contract, his wallet, and a booklet from his pocket and puts them on the table.)* There, read it! Here you are free as a bird in your role— "insurance agent," boy oh boy, but as far as me, pure slavery.

BAREFOOT DANCER *(noticing that door No. 4 is starting to open)*. Shh . . . Careful. *(Goes over to the buffet, opens it and goes over the dishes, making them tinkle a little and pretending to be putting them away.)*

AGLAYA KARPOVNA *(appears in the doorway of room No. 4, then in a sweet voice)*. Semyon Arkadevich! . . . You back already? . .

COMIC *(hastily jams the contract and the wallet into his pocket while the Romantic Lead grabs the booklet).* Aglaya Karpovna I *(Runs over to her. Obsequiously.)* Bon-zhur . . . komant alle voo? How's your health?

AGLAYA KARPOVNA *(nodding).* Not too good . . . slept badly again last night. I wanted to consult you again . . . *(The Barefoot Dancer covers the table with a cloth.)*

COMIC. At your service . . . my duty as a physician . . . so to say, the suffering of one's fellow man . . . But as for you, it's a pleasant duty indeed . . . you might say, the most pleasant . . .

AGLAYA KARPOVNA *(smiling).* You're such a big flatterer . . . Come to my room for a minute . . . *(Goes off to her room.)*

COMIC. With the greatest . . . *(Goes off after her.)*

BAREFOOT DANCER *(after their departure).* I only hope he doesn't pack her off to the next world.

ROMANTIC LEAD *(leafing through the booklet).* Meaning?

BAREFOOT DANCER. He's really been writing out prescriptions for her! He'll kill her, God forbid.

ROMANTIC LEAD. Don't worry, Dr. Fregoli's in charge of everything.

BAREFOOT DANCER. You can't keep track of such people. What's that booklet he left?

ROMANTIC LEAD *(reads the booklet's title).* "A Treasury of Witty and Amusing Jokes" . . . *(He laughs.)* So this turns out to be the source of his "inexhaustible humor."

(The Typist appears at the kitchen door at the end of the hall.)

TYPIST *(standing in the kitchen doorway, turning to her mother, who is not visible).* All right, Mama, all right . . . What did you say? . . *(She returns to the kitchen.)*

BAREFOOT DANCER *(quietly, hastily).* It's the girl . . . quiet! . .

ROMANTIC LEAD. Wonderful. *(Sticks the booklet in his pocket.)* It's time now for my formal declaration of love. Dr. Fregoli said so. I've been preparing the ground for a month now . . .

BAREFOOT DANCER. Only please don't get carried away.

ROMANTIC LEAD *(laughs).* What do you mean "don't get carried away? . ." As an honest actor I'm supposed to get carried away.

BAREFOOT DANCER. You know very well what I mean.

ROMANTIC LEAD. Now listen, this jealousy of yours is absurd . . . I'm not jealous of you and that student.

BAREFOOT DANCER. That's all I'd need!

TYPIST *(coming out of the kitchen).* Aniuta! Mama wants you.

ROMANTIC LEAD. Go ahead.

BAREFOOT DANCER *(yells).* I'm coming! *(To the Romantic Lead.)* Watch out now! *(Runs off to the kitchen.)*

TYPIST *(entering)*. Now then, are you going to take a lesson on the typewriter today? *(Sits at her typewriter table.)*

ROMANTIC LEAD. Of course . . . You're such a wonderful instructor . . . Everybody at the office knows how except for me. And so fast, you know . . . But me and my handwriting—a regular disaster . . .

TYPIST. Sit down then and let's not waste any time. We'll finish before dinner.

ROMANTIC LEAD. Wonderful! *(Takes a chair and sits close to the typewriter table.)* Lesson Five today.

TYPIST. Four.

ROMANTIC LEAD. Absolutely correct.

TYPIST *(instructing)*. Your biggest mistake is not using the punctuation keys properly. You've got to tap them ever so lightly, otherwise they punch holes in the paper and make marks on the roller. Besides that, the shift key—you keep forgetting—has to be pushed all the way down, otherwise the capital letters come out above the small letters. *(Clicks away a little.)* Is that clear? . . *(Gets up.)* First type out a line of words separated by commas . . . Only don't get mixed up or leave any out.

ROMANTIC LEAD. Yes ma'am. *(He sits in her chair and types.)*

TYPIST *(while he types)*. Like that . . . Well, why are you hesitating? . . Don't get your fingers mixed up: your left little finger should hit only Q, A, Z, and no other letters . . . It's all got to be done automatically . . . that's the whole secret . . .

ROMANTIC LEAD *(gets up)*. All done.

TYPIST *(sits at the typewriter and reads)*. When . . . comma . . . you . . . type . . . I . . . you missed one . . . always . . . comma . . . am . . . comma . . . fascinated . . . by your hands. *(She blushes somewhat.)* So . . . not bad . . . only you spend too much time looking for the keys, it's got to be automatic. Like this. *(She sits down, types something very quickly and gets up.)*

ROMANTIC LEAD *(sits close and reads)*. "Flattery doesn't appeal to me, and if you're laughing at me, may God punish you, for I'm unhappy enough as it is . . ." *(To her.)* Let me try one more time.

TYPIST. Fine; only do periods this time instead of commas.

ROMANTIC LEAD. Yes ma'am. *(He types. She watches with burning eyes and uneven breath. The Barefoot Dancer enters, gets a salad bowl and a platter from the buffet, looks around jealously at the couple and goes off to the kitchen.)* There! I typed it. All right?

TYPIST *(reads)*. "I'm an enemy of flattery. Truth, sincerity, and kindness—that's what I value in a person. I found these qualities in you and that's why you mean more to me than a thousand soulless dolls." *(She laughs, embarrassed, tries not to give herself away.)* Fine . . . almost perfect . . . but what happened to the periods after each word?

ROMANTIC LEAD *(deliberately, smoothly).* They're at the end . . . Dot, dot, dot . . . *(Takes her by the hand.)* Isn't it all the same? *(The Barefoot Dancer comes in and starts setting the table for dinner: gets the plates, glasses, and so forth out of the buffet and puts them on the table. The Romantic Lead coughs a little as if to let her know that the presence of a servant is not desired.)*

TYPIST *(softly).* I'll answer you. *(Types.)* There . . .

ROMANTIC LEAD *(reads).* "I'm afraid to believe you. You . . ."

TYPIST *(interrupting).* Shh . . . *(Softly.)* To yourself! . . *(The Romantic Lead reads to himself; she coughs a little, turning slightly in the servant's direction.)*

BAREFOOT DANCER. What's this, miss, coughing again? Should I run get your cough medicine?

TYPIST. Yes, please do. *(The Barefoot Dancer goes off to room No. 3.)*

ROMANTIC LEAD *(finishes reading, then gets up).* Lidia Fedorovna, in reply to your question I can say only one word, but that word includes the deepest feelings in my heart. *(Standing, he types three letters.)*

TYPIST *(reads).* "Yes" . . . *(A pause. Softly, out of breath, not daring to believe.)* Yes?

ROMANTIC LEAD *(with convincing tenderness).* Yes. And if you get to know me well, then you won't have any doubt of it.

TYPIST *(with trembling hands takes the paper out of the typewriter).* I . . . I'm afraid to believe you . . . I . . . don't know, I . . . *(Presses the paper she's taken from the typewriter to her lips, raises her shoulders for an instant, then lets them fall again. She stares off into space with wide-open eyes full of tears.)*

ROMANTIC LEAD *(after a moment of indecision).* You must believe me . . . Listen . . . *(Takes her by the hands, puts them beside her and kisses her. The Barefoot Dancer appears with a small bottle of medicine in doorway No. 3. She stops as if petrified. The Romantic Lead quickly leaves the dining room and disappears into his own room, No. 8. The Typist, scarcely believing what has happened, sinks weakly into her chair.)*

BAREFOOT DANCER *(going over to her, at first distraught, but then getting a grip on herself).* Here's your medicine . . . *(Sets the bottle on the typing table.)* Would you like some water? . .

TYPIST. Oh no, that's not necessary . . . thank you . . . no thanks . . . *(Convulsively sticks the paper with the typing in her bodice, tries to say something more to the maid, but losing control, drops her head into her hands, which were attempting to reach the typewriter keys, then sobs like a little girl.)*

BOARDINGHOUSE LANDLADY *(comes in from the kitchen to get something from the buffet and notices her daughter crying).* Lida . . . what's the matter? . . Lida! . . *(To the maid.)* What's the matter with her?

BAREFOOT DANCER. I don't know, Madam . . . I offered her some water, but Miss Lida didn't want any . . . so . . .

BOARDINGHOUSE LANDLADY. Lord in heaven . . . Lida . . . *(To the maid.)* Step into the kitchen . . . Take a look at the roast . . . *(The Barefoot Dancer goes off.)* Lida! . . What's the matter? *(Kisses her with great agitation.)*

TYPIST. Mama . . . dear . . . dear Mama . . . Hit me, beat me, it's all too wonderful . . . *(Laughs through her tears and smothers her mother in embraces.)*

BOARDINGHOUSE LANDLADY. Goodness me! . . Oi, you're smothering me, you mad girl! *(Voices are heard behind door No. 4. The Typist rushes headlong to her own room, No. 3. Her mother moves her hands apart in resignation and follows her daughter.)*

COMIC *(entering from room No. 4 with Aglaya Karpovna).* You are quite right: the main thing is routine. Routine, diet, and walking—those are, so to say, the three whales that support the world of our health. As for the medicine I prescribed you needn't take it any more: I was just testing your organism. If the organism wouldn't tolerate the prescription then we would have to deal with a purely nervous condition. *In corpore sano mens sana.* Right? And so valerian drops, routine, diet, and walking—that's all I can prescribe for the present.

AGLAYA KARPOVNA. Thank you, doctor . . . *(Rummages in her purse.)* I hope you won't be angry, *mon cher docteur*, that I'm a little shy about undressing. I realize that a doctor is only a physician to his patient, not a man, but just the same, I was always taught . . .

COMIC *(shaking his finger at her).* A coquette, you're a real coquette.

AGLAYA KARPOVNA *(embarrassedly thrusting the money at him).* I still owe you, doctor . . . for the call . . .

COMIC *(overly ceremonius).* Oh come now, please . . .

AGLAYA KARPOVNA. *Non, non, sans blagues!* I beg you. Any labor must be remunerated, especially a physician's . . .

COMIC. But after all, I . . .

AGLAYA KARPOVNA. Don't be so stubborn . . this is for four consultations. Otherwise I'll be offended . . .

COMIC. Well, if you're going to be offended . . *(Takes the money and puts it in his pocket.)* Gran—mersee. *(Kisses her hand.)*

AGLAYA KARPOVNA *(directs the Comic's attention to the hallway where the Student has come out of his room and is heading for the kitchen).* Look, doctor, look how our suicide has gone off to the kitchen again to "enlighten" the masses.

COMIC. A real democrat, damn it! How can you not be with a pretty servant girl around the house.

AGLAYA KARPOVNA. Around a family home you should say! And have you observed, doctor, how often he's been drinking water lately? They say that's the first symptom of lover's fever . . . he who's fallen in love, so I've heard, drinks a lot . . .

COMIC. Of water? . . First time I ever heard that. Vodka, maybe?

AGLAYA KARPOVNA. No indeed, water.

COMIC. Are you sure of that? . . In that case . . . *(Goes over to the buffet, pours himself a glass of water, raises it as if to toast Aglaya Karpovna and downs it in one gulp.)*

AGLAYA KARPOVNA *(blushes).* Oh, you wicked fellow! I'm too wise to take that as the genuine thing.

COMIC. Too wise? . . Well, I guess Griboyedov was right then.

AGLAYA KARPOVNA. In what sense?

COMIC. In the sense of "Woe from Wisdom."

AGLAYA KARPOVNA. Woe from Wisdom?

COMIC. Yes ma'am, I suffer *woe* as a result of your *wisdom*, in as much as you're unwilling to accept as the *genuine* thing my *genuine* feeling for you. It just seems to me that he who loves tenderly ought to be drinking not a glass of water—that sounds rather *coarse*, but a wee shot of vodka—now that sounds much more tender.

AGLAYA KARPOVNA. But it's very harmful, you know!

COMIC. For the sake of one so dear, I'm prepared even to risk an early departure for the next world . . .

AGLAYA KARPOVNA. Oh you flatterer! Incorrigible, that's all! *(Turns toward the hall and notices the Romantic Lead heading for the kitchen.)* Look at that, our "insurance agent" is off to the kitchen too. Why are they all so interested in that wench? . .

COMIC. It's the age of democracy—that's all there is to it.

AGLAYA KARPOVNA. I'll call her. *(Goes over to the bell button by the door.)*

COMIC. Don't!

AGLAYA KARPOVNA. No, no. We've got to give her a ring, or they'll get in an argument and she'll have to stop it and then the roast'll get burned. *(Pushes the button. A long ring is heard.)* Heavens above! What sort of place have we stumbled upon? A regular den of iniquity, not a respectable boardinghouse.

COMIC *(looking at his watch).* The main thing is that delaying dinner is really a dirty trick.

AGLAYA KARPOVNA. That's only a minor misfortune, of course. But what would you say if you knew—*mais c'est un grand secret*—that this trollop has been sleeping, not in the kitchen, but . . . I've been keeping my eyes open.

COMIC. Where? . .

AGLAYA KARPOVNA. In the "insurance agent's" room.

COMIC. Now she's done it! That is . . . I meant to say: that's an idealist for you!

AGLAYA KARPOVNA *(astonished)*. Idealist?

BAREFOOT DANCER *(entering)*. You rang, madam?

AGLAYA KARPOVNA *(severely, emphatically)*. Yes. We did.

COMIC *(taking care of the whole mess)*. About the dinner. The landlady promised a little vodka. That's it . . . be sure to remind her.

BOARDINGHOUSE LANDLADY *(entering, overjoyed, from room No. 3)*. Right away, right away . . . Dinner, vodka, everything . . . I give in—drink then if you're so happy. Aniuta! Dinner! *(The Barefoot Dancer meets the Romantic Lead and the Student in the hall as she goes off to the kitchen.)* Only I don't know what we should do about Mr. Schmidt? *(Goes over to the buffet.)* He's always been right on time, but today . . . *(The Romantic Lead and the Student appear in the doorway whispering merrily over the Comic's booklet which the Romantic Lead is lending to the Student.)* Fedya, tell your father it's time for dinner. *(Sets on the table a decanter of vodka and a bottle of wine, both of which she had playfully extracted from the depths of the buffet. The Student goes to room No. 9. The Romantic Lead comes downstage. The Comic rummages in the side pocket of his jacket, then comes over to the Romantic Lead.)*

COMIC *(confidentially)*. Where's my book?

ROMANTIC LEAD. Which one?

COMIC. The jokes.

ROMANTIC LEAD. Which jokes?

COMIC. Don't play the fool! You took it yourself, don't pretend. *(The Typist, who has changed into another dress, calmed down and brightened up, comes out of room No. 3. Aglaya Karpovna goes over to her and a question is heard: "Well, are you all right now?" Answer: "Look at me," and the observation: "Well, thank the Lord." Aglaya Karpovna sits at the table, having first fastidiously brushed the dust off her chair and having wiped her plate with a napkin. The daughter assists her mother in the pre-dinner arrangements.)*

ROMANTIC LEAD. *Ah, that rubbish? I gave it to the student. Roman law's not very amusing, and so I . . .

COMIC. You're out of your mind! I've got to refresh my memory on some joke for dinner, and he gives it away; forgot, I suppose, what my contract requires?

ROMANTIC LEAD. . . . . Come up with a new joke every day? I remember.

---

*This dialog is of secondary importance, but it should not be cut. The director will note that it serves to cover the entrances of the daughter, the retired civil servant, and the student. *N.E.*

But the ones in that collection are old. Last year's edition. *(The bell is heard. The maid runs off to open the entryway door.)*

COMIC. What's it to you? *(The Retired Civil Servant and the Student enter and the former sits at the table.)*

ROMANTIC LEAD. Oh no, my friend, if you're going to insist the contract requires "Aniuta" to clean your shoes, then allow me to insist the contract requires you to deliver brand-new jokes, and not last year's.

COMIC *(venomously)*. Are you trying to do me in? Take care, my friend, I don't do you in, you wretched idealist. *(Goes off to the door of the entryway, glances into it, then runs almost at a gallop to the gramophone and shouts with affected good cheer.)* Mr. Schmidt is here! Let's have some music! . . We ought to put on . . . a welcoming march. *(Puts on a record.)*

BOARDINGHOUSE LANDLADY. Ah, at last! And we were afraid . . .

TYPIST. Karl Ivanych? Well then, that makes everybody.

ROMANTIC LEAD. That's what I call being on time . . . A real fine fellow, by God, just in time for dinner. *(The gramophone plays a smashing, exuberant march. Mr. Schmidt—Dr. Fregoli, that is—marches in from the entryway, that is from door No. 1, with his right hand making a sort of salute and his left holding a round bundle of records against his heart. His appearance has changed somewhat: his hair is curled in lovely ringlets, there are sideburns on his cheeks, a gold pince nez on his nose, and he's dressed in a Hungarian style jacket. He gaily walks around all those present and greets them, beginning with the ladies, giving each a smile and a friendly greeting. Right behind him the Barefoot Dancer comes in with a package wrapped up in newspaper. She unwraps it on the buffet, revealing candy and fruit, hastily puts them in glass bowls and is about to crumple up the newspaper which had served as a wrapping, when she notices something on the last page and finds herself—to her surprise—engrossed in it.)*

ROMANTIC LEAD *(enthusiastically greeting Schmidt downstage)*. Greetings to the esteemed supersalesman from the Chicago record company. Long live Edison and Schmidt, his devoted popularizer!

SCHMIDT. Greetings to the most honored agent of the glorious Double Salamander insurance company! *(Mock-ceremonial handshake.)*

ROMANTIC LEAD *(pointing to the round bundle)*. A surprise?

SCHMIDT *(patting the bundle)*. Top quality.

ROMANTIC LEAD *(confidentially, leading him to the left downstage corner)*. I've got a surprise too! I didn't want to tell you about it until now. *(Aglaya Karpovna, who has stopped up her ears and displays a strained smile, goes over to the gramophone, stops it—the selection is apparently not to her taste—and returns to her seat.)*

SCHMIDT. What is it?

ROMANTIC LEAD. I got a letter from the fortune-teller yesterday. It's super-natural.

SCHMIDT. What does she predict this time?

ROMANTIC LEAD. Swear you won't tell anybody!

SCHMIDT. I swear. After all, I haven't told anyone you're a detective aspiring to be another Sherlock Holmes.

ROMANTIC LEAD. Shh . . . Damn it—I can't keep anything from you—you're such an incredibly nice person, and on top of that you give such terrific advice.

SCHMIDT. Glad to be of service. What's going on?

BOARDINGHOUSE LANDLADY *(calling them).* Dinner's on the table, ladies and gentlemen! *(She goes off to the kitchen. The Comic has already poured himself some vodka and drinks to Aglaya Karpovna's health. She decisively rejects the life-giving moisture offered her.)*

ROMANTIC LEAD *(to the Boardinghouse Landlady).* In a minute, in a minute! *(To Schmidt.)* The fortune-teller writes . . . go ahead, read it . . . *(Hands him the letter.)*

SCHMIDT *(reads sotto voce).* . . . Hm . . . "Coffee grounds reading . . . The golden cupolas of Moscow . . . that's where she is . . . The name of Zinaida Belkina appeared on the alphabet plate . . ."

ROMANTIC LEAD *(overjoyed, hardly restraining himself from shouting).* The third wife's been found! You understand . . . I'm getting very close to the goal now . . .

SCHMIDT. Unbelievable. But what about the address of the polygamist, the criminal?

ROMANTIC LEAD *(takes the letter from him and puts it in a pocket).* Don't have it yet. But I have great faith in this fortune-teller, just like in God. She'll find the rogue, it'll come to her!

SCHMIDT. Miraculous!

ROMANTIC LEAD *(hastily).* Yesterday his first wife and I visited the second one, the deaf-mute, who, as you know, has just arrived from abroad—great party we had together—they both think I'm some kind of magician . . . Sent off an address inquiry to the Moscow information bureau, we'll get the third wife here . . . and then all of us together . . .

TYPIST *(coming up to them and interrupting).* Gentlemen, dinner's on the table! Come on!

BOARDINGHOUSE LANDLADY *(returning from the kitchen).* Aniuta! Aniuta! . .

ROMANTIC LEAD *(heading for the table with Schmidt).* I need to have a little talk with you. *(Sits at the table with the Typist as soon as she frees Schmidt of the bundle and puts it on the gramophone stand.)*

BOARDINGHOUSE LANDLADY. Heavens, Aniuta, here you are, and I was looking for you in the kitchen.

COMIC *(leaping over to the Barefoot Dancer)*. Bring on the meat pie. *(Sits at the table.)*

COMIC *(tears the newspaper from the Barefoot Dancer)*. Attendez m'amselle! Allow me to have a look! *(The Barefoot Dancer departs. The Comic reads closely some article on the last page of the newspaper.)*

TYPIST *(at the table)*. Well, what will you have, ladies and gentlemen? *(To the Romantic Lead.)* A little vodka?

ROMANTIC LEAD. No thank you.

TYPIST. But I hear you have a drink every now and then.

ROMANTIC LEAD *(laughing)*. Well, in that case, I'll have some!

TYPIST *(to Schmidt)*. How about you?

SCHMIDT. I always like to be part of the crowd. *(The Typist pours them some vodka. They clink their glasses and drink. The Barefoot Dancer brings on the pie. The Boardinghouse Landlady puts portions on the plates and hands them to the Barefoot Dancer who then serves them to everyone.)*

AGLAYA KARPOVNA *(to Schmidt)*. Even if it's a nasty crowd?

SCHMIDT. I don't associate with nasty crowds.

AGLAYA KARPOVNA *(using her eyes to indicate those seated at the table)*. But I have to.

SCHMIDT. In that case I feel sorry for you.

ROMANTIC LEAD *(rising)*. Now *he's* immersed in the newspaper. *(Goes over to the Comic.)* What is it! He's even neglecting his vodka! *(The Comic shows him something in the paper, they read it together.)*

AGLAYA KARPOVNA *(not letting Schmidt off the hook)*. And can you always tell which is bad and which is good?

SCHMIDT *(with all the sweetness and glitter of a well-sharpened razor)*. On that score, madam, I always make it a rule to try to change the bad into the good.

AGLAYA KARPOVNA. But is it worth soiling oneself? Consider the cost?

SCHMIDT. The gardener isn't finicky about the manure when he grows roses.

AGLAYA KARPOVNA. Sophistry.

SCHMIDT. You think so? *(Whispers something in her ear, she laughs affectedly.)*

COMIC *(putting his finger on the article in the paper, touched, to the Romantic Lead)*. They remembered me . . . they're sorry I'm gone . . .

ROMANTIC LEAD *(reading)*. . . . one can only regret deeply the absence from the troupe of the talented comic Deryabin, who would undoubtedly, had he been present, have been a big hit in the otherwise miserable production of *Quo Vadis*, that immortal work of Sienkiewicz, whose pen . . .

ACT THREE

COMIC. The rest of it is not important. *(To the Romantic Lead and the approaching Barefoot Dancer.)* Ah, my friends, I miss the applause! By God, I don't know about you, but I miss it.

BAREFOOT DANCER. Shh . . .

SCHMIDT *(coming over to them)*. Now what sort of wretched newspaper did they foist off on me for a wrapping?

BOARDINGHOUSE LANDLADY *(interrupting)*. Aniuta! Bring on the soup! *(The Barefoot Dancer goes off to the kitchen.)*

ROMANTIC LEAD. It's an old review . . . *Quo Vadis* was a flop, even though it was a benefit performance. *(Schmidt reads.)* And how did we miss it?

COMIC *(with mock sadness)*. Of course, we don't get the paper here. Nobody's interested. Who would appreciate true theater criticism anyway! . . Oh, Sashka, Sashka—there's a reviewer for you. Oh, the vodka we've drunk together . . . God Almighty! But he sure knows how to write . . . he remembered me. *(Wipes his eyes with his handkerchief.)* I'm really touched, the old rascal . . . "one can only regret," he says, "the talented comic." *(Pokes himself in the chest and blows his nose through his tears. The Barefoot Dancer brings the soup, the Boardinghouse Landlady ladles out some in bowls for the Barefoot Dancer to pass around, while the Typist goes over to the group clustered around the newspaper.)*

TYPIST. If I may be so curious, my friends, what is it that's so interesting?

BOARDINGHOUSE LANDLADY *(shouts reproachfully)*. Ladies and gentlemen, the soup's getting cold! *(Those who had left the table now return.)*

SCHMIDT *(to the daughter)*. Oh nothing . . . an untalented review of an untalented show, produced by an untalented regisseur for the benefit of an untalented actor. *(Crumples up the newspaper.)*

ROMANTIC LEAD *(to the Typist)*. Remember, we were going to *Quo Vadis*, but something came up . . .

SCHMIDT. Thank the Lord for that . . . *(Hands the crumpled newspaper to the Barefoot Dancer.)* Here, take it, Aniuta, and don't ruin your eyesight reading trash like that . . . To be sure, the shopkeeper who wrapped the merchandise for me in it made better use of it than you did, my friends. *(Claps the Romantic Lead on the shoulder.)* Admit it . . .

COMIC *(somewhat hostile, provocative)*. I don't agree . . .

SCHMIDT. So much the worse for you.

COMIC. You think so? *(With malice ill-concealed by his joking tone.)* And you know something? The worse for me, the worse for you too.

SCHMIDT. I don't understand.

COMIC. Ha, ha . . . I could repeat your own words: so much the worse for you if you don't.

95

SCHMIDT. You speak in riddles, when, if I'm not mistaken, you're supposed to be telling us a joke over our soup.

TYPIST. Yes, yes, please do! Dear Semyon Arkadevich!

ROMANTIC LEAD. Yes, doctor, it's time for a joke.

COMIC. Fine. But why "supposed to," as Mr. Schmidt put it?

SCHMIDT *(catching himself)*. Don't argue over semantics!

BOARDINGHOUSE LANDLADY. You promised it yourself.

COMIC. All right, "promised" then, not "supposed to."

BOARDINGHOUSE LANDLADY. Lord in heaven, I almost died laughing yesterday. What was it the seminary student answered at the examination: "That, your excellency, was not a miracle, just pure luck the man wasn't killed when he fell out of the belfry." *(She laughs.)*

ROMANTIC LEAD *(interrupting)*. No, no, let's have a new one today. The doctor himself promised us a new one every day. We're all ears, oh "fount of inexhaustible humor"!

SCHMIDT *(rings his knife on his plate)*. Quiet, everybody! Go ahead, doctor!

COMIC. Hm . . . *(coughs.)* There was a certain Jew . . . Hm . . .

ROMANTIC LEAD. That's right—a certain Jew, not an uncertain one.

TYPIST. Don't interrupt.

COMIC . . .who was travelling on the train without a ticket, and when the conductor asked him . . .

ROMANTIC LEAD. You told that one day before yesterday. *(The Barefoot Dancer bursts out laughing at the Comic's plight.)*

COMIC. So I already told that one? In that case . . . hm . . . let me . . . *(Thinks.)*

SCHMIDT. We're listening.

COMIC *(downs a small glass of vodka)*. Hm . . There was a certain lady, very nice-looking, who, when she realized that . . . hm . . . she was in an interesting condition . . .

ROMANTIC LEAD. Wait a minute, doctor . . . there are young ladies present . . . it's not appropriate. This isn't a stag party.

COMIC. But you don't know the punch line!

ROMANTIC LEAD. We know, we know, what kind of punch line you come up with in the case of an "interesting condition."

BOARDINGHOUSE LANDLADY. No, let's hear another joke! . . Aniuta, dear, clear away the soup bowls! *(The Barefoot Dancer clears away the soup bowls and takes them to the kitchen.)*

COMIC *(getting up his courage)*. All right. If you want another one, fine. This officer had a certain orderly—this was back in the days of Nikolai the First—who poured himself a glass of vodka and said "God's servant Ivan is being joined to God's servant vodka glass." So he drinks the glass down in one gulp. At this moment the officer suddenly materializes from nowhere. The orderly is dumbfounded. The officer takes out a rod and says "God's servant Ivan is being joined to God's servant birch rod. Can any man say why these two should not be united in holy matrimony?" "Oh yes, your excellency," says the orderly, "the groom's ag'in it." *(Except for the Romantic Lead, the Student, and Schmidt, those present break out in forced laughter.)*

ROMANTIC LEAD. Oh, that was a real old one. You ought to be ashamed.

STUDENT *(seconding)*. And not at all witty either!

AGLAYA KARPOVNA. Oh no, very witty! Hurray for the clever orderly! In the old days authority was respected and people always had a witty comeback, not like today.

COMIC *(encouraged)*. "The groom's ag'in it" . . . Isn't that something! . . Heh, heh . . . Listen, Lydia Fedorovna, it sometimes so happens that the groom's ag'in it. What do you think about it?

TYPIST *(embarrassed)*. I'm not getting married . . . why should I think about it, I don't understand?

COMIC. Don't you remember our talk a little while ago?

TYPIST. What of it?

COMIC. Just this: *(starts singing the Mephistopheles theme from Gounod's Faust)* "Never kiss the man before you are betrothed." Ha, ha, ha, ha, ha . . . ha, ha, ha, ha.

SCHMIDT. By the way, Marya Yakovlevna, this is mighty strong vodka you have around here. Makes people not only sing, but the wrong opera as well.

COMIC *(to the Typist)*. So you're not getting married . . . Too bad . . . And I was all set to drink "the health of someone who loves someone."

ROMANTIC LEAD *(getting halfway up)*. In that case allow me to drink *(to him)* to your health. And *(to Aglaya Karpovna)* to yours.

AGLAYA KARPOVNA *(scandalized, but flattered)*, Mais vous êtes fou, mon cher! Marya Yakovlevna, your vodka really is too strong. *(The Barefoot Dancer brings on the roast, the Boardinghouse Landlady puts portions on the plates, the Barefoot Dancer serves them.)*

RETIRED CIVIL SERVANT *(rises)*. I would like, from the bottom of my heart, to raise a glass to the one who has lightened my old age with his presence, who doesn't mind chatting with me, who consoles me in my sorrows, who plays a little chess with me on occasion, and who shares the bath house with me. The heart of an angel . . . I drink to his angelic heart, to the most noble, the most kindhearted lodger we have, to that physician and healer of human souls, to Semyon Arkadevich, may God bring him the greatest good fortune. *(Clinks his glass with the Comic's as Aglaya Karpovna, the Boardinghouse Landlady, the Typist, and Schmidt all applaud.)*

COMIC *(touched, rises, and forcefully embraces the Retired Civil Servant).* Overwhelmed, by God, I'm overwhelmed! . . I don't deserve it, although I've tried to . . . Ladies and gentlemen! . .*(Raises his glass.)* I'm deeply touched . . . at last I hear some applause in this house . . . makes me tremble! Tremble, like an old war horse hearing the horn blow. *(Schmidt coughs loudly and meaningfully.)* Sorry! I got a little carried away . . . Happens to me quite often. I remember when I was just a pupil in the army medical institute . . . *(Schmidt again coughs a warning.)* Eh-h . . . yes, of course, first I finished at the army medical institute, then I went off to the university and so forth . . . Anyhow, it so happened we had to report to the commanding officer— they were very strict about it, so it was easy to overdo it. But I was a real spoiled brat, as they say, and for me subordination was worse than pulling teeth. Well sir, those days, you all know, are not like today, you had to pay for irresponsible behavior . . . So they'd report on our fannies—still makes me sore to think about it. But people made out all right, just the same. *(Thumps himself on the chest.)*

AGLAYA KARPOVNA *(sighing tenderly).* And such nice people!

COMIC. That's precisely it ma'am, the old-fashioned upbringing tempered a man. No matter how hard they beat me, not a word! Kept it all to myself just as if I had a mouthful of water. Our inspector—even he was amazed. "Here's a rascal for you," he says, "look at him pretend . . . as if it didn't hurt," he says, "he doesn't even show a trace of pain! An actor," he says, "a real actor." And these words made such an impression on me that the minute I finished the medical institute, I couldn't think of anything but a career on the stage . . . *(Once more Schmidt coughs loudly.)* Eh-h . . . yes, of course! But, you understand, common sense prevailed and I went into medicine instead of acting. That's the way it was, all right. And so, allow me, as a doctor, that is, as a person concerned about health to drink to the health of those present. *(Clinks his glass with everybody's. The Typist puts her napkin on the table in order to clink glasses with the Comic. The instant their glasses meet, Aglaya Karpovna seizes the napkin and begins examining it closely.)*

TYPIST *(to Aglaya Karpovna).* Pardon me, but that's my napkin! You've gotten them mixed up!

AGLAYA KARPOVNA. I realize it's yours. But what is it you've soiled it with?

TYPIST. Oh please, give it back!

AGLAYA KARPOVNA. Red, ve ry red . . . Hmmph! Why, this is some kind of lipstick. Are you painting your lips?

TYPIST. What business is it of yours? *(Takes the napkin back.)*

AGLAYA KARPOVNA. Well, should a young girl paint her lips? . . I told you. It's absurd, *ma chere*, and even worse—*artificial!* You should be ashamed of yourself!

TYPIST (*pathetic in her embarrassment, blinking her eyes tearfully*). My lips get cracks in them . . .

AGLAYA KARPOVNA. And so you've got to paint them? How many times have I explained to you that only the natural is good. As a matter of fact you've become rather artificial all over recently.

BOARDINGHOUSE LANDLADY. That's enough, Aglaya Karpovna, why do you keep on . . .

AGLAYA KARPOVNA (*interrupting*). But if you as a mother are not going to set this young lady straight, then other people jolly well are entitled to.

SCHMIDT. I'm not going to. (*A pause. All look at him with anticipation.*) I love artificiality and cherish it from the depth of my heart, when it beautifies our life.

AGLAYA KARPOVNA. Yes, but artificialty is based on lie, on falsehood!

SCHMIDT. What of it? And do you suppose speaking the plain truth in public is such a great idea? . . Why, if I were to be utterly frank with you, you'd never speak to me again!

AGLAYA KARPOVNA. Why not? Be frank, go ahead!

SCHMIDT. Oh come on! Can it be you're not aware that people are sometimes forced to conceal their age, social origins, poverty, physical disabilities, physiological needs! That, in so concealing, people are forced to lie and to behave artificially?

AGLAYA KARPOVNA. It's too bad then they're brought up so poorly.

SCHMIDT. But, you know, all our upbringing boils down to learning how to restrain one's natural impulses, *emulating* an ideal so difficult to achieve. Our entire upbringing is nothing more than studying the role of a sweet, kind, thoughtful person, the role of an altruist, or if you prefer, the role of a courageous person, a likable person, or simply a person with all the social graces, studying that role until it becomes second nature. Children, after all, are by nature nothing remotely like what parents, governesses, or deportment mistresses make out of them. You apparently have never stopped to think what the natural is in all its nakedness.

AGLAYA KARPOVNA (*stubbornly*). I only know that its every person's duty to be natural, that is, every person who doesn't wish to be taken for a fraud or a painted doll.

SCHMIDT (*rises, looking quite merry*). All right then . . . would you like an example to convince yourself what a lovely thing the natural is in its purest form?

AGLAYA KARPOVNA. You won't change my mind.

SCHMIDT. Viktor Antonovich! . . Semyon Arkadevich! . . Let's show Aglaya Karpovna how people act when they're natural! All right?

COMIC. Great! *(Gets up.)*   —Simultaneously.

ROMANTIC LEAD. Marvelous! *(Gets up.)*

COMIC *(as if preparing himself)*. You want full blast, or only half natural?

SCHMIDT. Full blast! . . *(By this time the Barefoot Dancer has come in with a platter covered with tasty-looking meringue shells filled with whipped cream.)*

COMIC *(rushes at the "Maid," seizes some meringue shells with both hands, stuffs them in his mouth, and winds up by taking the whole platter.)* Mm-mm! My favorite dessert! I could eat a dozen and still not choke on 'em. *(Gulping down another one.)* A man could get a belly-ache like this! Hell with belly-aches! *(Goes over and sits down by the typewriter table.)*

SCHMIDT *(takes off his jacket, leaving him only in shirt and trousers)*. You really turned up the heat today, Marya Yakovlevna! Must be ninety! . . And vodka on top of that . . . *(Stretches out in a completely relaxed pose on the ottoman.)* Am I pooped . . . *(Yawns loudly, picks his teeth and spits.)*

COMIC. He's right about the heat . . . My armpits are soaked. *(Unbuttons his jacket and kicks off his right shoe.)* And my corn's raising hell again, goddamnit! . . It's that bastard shoemaker . . . Hic . . . hic . . . *(Hiccoughs and belches simultaneously.)* Money is all he thinks about . . . Hic . . . about overcharging everybody . . . *(Fingers his sore corn gingerly. Meanwhile the Romantic Lead has come up behind the Typist, pulled her head back and given her several enthusiastic kisses on the cheek and mouth.)*

BOARDINGHOUSE LANDLADY *(leaps up)*. My heavens! . . Have you gone out of your minds? . . Stop it! . . That was some nice stunt you dreamed up! . .

ROMANTIC LEAD. You should be overjoyed, Aglaya Karpovna, I took off all her lipstick. So now, long live the natural! . .

STUDENT *(to Aglaya Karpovna)*. Now are you convinced?

AGLAYA KARPOVNA. I was talking about the natural in the sober version, not the inebriated.

STUDENT. Yes, but the classics teach us *in vino veritas!*

SCHMIDT *(to Aglaya Karpovna)*. Well now, is that enough or shall we continue?

BOARDINGHOUSE LANDLADY. It's enough, it's enough!

TYPIST *(having recovered from her embarrassment, in merry, coquettish tones)*. Let's save a few sweets for next time! . . *(Schmidt puts on his jacket and the Comic his shoe.)*

AGLAYA KARPOVNA. Sweets? . . I'd call it bitters.

SCHMIDT *(setting the bowls with candy and fruit on the table.)* In that case wouldn't you like to sweeten them up a little? *(Meanwhile the Student takes the platter from the Comic and hands it to the Barefoot Dancer.)*

TYPIST. Karl Ivanych! You made a promise and I'm still waiting! . . *(She unwraps the package of records. The Barefoot Dancer notes that the Student has gotten whipped cream on his jacket, so she heads off for the kitchen. The Student follows her out and then goes to room No. 9.)*

BOARDINGHOUSE LANDLADY. That's right, you promised us some new records today! That's much more interesting that all this "natural" stuff.

SCHMIDT *(cranking the gramophone)*. Allow me first to play a rather old one . . . some Shakespeare . . . Jacque's soliloquy! *(Finds the necessary record and reads the title.)* As You Like It . . . In my opinion . . . *(Puts the record on the turntable.)* this has a direct bearing on the subject of our discussion . . . *(The Comic sits fondly against Aglaya Karpovna, who reproachfully shakes her head at him as he pours out the apologies he pretends are so tender.)*

GRAMOPHONE *(declaiming in noble, lofty tones)*:

> All the world's a stage,
> And all the men and women merely players:
> They have their exits and their entrances,
> And one man in his time plays many parts,
> His acts being seven ages. At first the infant . . .

AGLAYA KARPOVNA *(interrupting)*. We've heard that before! It's boring! Put on something new instead! Something musical! Something noble!

SCHMIDT *(stopping the gramophone, ironically)*. Well, if Shakespeare's boring, then . . .

TYPIST. Let me pick one! *(Rummages among the records Schmidt has brought. The Student by now has brought in a chessboard and starts setting it up on the table in front of the Retired Civil Servant.)*

RETIRED CIVIL SERVANT *(to the Comic)*. Doctor, would you like a game? *(The Student goes over to the buffet and drinks some water.)*

COMIC. A little later, if that's all right. My head's not functioning very well. *(Continues to dote upon Aglaya Karpovna.)*

RETIRED CIVIL SERVANT. And you, Marya Yakovlevna?

BOARDINGHOUSE LANDLADY *(laughing)*. All I know how to play is checkers.

RETIRED CIVIL SERVANT. That's all right! Come on anyway. *(They play.)*

TYPIST *(who has picked out a record)*. This one! *(Schmidt puts on the record she selected. Aglaya Karpovna and the Comic move over and sit on the ottoman.)* Only I prefer to listen from a little way off. *(She goes left to her work table and sits down by it. The Romantic Lead grabs a chair, follows her and sits beside her. The gramophone plays the Faust-Margarita duet from Boito's opera Mephistopheles: "There's a beau-*

tiful far distant land . . ." The maid brings in some hot water and uses it and a handkerchief to clean the sweet, sticky spot on the Student's jacket. Her presence makes him breathe irregularly. Schmidt stands by the gramophone and contentedly watches the four couples as the enchantment of "that beautiful land" descends, that land of which Faust and Margarita sing with such tenderness and ecstasy.)

CURTAIN.

ACT FOUR

The same place, the last day of Shrovetide. The dinner table is placed against the wall left and is set with bottles of wine and lemonade, cold hors d'oeuvres, fruits. A vase of flowers also graces the table and one finds it difficult to distinguish the real flowers from the artifical ones. Bright, fantastic festoons consisting of small flags, paper flowers, serpentine ribbons, strings of multi-colored electric lights stretch from above the ceiling light to the corners of the room. A poster of Pierrot being attacked by little devils is hung above the center door. A poster depicting a tender Columbine-Harlequin scene is hung above the ottoman. The face of the Carnival Prince laughs above the entryway door. There is a red heart under a black mask above door No. 3. The face of the typical commedia dell'-arte doctor looks out from above door No. 4. All in all the stage—bathed in a not too bright pink light—produces a confusing, phantasmal impression. To the left and nor far from the buffet the Barefoot Dancer stands on a chair as she fastens the lamp end of a festoon stretching to the corner of the dining room. She is partly costumed in a short Columbine's skirt, in black stockings with arrows, in patent leather slippers with red heels and red pompons. The Comic wears a commedia dell'arte doctor's costume and has a mask bobbing on a string at the back of his head. He puts the bottle and victuals on the hors d'oeuvres table in a conventionally "pretty" arrangement. The Romantic Lead and the Typist—merrily trying to maintain their equilibrium as they stand on the ottoman—pin up some posters on the wall. The Boardinghouse Landlady stops in the doorway as she comes out of room No. 3. She is hastily sewing some lace onto a black half mask. A happily excited Schmidt stands in the center of the room and is giving his final instructions on the room's decoration.)

SCHMIDT *(to the Barefoot Dancer)*. Make it a little tighter yet . . . it's sagging . . . Like that . . . That's enough, enough! . . Tied well now? . . Watch your step . . .

BOARDINGHOUSE LANDLADY *(glancing out at the decorations)*. You're a regular magician Kar! Ivanovich! . . Transforming a room like that! "Her own mother'd never know her." *(She laughs.)*

SCHMIDT *(to the Comic)*. Are the bottles all uncorked? . .

COMIC. Every last one, sir.

BOARDINGHOUSE LANDLADY *(to Schmidt)*. But just think how much all of this must have cost you! . .

SCHMIDT *(to her)*. Shrovetide demands a sacrifice, Marya Yakovlevna . . . Prince Carnival will not forgive any disrespect to his august personage . . . *(To the Typist.)* A little more to the left! . . That's it! . . *(The Typist straightens up the poster until it's level.)* A little more! . . Fine . . .

COMIC *(walks away from the table and looks at the poster under discussion)*. Terrific! . .

I recognize our set man's hand all right . . . Only the painting here looks like something entirely different . . . A work of inspiration, by God! . . Hic . . . I sure had enough bliny today . . . *(Schmidt gives him a severe look.)* I beg your pardon . . . *(A sly, drunken grin comes over his face.)* I had a little to drink . . . that's true . . . but I couldn't wait any longer—the last day of Shrovetide . . . You do understand, Mr. Schmidt, it's the last day of Shrovetide! . . *(Slaps Schmidt on the shoulder and speaks in his ear.)* I need to have a little talk with you.

RETIRED CIVIL SERVANT *(appears in the center doorway and admires the decorations).* What beautiful decorations . . . they did a lovely job . . . What a man, that Karl Ivanych . . . And Fedya's lending a hand too! . . It looks as if Shrovetide had really arrived all right . . .

STUDENT. Have you seen the costume I fixed up for Aglaya Karpovna, gentlemen? . .

RETIRED CIVIL SERVANT *(laughing).* Let's see it, let's see it! . .

STUDENT. Be right back . . . *(Assists the Barefoot Dancer-Maid down to the floor and then goes off to his room.)*

SCHMIDT *(to the Maid, indicating the festoon stretching to the left downstage corner of the room).* Tighten that one a little more . . . See how loose it is? . . *(With Schmidt's help, she carries the little table and chair to the downstage left corner.)*

COMIC *(softly, teasing, to Schmidt).* Ah yes, twenty years on the stage and I've never once performed with a set like this . . . *(To the Retired Civil Servant, who is approaching them.)* Aren't you about ready for another glass? . . *(Pours him one. The Romantic Lead and the Typist have by now gotten down from the ottoman and are admiring their work.)*

REITRED CIVIL SERVANT. I'll have one because I'm so happy . . . Fedya's certainly been a great comfort to me lately! . . God bless him! . . Has begun playing chess with me again! . . And doesn't frown anymore and he looks you straight in the eye, too. *(Eats and drinks.)*

SCHMIDT *(looking at his watch).* But come now, gentlemen, shouldn't you be getting in your costumes? The guests will be totally confused if they arrive and find you here like this. The doctor's already "prepared" . . . *(Taps himself on the neck to indicate a lot of drinking.)* And you, my friends? . . *(Assists the Barefoot-Dancer-Maid in getting up on the small table.)*

ROMANTIC LEAD. Yes, it is time . . . although, actually, one minute is plenty for me . . . we'll make it! . .

STUDENT *(enters carrying a pole with an angry, toothy skull mask on it and a long white shroud).* You think it's good enough for our old witch? . . *(General amazement, mixed with fright and laughter.)*

SCHMIDT. But won't she be offended?

BOARDINGHOUSE LANDLADY. You just can't take your mind off death, Fedya! . .

STUDENT. For heaven's sake, Marya Yakovlevna, isn't Aglaya Karpovna the true *mortifying aspect of life?* "If the shoe fits, wear it . . ." *(To the Typist.)* Is she home? . .

TYPIST. I don't think so . . .

BOARDINGHOUSE LANDLADY. She went out! . . 'll be back shortly.

STUDENT. I'll put her costume in her room . . . what she does with it is her business! . . *(Heads for No. 4.)*

BOARDINGHOUSE LANDLADY *(trying to stop him)*. Fedya, stop it, it's not a good idea! *(The Typist goes to room No. 3.)*

RETIRED CIVIL SERVANT *(interrupting)*. It's all right, Marya Yakovlevna . . . Let him have a little fun—it's only a joke! . . It's all because he's so happy, my dear, we got a letter from Volodya; he'll soon be back from the high seas! . . *(To the Comic.)* A fantastic chess player too, I tell you . . . At least there'll be someone to take your place, now that you're leaving . . . that's one consolation! . .

BOARDINGHOUSE LANDLADY *(interrupting)*. What's come over all of you— it's like you all agreed to leave at once? . . Even Aniuta's getting ready to go! . .

SCHMIDT *(looking surprised)*. Aniuta? . . *(The Student returns and takes Schmidt's place supporting the chair on which the Barefoot Dancer-Maid is standing.)*

BOARDINGHOUSE LANDLADY *(resigned, sadly)*. What can she do: she just heard from the country that her old mother's ill.

BAREFOOT DANCER. They need a hand around the house . . . I'd be more'n happy to stay, but I'il sister's such a tiny thing, y'know, house is too much for her . . .

SCHMIDT *(smiling)*. You're right, looks like they all made an agreement!

TYPIST *(coming in from No. 3 with a tangle of ribbons)*. Time's a-wasting, people, and here nobody's giving a thought to this room. If we're going to make it into a real salon, then . . .

BOARDINGHOUSE LANDLADY. We've got to rearrange the furniture . . .

TYPIST. And find something to cover up this awful chest of drawers.

BOARDINGHOUSE LANDLADY *(bustling about)*. In a minute, in a minute . . . *(Goes off to No. 3.)*

SCHMIDT. We'll help you! Semyon Arkadevich, let's go! . . *Eins, zwei, drei* and presto-chango. Isn't that the way? . .

COMIC *(following him into No. 3)*. Right, drink my blood! . . it's not long now: the last day is upon us . . . *(Goes off.)*

STUDENT *(to the Barefoot Dancer-Maid)*. What's this? . . Got them all tangled up . . .

BAREFOOT DANCER *(untangling the festoon)*. A little . . . Be patient! . . Don't get upset.

RETIRED CIVIL SERVANT *(eagerly)*. What do you think, Fedya, should I wear my new shoes? . .

STUDENT. Absolutely, Papa! . . When, if not today!

RETIRED CIVIL SERVANT. Right! *(Goes off to his own room.)*

TYPIST *(sitting on the ottoman, with her back to the two on the left; softly)*. Help me get it untangled! *(Indicates the tangled ribbons.)*

ROMANTIC LEAD *(sitting by her)*. All right! . . Is it for a costume?

TYPIST. For the cotillion.

STUDENT *(to the Maid)*. So you're leaving then? . .

BAREFOOT DANCER. I'll write you.

STUDENT. Thank you . . . But couldn't I visit you in the country? . . You'll give me your address?

BAREFOOT DANCER. They'll make fun of me back home! . . They'll say: got seduced in the big city . . . And the mails are just awful where we are . . . Be better if I come see you sometime.

STUDENT. You promise? . .

BAREFOOT DANCER. If everything goes all right, I sure will . . . Only you must be patient.

TYPIST *(to the Romantic Lead)*. You're leaving tomorrow? . .

ROMANTIC LEAD. Tomorrow.

TYPIST. I'll see you to the station.

ROMANTIC LEAD. Oh no! . . That's a bad omen! . . And here I am going to see my sick wife . . . I know it's only superstition, but . . .

TYPIST. But why didn't you tell me you were married? . . I didn't understand until now . . .

ROMANTIC LEAD. I . . . I thought you'd leave me if you knew I was married, "already sliced off the old loaf"! . .

TYPIST *(cuddling up against him)*. Silly, could you really be guilty in my loving eyes for having found another woman before you found me? . .

ROMANTIC LEAD *(embracing her tenderly)*. But I do feel guilty just the same.

STUDENT. Be patient, you say . . .

BAREFOOT DANCER. That's the main thing.

STUDENT. I'm patient enough . . . only will you think about me?

BAREFOOT DANCER. Why do you ask? . . You know the answer as well as I do! . .

STUDENT. I want to believe you, but . . .

BAREFOOT DANCER *(interrupting)*. And will you think about me? . .

STUDENT. Me? . . All my life! . . all my life! Now I have something to live for . . . Yes, I do . . . Your memory will keep me alive . . . *(The Barefoot Dancer-Maid slips down from her improvised platform.)*

ROMANTIC LEAD *(continuing to embrace the Typist)*. What's that rustling in your blouse?

TYPIST *(smiling)*. Hm . . . something no one will ever again ask me about! . .

ROMANTIC LEAD. What is it then? . . *(The Typist takes a piece of paper out of her blouse and shows it to him.)*

ROMANTIC LEAD. Ah . . . my declaration of love! . .

TYPIST. Your fourth lesson on the typewriter! . . *(Kisses the paper and conceals it again. Meanwhile the Student and the Barefoot Dancer carry the small table and the chair, which had served as scaffolding, off into the entryway.)*

ROMANTIC LEAD *(sees that they are alone, kisses the Typist repeatedly)*. Why do you suppose no one will ever ask you again? . .

TYPIST. . . . what's rustling in my blouse? . .

ROMANTIC LEAD. Yes . . .

TYPIST. Because no one will ever in my life embrace me again *(with tears in her eyes)*, because nobody needs me! . . and you're going back to your wife . . .

ROMANTIC LEAD. But you know perfectly well . . .

TYPIST *(interrupting)*. Oh, I'm not jealous! . . I don't have the right to be jealous . . . But at the same time I regret the past and I love you all the more and I'm happy in my love! . . *(Weeps softly.)*

ROMANTIC LEAD *(kissing her ever so tenderly)*. Well, if you want, then I won't go! . . I'll stay, all right? . .

TYPIST. No, no, I'm not that selfish . . . Your wife is waiting for you . . . sick, probably unhappy! . . And sooner or later you'd leave me anyway . . . And I'm grateful even as it is for the happiness you've given me . . . You were my beautiful, bright dream! . . Yes, a beautiful, bright dream that makes you wake up happy for the rest of your life . . . *(Kissing his hands)* for the rest of my life . . . Thank you dearest, beloved, my only . . .

BOARDINGHOUSE LANDLADY *(appearing on the threshhold of door No. 3)*. Lidochka . . . what about the ribbons? Got them untangled yet? . .

TYPIST *(gets up)*. In a minute, Mama . . .

BOARDINGHOUSE LANDLADY. Karl Ivanych is waiting . . . And it's time to change already . . . *(She goes off.)*

TYPIST *(laughing through her tears)*. Some untangling! Look . . . *(Indicates the tangled ribbons.)* We got them tangled up even worse. *(He laughs in reply. She goes to No. 3 and looks around.)* Heavens! . . What a strange room! And the lighting . . . So weird . . . Is this *our* room? . . Is it true you love me? Is it true you're leaving? . . Am I dreaming or is it really happening? I'm getting all confused . . . What is this? . . Was it happiness . . . or only a phantom of happiness? . .

VOICE OF THE BOARDINGHOUSE LANDLADY. Lidochka! . . What's the holdup? . .

TYPIST *(as if suddenly awakening, smiling)*. Coming, Mama, coming . . . *(Goes off to No. 3 with the Romantic Lead behind her. From the entryway left enter the Student and the Barefoot Dancer. The Student pulls her by the hand to the hors d'oeuvres table.)*

STUDENT. Well, go ahead! . . I beg you! . .

BAREFOOT DANCER. It's not a good idea . . . the lady'll see . . .

STUDENT. So what if I'm having a drink with you? . . Why shouldn't I? . . *(Pours two glasses of madeira.)* I believe in equal rights! . . Your health! . . and you must drink to my heroism! . . *(They clink glasses and drink.)*

BAREFOOT DANCER *(surprised)*. What heroism? . .

STUDENT. At the office today, the very office where they fired my father for no good reason, I stood eye to eye with the boss, the first-class swine, and slapped his face. And what a slap! . . If you'd only heard it! . . Sppplat! . . *(He laughs.)* True enough, God only knows what heroism there was to it, but just the same it's good enough to drink to! . . *(Pours himself another.)* Your health! . .

BAREFOOT DANCER *(laughing)*. What do I have to do with it?

STUDENT. You've given me wings! . . Yes, that's it! . . Don't laugh! . . You . . . I don't know how to explain it, Aniuta, but you are one of the sources of my "will to life" . . . And life means struggle, means standing up for myself, for the ones I love, for justice . . .

BAREFOOT DANCER *(laughing)*. You're so eloquent, my heavens, such a philospher . . . but in my heart I understand . . . *(Clinks her glass and drinks.)* I understand everything . . . Except for one thing, what made you lay hands on yourself that time? . . The devil must have put you up to it, or else . . .

STUDENT. Not the devil, Aniuta, but . . . *(Turns away, tears ready to fill his eyes.)*

BAREFOOT DANCER. If it's so hard for you, don't tell me then, but I'm leaving tomorrow, you mean I'll never know? . .

STUDENT *(after looking around carefully)*. You swear my father will never learn?

BAREFOOT DANCER *(surprised)*. Your father?

STUDENT. If you say a word, you just might as well cut his throat! . .

BAREFOOT DANCER. Lord Almighty, how awful! . . You mean that you . . .

STUDENT. Don't worry . . . I didn't rob a bank, or lose a fortune at cards, I . . . *(Stops, breathing heavily.)* Volodya, my brother . . . listen, Volodya, the one out on the high seas . . .

BAREFOOT DANCER. Yes, yes? . . *(Suddenly.)* Master, dearest, don't cry . . . what's the matter? . . *(Strokes his back.)* Please don't . . . if it's so hard, don't tell me then! . .

STUDENT *(after getting a grip on himself)*. He's dead . . .

BAREFOOT DANCER. Dead? . .

STUDENT. Yes . . . it's been over six months now . . . My father doesn't know! . . The news of his death fell, fortunately, into my hands . . . My father would never have survived it . . . And so I began to conceal things . . . pretend . . . even forge letters . . . as if Volodya were writing, even though he's been at the bottom of the sea all this time . . . I'm performing . . . you see, like an actor . . . want to say one thing, but say another instead, want to mourn my brother, but have to smile, be hopeful . . .

BAREFOOT DANCER *(sympathetically, deeply touched)*. God in heaven . . .

STUDENT. It's a difficult role . . . God forbid anybody else . . . most people wouldn't last . . . even I at first was ready to walk off the stage before finishing the play . . .

BAREFOOT DANCER *(after a pause)*. Everyone has his own cross to bear.

STUDENT. That's right! But bless him who helps another to bear his cross! . . *(Takes the Barefoot Dancer by the hand.)* Thank you for the kindness you showed me, for the strength I soaked up at the sight of you working here, such long hours with never a complaint! . . We're all the Lord God's actors . . . Who knows, Aniuta, maybe we're to be rewarded with better parts to play in the next world, but in the meantime . . . we'll put up with our earthly roles the best we can, Aniuta, we'll do what we can and try to help one another! . .

BAREFOOT DANCER *(draws him to her and kisses him passionately)*. That's right, that's right! Dearest! . . Wonderful . . . *(The Romantic Lead's entry from room No. 3 interrupts the kiss and forces the Student to take refuge in his own room.)*

ROMANTIC LEAD *(with friendly irony)*. "Transformation through transfiguration," as Dr. Fregoli has been preaching? . .

BAREFOOT DANCER. Aren't you ashamed of profaning such words?! I could say the same to you . . .

ROMANTIC LEAD. If you had actually been jealous . . .

BAREFOOT DANCER. How do you know I wasn't? . .

ROMANTIC LEAD. Come, come! . . of someone like Lidochka *(turning toward No. 3)*, you can't be jealous . . .

BAREFOOT DANCER. And of someone like Fedya? . . *(She smiles.)*

ROMANTIC LEAD. Hm . . . you play your part so well that you don't know where the play ends and reality begins . . . Damn it all, I'm beginning to believe you really are an actress by the grace of God . . . *(Draws her close.)*

BAREFOOT DANCER *(laughing).* "An actress of mercy" . . .

ROMANTIC LEAD. Only not to me! . .

BAREFOOT DANCER. Are you jealous? . .

ROMANTIC LEAD. What do you think? . .

BAREFOOT DANCER *(happily, ecstatically).* Really? . . you mean you love me? . . you do? . .

ROMANTIC LEAD. I've always loved you, but now . . . *(kisses her)* now I've learned to appreciate you and cherish you . . .

BAREFOOT DANCER. You're not acting now? . .

ROMANTIC LEAD. And you? . .

BAREFOOT DANCER *(laughing and kissing him).* Stupid, can't you tell? . .

COMIC *(entering from room No. 3).* Ye Gods, look at that! . . carrying on like they were in their own bedroom. Happy, no doubt, the play's nearly over. *(A bell is heard from the entryway.)* Yes-s-s indeedy, it's been a tough season! . . But thank God today's the last day and then *finita la commedia!* Tomorrow's the beginning of Lent, free again, and long live free art! . . Where are you *engagé?* . . I'm thinking about starting my own theater! By God! . . Would you like to throw in with me? . . *(Aglaya Karpovna, in raincoat and hat, enters from the entryway.)*

AGLAYA KARPOVNA *(looking the room over).* Au nom de Dieu! What kind of circus do we have here?! *(The Barefoot Dancer passes from the entryway to the kitchen.)*

ROMANTIC LEAD. And you visit the circus frequently? . .

AGLAYA KARPOVNA. I am not speaking, sir, to you.

ROMANTIC LEAD. Sorry! But I thought once your tongue got to work on a metaphor like that, why . . .

AGLAYA KARPOVNA *(interrupting and sneering through her lorgnette at the Comic's costume).* Doctor, what on earth are you doing? . .

COMIC. And there's a cute little costume ready for you . . .

ROMANTIC LEAD. Allegorical! . .

COMIC *(as if excusing himself).* Everyone's wearing masks today. So, just like everybody else, I was forced . . .

AGLAYA KARPOVNA. But I won't be forced, you can be sure of that! *(The Boardinghouse Landlady and Schmidt appear in the door of room No. 3.)* Every man has principles, Semyon Arkadevich, and as for mine, the principle of illusion, even if only in jest, is not one of them . . . *(To the Boardinghouse Landlady.)* Marya Yakovlevna, it seems you're expecting guests? . .

BOARDINGHOUSE LANDLADY *(timidly).* And so?

AGLAYA KARPOVNA. Be so kind as to warn them that I have a headache and request that they not make too much noise . . . *(Goes into room No. 4, slamming the door behind her.)*

BOARDINGHOUSE LANDLADY *(after an unhappy, confused pause)*. Always poisoning everybody else's fun . . .

SCHMIDT. That's her parting shot, Marya Yakovlevna! Because she's so mad the five months she paid for here are almost over! . .

ROMANTIC LEAD. Yes, I don't envy the people she goes to next! . .

BOARDINGHOUSE LANDLADY *(to the Comic)*. I'm afraid she'll create some sort of scandal yet. For God's sake, doctor, go to her, calm her, give her something soothing . . .

COMIC *(drawing his hands apart in a gesture of helplessness)*. What's left for me to try on her! . . I've been prescribing buckets of Valerian drops. Bromide! Opium! Nothing has any effect . . . Maybe I should try chloral hydrate! . .

BOARDINGHOUSE LANDLADY *(beseeching)*. Why don't you simply go see her! . . You'll be better for her than any medicine . . . that is, have a better effect on her, I mean . . .

COMIC. I can do it, all right, but chloral hydrate would be a terrific joke! . . *(Knocks on No. 4.)*

TYPIST *(backstage, from room No. 3)*. Mama! . .

BOARDINGHOUSE LANDLADY. Coming, coming . . . *(Goes into No. 3.)*

AGLAYA KARPOVNA *(backstage, from room No. 4)*. Come in! *(The Comic goes in room No. 4.)*

ROMANTIC LEAD *(in the direction of the departed Comic)*. What are you doing letting him prescribe opium? . . He might poison her by mistake in a drunken stupor . . .

SCHMIDT. Don't worry! . . I dilute his potions to a harmless level.

ROMANTIC LEAD. So that's it? . .

SCHMIDT. On the sly, of course, so as not to offend his professional pride. But how about you? Don't you need a little something soothing? . . You seem extraordinarily nervous today!

ROMANTIC LEAD. Of course! . . Suppose this fortune-teller is putting one over on me! . . What an idiot I'll turn out to be then!

SCHMIDT. Let me see the letter one more time! . .

ROMANTIC LEAD *(taking the letter from his pocket and handing it to Schmidt)*. I can't imagine who it could be! Someone from the theater? . . One of my friends? . .

SCHMIDT *(taking the letter out of the envelope)*. Did you invite everybody today? Or . . .

ROMANTIC LEAD. Almost the whole troupe; only some will be here before the show and others after . . .

SCHMIDT *(reads the letter)*. "There will be a great many people in disguise at your place on the twentieth of February. Among them will be someone

disguised as a monk. *He is the one.* Invite his wives to the masquerade . . .
Catch him red-handed! . . Good luck." Hm . . . what time did you invite
the wives to come? . .

ROMANTIC LEAD. By eleven. All three will be dressed in black dominoes.
They'll arrive by carriage. We'll grab the bird and whisk him right off to
the Detective Bureau! . . And so I could get the reward and be rich and the
most famous of detectives!

SCHMIDT. You're not going to be fooled? . .

ROMANTIC LEAD. By who? . . The fortune-teller? . .

SCHMIDT. No, his wives. I suppose it must have been difficult to persaude the
deaf-mute? Are you sure of her? . .

ROMANTIC LEAD. True. The third wife didn't agree right away either. Even
though she's a prostitute, she's afraid of raising a scandal, she feels sorry for
him, says *he* married *her* purely to save her from her shameful profession,
that he was the only one who ever kissed her soul rather than her body, that
she is more guilty than he, since she foresook her vow of chastity and thus
drove him away, in short, if she were to appear here it would not be for the
purpose of betraying him into the hands of the law, but for the purpose of
saving him . . . How does all that strike you?

SCHMIDT *(bites his lip).* You didn't tell me about any of that! . .

ROMANTIC LEAD. Didn't have time! The personality of this trigamist
assumes such a mysterious character that the devil himself'd go mad trying to reconcile what the three wives have to say! . . Unbelievable
contradictions . . .

SCHMIDT *(looking at his watch).* You'll be dressed as Pierrot?

ROMANTIC LEAD. Yes.

SCHMIDT. And your wife? . .

ROMANTIC LEAD. As Columbine. And you? . .

SCHMIDT. As Harlequin. I told you! . .

ROMANTIC LEAD. Did you get a costume? . .

SCHMIDT. I did indeed.

COMIC *(entering).* Sweet-talked her into it! . . She even promised to get into
costume. Said she didn't mind a death costume, since the ancient Egyptians
used to bring in a mummy right in the middle of their feasts! . . Quoth
they, life is not just "tra-la-la," but something more serious . . . A really
deep thought, I'd say. *(Goes over to the table and drinks.)*

ROMANTIC LEAD *(looks at his watch).* Well, I'd better go change . . . . *(Goes off
to his room.)*

SCHMIDT *(to the Comic).* You haven't been courting her properly lately! . .
(Makes a motion in the direction of room No. 4.)

COMIC *(working on the hors d'oeuvres, familiarly)*. No more and no less than the contract requires.

SCHMIDT *(approaching him)*. Did the contract require you to ask her for a 5000 ruble loan? . .

COMIC. But look at the trash you assigned me to make up to! Even intimate matters like that she can't keep quiet about! . . *(Door of room No. 4 opens a crack revealing Aglaya Karpovna eavesdropping.)*

SCHMIDT *(standing with his back to door No. 4)*. She suspected that you took an interest in her because of her money and turned to me for advice . . .

COMIC. The old harpie! . . *(Aglaya Karpovna displays by various facial expressions her reactions to the revelations in the entire following scene.)*

SCHMIDT. I, of course, talked her out of the loan, since I had brought you here not for the purpose of exploiting the lodgers!

COMIC *(angrily)*. So, it's thanks to you that I've been made an ass of? . .

SCHMIDT. I told her "he should take an interest in you even without any money involved."

COMIC. Should?!

SCHMIDT. Of course! . . In the first place, because of the contract, and in the second place because she is entirely worthy of the attention of such fine people as Your Worship.

COMIC. All right, Dr. Fregoli, that's enough! . . All jokes aside! . . I need the money because I've been planning for a long time to start my own business.

SCHMIDT. A pothouse? . .

COMIC. No sir, not a pothouse, a theater. Not the sort of trivial, no-account theater you've set up here, to be sure, but a real, honest-to-God theater, headed by me, as the guiding force . . .

SCHMIDT *(sighing)*. The poor audience! . .

COMIC. And I'll tell you one thing: if you don't get me my 5000 back again I'll put on a benefit performance here that'll make your teeth rattle.

SCHMIDT *(cooly)*. According to the contract, if I'm not mistaken, you're not expected to put on any sort of benefit? . .

COMIC. To hell with the kind of contracts that allow you to make fun of people.

SCHMIDT. Make fun? . .

COMIC. Yes sir, make fun! . . I'm going to expose you this very day and reveal to one and all how it was all only theater . . . only the "stage of life" as you put it . . . that I'm no doctor, but a comic in the local theater, that the insurance agent is no more an insurance agent than I'm the Emperor of China, that you aren't Schmidt, but Fregoli, that . . .

SCHMIDT *(interrupting angrily).* You wouldn't dare!

COMIC *(insolently).* Who's going to stop me? . .

SCHMIDT. Your conscience, I would hope!

COMIC. Conscience obliges one to tell the truth . . .

SCHMIDT. But not during the play, if you're acquainted with theater ethics . . Without the risk of destroying the illusion, you wouldn't dare announce on stage "That's not Hamlet, that's Ivan Ivanich, my old drinking buddy."

COMIC *(spitefully).* All right then, *after* the play? . .

SCHMIDT. Hm . . . you're right. I forgot about that. However, when you make a deal with a scoundrel you never know how to write a contract without any loopholes. Fortunately, your colleagues have played their roles so well that your betrayal will be of no avail! . . The spell they cast is a perfect shield against such "truth-lovers" as your lordship! . .

COMIC. Do you think so? . .

SCHMIDT. I'm positive! . . Who's going to believe a pitiful old drunken sot like you, who's been spouting the most absurd nonsense ever since he's been here! . .

COMIC *(biliously excited).* They'll believe me all right! . . Yes sir, they will, don't worry about that . . . I'll bet anything you want on it!

SCHMIDT *(looks at his watch).* Oh, stop it! . .

COMIC. Would you like to try 5000 rubles? . .

SCHMIDT. You'll lose! . .

COMIC. I'll win easy as falling off a log! . . *(Runs over to door No. 3)* I'll win this instant! . . Is the bet on? . . *(Aglaya Karpovna with the distorted face of the betrayed witch, sways as she disappears behind door No. 4.)*

SCHMIDT. The bet's on, but only to teach you a lesson . . .

COMIC *(knocks on door No. 3).* Fine, we'll see who'll teach whom!

TYPIST *(almost completely decked out as a "marquise," appears in the doorway with her mother).* What's going on? I'm not ready yet . . .

COMICLydia Fedorovna! . . Marya Yakovlevna! . . My friends! . . My dears! I have an apology! . . We've deceived you! As God is my witness! Deceived you, made fools of you, put on a show! . .

BOARDINGHOUSE LANDLADY *(not understanding).* A "masquerade" you mean? . . What of it? . .

COMIC. A "masquerade" all right . . . I'm not a doctor at all, but a comic in the local theater . . . Karl Ivanich *(turning in Schmidt's direction)* is not Karl Ivanich Schmidt, but Dr. Fregoli, who hired us all to work here! Honest! Hired us as actors! . . And Svetozarov's an actor and his wife who's been working here as a maid, we're all actors! There isn't any insurance agent here, there's only Svetozarov, an actor who plays romantic leads, who was hired to love you, now do you understand? . . He was only playing a part! . . A part, sweetheart! . . That's his specialty, playing lovers! . .

BOARDINGHOUSE LANDLADY. I don't understand a word of it! . .

TYPIST. What do you mean? . . What sort of lovers are you talking about? . .

COMIC. The insurance agent . . . Viktor Antonovich . . .

TYPIST *(angrily)*. Well? . . What about him? . .

COMIC. Now don't be angry! . . I'm just telling the truth! . .

TYPIST. What truth? . .

COMIC. That he's a lover! . .

TYPIST. My lover? . . He is? . .

COMIC. A lover in general! . .

TYPIST. Oh, you base man! . . How dare you slander Viktor Antonovich, and behind his back at that, a man who is faithful to his wife, when you aren't worth his little finger . . .

SCHMIDT *(soothingly)*. Don't be upset, Lydia Fedorovna! . . You can see for yourself that the doctor overdid Shrovetide a little! . .

BOARDINGHOUSE LANDLADY *(slapping the Comic on the shoulder)*. Go on, my dear, why don't you take a little nap . . . there's enough time before the party! . .

COMIC *(distraught)*. But I'm not drunk at all! . . You've got me all wrong! . .

TYPIST *(hotly)*. We've got you perfectly, and figured out what sort of bird you were long ago! . . *(Goes out.)*

BOARDINGHOUSE LANDLADY. Lydia, stop it! . . Come now, doctor! . . That was not nice, by God, not nice at all! I wouldn't have expected you to say such things to a young lady! . . *(Goes off and closes the door behind her.)*

SCHMIDT *(to the Comic)*. Well now? . . . I was right, eh? . .

COMIC *(clenches his teeth)*. The idiots! . .

SCHMIDT. Lost the bet, so all you have left is yelling at people . . . "You are angry, Jupiter, ergo you must be wrong."

COMIC. I haven't lost yet, there's still the deportment mistress, the student, the clerk . . .

SCHMIDT. But you, I hope, see now that illusion on the stage of life is more convincing than on the theater stage? . .

COMIC. Nothing of the kind! . . *(Goes over to the table and pours himself some vodka.)* You forget I'm a famous comic . . . *Everybody* knows me . . . twenty years on the stage . . . Thousands of witnesses can swear I'm an actor, not a doctor . . .

SCHMIDT. You really are a comic, if you can't see what a comical position you're in now . . . *(Goes off laughing to his own room across the hallway.)*

COMIC *(downs his glass and sways slightly)*. "In a comical position"? We'll see yet who's going to wind up in a comical . . . *(He turns and see a strange picture: a shroud, topped by a skull mask, slips out of door No. 4. The ghostly light which fills the room dims somewhat and flickers mysteriously.)* Ss . . . ss . . . sorry, Aglaya Karpovna, is that you? . . Already dressed up? . . heh, heh . . . all disguised? . . . *(Timidly approaches the phantom.** And I was just getting ready to drop in and let you in on some sensational news . . . Why are you swaying like that, my dear? Or am I just imagining things? . . I—*pardonnez moi*—drank a little to your health today . . . I'm not seeing too well and my head's a little dizzy . . . What? . . Did you say something? . . You didn't? I must have imagined it . . . I'll be brief . . . You refused me the five thousand and you were right: it's rather difficult to entrust a doctor with a modest practice with a loan of that size. On the other hand, a famous comic in the theater, a star with twenty years on the stage, who could make millions any time he pleased would, of course, be able to pay you back! . . Right? . . . *(Goes right up to her.)* Here's the story, Aglaya Karpovna! . . You've put on a disguise, but I, on the contrary, have taken mine off . . . Yes indeed! I'm not a doctor, but a famous comic in the local theater! . . A first-class actor, adored by the public. What? . . You're amazed? . . Dumbfounded? . . You'd have never guessed? . . *(Tries to take the phantom by the waist, but not feeling anything under the shroud, yells bloody murder. The light on the stage goes out for a moment, the phantom disappears. The room again fills with light, not a flickering light this time, revealing a comparatively more realistic setting. The Student runs in from the center doorway disguised as a wood goblin. The Comic lets out his second shriek of terror as the Student appears.)*

STUDENT *(removing his mask).* What are you screaming about? . . What happened? . . What's the matter?

COMIC *(wiping the sweat off his forehead).* Ah, so it's you? . . I'll be damned! . . My nerves have gotten really shot around here . . .

STUDENT. What's the matter? . . You don't feel well? . .

COMIC *(indicates door No. 4).* There . . . over there . . . something awful . . . I have this feeling . . . A vision . . . A ghost . . . *(A bell is heard in the entryway.)*

TYPIST *(appears in doorway No. 3 in a black half-mask and dressed as a marquise—which suits her very well indeed, holding a small bag of confetti and ribbons in her hands).* What's happened now? . . Fedya! . . You're so funny in that outfit! . . *(Laughs heartily.)* A real goblin. *(Covers him with confetti.)*

BOARDINGHOUSE LANDLADY *(has come in right behind her daughter wearing a festive head-dress and her best dress).* A regular goblin, sure enough . . . Was that you screaming? *(The bell in the entryway is heard again, insistent but at*

---

*The phantom is a rather primitive creation, consisting of a pole stuck out the door with a skull mask on the tip and a shroud hung on a cross piece serving as shoulders. N.E.)

amusing intervals. The Barefoot Dancer, dressed as Columbine, runs from the kitchen to the entryway.)

COMIC *(to the Student, pushing him toward door No. 4).* Let's go in there! . . We've got to find out! I'm afraid by myself . . . *(The Student knocks on door No. 4.)* No use knocking! Maybe there's no one there to answer! . . *(Pushes the Student through the door and timidly follows him in. The Boardinghouse Landlady and her daughter are on the verge of following them in, but the Romantic Lead has appeared by now, dressed as Pierrot and wearing a narrow black half-mask. He attracts their attention with an impudent, merry yell, and with his traditionally long sleeves flapping in the air.)*

ROMANTIC LEAD *(glances into the entryway, where a happy hum of voices is heard).* Oh ho . . . Ooh la la! . . Welcome! . . Ring, bells! . . Bloom, flowers! . . Rejoice in the coming spring, eternally youthful heart! . . *(Winds up the gramophone. The old Retired Civil Servant appears in the center doorway wearing his new shoes and bows to all present with a merry smile and a comical shuffling of the feet, aimed at directing everyone's attention to his new shoes. The Typist-marquise throws ribbons at Pierrot, lovingly tying him up in momentary knots. The gramophone plays a bravura polonaise. Pierrot yells.)* Long live Carnival! Beat, drums! . . Ring, bells! . . Shine on, sun! . . Dance, stars! . . *(A crowd of masqueraders, among whom may be seen the Quo Vadis costumes of Act II, enter in a decorous but merry polonaise from the entryway, covered with confetti strewn by the marquise, and greeted by the Boardinghouse Landlady. The old Retired Civil Servant seizes the latter by the hand and they form another couple in the polonaise. Pierrot and Columbine, that is, the Romantic Lead and his wife, follow their example, ending the procession with all the polish of actors worthy of the name. Laughter, joking, shrieks, wisecracks, confetti, and ribbons . . . Suddenly the Comic and the Student burst in from room No. 4 with pale, alarmed faces.)*

COMIC *(shouts).* Ladies and gentlemen! . . A tragedy! . . *(Some sort of piece of paper rustles in his hands.)*

STUDENT. Stop the music! . .

COMIC. There's been a death in the house! . .

STUDENT. Suicide! . . *(General tumult. Everyone stops as if struck by lightning. Barefoot Dancer stops the gramophone.)*

BOARDINGHOUSE LANDLADY. Aglaya Karpovna? . .

STUDENT. She . . .

TYPIST. Even this time she couldn't resist poisoning everyone else's happiness! . . .

COMIC. Poisoned herself! . .

STUDENT. Swallowed a whole vial of opium . . . And she laughed at me! . . And then went and did it herself! . .

COMIC. Open and shut case of suicide! . . Here's her final note! . . No point in a physician trying to help! . . I'm not a specialist in poisons! . .

BAREFOOT DANCER. What did she write? . .

ROMANTIC LEAD."I blame no one for my death"? . .

COMIC. Just the opposite! . . *(To the Student.)* Read it . . .

STUDENT *(takes the note and reads).* "I blame *everyone* for my death!" . .

ROMANTIC LEAD. God damn! . . *(Stops as he realizes the unfortunate implications. Everyone is stunned for another moment. A bell is heard in the entryway. Barefoot Dancer—Columbine rushes off to open the door.)*

BOARDINGHOUSE LANDLADY *(rushing toward No. 4).* Perhaps there's still a chance . . . *(Goes into room No. 4 with everyone else making a general anxious hum, in the midst of which one hears such exclamations as: "how awful" . . "was she very young?" . . "there was a feast on the table, now there's a coffin" . . "that's an interesting case for you" and so forth. As the last of the masqueraders are on the verge of disappearing into room No. 4, a new couple of masqueraders flies in shouting and laughing merrily and strewing a cloud of multicolored confetti. People shout at them "shhh . . . there's been a death in the house." They lapse into an embarrassed silence and follow the others into room No. 4. Just as Barefoot Dancer-Columbine is about to do likewise, another bell from the entryway summons her to her duties again. The stage is now empty. In the hallway a mysterious monk in Capuchin habit appears, with a cowl pulled around his face. He steals into the dining room and glances into the entryway, then quickly steps over to door No. 4 and locks it with a key.)*

MONK *(coming to the center of the room).* Aniuta! . .

BAREFOOT DANCER-COLUMBINE *(in the doorway leading to entryway).* Who called for me? . .

MONK. It was I. Come here! . .

BAREFOOT DANCER-COLUMBINE *(running over to him).* Who are you? . . *(The Monk, with his back to the audience, points to his face under the cowl.)* Good heavens! . . You were supposed to be Harlequin.

MONK. Shhh! I'll explain later. Go into the entryway and allow no one else in. I need two or three minutes alone with these ladies. *(Motions in the direction of the entryway.)*

BAREFOOT DANCER-COLUMBINE. Yes, but suppose . . .

MONK. Don't argue about it . . . Ask them to step over here and then guard the door! . . *(Barefoot Dancer-Columbine shrugs her shoulders, goes back to the entryway and curtsies as she invites the latest arrivals to step into the room. Three "Black Dominoes" appear on the stage, one with a little dog on an elegant leash easily revealing the owner's identity. Barefoot Dancer-Columbine disappears into the entryway.)*

MONK. Come in, my dearest wives! . . Come in! . . Don't be afraid! . . I'm so

glad to see you, especially since you made such an effort to find me! . . .
(Removes the cowl from his face. The "Black Dominoes" shriek in amazement.)
LADY WITH THE SMALL DOG. Ah! . . It's you, you sneaky crook?! . . .
Caught at last! . . Finally caught you? . . *(Takes off her mask. The Deaf-Mute
follows her example.)* I don't suppose you thought the law would catch up
with somebody like you!? . . The dove sang so beautifully! . . And such
fine words too . . . and I, the idiot, listened! . . And believed! . . And went
limp! . . And brought my whole soul to the altar of love! . . And look how
he paid me back . . . look how he paid his debt! . . . Says "the law doesn't
apply to us." Spit on the law?!. Wrong, my friend! . . The law will triumph! . . And you'll answer to it . . . sure as hell you'll answer to it! . . .
(Meanwhile Paraclete has been conversing in sign language with his second wife.)
FALLEN WOMAN *(yells at the Lady with the Small Dog).* Shut up, you wicked
old sinner! *You* talk about the law? . . And to *him*, who raised his love above
the law, like some higher law?! . . *(Tears off her own mask.)*
LADY WITH THE SMALL DOG *(amazed beyond belief).* Have you gone out of
your mind, my dear!?
FALLEN WOMAN. Your fat has gone to your head if you place some pitiful,
formal law higher than the man who once saved you, like the handsome
prince and Cinderella . . . You were defenseless then, and he gave you
strength! . . She *(motioning in the direction of the Deaf Mute who is still conversing
in sign language with Paraclete)* was unhappy, and he made her happy! . . I was
a pitiful fallen woman and he raised me up to his level! . . *(Falls at Paraclete's
feet and kisses them in self-oblivion.)* Master! Master! Forgive her her insults
and her lies! . . She knows not what she does nor where she's going . . .
*(Her thick, long hair comes out of her cowl and covers Paraclete's feet with a shining
wave.)*
MONK. All is for the best, Maria! . . Rise, rise, I'm not God! . . *(Raises her up.)*
Let justice take its course and let me be punished for the compassion that
drove me to save all of you! . . Perhaps prison is really the place where I
belong! . . There are so many there in need of Paraclete, in need of a coun-
seler, a helper, a consoler! . . Paraclete's road always leads to Golgotha! . .
That is in the nature of things.
FALLEN WOMAN *(seizing the Deaf-Mute's hand).* Only we won't let him go! . .
LADY WITH THE SMALL DOG. He should simply return to the "bosom of
married life" . . . What does he need a Golgotha for?!.
FALLEN WOMAN *(sneering, crudely).* You said it that time!
LADY WITH THE SMALL DOG *(to her).* You traitor! . .
MONK *(to the Lady with the Small Dog).* Well, all right then . . . only "married
life" with whom? . . With you? She *(motions in the Fallen Woman's direction)*

would object! With her? You would object! . . With the deaf-mute? *(Motions toward the Deaf-Mute.)* Then both of you would object! . . *(A bell is heard in the entryway as well as some altercation between the Barefoot Dancer-Columbine and the new arrivals.)* You're not Moslem enough for life in a harem! . . And I don't know any other way out! . . Consider I'm dead! . . That I'm lost forever! . . That I entered a monastery and that this robe is the one actually worn in my order! . . I gave you everything I could! . . Don't ask for more, for that needed by others who haven't yet had a crumb from me.

LADY WITH THE SMALL DOG *(nervously glancing around).* Where's this Svetozarov? . . Where's my detective and his gendarmes? I see that without the arm of the law we're never going to get anything out of him! . .

MONK. Svetozarov is *my* agent, madam! . . And it wasn't he who summoned you here, but I . . . Yes, I, so as to help you conquer the beast within. You'd do better to think of the gendarmes of heaven than those of earth, in that sacred place where one speaks not of men, but of human beings! Fortunately I have found among you one who will speak for me *(motions toward the Fallen Woman),* relieving me of the necessity for unworthy self-justification . . . *(Insistent, uninterrupted ringing from the entryway and pounding on door No. 4, trembling under the blows directed at it by those trying to open it.)* There's no time left! . . It's all been said! . . Go and curse not the one who has given his soul for your happiness! . . My final gift: I will pay Svetozarov for his investigative efforts! . .

LADY WITH THE SMALL DOG. There's nothing to pay him for! . . We've been deceived! . .

FALLEN WOMAN *(handing a roll of bills to the Monk).* Here's his fee! It's our debt, not yours!

LADY WITH THE SMALL DOG. Why is that? . .

FALLEN WOMAN. One must be honest, madam! . . One must be thankful! . . Farewell, my Master! . . Thank you for the happiness of this meeting . . *(To the other wives.)* Let's go! . . . Let's not hinder him! . . There are many of us and only one of him! . . *(Goes off left, the Deaf-Mute follows, to whom Paraclete bids farewell in sign language.)*

LADY WITH THE SMALL DOG *(taking the dog in her arms).* Mimi, what has life come to, when some trash for sale has the brass to teach us about honesty and gratitude! . . *(Tearfully kisses the dog's face as Paraclete goes over to door No. 4.)* My treasure! You're the only consolation I have left. You won't betray me? . . Well, answer me!. Answer me! . . Answer me! . . *(Goes off, passionately pressing the dog to her face at the very moment Paraclete, in the guise of the Monk, opens door No. 4.)*

STUDENT *(perplexed, worked up).* Who was it locked the door? . .

MONK. What's the matter? . .

STUDENT *(somewhat amazed).* Oh, it's you, Karl Ivanich? . . We need some water right away! . . We've got to revive the suicide . . . *(Takes a water pitcher and a glass from the buffet.)*

MONK. The suicide? . .

STUDENT. Don't worry! . . It turned out to be a false alarm! . . *(Runs off into room No. 4 at the same time several actors in masquerade and the Provincial Theater Director and the Regisseur come in from the entryway. The Provincial Theater Director is dressed as a Roman Senator and the Regisseur as the Poet Lucan.)*

MONK *(pulls the cowl around his face, then addresses the Senator in sanctimonious tones).* Quo vadis, domine?

DIRECTOR-SENATOR *(peeping under the Monk's cowl).* Ah! . . So it's you? . . *(Laughs loudly.)* Did you recognize us? . . *(Raises his own mask.)*

MONK *(raising his cowl enough to reveal his eyes).* Well, of course! . . *(Laughs. Several of the new arrivals gratify their curiosity by looking over the dining room, then pass into room No. 3. The others soon follow them.)* And so, wither goest thou?

DIRECTOR. I am going to the last act of the comedy which you have produced on the stage of life.

MONK. Do come in! . .

DIRECTOR. Is the play having a good run? . .

MONK. Terrific. And how's yours doing? . .

DIRECTOR. Not so great . . .

MONK. Poor house? . .

DIRECTOR. Not exactly mobs . . .

MONK. If the mountain won't come to Mohammed, then Mohammed will come to the mountain. If the audience won't come to you, then you should go to the audience, like me! . . *(He laughs.)*

DIRECTOR *(laughing back).* Here I am, as you see! . . I'm not too late?

MONK. You've arrived right at the denouement.

DIRECTOR. Is it an interesting finale? . .

MONK. That's hard to say, it's so drawn out I'm afraid you and I won't live to see the final curtain.

DIRECTOR. No, all jokes aside, are you satisfied with the *results* of your enterprise? . . Of the realization of your *idea?* . .

MONK. And aren't you an Hegelian? . .

DIRECTOR. In what sense? . .

MONK. Hegel holds that when it comes to *idea*, the only important thing is the process, that the "result". is only a lifeless corpse, forsaken by the living soul, by the tendency . . .

DIRECTOR *(not understanding).* What do you mean? . . Your play is tendentious? . .

MONK. There's no such thing as a non-tendentious play, even one that's pure farce! . .

DIRECTOR. "Pure farce"? . . But the highest purpose of art . . .

MONK. The highest purpose of art is to fill life with its being, the way a flower fills the air with its aroma! . . To transform life into art! . . To attain an art of life! . . Had you ever thought of that, you, the old helmsman of the vessels of theater? *(A mob of guests and boardinghouse lodgers emerge from room No. 4. The Monk lowers his cowl over his face but remains in full view by the footlights.)*

BOARDINGHOUSE LANDLADY *(heaving a sigh of relief)*. Well, thank the Lord it all turned out all right! *(To her daughter.)* What kind of "theater" was it she was asking the doctor about?

TYPIST. The doctor was drunk and made up some fantastic story. I wasn't taken in—I'm not that gullible . . . But *she* was.

PIERROT-ROMANTIC LEAD *(to her)*. "In every wise old head there's plenty of stupidity." *(Notices the Monk and lets out a gasp of astonishment and grabs him by the arm.)* Who are you? . . Speak up! . . Ladies and gentlemen, stop where you are!!! In the name of the law! *(All freeze as they crowd around Pierrot-Romantic Lead and the Monk, and all stop talking.)*

MONK *(to him, in a different voice)*. Relax! . . I'm the very one you've been looking for throughout the four acts of this play . . .

PIERROT-ROMANTIC LEAD. What is your name? . .

MONK. "As to what ye shall call me," it's plain the fortune-teller's words have now come true.

PIERROT-ROMANTIC LEAD. Fortune-teller? You know about her predictions?

MONK. Just as I know you're expecting a big reward if your investigation is successful! . .

PIERROT-ROMANTIC LEAD. I'll be damned! . .

MONK. And here it is, my friend, count it! . . *(Hands him the money.)*

PIERROT-ROMANTIC LEAD *(takes the money with trembling hand)*. Who are you? . . I must be going out of my mind . . .

MONK. As for my identity, you must guess that yourself; and as for yours there's nothing to guess.

PIERROT-ROMANTIC LEAD. Just who am I then, in your opinion? . .

MONK. You're Pierrot, and you've been made a fool of.

PIERROT-ROMANTIC LEAD. A fool? . .

MONK. Of course! That's your fate, you know, if you're Pierrot, that is a simpleton who's always getting into a jam when he pokes his nose in somebody else's business.

PIERROT-ROMANTIC LEAD. What *is* my business, in your opinion? . .

MONK. Love! Hundreds of commedia dell'arte, hundreds of harlequinades testify to that . . .

PIERROT-ROMANTIC LEAD. But if I'm Pierrot, then only Harlequin can make a fool of me! . . Hundreds of commedia dell'arte, hundreds of harlequinades can also testify to that! . .

MONK. He stands before you! . . *(Throws off his monk's habit. As it falls to his feet it reveals a harlequin in a shiny, blindingly bright costume.)*

ROMANTIC LEAD-PIERROT. You? . . Is it you? . .

HARLEQUIN *(ringing the bells on his sleeve).* Yes, my dear, here I am, here you are, here she is. *(Barefoot Dancer-Columbine has come up to him and he takes her hand.)* And here he is! . . *(Motions toward the Comic-Doctor who has just come out of room No. 4 in a mask and with the traditional syringe in his hands.)* We're all here! . . Count 'em: Harlequin, Pierrot, Columbine, and the Doctor from Bologna—the most beloved characters in the merry harlequinade . . . *(They line up in a motley row at the footlights and all join hands.)* We've come to life again, my friends! . . Come to life again! But not just for the theater, but for life itself, distilled without our pepper, salt, and sugar! . . We've mixed ourselves into the pie of life, like the seasoning which saves the pie from tastelessness, we've browned it with the fire of our love, like a roll in the oven! . . Glory to us, the eternal players of the sun-drenched South! . . Glory to the real actors, who use their art to save the pathetic comedies of miserable dilletantes! . . *(Leaping onto the prompter's box, to the audience.)* Glory to you, ladies and gentlemen, if you manage to carry away in your hearts a memory of *the main thing*, which we have not merely discussed here, but demonstrated! . . The play is over, and if you have no objections to the curtain, then we'll lower it with the appropriate pomp! . . But if the main thing for you is not what has been presented, but rather the resolution of the intrigue, which everyone expects in the sort of theater run by knowledgable, experienced people acquainted with public taste, then . . . all right, ladies and gentlemen, if you please, it won't cost us anything to finish the play any way you want it! Would you like Svetozarov to divorce his barefoot dancer wife and marry Lidochka, and for Fedya the student to marry the barefoot dancer? . . Or, if you like, for Fedya's father, the clerk, to go back to work and even to marry Lidochka's mother? . . Or maybe something else, for instance—it'd be a great finale for a play, too—Lidochka finds out that Svetozarov's not an insurance agent but an actor in the local theater, so she *forgives* him his great performance and transfers all her love to dramatic art and eventually becomes an actress? . . It's still not too late to bring Dr. Fregoli before the bar of justice, perhaps it's even necessary, because trigamy, after all, no matter how you look at it, isn't and can't possibly be the slightest bit praiseworthy? . . Would you like us to finish the play like that? . . No sooner said than done! . . It's no effort for us. Or we could even give it a tragic ending . . . If it's drama you want, we'll give it to you. Would you like Aglaya Karpovna, who's eavesdropped, as you saw, on the conversation between the comic and Dr. Fregoli, to squeal on Paraclete and reduce to nothing his whole philosophy that illusion on the stage of life is more convincing than illusion on the stage of the theater? . . .*

DIRECTOR *(comes up behind, puts his hand on Harlequin's shoulder).* Listen to an old, experienced producer! . . The main thing is to finish the play on time . . The hour is late, the audience is anxious to get home, lots of them have to go to work early tomorrow! . . What's more, the trolleys only run up to a certain time! . . You've acted enough for one night! . . Can't you see how the audience is getting restless over the overcoats, galoshes, and so forth? . .

REG ISSEUR *(approaching Harlequin from another direction and bending near his ear).* The main thing is to have a smash ending for the play. Everybody dance! . . A burst of laughter! . . Something like that! And if this is going to be a work of art, then one shouldn't hesitate to light up the stage properly! Apotheosis is always appropriate! . . I purposely carry a few "sparklers" around with me just for occasions like this! . . Here, hold it! . . *(Takes a box of sparklers out of his pocket, hands it to Harlequin and lights one with a match as he shouts to all around him.)* Let's everybody dance! . . Music! . . Play! . . Laugh! . . Throw confetti! . . More life! . . Audacity! . . Merriment! . . Youthfulness! . . Cur-tain! . . *(With an indulgent smile Harlequin uses a sparkler to Illuminate the deliberately artificial merriment of the actors as they waltz to a dance band playing a bravura waltz.)*

CURTAIN.

---

*Translator's note: At Evreinov's suggestion this speech in the 1926 Broadway production was accompanied by a pantomime by several characters of the proposed variant endings.

THE SHIP OF THE RIGHTEOUS

A Dramatic Epopee in Three Acts

Dedicated to Anna Alexandrovna Kashina-Evreinova, dearer than a wife, closer than a sister, and more than a friend.

N. Evreinov

CHARACTERS

The One Called Madman (Maestro Isai)

The One Called Dream (Anna Reving)

Captain of the Hermit-Ship *Anchorite*

Elsa, his daughter

Dr. Weiss, a physician

Barbara, his wife

Maria, her elder sister, a physician

Vitalius, a sailor

Irina, a nurse

Sorokin, a nobody

Professor of Eugenics, an anybody

Engineer Ivanov, a somebody

The Walking Joke

A very young chambermaid (Olga)

Citizens of the country of Anchorite, sailors, workers, and others.

The Time: The 1920s.
The Place: Act I—the Transcaucasian Black Sea shore.
 Acts II and III—the sea.

ACT ONE

The Transcaucasian Black Sea shore. Spring. Shortly before sunset.

The action takes place in a boardinghouse for invalids and tourists. A large room serves both as a hall and as a dining room. It is furnished very modestly, with high, gray, slightly cracked walls.

An enormous Venetian window at center is wide open, giving a view of the sea and a large ship anchored quite close to shore. In some respects it resembles an ocean liner and in others a gigantic sail-and motor-driven schooner.

Outside, the lovely, whimsical line of some lush, barely blooming wisteria hangs over and partially covers the window.

A narrow staircase by the wall at stage right begins downstage and rises upstage to the second floor.

A high entrance door upstage left, leading off to an anteroom, remains wide open almost the entire time, whereas the low door under the staircase right remains closed.

A rather large dinner table spread with a patterned tablecloth stands in front of the window; at each end is an enormous, beautifully arranged bouquet of crimson roses. Behind the table, almost as long as the window is wide, a soft narrow ottoman is pushed against the wall under the windowsill. There are several chairs around the table.

A piano, with its back pushed at an angle under the staircase, stands farther downstage right.

Well downstage left is a small table with two stools.

A small chandelier hangs overhead.

As the curtain rises Anna Reving—wearing a modest rehearsal dress and appearing to be a sort of embodiment of "the enchanting dream"—is dancing "The Farewell Waltz." Accompanying her on the piano, glancing at the score only occasionally, Maestro Isai—the One Called Madman—is playing romantically. He is a lean, tall, middle-aged artist with a shock of long black hair and a feverish look in his enormous, burning eyes. Dressed shabbily, with a Bohemian's characteristic carelessness, he—both in his movements and in his manner of speaking—reveals both a certain reserve and the indomitable temperament of a southerner. There is something Quixotic about him, about all his behavior, which easily justifies the sobriquet "madman."

The Madman begins the final part, then suddenly breaks off in the middle of a phrase.

MADMAN *(turns on his stool in the direction of Dream)*. Keep in mind, Anna, that the tempo at the end of the second part retards, but increases on the repeat!

DREAM. I remember.

MADMAN. Don't get it confused, because I make it very distinct in the orchestra.

DREAM. Fine. Once more! (*The Madman plays the second part of the waltz. Dream repeats the appropriate part and makes the required emphasis. At the top of the stairs appears Barbara, the wife of Dr. Weiss. She is wearing a coquettish, yet simple spring outfit. She comes halfway down the stairs and watches the dance, smiling and drinking in the music. Her beautiful, nervous face shows traces of her recent illnesss. It is neither quite mournful nor meditative, and the smile wandering over her sensitive lips seems strange and enigmatic. After the dance is over, she faces the musician and comes down another two or three steps.*)

BARBARA. What did you name that waltz, Maestro Isai?

MADMAN. "The Farewell Waltz."

BARBARA. Farewell?

DREAM. Because in this waltz we bid farewell forever to our audience! . .

BARBARA (*approaching the piano*). Is it really forever, Maestro Isai?

MADMAN. Forever, Barbara Nikolaevna.

BARBARA. You really are a madman! . . I'm so terribly sorry that I can't be at the theater this evening.

MADMAN. The fever again?

BARBARA. I'm always worse in the spring . . . And a year ago—you remember?

MADMAN. The roar of the wings of Death! How could one forget that!

BARBARA (*at the window*). I'm eternally grateful to the Black Sea shore! It's a real paradise here in the Transcaucasus! . . The flowers alone! . . the sea! (*Turns around.*) But where are the others?

MADMAN. Almost all of them went to town! A half-hour ago at least!

BARBARA. To the theater?

MADMAN. Probably, although it's still terribly early.

BARBARA. But you? You aren't afraid of being late for your performance?

MADMAN. We're waiting for the motorboat. (*Barbara goes over to the table, drinks in the fragrance of the crimson roses, almost presses one of the bouquets to her breast.*)

DREAM (*sits next to the Madman and points to one of the pages in his notebook*). Do this part over again! . . I want to be really sure . . . (*The Madman plays the last part of "The Farewell Waltz," not at full volume, hardly touching the keys. Dream sits and listens, going over her dance in her mind.*)

BARBARA (*goes to the window and kneels on the ottoman*). Such an early spring this year! . . The wisteria is already completely out . . . (*Turns halfway.*) I might not have seen them again! . . (*Dr. Weiss appears at the top of the stairs.*

He is elegant, elderly, blond, with a pince nez. He wears a small beard and a neatly trimmed moustache around his energetically outlined mouth.)

DR. WEISS *(not coming down the stairs)*. Bobbie! Where did you put my sweaters?

BARBARA. What?

DR. WEISS. Sweaters.

BARBARA. Why do you ask?

DR. WEISS. I need them; where are they?

BARBARA. You pack like you were going to the North Pole . . . *(The Madman stops playing the piano.)*

DR. WEISS. I may be gone a little longer . . . Nights at sea are cold . . . Where did you put them?

BARBARA. In the bottom drawer. Where the gloves are . . . But listen . . . *(He goes off.)* Gone. *(The Madman is on the verge of playing once more, but she interrupts him.)* You know, I'm beginning to wonder. Seriously . . . what does it all mean? This mysterious Captain with his unbearable daughter arrives from England and everybody goes mad. My husband's leaving, both of you are leaving, nurse Irina too . . . What's going on? And everybody on that ship . . . It's no joke the way it's beginning to affect my nerves . . . "A Scientific Expedition? . ." I find it hard to believe . . . And that strange name . . . "Anchorite" . . . *(She looks out the window at the ship.)*

MADMAN. What's so strange? "Anchorite" means "hermit" . . . You couldn't find a better name for a ship going on a scientific expedition . . .

BARBARA. When are you leaving tomorrow?

MADMAN. In the morning . . . at sunrise.

BARBARA *(glances out the window)*. Vitalius! . . Where are you heading? . . To see us? Practice over? . . Then come! . . What? . . Have to change first? . . Don't bother!—There's no one else here! . .

DREAM *(to the Madman)*. We won't be late?

MADMAN *(looking at the clock)*. No, there's still lots of time . . . The motorboat will have us there in a flash . . . *(Vitalius enters—a strapping, nice-looking youth with the typical bearing of a Black Sea sailor. The collar of his faded sailor's blouse is open wide, his sleeves and patched bell-bottom trousers are rolled up. He wears work shoes without socks. A short little pipe in his teeth puffs away.)*

VITALIUS. Hi there! Is nurse Irina home? *(Greets those present.)*

BARBARA. What do you need her for? . . She's probably packing . . .

VITALIUS. I need a little iodine. Stuck a nail in my foot . . .

BARBARA. It gets worse by the hour! One of these days you're going to get your head knocked off in this repulsive sport! . . *(To Dream.)* Anna, is the nurse downstairs? *(Vitalius sits with his legs stretched out on one of the stools at left and leans against the wall.)*

DREAM. I'll run get her. *(Runs off right.)*

BARBARA. Oh no! I merely asked . . . God, what a . . .

VITALIUS *(to the Madman)*. Say . . . are you going tomorrow?

MADMAN. Yes, I am . . .

VITALIUS *(grins at his own thoughts)*. Hm . . . that's funny!

MADMAN. What's funny?

VITALIUS. Well, that they built a ship like that . . . First time I've seen one like it. A real frigate.

BARBARA. Just like any other ship . . .

VITALIUS. The hell it is . . . a lot you know . . . An electric winch for raising the sails? . . Who ever saw anything like that before? And the kind of engineering plant that hardly needs a human hand? . . *(Throws one leg over the other and makes a face.)* Damn . . .

BARBARA *(sympathetically)*. Does it hurt?

VITALIUS. Mm . . . it's annoying . . .

BARBARA. Where can nurse Irina be?

MADMAN *(gets up)*. Where do you suppose she's gone? . .

BARBARA. She's probably packed up the medicine chest already . . .

MADMAN. Wait a moment. I'll find out! . . *(Goes off right.)*

VITALIUS. Is nurse Irina leaving too?

BARBARA. Oh yes. *(She laughs happily.)* They're all leaving! No one left but us! . . *(Presses against him.)* Just us! . . Just us! . . *(She kisses him passionately and he responds.)* Oh! . . What have you done to me this past year! . . Sh! . . I'd do anything for you, anything! . . do you hear? And I forgive you everything, everything, you scoundrel! And you take advantage of it!

VITALIUS *(lighting his pipe)*. What do you forgive me? What am I taking advantage of? . .

BARBARA. Come now . . . Don't play innocent! . . Some nice-looking wench shows up and off he goes! . .

VITALIUS. Who? . . You mean Elsa? . . I wouldn't have paid the slightest attention to small fry like that, if . . .

BARBARA. "If" what?

VITALIUS. . . . if I hadn't wanted to look over the "Anarch—" . . . the "Anchorite." What a name! The men on watch, damn 'em, wouldn't let me on— sons-a-bitches! . . So that's how I came to make up to the Captain's daughter.

BARBARA. Sure—keep talking! I see it all now.

VITALIUS. Cut the nonsense! . . In the first place, she's leaving tomorrow, and in the second place, what devil instilled this idiotic jealousy in you?

BARBARA. And he still has the nerve to ask!

VITALIUS *(laughs kindly)*. Why are you staying at home? You wanted to take in the theater today!

BARBARA. I'm not going!

VITALIUS. God in heaven! Why not?

BARBARA. Just because! . .

VITALIUS. I can't argue with that! *(Sorokin, with quick, mincing steps, bustles in from left. He is a bald, rosy, well-fed man with a large belly poorly masked by an expansive, generously cut suit. He gives an instant, profound impression of a comedian playing the role of "the bourgeois who hasn't been caught yet." Waving a straw hat in front of him, he rushes over, very businesslike, to the door right and yells.)*

SOROKIN. Maria Nikolaevna! . . He's here! . . With the things! . . *(In the direction of those present.)* Where's Olga? Have you seen her? Maria Nikolaevna! . . *(He runs off right.)*

VITALIUS. Who the hell is coming now? . .

BARBARA. How would I know!

VITALIUS. This Sorokin rejoices over every new dog . . . Deliberately sits for hours at the gate, waiting for someone to come along! . . *(Engineer Ivanov, in a coat and visored cap, appears in the door at left. He has two suitcases in his hands and a handbag over his shoulder. He's rather "ordinary" in appearance: Middle-aged, blond, a weathered, sun-tanned face, a small moustache under his slightly snubbed nose, and a straightforward look in his small gray eyes that makes you want to like him. Hardly has he appeared before Maria rushes in from right as if to meet him. Barbara's elder sister is not beautiful, but is a pleasant-looking and energetic woman in a modest, dark-colored dress. Her short hair is smoothed down neatly. With a nervous, feminine motion she takes off her pince nez on the run. Sorokin comes in smiling right behind her.)*

MARIA *(extending both hands to Engineer Ivanov)*. Ahh! . . Welcome aboard! . . *(She turns around.)* Olga, Olga! . . *(To him.)* So glad you're here! *(Firm handshakes with Engineer Ivanov.)* I'm so delighted! . . Right on time, as usual! *(A nice-looking young Chambermaid with closely cropped, light-colored hair rushes in barefoot.)* Olga, take the things! Upstairs! Room fourteen. Is it made up?

CHAMBERMAID. Yes it is. *(She starts to take both suitcases.)*

ENGINEER IVANOV. They're heavy! I'll do it . . . *(The Chambermaid carries one of the suitcases off upstairs.)*

MARIA *(to Sorokin)*. Have you met? Mr. Sorokin, a tenant here, Bogdan Bogdanich Sorokin! . . *(They shake hands.)* And this is my sister—do you recognize her? Barbara! *(She laughs.)* What? You don't? . . Barbara! This is Engineer Ivanov, Pavel Semyonovich Ivanov . . . Remember, when you were little how he used to come to see us when he was a student?

BARBARA *(smiling)*. Vaguely . . . *(Greets him.)*

MARIA *(to him)*. And now she's already married . . .

ENGINEER IVANOV. Really? *(He and Vitalius introduce themselves to each other, mumbling their names in the process.)*

MARIA *(without pausing)* . . . to Dr. Weiss. Have you heard of him? He's a celebrity around here! *(To the others.)* Comrade Ivanov from Rostov . . . Assigned to build a road along the shore . . . But in his spare time has promised to help us "sinners" with the renovation . . . *(To Engineer Ivanov.)* Now you know, I've really decided to change this boardinghouse into a sanatorium . . . *(The Chambermaid comes running down the stairs. To her.)* Olga! Heat up the supper right away! You're probably starving . . .

ENGINEER IVANOV. Oh no, I had a bite at the hotel.

MARIA. Well, that doesn't count. *(To the Chambermaid.)* Hurry! *(The Chambermaid runs off right.)* In the meantime perhaps you'd like to wash up, take a look at your room and . . . Bogdan Bogdanich, show the guest up—be so kind! . .

SOROKIN. With pleasure! *(Engineer Ivanov picks up his suitcase.)* Follow me! *(They both go up the stairs. Sorokin turns to Maria.)* And how about the theater? Are you going anyway?

MARIA. I'm just waiting for the motorboat. Don't be angry now, Pavel Semyonich! Today they're having a program for the benefit of the Tuberculosis League . . . I've got to be there!

ENGINEER IVANOV. Please, go right ahead! We've plenty of time to talk yet!

MARIA. Bogdan Bogdanich will take care of you. *(To Sorokin.)* Can I rely on you?

SOROKIN. Absolutely. *(Smiles pleasantly and disappears above with Ivanov. Maria runs right and collides at the door with nurse Irina, who is followed by the Madman.)*

MARIA. Well? All packed?

IRINA. *(She is about forty, her dark face still preserving some traces of beauty. She has a bottle of iodine and an applicator in her hands.)* What's all this! We had to go and unpack again! *(To Vitalius.)* Are you such an important big shot that you can't come yourself and have to send emissaries instead?

VITALIUS. But I only needed some iodine; I'll put it on myself. *(Maria goes off right.)*

IRINA. Let's see it! Where is it?

VITALIUS. Here! *(Kicks off his left shoe.)*

IRINA *(kneeling by his feet and examining the bottom of his foot)*. Nice! . . Stepped on a nail, eh? . . A rusty one, no doubt? . . *(Smears iodine on the wound.)*

VITALIUS. Who the hell knows? . . Ow! . . That stings, damn it! . .

IRINA *(blows on the bottom of his foot)*. Now you just hold on! You're pretty good at making others suffer, now it's your turn!

VITALIUS. Who have I made suffer?

IRINA *(with mock bitterness)*. You don't even know! . .

VITALIUS. Well, who? . .

IRINA. I suppose you weren't the one that bragged about how in the war . . .

VITALIUS *(interrupting)*. That's something else! You had to remember! . . You've really got a sick imagination! *(Puts on his shoe.)* A real passion for seeing horrors all over the place! Makes your mouth water just talking about them!

BARBARA *(to Irina)*. Remember how he was the first to jump in the storm to save the people from drowning!

IRINA. A sailor, and a swimming instructor at that, could hardly just sit there with his arms folded while his comrades were drowning!

MADMAN *(smiling)*. Wait a minute, my friends! As you well know I am inclined to see symbols everywhere! . . And so in this instance I consider that the name Vitalius *(puts his hand on Vitalius' shoulder)* wasn't given him for nothing! *"Vitalis"* means "lively," from *"vita,"* which means "life." And sure enough, here he is—the embodiment of life itself—of life, where light and shade, good and evil play against each other like two voices in the same musical composition, or, if you prefer, like major and minor keys. Allow me to illustrate this point. *(He sits at the piano and plays fervently a piece in which dual tonality is sharply outlined.)*

IRINA *(after the music ends)*. Such sad music!

MADMAN. That's because you're only hearing the minor!

VITALIUS. I'd call it terrific! Makes your blood boil!

MADMAN. That's because you're catching the major!

BARBARA. It's a deceitful life, if it's like your music!

MADMAN. Deceitful? *(Laughs loudly.)* But if life is deceitful, then we have a right to pay it back!

BARBARA. Meaning?

MADMAN. To deceive it, the way it deceives us! Tit for tat!

BARBARA *(with a grin)*. Hm . . . only a poet—or should I say madman, would say that!

MADMAN. Only our sense of fair play—or should I say pride, would say that! *(Meanwhile Sorokin and Engineer Ivanov have been slowly coming down the stairs; the latter has apparently had time to clean up and change clothes since arriving.)*

VITALIUS *(notices them)*. Well, I'm going to change. *(To Barbara.)* So you're not going to the theater?

BARBARA. I told you!

VITALIUS. All right . . . *(He limps past Irina and bows to her.)* Thank you, nurse!

IRINA. Be careful now you don't make your foot any worse! *(Heads to the door right.)*

VITALIUS. It's all right! It'll heal! I won't die of it! *(He laughs.)* My name is Vitalius! And that's like "life." Right, Comrade Isai?

MADMAN. Right, my friend! And when you limp you're even more like life, since life, as I see it, always limps, even needs crutches some of the time.

VITALIUS. You're a cheerful one! *(All laugh. Vitalius disappears through the door left, at almost the same time Irina disappears through the door right. Barbara goes over to the window and looks out to the left.)*

SOROKIN *(by this time has walked over to Engineer Ivanov and the Madman).* Allow me to introduce you two! . . Engineer Ivanov . . . Maestro Isai . . . the moving spirit of the group here, musician, composer, poet, and philosopher; goes by the name of—you won't be offended?—"madman" . . .

ENGINEER IVANOV. Madman?

MADMAN. Is that bad? . .

> It's great to be a madman,
> It's bad to be a lunatic,

as one poet put it, and I agree with him completely. *(Meanwhile Barbara has wiped her eyes with a handkerchief, taking care that the others not see her and then nervously walks off left.)*

SOROKIN *(as if apologizing to Ivanov for Maestro Isai).* A real character . . .

MADMAN. Are you an engineer? . .

ENGINEER IVANOV. Yes, a civil engineer.

MADMAN. What's the rest of your name?

ENGINEER IVANOV *(with a smile produces his calling card).* Pavel Semyonich . . . my card *(gives it to the Madman)* lists my profession, place of employment, and so forth.

MADMAN *(sitting at the piano).* And here's mine, if you'd like to know who I am! *(Improvises his characterization on the piano. Meanwhile the sky outside the window has turned to a crimson sunset.)*

ENGINEER IVANOV *(clicking his heels gaily).* Very glad to meet you. *(The Chambermaid sets a modest supper on the table at left.)*

SOROKIN *(again as if apologizing for the Madman).* He tries to put everything into music . . . words are just not adequate! . . *(The Madman looks at his watch.)* Supper's on the table already! *(Takes Engineer Ivanov by the arm.)* Sit down and go to it! *(To the Chambermaid.)* Kindly bring us a bottle of red wine! . .

CHAMBERMAID. Right away. *(Runs off right.)*

SOROKIN. The wine here is marvellous! *(To the Madman.)* Won't you join us? For the company? *(He and Ivanov sit down at the table left.)*

MADMAN *(putting the sheet music standing on the piano into a folder)*. I'm sorry, I have to hurry off . . . . it's time to be getting ready . . . *(Goes to the door right.)* Anna! . . Get dressed! . . It's time to go! *(Goes off right.)*

ENGINEER IVANOV *(laughs)*. Are you recuperating here or just resting?

SOROKIN *(sighing)*. Getting over the traumas I've been through.

ENGINEER IVANOV. Traumas?

SOROKIN. Good heavens, can it be you haven't heard how the *Mon plaisir* theater went broke?

ENGINEER IVANOV. You're an actor then?

SOROKIN *(proudly)*. A producer whose faith in the public has caused him much suffering!

ENGINEER IVANOV. And you're not bored here?

SOROKIN. I'm living here on a complimentary ticket, so to say! An old habit of us producers. *(Leaning toward him.)* And what a show is on here! *(Kisses his fingertips.)* Sheer delight!

ENGINEER IVANOV. So why didn't you go to the theater today?

SOROKIN. Oh, hell with it! . . I'm talking about life here, life in this boarding-house!

ENGINEER IVANOV. I don't understand!

SOROKIN. I didn't understand it at first myself! Unbelievably complicated plot! Love, betrayal, jealousy, a group departure on a mysterious ship, hints of some fantastic plans!

ENGINEER IVANOV. Hm . . . interesting!

SOROKIN. Life is theater, my good man! And theater is a very interesting thing, if you're not risking losing your producer's shirt! . . You've arrived at the height of the action! . . That is, at the very moment when the denoument of our little drama is at hand! The events in this house are rushing onward madly! . . Any moment now we may expect the most unusual climax! I can sense it! You can trust an old producer's instinct! *(The Chambermaid brings in a bottle of wine.)*

IRINA *(appearing in the doorway right)*. Olga, help me get these bags shut!

CHAMBERMAID. Right away! *(Runs off right.)*

SOROKIN *(jumps up and runs over to Irina)*. Nurse! *Pour un moment!* . . Can it be that you are really abandoning us? . .

IRINA *(smiling)*. Yes I am, my friend, I am! *(Goes off with the Chambermaid.)*

SOROKIN *(returning to his seat)*. No luck, damn it all to hell! I tried to intervene personally in this little production and it was a fiasco!

ENGINEER IVANOV. But what did you have in mind?

SOROKIN. Marriage! . .

ENGINEER IVANOV. To whom?

SOROKIN. Have you gone blind or something. Why, that's no woman, it's a keg of pure condensed passion!

ENGINEER IVANOV. That nurse?

SOROKIN. Who else then! . . Have you ever seen anyone so well preserved? . .

ENGINEER IVANOV. Yes, she does look youngish!

SOROKIN. Looks are nothing! Just talk to her . . . about suffering, sacrifice, strong feelings, anything you want! A volcano waiting to erupt! That's what she is! I, my good man, can sense these things. *(A prolonged blast of a motorboat's horn is heard.)* Ah! The motorboat! *(In a loud, almost melodramatic whisper.)* The Captain of the Anchorite, every bit as mysterious as his ship, has returned! *(Dream runs in. She is wearing a summer coat, a shawl on her head and has a bundle in her hands. She looks through the window left into the distance.)*

SOROKIN. And this is The One Called Dream! Have you met?

ENGINEER IVANOV. No . . .

DREAM *(shouts through the door right)*. Let's go! . . We're late! . . *(Maria enters in a dark evening dress with a coat folded over one arm. With her is the Madman in a hat and cloak. Irina follows them in.)*

MADMAN. Let's go, let's go! *(Maria rushes over to Engineer Ivanov and offers him her hand.)*

IRINA *(taking her leave of Dream)*. You won't get detained at the theater now?

MADMAN. Don't worry!

DREAM. I already agreed that when my number . . .

MADMAN. She's dancing at eight-thirty sharp and twenty minutes later we'll be home!

MARIA *(to Engineer Ivanov)*. Good night! . . I'll be home quite late, since our guests here will insist on staying to the end of the show . . . you'll already be asleep. *(Dr. Weiss comes down the stairway.)*

MADMAN *(to Maria)*. Maria Nikolaevna! Let's go, dear!

MARIA. Coming, coming! *(Goes off left with Dream and the Madman. Irina looks out the window and bows to those departing.)*

DR. WEISS *(to Sorokin)*. I did hear the horn, did I not?

SOROKIN. You're meeting the Captain on the way? *(Introducing Engineer Ivanov to the Doctor.)* Dr. Weiss . . . Engineer Ivanov.

IRINA *(turns around)*. There's a real mob with the Captain!

SOROKIN *(to Dr. Weiss)*. I hear that you're having a big gathering today?

DR. WEISS *(with a strained smile)*. How do you know so much?

IRINA *(laughing)*. You can't hide anything from him! . .

SOROKIN *(slightly high).* That's nothing! . . In town I found out all about . . . well, the Captain, for instance . . .

DR. WEISS *(with mock amazement).* The Captain?

SOROKIN. Yes sir . . . I now know, for instance, why no one has ever seen a smile on the Captain's face! . .

DR. WEISS *(smiling in disbelief).* All right then, why?

SOROKIN. Because on the very day he received the inheritance from his father, with whom he had quarreled, his young wife died in desperate poverty, having just given birth to Elsa, whom he now dotes upon . . . He was so shaken by the horrible trick that fate had played upon him that he suffered a stroke, after which the muscles in his face no longer allowed him either to laugh or to smile . . . *(Voices are heard left.)*

IRINA. Shh . . . it's him! . .

SOROKIN *(to Engineer Ivanov).* Interesting story, isn't it? . . *(Softly.)* Just see what a terrible face he has! . . *(The Captain and his daughter Elsa enter with their arms around each other. The Captain—a tall, elderly man—has a sickly expression on his gloomy, nearly immobile features. Elsa—a nice-looking girl of about eighteen—looks like an Englishwoman; her eccentric clothes announce her "independence.")*

DR. WEISS *(with a smile, to the Captain).* Are you tired? . .

CAPTAIN *(not smiling, speaking with the slight accent of a man who has lived abroad for a long time).* A little. It's a terrible thing, my dear doctor, to have a bad heart . . .

ELSA *(like the Captain, she pronounces her words with a touch of the foreign).* Papa's got to rest a little before the meeting . . .

DR. WEISS. And where are all the rest? . .

CAPTAIN. In the garden . . .

ELSA. What a marvelous evening! . . Couldn't we have the meeting in the arbor?

CAPTAIN. No, my friend . . . there might be other people nearby and that would inhibit us . . .

SOROKIN *(taking the hint, to Engineer Ivanov).* Would you care for a walk?

ENGINEER IVANOV. Love to! *(They go off left.)*

DR. WEISS. Did you get the style of type you wanted?

CAPTAIN. Yes, but not much of it . . .

ELSA. What pitiful print shops they have around here!

IRINA. Is it really true a newspaper is going to be published on board?

CAPTAIN. Newspapers, magazines, anything you want! . .

DR. WEISS *(to Irina).* It's a whole sovereign state, nurse! How are you going to get along without the press?

IRINA. My God! Your ship is a pure wonder!

CAPTAIN *(correcting her).* Our ship, nurse, I hope! *(Barbara enters nervously from left, pale, with eyes full of tears. Breathing irregularly, she walks past quickly to the stairway. Dr. Weiss seizes her by the hand at the bottom of the stairs.)*

DR. WEISS *(to her, with deep concern).* What's the matter? Why are you so upset? *(She doesn't answer, is on the verge of tears and tears her hand from her husband's. Meanwhile Elsa makes a sign with her head to someone outside the window, all of which does not escape Irina's notice.)*

BARBARA *(almost begging).* Let me go! . . *(Runs up the stairs and disappears beyond the door above.)*

CAPTAIN *(to Dr. Weiss).* She's sorry you're leaving? . . angry? . .

DR. WEISS *(with a nervous smile).* Apparently . . .

CAPTAIN. I've heard so many nice things about your wife . . . It's such a pity you can't find a way to bring her onto the ship!

DR. WEISS *(smiling, but painfully).* It's not a question of my desires . . . you have to reckon with her desires . . .

ELSA *(leaps over to her father and takes him by the arm).* Listen, Papa, you've got to rest! Otherwise you'll be tired: it'll soon be time for the meeting!

CAPTAIN. I'm going, my friend . . . don't worry!

ELSA. I'll go with you!

IRINA *(to the Captain, with deliberate sweetness).* Is Elsa a lot like her mother?

CAPTAIN. Oh yes! . . the same heart, the same soul! . . *(He kisses his daughter tenderly.)* She's very much like her mother and mine too . . Double happiness! I understand your question . . . No, no! If I had found even the slightest trace of my father, who nearly wrecked my life, as you know, I wouldn't be able to breathe in this world, where the human herd tramples on high ideals . . . *(He and Elsa go off right. By now the light of sunset has given way to dusk, which quickly fills the room. The daylight beyond the window dies and is replaced by moonlight. A seascape in all its beauty faintly recalls an old lithograph titled "A Wonderful, Moonlit Night." Dr. Weiss is about to go up the stairs; Irina restrains him.)*

IRINA. One moment! . . A certain note has fallen into my hands . . . Don't interrupt me! . . Yes, yes, I'm prepared even to spy for you and I see nothing—but good—in it . . . My love for you is above ordinary morality . . .

DR. WEISS. What is it? Come to the point, Irina! . .

IRINA *(thrusts a note into his hand).* Read it! . . She dropped it, I picked it up! . . Blame *me*, not yourself . . .

DR. WEISS *(reading).* "My darling little bird!" *(Irina runs over to the light switch and turns it on, partially lighting up the room.)* "You flew here with the spring and the two of you inspired new joy in me" . . . *(Reads rapidly to himself. His face is distorted with pain. He convulsively crumples the note. Irina turns off the lights.)* I'll shoot him!

IRINA *(agitated, breathless, she goes over to him)*. As you see, unfortunately, I was right! . . You didn't believe me!

DR. WEISS *(through his teeth)*. I knew he was a nonentity, but anything this despicable . . . *(Trembles nervously.)*

IRINA. Get hold of yourself!

DR. WEISS *(hollowly)*. I'll shoot him! There's no other way . . .

IRINA. Shhh . . . They'll arrest you!

DR. WEISS *(softly, with restraint)*. Rubbish! A husband killing his wife's lover is hardly ever convicted! . .

IRINA. You forget that our ship is going to sea tomorrow!

DR. WEISS. So much the better! Then I'll be able to hide on it today.

IRINA. But you've forgotten . . .

DR. WEISS. I remember one thing: it'll be easier for her with him dead, than . . .

IRINA *(hearing light footsteps approaching from right)*. Shh . . . let's go upstairs! *(They go up the stairs almost noiselessly and stop on the second floor, while Elsa comes in right and approaches the window.)*

ELSA *(looking through the window toward the left and down)*. Are you still here?

VITALIUS' VOICE. Here.

ELSA. What are you doing?

VITALIUS' VOICE. Thinking about you.

ELSA. That's a fine way to spend your time!

VITALIUS' VOICE. Give me something else then!

ELSA. Like what?

VITALIUS *(scrambles up on the sill like a gymnast. He has changed into a double-breasted naval uniform jacket and looks like a dandy)*. You know!

ELSA. Take you on board the Anchorite as a seaman?

VITALIUS. As anything you want! Just to be near you!

ELSA. Alas! . . I already told you . . .

VITALIUS. Why is the Captain so damned stubborn?! . .

ELSA. Ask him yourself!

VITALIUS. And you'll come back here?

ELSA. Not very likely . . .

VITALIUS. I'll send you dispatches! All right? I just happen to be working at the radio station right now . . .

ELSA. There isn't any radio on our ship! . . Didn't you notice?

VITALIUS. Why not?

ELSA. Because we want to cut ourselves off from the cares of the world.

VITALIUS. How idiotic! . . And if you have a shipwreck, how would you call for help?

ELSA. We'd just perish quietly . . . without any complaints over the airwaves!

VITALIUS. Phew! Proud as hell, all of you! *(Tries to take her by the hand; she skips away.)* Cruel woman!

ELSA *(coquettishly, with a mock curtsy).* But you are very kind, sir!

VITALIUS. What's that shining on your wrist?

ELSA. The phosphorous on my watch. *(Looks at her wrist watch.)*

VITALIUS *(slipping into the room).* A regular firefly . . . Let me see it! . . *(Comes up to her and embraces her in a friendly way.)*

ELSA. Eight-thirty . . . *(Looks meditatively into the distance, as if seeing some vision, and speaks slowly, yet with excitement.)* Anna Reving, the One called Dream, is now dancing her last waltz for the audience! . . her last waltz! . . *(Darkness. Orchestra music is heard. As the light flare up in a theatrical pink the audience seems to have been transported into another theater and before it rises a shallow stage taking up only the proscenium and the downstage area. It is bounded by a backdrop covered with stylized tongues of orange flames dotted with red. The streams of smoke from the flames flow together at the top and form an enormous tragic mask. Dream, in a smoky mourning tunic and with a veil of mourning over her face, is dancing The Farewell Waltz. She dances with tragic sorrow and the unswerving resolve of a person departing forever. In the finale she removes the crepe from her head and throws it to the audience to remember her by, then disappears backstage. Applause breaks out, she reappears, bowing, and leading the Madman out by the hand. The Madman in turn bows to the audience and speaks a word of farewell.)*

MADMAN. Farewell, dear audience! . . Today Anna Reving has danced for you the last time! . . What she wished to say to you in farewell, she has said fully in her Farewell Waltz, and it's no fault of hers if now, just as before, she is not understood! For many years now her inspired dance has called you to the path of good, where her winged legs cavort so freely! . . Dirty, suspicious, deaf, you would not follow her! . . Rhythmically infecting you with the purity of her thoughts, she expected to reduce the sum total of vulgarity on this earth by at least a tiny bit! . . But actually she increased it, merely appealing to your lust! . . Entertaining you was the last thing she wanted! There are enough cute little dolls on the stage and in life without her! She hasn't the strength! It hurts! Look! She has tears in her eyes! . . See how pitiful she is in her disappointment! Look upon this image of Dream unrealized and remember it!

DREAM *(hollowly, with restraint).* Farewell! . .

MADMAN *(loudly, coldly, proudly).* Farewell forever! *(Darkness. It's sudden arrival corresponds with a loud revolver shot. Elsa's scream is heard, as well as feet running downstairs, a general uproar, and here and there the voice of Dr. Weiss: "Let me go! . . Stop it, I say! . . Let go!" As the stage lights up again, the audience once more sees the inside of the boardinghouse. Dr. Weiss tears his hand with the revolver away from the grip of Irina's hands as he comes off the stairs. In the opposite corner of the room Elsa shields Vitalius from Dr. Weiss.)*

ELSA *(to Vitalius).* Get out of here! . . You can explain later! . . Go! You can see he's not himself! . .

VITALIUS *(who has quickly taken his own revolver out of his pocket).* You go! God damn it! Crazy! . . I'm not a coward to go running away! . .

DR. WEISS *(to Irina).* Let go! . .

VITALIUS. The man's gone mad! *(Tears loose from Elsa.)*

DR. WEISS. Killing would be letting him off easy! . .

VITALIUS. What for? . . What's going on? . . *(Barbara appears at the top of the stairs.)*

BARBARA. What's all this about? . . What happened? . .

VITALIUS *(to her).* Your husband took a shot at me! . .

BARBARA *(running over to Dr. Weiss and grabbing the hand with the gun).* My husband? . . What for? . . *(To her husband.)* You? You could come to this? . . *(Pause.)* You? If you lost faith in me, if you suspected . . . You're not some savage, after all! . . You could have divorced me! . . You could have . . . Why he . . . What a nightmare! . . Blaming him, when I'm the one responsible! Me, me! Ask *me* about it! . .

VITALIUS. I'm quite capable of taking the responsibility myself! *(The Chambermaid appears in the doorway right.)*

BARBARA *(restraining her agitation, turns to Vitalius, with firm conviction).* Vitalius Ivanych, get out of here! Do you hear? I ask you to leave this instant! . .

CHAMBERMAID *(somewhat confused).* The Captain's worried about the shooting! . . *(Turns on the switch to the right of the window and fully illuminates the room.)*

ELSA. Did Papa wake up? *(Runs off right drawing the Chambermaid after her.)*

BARBARA *(to Vitalius).* Leave, I repeat, if a woman's entreaties mean anything to you! *(By this time several new faces have appeared in the door left.)*

VITALIUS *(putting his revolver in his pocket and walking off left).* Let's go, fellows! . . We've been asked to leave! . . *(Shuts the door behind him.)*

VOICES OFF LEFT. What happened? . . What's the shooting about? . .

VITALIUS' VOICE. Nothing at all! . . Didn't know how to use a gun! *(Dr. Weiss, exhausted from emotion, throws the gun on the floor. Irina quickly picks it up and puts it in her pocket.)*

BARBARA *(to her husband).* What a terrible thing! . . That you should descend to such barbarism! . . And a man who has always been a model of goodness! . . Try to murder somebody! . . A real executioner! . . There was no other way out! . . Grew cold to me long before! . . Going away for God knows how long! . . And all of a sudden . . .

IRINA *(greatly agitated, in no condition to restrain herself, bursts into Barbara's speech).*

Stop it! . . . You don't know anything! . . I can't listen to these reproaches
any longer!

BARBARA *(amazed)*. What? . . I "don't know anything"? . . And you? . .
What business is it of yours?

IRINA. It's my business because I can't listen to any more reproaches based on
pure delusion . . .

BARBARA. I don't understand you . . .

IRINA. Can you really imagine that he, *he*, a man another wife would idolize,
could be driven to revenge out of jealousy! . .

DR. WEISS *(to Irina, seizing her hand)*. No, nurse, don't! . . She doesn't need to
know that! . .

IRINA. No! Kill me if you must, but I'll tell her everything! . . Everything! . .
She doesn't dare sneer at you when she ought to be bowing down before
you! *(Dr. Weiss sinks helplessly onto one of the chairs by the piano.)*

BARBARA. I'm not sneering at him! . . I'm merely amazed that a cultured
man . . .

IRINA *(interrupting)*. Shut up? You don't know anything! . . He's been watching your affair for a long time! . . He couldn't not know about it, because
he started it himself! Do you hear?

BARBARA. What?!

IRINA. You were ill . . . Being a doctor he knew that no medicine, no change
of climate would save you from tuberculosis, if there was no will to live,
that powerful, all-conquering will! . . He knew that only love, passionate
love, inspires that will . . . He knew that he himself could not inspire in
you that love and made the sacrifice only a real hero could make! . .

DR. WEISS *(almost with a groan)*. Stop it, nurse, we don't need the details! . .

BARBARA. What sacrifice? . . What are you talking about?

IRINA *(pale, with eyes wide open)*. He himself gave the man you liked permission
to make love to you! . .

BARBARA. Who? Vitalius? . .

IRINA *(passionately)*. Who else? . . *(Pointing to Dr. Weiss.)* He himself gave up
his rights as a husband, thinking only of your salvation! . . And you recovered . . . You were resurrected into life!.

BARBARA *(almost staggering)*. What am I hearing? . .

IRINA *(energetically takes Dr. Weiss' hand)*. Look! I kiss the hand of this man,
who suppressed his male instincts in the name of a higher love! . .

BARBARA *(perplexed, as if trying to grasp something)*. You mean Vitalius didn't
love me? . . He was only an actor? . .

DR. WEISS. Wrong! . . He did love you! . . And loved you passionately! . . *(In*

Irina's direction.) She exaggerated my contribution! . . In fact, I didn't make any contribution at all!

IRINA *(with great indignation, to Barbara).* What an outrage! . . You're thinking about the love of another man, when that love ought to fade into nothing next to the love of your husband!

BARBARA. No, no . . . I'm merely asking . . . Why did you shoot at him? . .

IRINA. Why! . . Because your husband loved you and couldn't bear to have you know the torments of jealousy such as had befallen him!

BARBARA *(hardly audible, dumbfounded).* Jealousy . . . Over whom?

IRINA. Elsa, for instance, that girl Vitalius has been chasing, breaking the promise made to your husband!

BARBARA *(as if in a dream).* Elsa? . . Yes, yes, I understand . . . he was avenging me? . . *(A heavy pause. Barbara looks steadily ahead, seeming to weigh all she has heard. She begins to breathe rapidly and her bosom heaves. She goes over to Dr. Weiss without saying a word and drops—as if shot—to her knees. Dry sobs shake her body, so pitiful at this moment.)*

DR. WEISS. Get up! . . get up! . . What's this for? . . *(He lifts her to her feet.)*

BARBARA *(suppressing her sobs).* Darling! . . dearest! . . Forgive me the pain I caused you. Forgive me! . . Come back to me! . . I won't survive away from you now . . . I swear by my honor, my mother, my love for you, I was never unfaithful! Never! . . Never! . .

DR. WEISS. I don't need to be consoled! You needn't lie. I love you anyway and . . . I sympathize!

BARBARA. I swear! . . Believe me! . . I was on the verge of betraying you, but managed to restrain my passion . . waiting for you to leave! . . And that made him mad! . . He left me for another out of revenge . . . tormenting me and tormenting himself! . . . What madness! I wanted to betray you! You! You, who sacrificed everything for me! . . My sweet, darling! . . Don't leave me! Take me with you! . . I'll die without you . . Your love, a love like that, is the greatest life-giving force there is! A love like that could raise the dead! . . Oh, give me the happiness of being with you always! Now I know who you are! Who you really are! . .

DR. WEISS *(pressing her to him with inexpressible tenderness and covering her face with kisses).* My love! . . My infinite love! . . My inexpressible! . . *(Elsa and the Captain appear in the doorway right. He has a briefcase in his hand.)*

ELSA *(loudly, to Irina).* I'll go call the meeting! All right? . . It's high time! . .

IRINA. Of course, of course! . . *(Goes over to the Captain.)*

BARBARA *(deeply happy, smiling through her tears).* What sort of meeting is it? . . Will I be in the way? . . *(Elsa runs across the room and out the door left.)*

DR. WEISS *(to the Captain).* Captain, your wish has been fulfilled! . . My wife is coming with us! . .

CAPTAIN. I am most happy to welcome the new member of our community! . .

BARBARA *(smiling).* What community? . .

IRINA *(to the Captain).* She doesn't know yet! . . *(To her.)* You are now a citizen of the country of Anchorite!

BARBARA. Anchorite? . . That ship there?

CAPTAIN. Our group is a community of the righteous! . .

BARBARA *(with a smile).* But I'm afraid . . . I'm not a saint, you know! *(Sorokin and Engineer Ivanov enter left.)*

SOROKIN *(indecisively bowing to nobody in particular).* Are we interrupting something?

CAPTAIN. You must excuse us, we're having a meeting.

SOROKIN. Marvelous! *(Motioning toward the stairs with his hand.)* Let's go, Pavel Semyonich! *(To Irina, leading her off to the side, in curious, eager whispers.)* Excuse me for asking, but was there a shooting here?

IRINA. It was an accident.

SOROKIN. Ahh! . . Well, thank God! . . *(Softly, confidentially to Ivanov as he joins him on the stairs.)* Wanted to kill his *wife!* Can't fool me . . . I told you you had arrived right at the denouement! . . I can sense these things! *(They go off.)*

BARBARA. And you've decided to leave! For a long while?

CAPTAIN.

DR. WEISS. —Forever!

IRINA.

BARBARA. What do you mean "forever?" *(Enter two young ladies, an elderly lady, two sailors—one in a red beard, the other in glasses—then the Professor of Eugenics—a gray, bearded man with enormous glasses—and "The Walking Joke"—a stately, sweetly handsome mountaineer from the Transcaucasus, wearing a Circassian coat, with his right arm in a black sling. Elsa follows them in. The Captain goes over to meet them on the way in.)*

ELSA. Welcome! . . These are all "members of the family"! . .

CAPTAIN. But where are the rest? *(To Barbara.)* Please introduce yourself! . . *(Dr. Weiss introduces his wife to those who have just arrived.)*

ELSA. They went to meet our "madman" and his lovely "dream." *(A long blast on the motorboat horn.)* Ahh! . . Speak of the devil! . . I'll run and hurry them along! . . *(She runs off left. The two young ladies, the elderly lady, and the Captain all cluster in the rear of the room, in the window's embrasure, while the Professor of Eugenics and the Walking Joke are taking positions downstage.)*

BARBARA *(cautiously shaking hands with the Walking Joke, who has removed his arm from his sling for the occasion)*. Did you hurt yourself?

WALKING JOKE *(with the slight, barely noticeable accent of a Caucasian)*. God forbid! . . *(He laughs.)* I carry my arm in a sling just to keep from having to offer it to all sorts of scoundrels! . .

PROFESSOR *(to Barbara, as he sits down)*. Been suffering for two years, but won't betray his principles! . . What a man! *(Laughs good-naturedly.)*

WALKING JOKE. My sufferings end tomorrow.

IRINA *(to the Professor, indicating Barbara)*. Here's a brand new one.

DR. WEISS. My wife! . .

IRINA. She trusts us without even knowing the history of our Community of the Righteous.

PROFESSOR. Well, what is there to know! . . It's all so simple, so obvious!

IRINA. Tell her in a couple of words!

PROFESSOR *(laughs)*. Gladly! . . The pure decided to part from the impure, the good from the evil, the wise from the stupid . . .

BARBARA. But how, I don't quite understand?

PROFESSOR. Like this! . . A group of good people—that is, those who have conquered their animal instincts—despairing at last in the struggle with those who have not completely conquered, simply decided to Isolate themselves forever.

BARBARA *(to the Professor)*. But aren't you afraid that—don't be angry, Professor—that it's all just a utopia?

PROFESSOR. What? The country of Anchorite? Our Community of the Righteous?

BARBARA. Yes.

PROFESSOR *(rises)*. That's what we're going to find out! What are we risking? The ship is at our disposal! In two years the owner—now incognito—has promised the Captain to "nationalize" the Anchorite for the benefit of the community! We're obviously people of great good will. The cast has been carefully selected. We should not keep on writing plays for the theater forever. As our chief source of inspiration once said . . .

BARBARA. Who?

DR. WEISS. Maestro Isai.

BARBARA. I thought so.

PROFESSOR. . . . the time has finally arrived to write a play for life, a good play, a play full of fun and ideas . .

BARBARA *(trying to comprehend the meaning of these words)*. For life?

PROFESSOR. Of course! And once it is written, devote our common efforts to performing it! *(From the left, the laughter and merry shouts of an approaching group of people is heard. The voice of the Madman is clearly distinguishable.)* Here he is himself! *(Several of those present look out the window, others stand at the door; all are filled with joy and excitement. Only Dr. Weiss and his wife remain downstage, kissing passionately.)*

BARBARA *(between kisses).* And I'll have time to pack?

DR. WEISS *(laughing).* We wouldn't go without you.

BARBARA *(barely managing to be heard above the happy noise made by the approaching group).* What is it—a gathering of the whole community?

DR. WEISS. No—just the committee.

BARBARA. The executive committee?

DR. WEISS. The only committee we have. *(About twenty people enter, men and women of various ages. Several fishermen and sailors are especially noticeable by their clothes and sun-tanned faces. At the head of the group is the Madman, arm in arm with Dream and Elsa. All are alive with excitement. Mutual greetings, passionate, hearty, with those present. The Captain and the Madman kiss.)*

CAPTAIN. Tired? No? Well? *(To Dream.)* Have you bid farewell to your public?

MADMAN *(emphatically).* We did.

CAPTAIN. Good show! *(To all, gesturing toward the table.)* Please take your seats! . . Is everyone here?

VOICES. Yes, all of us! . . *(Those present move a small table from the left against the main table; some take their seats in the chairs at the table and around the table; others sit on the windowsill, and still others on the stairs.)*

CAPTAIN. The meeting today, our last on dry land, will be the final session devoted to discussion of the first voyage of the Anchorite as a shelter for our community.

PROFESSOR. Long live the Community of the Righteous!

ALL. Hurrah! . . *(The Captain goes over to the light switch and turns the lights in the room off and on three times. In response to his signal two blue lights appear on the foremast of the ship, sending their bright beams off into the distance. Everyone greets the sight with joyous sighs.)*

MADMAN *(rapturously).* There they are—two fiery blue eyes, casting their mighty gaze into the future of mankind!

CAPTAIN. A gaze full of reproach and appeal!

DR. WEISS. Let us swear that those eyes shall henceforth never close! . .

ALL. We swear! We swear!

MADMAN. I propose that we here and now sing the song of our community, so that it will sound as a summons to all others on earth!

VOICES. Let's sing! . . Oh, please! *(The Madman sits at the piano. The men and women form two choirs.)*

ACT ONE

CAPTAIN. Attention everybody! Please rise! *(The Madman plays the introduction to the "Anthem of the Community of the Righteous."*

    MALE CHOIR
A hero be!
    FEMALE CHOIR
               'ro be!

    MALE CHOIR
In Love's victory!
    FEMALE CHOIR
               Victory!

    MALE CHOIR
Of sin be free!
    FEMALE CHOIR
               Be Free!

    MALE CHOIR
The good to see!
    FEMALE CHOIR
               At sea!

    MALE CHOIR
Find the right way!
    FEMALE CHOIR
               Our way!

    MALE CHOIR
Nevermore to stray!
    FEMALE CHOIR
               Hooray!

    MALE CHOIR
The crowd gainsay!
    FEMALE CHOIR
               Gainsay!

    MALE CHOIR
They're going the wrong way!
    FEMALE CHOIR
               We dare say!

    BOTH CHOIRS

March on, march on,
Down with yesterday!
Seek the new dawn,
Take the better way!

Find ecstasy
And saintly be!
'Mid friends in the
Community!
    MALE CHOIR
A hero be!
    FEMALE CHOIR
                'ro be!
(And so forth from the beginning.)
    BOTH CHOIRS
There where reigns the mighty ocean
Far from sinful land's desire
Where the waves in endless motion
Form with birds a joyous choir.

Having scorned this world's temptations
For a life on new foundations,
Heroes from the myths of yore,
We'll know bliss forever more.

         CURTAIN.

ACT TWO

A clear, sunny day on the deck of the Anchorite. The deep blue, nearly cloudless sky of the tropics. The sea is calm, the barely noticeable line of the horizon is imperturbably calm.

The rear of the stage is bounded by the starboard bulwark, that is, the bow of the ship is assumed to be stage right.

A platform, the lid of a large hatch, rises in the center of the deck. It is about five or six yards long and forms a stage of sorts. A short, wide ladder leads up to it.

To the left there is an enormous ventilator of the type usually found on ocean liners. It stands in front of one of the entrances through the curtains on that side.

To the right are the walls of the ship's salon, with curtained windows and a half-opened door. The roof of this above-decks structure is almost even with the lower edge of the main curtain above the stage.

Two or three large ropes slant upward from the bulwark.

The basic colors of the ship's painted surfaces, the curtains in the windows, etc., are turquoise blue, oak brown, and white.

As the curtain rises several girls are playing on the platform with large light blue balls. They are tossing them back and forth to some men—hardly visible to the audience—standing on the roof of the salon. Elsa is one of the girls; the Walking Joke is one of the men.

The girls, including Elsa, are each dressed in summer clothes to suit their own taste or in short sport tunics, with colors reminiscent of sailors' clothes. Some of them wear sandals, others are barefoot. Their hairdos, like their clothes, reveal their desire to be individual at all costs. The sun-tanned appearance of these young women of the country of Anchorite, the cut of their dresses, the style of their hair and sandals, their free, playful motions, laughter and way of talking—all combine to create an impression of the exotic, of strangeness, of whimsy, of something the audience is not accustomed to, of something not of this world.

As the curtain rises the sounds of the Ocean Waltz are heard coming from the half-open door of the salon.

The lively game of ball is apparently being scored in accordance with some rules governing missed balls agreed upon by the two teams—the women below and the men above.

Here and there one hears cries like: "Missed . . . that one doesn't count . . . seven . . . nice shot . . . eight . . . that's right . . . c'mon . . . aha . . . missed again . . . wrong . . . nine . . . what's that make it?. . . ten . . ."

ELSA *(clapping her hands).* We won!
FIRST GIRL. That's the third game!

MEN'S VOICES. Oh no! The first one didn't count!

GIRLS. What do you mean, didn't count? Silly boys! That was the third game. We won!

ELSA. We won, we won! . . *(The men protest, the girls insist. Laughter, argument, uproar, the triumph of the victors, who jump up and down from joy and throw the balls high in the air.)*

GIRLS *(drowning out the men's voices).* To the ropes! To the ropes! . . You lost! That's right—now you have to come down the ropes! *(The men finally throw down several balls to the girls and reluctantly disappear. As the men go, the girls tease them by thumbing their noses at them, sticking out their tongues and other gestures appropriate to be directed at a losing team. The victors look up impatiently, over the salon, in the direction of the farthest rope. It soon begins to swing, shake, and sag downward. For several seconds all is silent except for the sounds of the Ocean Waltz and the girls' excited breathing. Several men come down the farthest rope, one at a time. They are dressed in suits worn by the male citizens of Anchorite, a combination of fantasy, sports clothes, sailor uniforms.)*

GIRLS *(with mock taunts).* Ahhh! . . So, you rascals? . . Tit for tat! . . Going to brag any more? . . Enjoy the exercise? . . Isn't it a bit warm up there? . . Aren't you getting tired? . . *(The music stops.)*

ELSA *(yells off right).* Hey, what happened to the music? . . Maestro Isai! . . We want it, like in the circus . . . to music! I just adore that Ocean Waltz . . . *(She runs right and looks in the door.)* He's gone . . .

SECOND GIRL *(to Elsa).* He has some sort of rehearsal today. He warned us . . .

ELSA. Oh yes! I forgot! Why, we've been promised a surprise for this evening . . .

FIRST GIRL. The sun is nearly setting now . . . *(Meanwhile Irina has come in from the left. Like the girls she is dressed according to her own unique taste, but looks more mature—she is wearing a long dress with covered neck and arms, and a kerchief on her head. The nurse's red cross on her bosom has been replaced by a light blue cross. Her feet are bare and her entire appearance bespeaks the great feat of humility and selflessness. She seems on the verge of opening the briefcase in her hands, but quickly forgets her intentions when she spots the row of men coming, hand over hand, down the ropes.)*

IRINA *(shaking her head reproachfully).* Still at it, I see! *(To the Girls.)* Why all these cruel rules you have?

SECOND GIRL. What's so cruel about them?

IRINA. "What's so cruel?" In the first place they might fall and get smashed on the deck! And in the second place, it probably makes their hands burn, and in general it's exhausting!

FIRST GIRL. They lost!

SECOND GIRL. If we lose they make us scrub the decks.

IRINA. Well at least that's something useful and not a bit dangerous!

ELSA. But not any less unpleasant! Lectures, lectures, lectures! . . . You seem to forget that this is an anarchist society, where everyone is free to do as he pleases! . .

IRINA. True, but it also happens to be a community of the righteous! And here you are running around arousing your baser passions.

FIRST GIRL. We're *jok-ing!*

SECOND GIRL. It's a game!

IRINA. But aren't there any other games which . . . *(At this moment the last of the men coming down the rope, the Walking Joke, falls not far from the bulwark, arousing a general cry of alarm.)*

IRINA. Aha! I told you so! I warned you! . . *(Runs over to the victim.)*

WALKING JOKE *(gets up, rubbing his side)*. It's nothing! Still in one piece! Don't worry . . . It's all because of my arm! . . Wore it in a sling for two years and now . . . you see!

IRINA. All weak from lack of use? I understand. *(Reproachfully addressing the others.)* A man was almost killed! . .

ELSA *(to him, teasing, coquettishly)*. When are you ever going to reveal the secret of why you were so stubborn about not shaking hands on land?

WALKING JOKE. You mean I didn't tell you? I didn't want to soil myself shaking some scoundrel's hand! That's the whole story!

ELSA. But what started all this? Something must have happened? *(He laughs enigmatically and nods his head, as if recalling something.)* Tell us! We'd love to hear about it! *(She and the others sit down on the platform, half-lying, clustered together and in a relaxed position, forming a rather picturesque group. It is not difficult to observe which of the young men and women are attracted to each other.)*

WALKING JOKE. Well, what is there to tell! A rather brief story, more like an anecdote, only very sad . . . Mm . . . *(Looking love-smitten at Elsa.)* I fell in love one time . . . *(Thinks things over for a moment.)* Fine, Was so much in love that I dreamed about her all night, every night! . . Only don't think there was anything indecent involved, quite the contrary . . . Fine. One day I'm leaving for Kutais on business. I call my friend, I tell him: "Please take care of her and be sure nobody else messes around with her. Promise? . ." He gave me his hand, his eyes flashed and he says: "Here's my hand, you can count on me! Don't worry about a thing!" Fine. Off I go to Kutais and catch such an awful cold that I got stuck in bed for two months. I come back, meet my friend, I ask him: "Well? Keep your promise? Nobody else messed around with her?" And he answers: "Are you crazy? I would let *somebody else*, when I gave you my word? I married her m'self." That's the kind of rascal he turned out to be! *(General laughter.)* And even after shaking hands on it! Called himself a friend! . . *(Offended.)* What are you laughing for? It's a very sad story and it's nothing to laugh about: man must understand his fellow man in his hour of need and sympathize with him.

ELSA *(with well-disguised irony)*. We sympathize with you very much! Very, very much! . . You're a genuine hero! Just imagine—wouldn't give his hand to anybody for two years. Must have been very beautiful?

WALKING JOKE. My hand?

ELSA. Your fiancee!

WALKING JOKE *(with a big, stupid grin)*. Hm . . . like you! . .

ELSA *(smiling, hypocritically seems to be embarrassed)*. Oh, come now!

WALKING JOKE *(passionately)*. It's the God's truth! And, just like you, wouldn't let me sleep the whole night!

ELSA *(somewhat perplexed, rises)*. How so, I don't quite understand?

WALKING JOKE *(rises right after she does)*. Like this: shows up, like you do, every night, smiles at me, puts her little head on my shoulders, lets her hair fall on me, says tender words.

ELSA *(shocked)*. You mean I've been coming to see you? And at night? What are you talking about?

WALKING JOKE. In my dreams, in my dreams! . . It's in my dreams that you come!

ELSA. Ahh, that's something else. *(All laugh. Elsa and the Walking Joke, gaily talking about something, walk upstage away from the rest; soon they have slipped away left.)*

SECOND GIRL *(to Irina)*. Nurse, do you know how to interpret dreams? Last night I had the strangest dream again . . .

SEVERAL GIRLS. And I did too! . . Me too! . . Such an unusual dream! It even woke me up! . .

FIRST MAN *(to Irina)*. And you, nurse, do you dream too, or not?

IRINA. Depends on what kind of . . .

SEVERAL VOICES. Strange ones!

IRINA. What do you mean, "strange"? I'm a very well-balanced person, and . . .

FIRST GIRL. How about your romance with Sorokin? *(Light laughter among the others.)*

IRINA. Sorokin?

FIRST GIRL. Who else! The operetta producer! He has such a nice little paunch!

FIRST MAN. And such a fascinating bald spot!

SECOND GIRL. I hear he proposed to you twice! . .

IRINA *(reddening)*. What a nasty thing to say! . . In the first place, Sorokin is by no means as bad a person as you think . . .

FIRST GIRL. Well then, why isn't he here with us right now?

IRINA. . . . and in the second place, am I . . . am I too old to be interesting to a man?

FIRST GIRL *(suddenly realizes how offensive she's been)*. Nurse! We've offended you? . . Dearest, we didn't want to offend you! *(Unexpectedly drops to her knees in front of Irina and begs in almost painful tones.)* Punish me! Beat me! . . Hurt me, if I've offended you! *(The others grow silent during this little scene the way people do in the theater at dramatically tense moments.)*

IRINA *(breaking the tension with laughter)*. You forget our principle of non-resistance to evil!

FIRST GIRL. But your not taking revenge is a higher sort of revenge!

IRINA. I don't want revenge! And you must believe me if you respect me.

FIRST GIRL. I . . . believe you, I do! . . *(Bends over and kisses Irina's hand, then falls at her feet. At this moment the sun-tanned, dashing navigator crosses downstage from right to left. Two of the girls, one after the other, playfully throw their light blue balls at him. He laughs loudly and declines to join the game.)*

GIRLS *(shouting at him, interrupting each other)*. Navigator, come see us! . . Where are you taking us? Navigator, listen! . . Head for the Paradise Islands! For Samoa! . . . For Tahiti! . . For the South Pole!. No, that'd be too hot! Let's go to the north one! *(General laughter.)*

IRINA *(infected by the general gaiety)*. Wait, navigator! When are we crossing the equator?

NAVIGATOR. This evening. *(Goes off left, followed by a ball.)*

IRINA. This evening? . . *(Rising, to the others.)* Tonight we shall see the constellation The Southern Cross . . . You can only see it from the other side of the equator! . . Oh, at last!

SEVERAL. Hurrah! . .

IRINA. They say it's a spectacle of pure enchantment! . . And it always means something special for people who see it for the first time!

FIRST MAN. I already saw it! In a dream, that is.

SECOND GIRL. When?

FIRST MAN. Last night.

SECOND GIRL. And I saw you.

FIRST MAN. Again? . . That's strange! . . Me too . . We were inseparable! . .

SECOND GIRL. Then why didn't I see the Southern Cross?

FIRST MAN. Because you always drop your eyes around me.

SECOND GIRL. Of course! The way you behave in your dreams, I can hardly help . . .

IRINA. What does he do? *(To him.)* Aha, we caught you!

SECOND GIRL. I dreamed I was in a virgin forest and somebody was chasing me, something like a robber, or maybe a savage! . . Finally, I turn around and see . . .

FIRST MAN. Me?

SECOND GIRL. Yes, but looking so awful! . . Your nostrils all flared, your teeth bared, your eyes like some wild animal! . . .

FIRST MAN *(hotly)*. Then I grab you like this! . . *(Embraces her.)*

SECOND GIRL *(trying to free herself)*. See, he remembers everything! The scoundrel! . .

FIRST MAN. I squeeze you so hard you scream from the pain . . .

SECOND GIRL *(screams)*. A-ail . . Let go! . . *We're not dreaming now!* . .

(General laughter; she breaks out of his embrace and runs away.)

FIRST MAN *(To Irina)*. There! Explain this dream of ours.

IRINA. My friends, forgive me for saying so, but you don't do enough work, you sleep too much and what's more read all sorts of cheap books, inflaming your imagination with images of the past when you ought to be concentrating on images of the future.

ELSA *(enters with the same person she left with, and has a news sheet in her hands)*. What are you all discussing?

IRINA *(with dignity)*. The inner sense of duty.

ELSA. Saving people's souls? . . And I thought it was about the celebration tonight! Did you read about it? *(Shows the news sheet to the others.)*

SEVERAL MEN *(gathering around Elsa)*. What's this? An "Extra"? . . When did it come out? . .

IRINA *(striking herself on the head)*. Oh, unhappy woman! . . *(Swiftly takes several news sheets out of her briefcase.)* What a miserable woman! *(Distributes the news sheets to those present.)* Here I am peddling all kinds of stuff, talking about duty, with the briefcase in my hands, forgetting my own personal duty . . . *(To the Second Girl.)* Now it's your turn to forgive me! . . I was commissioned to hand out the Evening Edition, but instead . . .

SECOND GIRL. Well, its all right . . .

IRINA. Oh no, you must forgive me! Forgetting my own personal duty, I was on the verge of rebuking you.

SECOND GIRL. It was my own fault.

IRINA *(seizing her hands and kissing them)*. No, I must be punished. *(Falls to her knees and kisses the hem of the Second Girl's dress.)*

SECOND GIRL. Are you trying to outdo me in virtue?

IRINA *(getting up)*. I only want to be on the same level with you.

SECOND MAN *(reads the news sheet).* "Anniversary of the Day the Anchorite Left Land." . . . Can a year have gone by already?

ELSA *(reading).* "Celebration on the occasion of the Newly Born Member of the Community of the Righteous" . . .

FIRST MAN. That's Barbara's little boy.

IRINA *(ecstatically).* Perfectly charming baby!

ELSA. He's the first to be born in the country of Anchorite.

IRINA. What's more, the first one who was conceived on board. *(Suddenly realizing what she has said.)* But that's a minor detail.

FIRST GIRL *(reads).* "The traditional Dance of the Merry Anchorite celebrating the new born. A new ships's sacrament of Holy Baptism. Welcoming speeches. As a grand finale an excerpt from Maestro Isai's tragi-comedy will be presented: *Ham vs. Noah,* book and music by Maestro Isai. Celebration to begin at seven o'clock. To be announced by three blasts on the ship's horn."

FIRST MAN. And what time is it now?

ELSA *(looking at her wrist watch).* Quarter to seven.

VOICES. Ohh! . . Already? . .

SECOND MAN. Why did they wait so long to tell us about it?

IRINA. It's all my fault! . . I was too busy admiring all of you. And the "Extra" came out long ago.

FIRST GIRL *(interrupting her speech, almost at the beginning).* That's great! We've got to be in the dance! When are we going to have time to change, do our hair and . .

ELSA *(interrupting).* Let's hurry then! There's no time to lose! *(Runs off right downstage, drawing the others off with her. They are heard making remarks like "Oh, these surprises are getting a little tiring . . we'll manage . . . c'mon . . they won't start without us" and so forth.)*

IRINA. You'll make it! No need to get all upset! . . Oh, you young people! Always in a big rush! . . Hardly know what to do with all your extra energy! . . *(Sits down on the steps to the platform, takes a notebook marked "Diary" and a pencil from her briefcase, and quickly jots down something. From left are heard male voices. Irina turns, smiles as she nods her head and once more sets to work on her diary. The Captain, Dr. Weiss, and the Professor enter from left. All are dressed in the suits of the sailor citizens of the country of Anchorite, rather modest, nice-looking suits, what you would call "solid." The Professor has grown a long beard; he has some manuscript in a folder in his hands.)*

CAPTAIN *(continuing their conversation).* . . . no, no, my dear Professor, a public reading of the year's accomplishments would take up too much time and would seem boring in the sort of celebration we're having today . . .

PROFESSOR *(slightly high, overly careful in his speech)*. All right. In that case I could limit myself simply to extracts and the overall totals: how much scientific research accomplished, how many meters of yarn the female personnel produced, a report on how many fish were caught, how much canned, repairs to equipment, how much coal consumed and so forth.

CAPTAIN. That's all been written up in the paper.

PROFESSOR. Sure, but not the overall totals!

CAPTAIN *(to the Professor)*. We'll report it all tomorrow. All right?

PROFESSOR. Other items worth noting would be how many persons passed courses in eurythmics, music, fine arts during the year. *(To Dr. Weiss.)* Your wife, for example, has been playing the piano superbly the last month or two!

DR. WEISS *(jokingly)*. Don't forget to include yourself on the list of accomplishments! Your success with the guitar this past year has almost surpassed your success in the laboratory.

PROFESSOR *(smiling)*. I used to play when I was a student—so I was just reliving my student days. I love to remember the days of my youth.

DR. WEISS. I suppose you were a great drinker in those days?

PROFESSOR. How did you know?

DR. WEISS. I was going by your enthusiasm in remembering those days!

PROFESSOR *(laughing)*. Sinful . . . sinful . . .

DR. WEISS *(in his ear, theatrically conspiratorial)*. And you still haven't atoned for it! *(The Professor laughs loudly.)*

CAPTAIN *(to Dr. Weiss)*. Well, and what did you accomplish during the year?

DR. WEISS *(jokingly)*. My pyrotechnics, of course! . . I got so terrific at putting out firecrackers that . . . *(cuts himself off)*. Oh yes, by the way, Captain! I have bad news for you! We've been setting off firecrackers around here so often that we've run out of potassium nitrate. So that means the celebration today . . .

CAPTAIN. . . . will have to get along without any fireworks?

DR. WEISS. I'm terribly sorry.

CAPTAIN. That's too bad.

DR. WEISS. So I'm free this evening and can be on watch as usual.

CAPTAIN *(to Dr. Weiss)*. What! Your son is being given the Sacrament of Holy Baptism tonight and you're going to be on watch?! . .

DR. WEISS. For one thing, it'll be after the ceremony, and for another . . .

IRINA *(having finished her diary entry, gets up and finishes Dr. Weiss's sentence)*. . . . it'll be a good example. *(Emphatically.)* So many here need one!

CAPTAIN. Oh come now, nurse!

PROFESSOR *(after raising his eyebrows)*. "So many"? . . Who, for instance?

CAPTAIN *(to Irina)*. The spirit of criticism is rather overdeveloped in your case.

IRINA. Well, wasn't I right the time . . . Remember how we hadn't been at sea more than a couple months before we had to return to the Black Sea to disembark three people to avoid moral contamination.

CAPTAIN. I've been trying to forget the whole thing, but you and it are simply inseparable—you'd think you just loved it . . . *(The Madman comes in from the right, carrying an enormous pile of home-made animal masks. With him are two laughing sailors also loaded down with masks.)*

MADMAN *(more fantastically dressed than the other citizens of Anchorite, he turns to the sailors who are brimming over with child-like merriment)*. This way, this way! . . Put 'em over here! . . Only watch where you're going! *(All three dump their loads behind the platform and straighten up the piles, and merrily get the separate masks ready for use.)*

CAPTAIN *(to the Madman)*. Are you going to start soon? . . It's almost sunset!

MADMAN. In a minute, in a minute! *(With the help of the sailors takes one of the benches from the bulwark and sets it in the center of the platform.)* But where can the guest of honor be?

BARBARA *(entering left with an infant in her arms)*. I'm bringing him right now! . . *(All greet their appearance with joyous exclamations.)*

MADMAN *(impatiently)*. Please be so good as to be seated, dear citizen-parents! How many invitations does it take? *(He seats the Weiss couple and their child on the bench.)* Anna and her group of dancers have been waiting! . . Sit as festively as you can . . . *(All laugh.)* Remember that the sacred Dance of the Merry Anchorite will be performed in your honor. Hold the baby up higher! . . As high as you can! Everybody's got to see him! . . Like a banner! This is our pledge to the future! . . *(All laugh approvingly and applaud.)* I'll run and give the signal! *(Runs off right accompanied by both sailors.)*

BARBARA *(with child raised high)*. Oh, our happiness! . . A free citizen of the country of Anchorite! . . Dost thou feel the hopes that thy appearance on earth bringeth forth? *(Meanwhile the sides of the stage have gradually filled with citizens of the Community of the Righteous, mostly men. Some have climbed onto the roof of the salon and are sitting on it with their legs hanging over the edge. The Captain, the Professor, and Irina all head left; the Captain disappears for a moment and then brings in some folding stools. Irina and the Professor express their gratitude as they sit on the stools. The Captain disappears once more and gets himself something to sit on. Three mighty blasts are heard on the ship's horn. Instantly the sounds of music from a small orchestra to the right are heard. The orchestra is playing The Dance of the Merry Anchorite. A row of girls and young men, all dressed up for the occasion, with sea-weed wreaths in their loose, flowing hair, and with fantastic flowers pinned to their belts, burst out from right led by Dream. They whirl around the platform performing the rousing, graceful Dance of the Merry Anchorite. In contrast to the first two parts the third part is a solo danced in a very provocative, bacchanalian fashion by Dream. She dances between the two ranks formed by the other dancers at the right and left of the stage. As the dance goes back to the first part again the dancers unpin the flowers from their belts and throw them at the Weisses and their baby. The finale of the dance is accompanied by unanimous, enthusiastic applause by all present.)*

CAPTAIN *(mounting the platform).* Allow me, in place of some formal speech, to recall here today an event from my early youth. My friend Isai and I when we were schoolboys together decided to flee to the end of the world and found an anarchic community there. But since *(tries to laugh, but is unable to, and only mumbles some hollow, jerky sounds "hm . . . hm . . . hm . . ."),* since we couldn't find any "end of the world" on the map we simply decided to abandon sinful land, and save ourselves from the injustices of the world on a fishing schooner somewhere far away in warm waters . . . We swore to each other to make this dream come true at the first opportunity. While waiting we made a toy ship and put on it cardboard figures of our friends and ourselves. We had hardly launched our little ship in the river, when . . . *(once more makes an unsuccessful attempt to laugh, creating an awkward pause for his listeners, a pause just barely filled with some strange gutteral sounds)* when a gust of wind hit and scattered . . . *(another effort to laugh)* och, it was so funny, so pitiful and funny . . . scattered the passengers in all directions and turned our poor little ship upside down . . . *(again tries to laugh).* A tragedy and a farce! . . A great idea and a childish attempt—all at once! Och! I could have died laughing . . . And so today I would like to say this to you: think of this little event, remember it, even on the calmest day! Don't forget that such gusts of wind, such unexpected whirlwinds are part of history, that whole peoples have been scattered like those cardboard figures. Only dreams, sensible, righteous dreams, will withstand the winds of time! The abolition of slavery, torture, class distinctions, private property, all of these were only dreams for centuries on end. A dream defeats the reality of the future. *(Takes the baby from Barbara and raises it high.)* Here before you is that very reality, in the form of the fruit of our dreams! This child was conceived and born in the Community of the Righteous and seems to be saying to you that nothing is impossible for real heroes, faithfully devoted to their bright dreams. *(Kisses the baby once more, hands it back to its mother and descends the platform to the friendly applause of all present.)*

MADMAN *(mounting the platform holding some sort of amulet on a silk string).* Today is the anniversary of Anchorite's departure for the high seas. During that year only three of us were unable to resist the siren call of the land, only a possessed three wished to go back to shore again, forcing us to sail back into the stormy Black Sea. You may well ask, why recall this unhappy event? Because it underlines the steadfastness of all the rest of us in resisting the siren calls of land. We find ourselves in company with the wise Odysseus who also resisted the call of the sirens. We even did him one better, dispensing with the rope he used to lash himself to the mast and the wax he stuffed in the ears of his crew. I put a tiny bit of each of these substances into this protective charm to go around the baby's neck, as a symbol of that classic steadfastness in the presence of the enticing calls of the land . . . And so let us hear, with the proper feeling, the insidious Song of the Sirens, which shall be a part of the Sacrament of Holy Baptism in this community from this day forward. *(Claps his hands three times, then, using his hands for a megaphone, yells in the direction of the door right.)* Eh, sirens, give it all you've got! . . Your song will only strengthen the resolution of us Anchorites! *(Stringed instruments and a female trio are heard off right. During the music Maestro Isai reverently kisses the charm and lovingly puts it on the baby's neck.)*

THREE SIRENS. *(Their voices off right are alluring, voluptuous, enticing.)*

> Come, oh godlike Odysseus, thou glory of Peloponnesus,
> Sail over here in your ship and delight in the siren's
> > sweet singing;
> Never a sea-faring fellow in thousands of years has
> > sailed past us,
> Once he has heard o'er these waves the enchanting sweet songs
> > sirens sing him.

MADMAN *(to all)*. Allow me, on behalf of all of us, to congratulate this infant on the occasion of his baptism on board and of his formal admittance into the ranks of the citizens of the country of Anchorite!

VOICES. Yes, yes! . . What's his name? . . What have you named him?

MADMAN *(kisses the baby, bows to him, then turns to the parents)*. They want to know what his name is!

BARBARA *(lifts the baby up high and rises)*. His name is Felix. I named him thus because Felix means "fortunate one," and he is fortunate indeed to have been born in a country filled with honest, kind people, where people don't fight each other, where rivers of human blood don't flow into seas of mothers' tears. *(With blissful tears she kisses the child. Warm applause and cries of "Hurray for Isai," during which the Weisses and their child come down from the platform. Those present surround them, extending their heartfelt congratulations. Those nearest the baby play with him, kiss him, try to take him in their arms. Meanwhile, in accordance with Maestro Isai's instructions, the bench has been brought down from the platform by his helpers. Upon their request the Weisses sit on it, together with the Captain and Irina, who happen to be close by at that moment. The sun is close to setting, making the horizon a flaming, fiery red.)*

MADMAN *(jokingly parodying the country fair impressario, rings a small bell to bring everybody together, while the two sailors pile the platform with animal masks).* We now have the great honor of presenting to our esteemed audience an excerpt from the tragi-comedy *Ham vs. Noah,* a play no censor in the world would allow on stage . . . The cast consists of: the patriarch Noah himself, his son Ham, and the latter's two wives—one blessed by children and the other not blessed by them. The action takes place on the deck of Noah's ark, not long before sunset. Since illusion is not the least important thing in the theater, and is what transpired on the ark—you note, besides the dramatis personnae only animals and a few birds Noah caught—the "management" respectfully requests the esteemed audience to put on the forementioned masks, turning the theater into a regular zoo. *(Rings his bell.)* Another great first in the theater! Complete theatrical illusion is achieved. A show exclusively for animals, for the benefit of the Society for the Prevention of Cruelty to Animals . . . Please be so kind as to pick out whatever mask suits you best! . . *(Shouts off right as he rings the bell.)* Music, the introduction! . . The show is on! . . *(Disappears right, as those present merrily and laughingly pounce on the animal masks, excitedly pick out the ones they like. They then put on the masks and deploy themselves in various half-lying, half-sitting positions in front of the improvised stage the platform has become. In the middle of the masked audience the masks of Dr. Weiss and his wife are distinguishable: he as a rooster, she as a hen, the child as a baby chick. The Captain is masked as an elephant and Irina as a cat. The musicians, offstage to the right in the ship's salon, are playing a dance in some exotic, primitive arrangement for a small band. On the platform appears Ham's First Wife, dressed in an antedeluvian, Biblical outfit, and holding a seven-stringed harp in her hand. She listens to the music in the distance, waits a moment, then begins her doleful speech.)*

HAM'S FIRST WIFE. She's always making him happy with her wild dances—with plenty of hips and instep to excite him. All hot and sweaty, her hair stuck together, she's trying to bewitch him. And here I am, I, his first wife, who has born his children and am great with yet another, swallowing my jealous tears, watching their ecstasy. Oh woe, woe is me! . . I'll just sit down here, me and my sorrow, and through my sobs sing a little song my sorrow and grief composed together. *(Sits on the platform in a voluptuously mournful pose and sings.)*

> Darling . . . my darling doesn't love me!
> Oh-h-h-h-h-h-h—woe!
> Strength . . . may God Almighty grant me!

Oh-h-h-h-h-h-h—woe!
Passion, heed this woman's prayer:
And melt like wax!
Head with pretty long black hair,
Develop cracks!
Strength . . . may God Almighty grant me!
Oh-h-h-h-h-h-h—woe!

(Enter Ham, played by the Madman. Ham is a handsome, strapping lad, only half-dressed in some exotic clothes. He has long, rusty-red hair and a gold band around his head. With scorn and pity he looks at his wife and addresses her as he would a child he has gotten tired of.)

HAM. Art thou crying again . . . One flood isn't enough for thee!. Here thou art trying to cry up a new one! Stop it! . . Anybody else in thy position would be rejoicing that the dove flew off and didn't come back! That means the earth has appeared somewhere, is drying off and ready for habitation by man and beast once more . . . Now thy children can defecate on it, stomp on the flowers, knock down birds' nests and fight over every little trifle, just like they used to . . I can see a high mountain over there already. The water recedes, giving us back the land, so thy children can multiply there, so that their great-grandchildren can fight wars over the best pieces. The clever and the powerful will again lord it over the weak and the simple, setting up laws that help the rich and hurt the poor . . . Rejoice! . . Tomorrow we'll land on the shore and the whole mess can start all over again, all for the benefit of that evil jester Jehovah, and the patriarch Noah, and thee ultimately, bringing up thy children to be obedient.

HAM'S FIRST WIFE. This passion for that other woman has fogged up thy head entirely! . . Am I to disobey God and not teach my children obedience? Are they to follow thy example, thou who disobeyeth thine own father?

HAM. Thou speakest well, but art best when silent. Put down thy harp and go find thy snotty little brats, thirsting for thy bulging nipples!

HAM'S FIRST WIFE *(handing him the harp)*. I'm quite aware that thou art fond of certain other nipples—sharp, empty ones! But I'm not going to be jealous of some barren fig tree.

HAM. Then why dost thou cry?

HAM'S FIRST WIFE. Because I love thee but get no response.

HAM. Thy lips speak of love for our grandchildren! But her lips—for it was her fate to be barren—speak of love only for me.

HAM'S SECOND WIFE *(enters, charmingly played by Dream, with tambourines in her hands and decked out in necklaces, bracelets and ankle bracelets)*. What happened to thee, my sweet? . . Thy father wants to know if thou hast fed the beasts for the glory of God! *(To her rival.)* Thou? Why art thou here, when thy children are off starving like little puppy dogs?

HAM'S FIRST WIFE. I'm going! I couldn't hear the little darlings for all my crying. *(She goes off.)*

HAM *(to her, with malicious laughter, as she leaves).* Go on then! Thy love for children was always mightier than thy love for me. *(To his Second Wife.)* Not like thee! Right? *(Pause.)* Why dost thou not say something?

HAM'S SECOND WIFE *(lowers her eyes, sways her hips, casting a spell with her beauty).* My dancing tells thee what I am.

HAM. True. But convince me of it. Show me over and over again that thou lovest me not for the sake of posterity, but for me myself! *(Kneels on one knee and plays the harp. His beloved, shaking the tambourines, dances to the music he plays. At the end of the dance Ham embraces her fervently.)* I know! I do! Thou lovest me! Now I know again that thou lovest me. *(Kisses her and speaks rapidly and passionately to her as he importunes her.)* Well, hast thou decided? It'll be like paradise, once we challenge those condemned to suffering. Nobody in the whole world! Nobody! Just us! Nobody but us two: I, who has defied God, and thou, whose womb is doomed to barrenness.

HAM'S SECOND WIFE *(agonizing hesitation).* But I feel sorry for them! I feel infinitely sorry for them!

HAM *(with angry irony).* Sorry for them? . . How about me? Me, subject to the will of a father deaf to the song of freedom?

HAM'S SECOND WIFE *(stressing each word).* He's the patriarch.

HAM *(surfeited with scorn, he spits toward the stage entrance right.)* In other words, I am fated to be a slave? . . Fated to continue the antedeluvian way of life? . .

HAM'S SECOND WIFE *(glances off right).* Shh! . . He's coming this way. *(The ancient Noah—played by the Professor—enters right. He is wearing an antedeluvian, patriarchal robe. In his left hand he carries a basket of fodder, and in his right an old-fashioned umbrella, which he opens as he enters.)*

HAM *(to Noah, ironically).* Why be a laughing stock for the animals! The rain stopped long ago, but thou appearest with an umbrella!

NOAH *(gumming his words comically).* Stopped? . . But it seemed to me it was sprinkling again.

HAM. That was me spitting out of annoyance.

NOAH. Some spitter! . . Thou art a real master at it . . . *(Stands his umbrella on the floor.)* Ah well! Let it dry off a little. It's never had a chance to get good and dry . . . it poured like out of buckets for forty days and forty nights! Even with a raincoat on you got wet. *(Grabs the small of his back.)* Ah, this damned dampness! . . Rheumatism makes my whole back ache . . . *(He sneezes.*) And a cold on top of that . . . The punishment of the Lord, to be sure. *(Blows his nose rather crudely.)* Well? Hast thou fed the animals?

HAM. Dost thou hear any complaints?

NOAH. Well, I'll give them a little more. *(He feeds the animals, tossing cookies among those masked, producing a scramble to catch them, people sampling them, laughter, and approving remarks.)* Eat, my little animals! . . Chew heartily! Eat for your health, so that in your gratitude you may give us juicier meat, tastier milk, more eggs. Sheep, grow plenty of wool so you'll be worth clipping! Horses, grow stronger so as to suit the saddle and the plow better! Fatten up bulls, grow hides good for straps, whips, and shoes! . . Remember, if it hadn't been for me the sharks would have devoured you long ago! The Supreme Being saved me because of the saintly life I led! Just as I in my turn took mercy upon you.

HAM *(putting a hand on Noah's shoulder).* Enough lies there, old-timer! Makes me sick to listen. Don't believe him, animals! There were better people than Noah—not so rich, to be sure, as to own an ark this size! "Only fools are lucky," as the old saying goes. He lucked out, the others didn't! And that's the whole story of my papa's saintliness.

NOAH *(scratching himself).* God Almighty—just aching for a fight! If I curse thee, disown thee, it will be too late then!

HAM. Thy curse is a blessing to me. *(Laughs loudly.)*

NOAH. Rude! Arrogant! . . Why the hell did I take thee on the ark, thou monster?

HAM. Somebody had to be here to let you in on the truth! . . I couldn't leave it only to the insects to sting thee, in order to prove how nice it is for the victim whose blood is being drunk! . . *To his Second Wife, motioning toward Noah.)* Yech, scratching himself! . . And he had to go and save all those nasty fleas, lice, and bedbugs . . . But too cowardly to take along the ichthyosaurs and the brontosauruses, no mammoths either—he was too scared! If it hadn't been for me he'd have let the beautiful tigers and lions and eagles all drown. He can't stand strength and pride in independent creatures . . . Anybody else's greatness annoys him . . . The cockroach gets an honored place on the ark, but the mammoth—death in the watery abyss!

NOAH *(picks up the umbrella, folds it up very carefully and turns to leave).* Ah, just wait, young man, till the day people remember you as one of history's scoundrels! *(On the way out he grabs the harp and sticks it in his basket.)* Thou hast no common sense! That's why thou rebelest, to the everlasting sorrow of thy descendants . . . Give in while there's still time! Give in so I won't curse thee! Thou knowest well it costs me nothing! One, two, three, it's done! *(Goes off.)*

HAM *(passionately, to his wife)*. The sun's going down. See! It depends on us whether it'll come up tomorrow on a world free from tyranny and vulgarity! All we have to do is turn this pathetic ark into a coffin for Noah and his buddies, and then . . . thou and I shall reign over the earth, like Adam and Eve, with no thoughts of descendants . . . We'll slay them! We'll slay them this very night while they're having dreams about their beastly rule over the earth! We'll slay them so that suffering, repression, war, this vale of tears and grief shall disappear forever. We'll slay them, as a challenge to God, in the name of rebellion against God, in the name of higher beauty, of the perfect happiness of all-consuming love! *(The sun dips below the horizon and the bloody-crimson sky begins to fade into the onrushing twilight.)*

HAM'S SECOND WIFE. But darling, you mustn't cause *more* deaths! Don't be like the very God that you despise for repression! Don't continue his deluge with another—a deluge of blood! I don't believe in a happiness washed by the blood of the innocent! I believe that the spirit of thy rebelleion will not die in thy innocent children! . . I believe that in the course of centuries it will overcome the power of antedeluvian law! . . I believe that the fruit of thy loins will shatter the chains of slavery and bring happiness to all, Everybody! Not annihilation, but happiness, not destruction in Evil, but ressurection in Goodness! *(The lament of Ham's First Wife is heard off right: "Darling, my darling doesn't love me." It breaks off in the middle of the first verse. Ham's Second Wife bows to Ham, kisses his hand and slowly goes off right.)*

HAM *(stares ahead steadily and speaks slowly, deliberately, as if each word were being weighed carefully)*. What a great historical opportunity is being missed this night! Poor mankind! . . This contemptible pity! . . *(He leaves. A pause. The spectators, at first indecisively, then with increasing warmth, applaud. The four members of the cast come out and bow. Scattered voices, "author, author." The Madman responds to the cries and bows low to the audience. The windows and door of the ship's salon light up and the sounds of the Ocean Waltz are heard. One of the young men cries: "Bal masqué comme vous etes . . . Valse generale! . ." The spectators respond immediately and proceed in couples to the salon, waltzing as they go, still in their fantastic animal masks. Irina takes the baby from Barbara and, rocking him gently, carries him off left, while the baby's mother goes off to the salon with someone who has invited her to dance. Dr. Weiss glances at his watch, sits down and relaxes on the bulwark to the left of the platform. The Professor, with guitar in hand and his costume and makeup now off, appears shortly and sits by Dr. Weiss. A small cloud on the horizon has meanwhile blocked out part of the star-filled sky. Elsa and the Walking Joke, both in half-masks, accompany the Captain across the apron. The Captain is now free of his enormous elephant mask.)*

CAPTAIN *(kissing Elsa on the forehead)*. Go ahead, my dear, enjoy yourself! . .

ELSA. But what about you . . .

CAPTAIN *(interrupting)*. Don't worry! A little dizziness! I'm simply tired, that's all . . .

ELSA. You ought to lie down more often . . . and you shouldn't get worked up over anything.

CAPTAIN. Maybe I'll do just that . . . Spend a couple days in bed . . . Fine idea! *(Leading her off a little distance away from her partner.)* Tomorrow I'll give you all the documents . . . for the ship and the rest.

ELSA. What for?

CAPTAIN. In case anything should happen to me. *(Almost whispering, with a smile)*. I hope you're not going to blab about the secret of ownership . . .

ELSA. . . . of *our* ship? How could you have any doubts?

CAPTAIN. Remember, no sooner than two years from the day of departure!

ELSA *(passionately, interrupting him)*. Could you really not trust me?

CAPTAIN *(interrupting her in turn)*. I was just joking. Be sure and remind me tomorrow! *(Kisses her goodbye tenderly and walks off left.)*

WALKING JOKE *(taking Elsa by the arm)*. What's this? Your papa has a weak heart? Ill again?

ELSA. Oh no, he has a wonderful heart! . . The best in the world . . .

WALKING JOKE. Well sure, rather good, but very bad?

ELSA *(almost laughing)*. I would say—rather bad, but very good. *(They go off right to the salon, closing the door behind them and muffling the sounds of music.)*

DR. WEISS *(to the Professor)*. I fear that the Captain . . . that is . . .

PROFESSOR. Well, what?

DR. WEISS. Is not long for this world . . .

PROFESSOR. Yes, poor fellow looks bad . . .

DR. WEISS. The slightest disturbance and . . . *(Irina comes hurrying across the stage from left.)* Where are you going, nurse? Come over here and talk to us!

IRINA. No time now! Later!

PROFESSOR *(to her as she hurries off)*. Ah, busy as ever! *(To Dr. Weiss.)* Energy to spare! . . She's like a tightly wound spring! . . What she needs is a good man to unwind her, then she'd forget all these ideas about . . . *(Says something in Dr. Weiss's ear. Two sailors sneak in left on the apron. One has a red beard, the other wears glasses. They look around to see who is on watch.)*

FIRST SAILOR. Of course it's him! . . You're always arguing . . .

SECOND SAILOR. Is he the one they tried to get off watch? . .

FIRST SAILOR. So what! . . *(They go off left. The music in the salon stops.)*

PROFESSOR *(plucking the guitar strings, hums some ancient tune with a shaky voice)*.

I long for creaking masts and whistling shrouds,
For mighty waves to roil the ocean deep.

FIRST SAILOR. *(comes in from the left again with his fellow sailor. The other sailor makes some sort of reassuring gesture to someone offstage left.)* Pardon us, Doctor, are we disturbing you?

DR. WEISS. Not at all! What's up?

SECOND SAILOR. It's such a special day today . . . a "holiday," so to say . . .

DR. WEISS. Yes, and so?

FIRST SAILOR. We wanted to petition for an anmesty.

DR. WEISS. An "amnesty"? . . What sort of talk is that! Ask me for "amnesty"? . .

SECOND SAILOR. Not just you, but everybody . . .

DR. WEISS. What's it all about? . . What's happened? . .

FIRST SAILOR *(hesitantly)*. It was when we weighed anchor . . . In the Black Sea . . .

DR. WEISS. Well?

SECOND SAILOR *(getting ahead of himself, hurriedly)*. We did it out of kindness . . . He was so pitiful . . .

DR. WEISS. Who was so pitiful? . . What happened? . . Stop talking in riddles! *(The cloud on the horizon has drifted off upward in the meantime and has now uncovered the four bright stars of the Southern Cross.)*

PROFESSOR *(interrupting)*. Look! There it is, the Southern Cross! . .

DR. WEISS *(looking at the sky)*. Yes, yes . . . *(Pause.)* Beautiful . . .

PROFESSOR. Wonderful! . . *(Pause.)*

DR. WEISS *(to the Sailors)*. Well? Are you going to tell me or aren't you?

FIRST SAILOR *(after a short pause)*. There's a . . . a stowaway on board . . .

DR. WEISS

PROFESSOR A stowaway?

DR. WEISS. How did he get on board?

FIRST SAILOR. We smuggled him on board . . . when we anchored that time . . . He begged us . . .

SECOND SAILOR. He's a great guy . . . no worse than anybody else here, you'll see yourself.

DR. WEISS *(agitated)*. Where is he? Who is he?

FIRST SAILOR. Just a minute . . . *(Goes left with his comrade, then turns around.)* But first we request amnesty . . . it's such a big celebration today . . .

DR. WEISS *(interrupting)*. Tell him to come here! . . *(The Sailors disappear left and immediately return with a third, dressed as they are. Dr. Weiss freezes in astonishment. A pause. He speaks in a constrained voice.)* Is it you, Vitalius?

VITALIUS. Yes . . . it's me.

DR. WEISS *(deliberately)*. You . . . here?

VITALIUS. I . . . am here! . . *(At right is heard the mighty refrain of the Anthem of the Community of the Righteous: "There where reigns the mighty ocean, far from sinful land's desire . . ." and so forth. Those present freeze in calm, respectful poses. Both sailors take off their caps. Vitalius bows his head and follows their example.*

CURTAIN.

ACT THREE

DREAM. *(She appears in front of the curtain, which is trembling and waiting to rise. She turns sideways to the audience, and speaks offstage, half-begging, half-commanding.)* Don't raise the curtain! . . Don't! You hear? . . End the show! . . In the name of a higher truth I implore you. The truth of the creative imagination! Don't touch the curtain! Let it conceal the future! Leave it down, leave the curtain down! *(To the audience.)* Dear audience! This actress speaks to you from the depths of her heart! An actress who has blended with her role into one indivisible unity! An actress who believes in the triumph of the dream she embodies! Consider the show is over! It's not so hard, all you have to do is wish it so! *(Claps of thunder and the sounds of a rising storm at sea are heard.)* Leave this theater with a light heart before it is disturbed by the author, the actors, the director, all ready to raise the treacherous curtain . . . Oh yes, treacherous! Because that curtain conceals the betrayal of dream to desecration, to ridicule, to disgrace! . . I cannot, how can I perform in a play where the author says one thing in the beginning and another in the end I am an actress who lives her role, not a puppet who suffers no pain from being jerked hither and yon! And I'll warn you right now that I won't play the part any longer, a part where the author winds up leaving out the fiery words and putting in only pauses and silence in the presence of the voice of life! . . I'm not going to be silent in its presence! I'm not going to submit the way he does! I protest! I call upon you to revolt! The destruction of ideals has no place in the theater, where illusion, greater than truth, is inspired by dream! Revenge yourselves on the author, who has betrayed the very essence of theater! Leave this place as if the play had ended! Go away with your own illusions, if the author is unwilling to comfort you with illusion! Leave, before the curtain rises and before your very eyes . . . *(The curtain rises, revealing the scene for Act III. It is a foul, threatening, lead-gray day.)* Too late! . . Oh woe! Woe! . . The Anchorite will perish! My greatest achievement will perish! . . (She runs off. The threatening clouds disperse, but the horizon is still hidden behind a thick, rainy shroud, looking like some impenetrable fog. As the curtain rises voices off left are heard: "Over here! . . Quick!! Eh! . . Hold that line . . . don't let go! . . Secure it! . . Hurry! . . Damn! . . Are you blind or something?!. Take a strain! C'mon." Several men run out from behind the salon and head left, swaying from side to side, and answering "Coming! . . Hang on! . . Don't let go! . ." The Madman comes on right by the bulwark. Barbara catches up to him at the bulwark.)*
MADMAN. Courage! Courage! . . The wind is dying down! . . Don't be afraid, the danger has passed! . .

BARBARA. Thank the Lord! . . Where is my husband? . .

MADMAN. I just saw him on the mast . . . Calm down!

BARBARA. As if he were seeking out death! . . Why all this bravado! . .
Tell him! After all, he's not a sailor, to go . . . (*Her words are drowned out by a call* "*Isai*" *at left.*)

MADMAN (*shouting*). Coming! (*Runs off left accompanied by Barbara. The Professor and Elsa come out of the salon door right.*)

PROFESSOR. It's calming down I tell you! Can't you see? Have another cognac and your nervousness will go away! . .

ELSA. I've got to see Father.

PROFESSOR. Nurse Irina was just with him . . .

ELSA. Oh, this storm! . . Who could have imagined! . .

PROFESSOR. But it's already passed! What are you talking about? . .

ELSA. Father just got out of his bunk yesterday . . . He'd been there for two months! . . And then suddenly this storm . . .

PROFESSOR. Sit over here! . . You need some fresh air. Away with these fears! The Captain's an old sea-dog and storms mean nothing to him. Take a few deep, slow breaths! That'll relax you. (*He sits on the platform.*)

ELSA (*sitting next to him*). There was nothing like this, even on the ocean.

PROFESSOR. What do you expect? The Black Sea is famous for storms—you even read about it in schoolbooks.

ELSA. They say some of the fishing gear was carried away . . . one of the boats too, and it's banging against the side . . .

PROFESSOR (*reassuringly*). They'll recover it . . . Isai himself went to help them . . .

ELSA. Well, that's small consolation when *real* help is needed.

PROFESSOR. You don't have any faith in his great talents?

ELSA. Depends on what we're talking about!

PROFESSOR. You've changed a great deal recently.

ELSA. Not for the worse, I hope?

PROFESSOR. How shall I put it! . . You've grown old beyond your years!

ELSA (*half-offended, half-joking*). I never was a child!

PROFESSOR. Never? . . Then you're a miracle! (*They laugh.*) No, all jokes aside, you've become terribly serious! . . Your attitude toward administration, toward the community's property . . . simply unheard of at your age! You work at it as if the ship were *your private possession.* That, of course, is all very fine indeed, but . . .

ELSA (*bites her lip, gets up and hurriedly changes the subject*). What do you think, are we far from shore now?

PROFESSOR. I'm afraid we've been set back. However . . . Do you see how far off the rain is now! . . Don't you feel better now?

ELSA. Thank the L . . . thank who? The cognac? *(Vitalius comes in left near the bulwark. He is sweaty, tired, flushed.)*

VITALIUS. Whew! . . Damn it! . . Man, am I pooped! . .

PROFESSOR. Were you pumping the bilges?

VITALIUS. I'm dying for a drink.

ELSA *(leaping up)*. I'll get you one! *(Runs off into the salon.)*

VITALIUS *(sits in Elsa's place and wipes off his sweat)*. Damn it to hell, I thought I'd get a little rest and relaxation here! Instead, I've been working like a goddamn . . . We can't get there soon enough for me! Messing around for nothing—three months.

PROFESSOR. You should have asked to be left off before!

VITALIUS. It didn't suit me before!

PROFESSOR. Why not?

VITALIUS *(with a big, stupid grin)*. I wanted to have time to marvel at all of you.

PROFESSOR. Well, have you?

VITALIUS. Thoroughly. Too much!

PROFESSOR. Don't care for it?

VITALIUS. How about you?

PROFESSOR. Me? What a question!

VITALIUS. Oh hell, we've jabbered on about this enough already . . . Damn it to hell, you really put one over on me!

PROFESSOR. Me? How?

VITALIUS. And not only you! . . Great sport! Tried to get on this scientific research ship, learn a thing or two, but look what it turns out to be! . . A floating monastery of unearthly dreamers! . . *(Elsa enters with a glass of wine.)* Thank you! *(Takes the glass and drains it.)* That's good! . . *(To her.)* Well then, we're heading for shore? Eh? . . Had enough tripping around?

ELSA. Shh! . . You take everything seriously!

PROFESSOR. Perhaps I should leave? You have some private matters to discuss?

ELSA. Oh come now! . . Nothing of the kind! . .

VITALIUS. Tell me, citizens! Only mind you now, be honest! . . Aren't you really sick of all this nonsense?

PROFESSOR. What nonsense?

ELSA. What are you driving at?

VITALIUS. Driving at? . . And you stand there with a straight face! . . Tell me then, why they had to put the English sailors ashore? Eh? . . Why, there's only a handful of the crew left by now!

ELSA. That's not for you to ask.

VITALIUS. Why not?

ELSA. Because before you showed up there wasn't any fighting or drunkenness!

VITALIUS. Oh, so I was the one who did it? Very nice! And why are they putting the Russians ashore now? How many? Five, or is it more? You should know!

PROFESSOR. Well, my friend, when it comes to assaulting the girls, fighting over them, and debaucheries . . .

VITALIUS. And the reason for all this?

PROFESSOR. The "reason"?

VITALIUS. Do you know the boys have been making up stories about themselves and set up these debaucheries on purpose?

ELSA. On purpose? Worse yet.

VITALIUS. And why, ask yourself, why? *(Meanwhile the Walking Joke has entered right and is walking by the bulwark and looking jealously at Elsa and Vitalius.)*

PROFESSOR. All right then, why, in your opinion?

VITALIUS *(from the heart)*. Because it's so godawful dull around here! Killing boredom, stinking dreariness! There's nothing to struggle for! There's nothing to do here! There's nothing to gain! People make up awful stories about themselves, just to be saved as soon as possible from this damned paradise you've grown around here, like mould! Why, you've drowned in your "virtues," like kittens in a pot of cream! You're looking for a way out! I can tell.

PROFESSOR. What a metaphor!

VITALIUS. It's a lovely metaphor! The cream of virtue, like ordinary cream, turns sour in a storm!

ELSA. So you consider your appearance here to be a "storm"?

VITALIUS. There'd be plenty of "electricity" in the air even without me. Can't you feel how suffocating the air has gotten? You just ought to hear these "righteous" people around here tear each other apart! They can't speak frankly to you, but with me, who doesn't really belong here, they complain like mad!

ELSA. Well, what do they say then?

VITALIUS *(with a big, stupid grin)*. Hm . . . Are you really interested in what gossipy old women, people sick with envy, tattle-tales, slander-mongers, and malcontents have to say? . . You mean you've begun to relish gossip just like everybody else? *(He laughs.)*

ELSA. Of course not, but where's the proof? . . This is all totally unsubstantiated!

VITALIUS. Oh stop pretending, as if you yourself didn't know perfectly well! Just the nicknames around here say a lot! . .

PROFESSOR. What nicknames? What are you talking about?

VITALIUS *(laughing)*. All kinds.

PROFESSOR. Like what, for instance! This is amusing.

VITALIUS. "The Brandy Swiller."

PROFESSOR. What?

VITALIUS. "The Brandy Swiller."

PROFESSOR. Whose nickname is that?

VITALIUS *(laughing)*. Yours, it seems.

PROFESSOR. Ve-ry witty. Who thought that one up?

VITALIUS. Won't find me gossiping.

PROFESSOR. I know, but tell me anyway!

ELSA *(laughing)*. It was my idea. I just love the idea of swilling brandy! I was just joking.

PROFESSOR. A terrific joke, I must say.

ELSA *(to Vitalius)*. And what's mine?

VITALIUS. What do you want me to do? Get you at each other's throats?

ELSA. Won't bother me! Tell me!

PROFESSOR. Sure you won't get mad?

ELSA. I swear.

PROFESSOR. "Mademoiselle Bitch."

ELSA. Pooh, how idiotic! . . *(To the Professor.)* That's to pay me back for locking up the wine cellar, I suppose? Wasn't it?

PROFESSOR. In all probability.

ELSA. Well, Professor, I certainly thought you were more witty than that!

PROFESSOR. I had a different opinion of you too. *(A strained pause.)*

VITALIUS. Oh stop it! Why get all upset! . . The reason we're all bitter is this endless goodness we parade around like a child with a new toy! *(To Elsa.)* Get me something more to drink! . . only *(winking at her)* a little stronger this time! . . All right?

PROFESSOR. One for me too, while you're at it! . . On the occasion of our deliverance from the storm!

ELSA *(laughs poisonously)*. You want me to prove the absurdity of my nickname and the accuracy of yours? Very well! *(Goes into the salon.)*

PROFESSOR *(laughing)*. She was offended! . .

VITALIUS. Well, of course! She thinks she's perfect! . .

PROFESSOR. How about you? Disenchanted with her?

VITALIUS. Got a good taste of her.

PROFESSOR. Not so tasty?

VITALIUS. The yeast's gotten stale . . . bourgeois dough.

PROFESSOR. So-o . . . *(Looks into the distance.)* The sea has really calmed down a lot!

VITALIUS. We're probably in the lee of some hill now! . . The shore feels close by!

WALKING JOKE *(appears left upstage and immediately comes over and attacks Vitalius).* Why're you sitting there not doing anything? Promised to pay for the voyage with your labor, but spend your time turning girls' heads instead! . . Go on! They've got to re-load!

VITALIUS. Why the hell did they unload?

WALKING JOKE. They the hell unloaded so the ship wouldn't sink! . . A sailor and he doesn't know when to get rid of excess weight!

VITALIUS. Excess weight? . . They should have started with you! . . And now the ship's got a list on; they threw practically the whole library overboard! For the fish to laugh at! . .

WALKING JOKE *(caustically).* No point feeling sorry for harmful books any more than for harmful people! . . Get to work!

VITALIUS. Why is it they feel sorry for you, then?

WALKING JOKE *(restraining his ire).* Look here,, my *friend,* you don't know my temper very well, or you wouldn't talk that way!

DR. WEISS *(entering).* What's going on?

WALKING JOKE. The nets got snarled under the ship . . . we've got to hoist them up . . . otherwise they'll tear loose . . . and he's just sitting there! . .

DR. WEISS *(interrupting).* Let's go . . . I'll help! *(Elsa appears in the doorway of the salon with a bottle of wine and two glasses on a tray.)*

WALKING JOKE. How about him? Promised to work, but actually . . .

DR. WEISS. Don't force the issue! I'll help you! *(Leads him left.)*

PROFESSOR *(to Elsa).* And the third glass?

ELSA. I don't want any. *(Puts the tray on the platform.)*

PROFESSOR. We'll see about that. And if I get it myself? *(He rises.)*

ELSA *(starts to go).* All right! I'll get it myself.

PROFESSOR *(clicking heels and bowing).* No, Madam, allow me! *(Caustically.)* It's my rule always to repay kindness with kindness. *(Disappears into the salon. Elsa looks around, then quickly kneels by Vitalius, embraces him around the neck and gives him a long kiss.)*

VITALIUS *(gently).* Crazy woman! . . This is hardly the time or place!

ELSA *(tearing herself away from him exhausted).* Oh! . . You're really driving me crazy! . . And not just me either . . . All the girls are wild over you! . . You're like a movie-star! A real Don Juan! . . Or else we really have a craving for evil, sin, the abyss that makes your head whirl! . . You have aroused those instincts in everybody which we'd do better not to think about! . . You're terrifying! . . Utterly shameless! . . Yours is some terrible truth that forces one to run away from you and . . . to you! . . I don't understand anything! What have you done with all of us? Why do we put up with your contempt, your rudeness, and then fight each other for a glance from you?

VITALIUS *(laughing)*. What nonsense that is! I don't have anything special.

ELSA. But you have so much strength!

VITALIUS. Well, of course: the atmosphere here is so enervating that all of your men . . .

ELSA. Ah, no, that's not it.

VITALIUS. . . . have gotten soft in this life in a greenhouse! . .

ELSA *(kissing him)*. Shut up! . . You repulsive man! . .

VITALIUS. Well then, are you going ashore?

ELSA. Did you come here for *me,* or . . . for *her?*

VITALIUS. For who?

ELSA. Well, for that one! For your former lover?

VITALIUS. But I told you, we didn't have an affair! . .

ELSA. Oh sure, keep talking! . . That's why her husband took a shot at you! . . When you were first smuggled on board you were afraid to go after her! But then you worked up your nerve and . . .

VITALIUS *(half-offended)*. What's nerve got to do with it? My foot was hurt then so I was laid up! . . You don't know anything! . . And you don't know Barbara either, that's just a lot of empty talk!

ELSA. Well, of course! . . How can we compare to her! . . But why are you trying to lure *me* ashore?!.

VITALIUS. Why in the hell should you mope around here? . . We'll take your father with us! . . He can recover his health at a sanatorium and get a job taking people on boat rides.

ELSA *(laughs)*. What a wild idea! . . And the ship?

VITALIUS. And the ship too! Give up this crazy idea of his! We need coastal liners anyway!

ELSA *(half-coquettishly, half-seriously)*. So that's why you came to see us? I understand. *(Barbara appears left by the bulwark.)* Oh, you brigand! *(She embraces him.)* Aren't you ashamed? Aren't you? Speak up! . . *(Kisses him and then seemingly gets angry at herself.)* Do you seriously believe that a mere boy like you is going to get us all on your side?

BARBARA *(approaching them, with a smile)*. Well, if not everybody, then certainly some of us!

ELSA *(half-distraught)*. Ahh! . . Barbara Nikolaevna! What wonderful hearing you have! . . But why are you so pale? . . Are you not well? Wouldn't you like to have a little wine with us for your health's sake?

BARBARA *(evasively)*. There are only two glasses . . .

ELSA. The third will be here in a moment . . . *(In the direction of the salon door.)* Where did he disappear to?

BARBARA. Your suitor?

ELSA. I don't have any.

BARBARA. Think of that! And he considers himself . . .

ELSA. That's his idea! . . But you know they don't call him the Walking Joke for nothing! . . *(She yells off right.)* Professor! Where are you? . . *(Turns around.)* I'll run get him! . . *(Runs off right.)*

BARBARA *(laughs).* So? . . The women have been wearing you down? . . Eh? . . All tired out?

VITALIUS *(lights his pipe).* Too much time on their hands! . . There's nothing for them to do around here! . .

BARBARA. But just the same, you like her a lot? . . Right, a lot? Yes? Confess now, it was she that made you take the risk of coming here? Why don't you say something? . . I am not, my dear, going to get jealous, now that our relationship is over!

VITALIUS *(in a coarsely tender tone of reproach).* Barbara Nikolaevna, don't you torment me too! . . Why the hell this interrogation after I already explained . . .

BARBARA. Explained what?

VITALIUS. . . . explained to what lengths a man's egotism will drive him when he's been discarded like a piece of trash! . . *(Gets up.)* That's it! I couldn't, I wouldn't believe that you had ceased to love me!

BARBARA *(derisively).* And so, to convince yourself it was true . . .

VITALIUS. I stop at nothing . . .

BARBARA . . . you appear here and begin flirting with someone else, so as to arouse my jealousy? Wasn't that it?

VITALIUS *(half-offended).* Well, if you don't believe . . . if it's not perfectly clear to you what precisely drew me here.

BARBARA *(ironically).* Ah yes, the machinery! . . Now I remember! It was the latest model steam turbines! . . They fascinate you more than the women!

VITALIUS. To put it bluntly, a slick piece of machinery is more entertaining than a talentless coquette.

BARBARA. Oh, you're so right about Elsa.

VITALIUS. You've gotten to be a regular bitch! Really! This place has spoiled your angelic character for sure!

BARBARA. You think so?

VITALIUS. I hardly recognize you, honest to God! I'm really starting to be afraid of you!

BARBARA *(laughs).* You'd do better to be afraid of your Elsa's suitor. Out of commiseration I opened his eyes to your relations with her.

VITALIUS. So sweet of you! But why the hell start a fight! . . Actually I could care less what he thinks of me! I care about what you think of me.

BARBARA. What difference will it make, if we're just going to part again!

VITALIUS *(hotly)*. But I wanted to part as friends this time. You promised to give me a commission . . . to see what I could do to cheer up your sister who is waiting so impatiently for your return.

BARBARA *(with a mournful smile)*. Tell her I am happy, that I have a child . . . Yes, yes! Don't smile; I'm very, very happy! But . . .

VITALIUS. I'm listening.

BARBARA. And tell her also, so as to "cheer her up," that happiness without struggle, without a future, is a terribly wearisome happiness! . . . Although . . .

VITALIUS. Although?

BARBARA *(after a pause)*. Perhaps I'd better tell her myself.

VITALIUS *(dumbfounded, joyfully)*. You're going ashore? You are? . . Terrific! . . *(Out of the salon right come a group of girls led by Elsa and the Professor. The girls are carrying a decanter of wine and some glasses, the Professor a guitar. They all arrange themselves on the platform as for a feast, drink wine, clink their glasses noisily, and laugh. Vitalius turns to the new arrivals, then leads Barbara further downstage as he continues the speech he has begun.)*

VITALIUS. When you see how life has be reconstructed, how everyone is hard at work, how the level of culture has risen, how much has already been done while you were here . . There's no need to say more. You'll see yourself! Everywhere you look! . . You won't recognize the boardinghouse! Turned into a sanatorium! And what a sanatorium! That Ivanov turned out to be a genius of an engineer!

BARBARA. Is my sister marrying him?

VITALIUS. How did you know?

BARBARA. It's been going on for a long time! . . How about the others? You said that Sorokin . . .

VITALIUS. You'll die laughing! . . Got me to give a letter from him to nurse Irina . . . Promises to endow hospital beds in her name, invest in the sanatorium, if she'll only . . .

BARBARA. He wants to get married?

VITALIUS. That's right! He sleeps and dreams of nothing but her. Honest to God! Even got totally absorbed in his work out of sheer loneliness! and became a fantastic administrator!

BARBARA. Tomorrow's the second of May! My sister's birthday! . .

VITALIUS. The second of May?!. Today's the first?!. Damn it to hell! That's right! I've lost my memory here! *(Unexpectedly turns to the surrounding merrymakers.)* Hey, fellas, how about a little swim in the waves of Moscow radio?

PROFESSOR, ELSA, AND OTHERS. What's up?

VITALIUS. Today's the first of May! Spring is celebrating together with the working class! Speeches! . . meetings, music! . . What time is it?

ELSA *(looks at her wrist watch).* Exactly one o'clock!

VITALIUS. Just the time! *(To Barbara.)* Wasn't a bad idea bringing a radio aboard with me! *(Starts to go off left.)*

BARBARA *(restraining him).* Don't! There'll be another uproar! Don't you remember how Isai once and for all . . .

VITALIUS *(interrupts, laughing).* Baloney! He won't hear! And anyway— enough of this *Madman Dictatorship! (Runs off downstage left.)*

PROFESSOR *(tuning his guitar).* Barbara Nikolaevna! Would you like to hear a new chorus for the anthem? . . Come over here then!

BARBARA *(approaching).* For our anthem?

ELSA *(raising a glass of wine).* Your health, my fellow citizens! To our deliverance from death! *(She drinks.)*

BARBARA *(to the Professor).* Another parody?

PROFESSOR. A joke by some unknown author. *(He sings to a very simple, crude accompaniment on the guitar.)*

> There where reigns the mighty ocean
> Far from sinful land's desire
> Where instead of Good promotin'
> The crew now forms a looney choir.
>
> Relishing this world's temptations
> Laughing at high aspirations . . .

ONE OF THE GIRLS *(notices Isai and the Walking Joke approaching in the distance, then coughs loudly and raises her glass).* To our deliverance from death! *(She drinks. The Madman and the Walking Joke pass right upstage. The Madman goes off, the Walking Joke remains upstage with his arms crossed.)*

PROFESSOR *(as if nothing had happened, shifts without missing a beat into his sentimental rendition).*

> I long for creaking masts and whistling shrouds,
> For mighty waves to roil the ocean deep.

(General laughter.)

BARBARA. Parody seems to be the latest fashion around here! Why profane your own highest ideals? *(Vitalius enters left with a radio. He puts the receiver up on the platform and sets up an antenna.)*

PROFESSOR. You can't be wearing heroic masks all the time! People are people! . .

BARBARA. Oh, I've become more convinced of it here than anywhere else! But you aren't sorry for the dream? Aren't you sorry for those who tried to deceive life and then wound up being deceived by it?

VITALIUS. You won't deceive life! A hopeless task! That's why it and your "play" all turned out ridiculous—because you turned away from real life. *(Pointing at the radio receiver he has set up.)* Now then, fellas, would you care to hear how far we are from life?

WALKING JOKE *(familiarly approaching Vitalius).* Spreading propaganda again? You haven't spread enough confusion already?

VITALIUS. Mind your own business. Don't butt in! Let's be a little more polite around here!

WALKING JOKE. Your own words aren't enough, you've got to find somebody else's to seduce everybody?

VITALIUS. That's it. I wouldn't borrow them from you!

WALKING JOKE *(maliciously).* Clear out, I warn you, while I can still ask you honorably.

VITALIUS *(laughs good-naturedly).* Honor! That rubbish!

WALKING JOKE. What rubbish?

VITALIUS. Your honor stinks like garbage.

WALKING JOKE. Like what?

VITALIUS. Stinks of the Middle Ages.

WALKING JOKE *(To those around him).* The man's gone mad!

VITALIUS. Do you suppose that honor hasn't changed over the centuries like everything else? You lie, brother, everything changes, liberates itself from ancient superstitions. Only idiots fail to see it.

WALKING JOKE *(grabbing Vitalius by the sleeve and drawing him close).* I'm an idiot?!

VITALIUS. *(with his fist knocks the hand off his sleeve).* Let's be a little more careful there! *(The Walking Joke answers with a blow aimed at the face, but Vitalius dodges it, knocking his opponent back with a blow to the chest. The fight is on.)*

BARBARA *(yells).* You've both gone mad! . . Crazy! . . Stop it! . . *(To the professor.)* Stop them!

PROFESSOR. Oh no, excuse me, we have a principle of "non-resistance to evil" around here. *(Rescues the wine and the glasses and takes them into the salon while the girls eagerly follow the course of the battle.)*

FIRST GIRL. First time I ever saw . . . Is that boxing?

VITALIUS *(striking a blow).* Something like it! . .

BARBARA. How horrible! . . Such bestiality! We've got to get help! . . They'll cripple each other! . . *(Runs off left.)*

SECOND GIRL *(squealing)*. I'm scared! . .

ELSA. So why are you watching? Go away! *(She laughs.)*

SECOND GIRL. But I never saw . . .

ELSA. Then keep watching and don't squeal! . .

FIRST GIRL. *(after a blow has been struck)*. Nice one! . .

SECOND GIRL. How awful!

ELSA. Like it?

SECOND GIRL *(to Elsa)*. They're fighting over you! . .

ELSA *(flattered)*. The fools! . .

SECOND GIRL *(to her)*. You lucky woman! *(At this moment the Walking Joke lets out a yell.)*

WALKING JOKE. Stop! . . Damn . . . *(Grabs his right arm with his left.)* He hurt my arm! . . Oil . . You bastard! . . Pistols would be better with you! And here I am soiling my hands! . . Oi, it hurts! . . Where's nurse Irina? . .

BARBARA *(entering left with several men)*. Stop them! What an outrage! . .

VITALIUS *(approaching the radio)*. The program's over! . . The end! *(Looks at his watch.)*

BARBARA *(going up to the Walking Joke)*. Did you hurt your arm? . .

WALKING JOKE *(after a long moan)*. Where's my sling? . .

BARBARA *(leading him off to the salon)*. Let's go! . . I'll patch you up myself! . . Such animals! . . *(Goes off to the salon.)*

FIRST SAILOR *(runs in left and yells)*. All engines back full! Hey! On the helm! . . Stop! *(Runs off right.)*

ALL. What's this? What's going on?

SECOND SAILOR *(runs in left)*. Get the life buoys! . . Hey! . . *(To those present.)* C'mon, mates, we need help! . . Dr. Weiss fell overboard! *(Runs off right. General commotion. Everybody rushes left. Vitalius hides the radio under his clothes and quickly follows the others off. The sound of machinery changing the direction of the screws is heard. The stage, beginning with the upstage area is covered with a semi-transparent curtain of smoke. The Captain and Irina appear at the extreme downstage left in front of the curtain of smoke.)*

CAPTAIN. Well, that's some news you've told me! . . *(Glances at the billows of smoke.)* What's that? "All engines back full"? . . Run aground again? . . Oh, Isai, Isai! . . A fairy tale is the only place where a madman should take the wheel!

IRINA. Don't get excited! . . It might kill you! . . A man like you, who's been in bed two months, ought . . .

CAPTAIN *(interrupting)*. Stop it! . . I feel wonderful and if it hadn't been for this news of yours . . .

IRINA. I thought Elsa had prepared you . . .

CAPTAIN. What else have you to tell me? Give me the *coup de grâce!* I can take it.

IRINA. Captain . . . *(her voice breaks).*

CAPTAIN. I'm listening.

IRINA *(getting control of herself)*. Captain . . . is there really no truth in this world?

CAPTAIN. What's this about?

IRINA. I was convinced that all of us were here because of an ideal! Because of some lofty ideal!

CAPTAIN. Well, of course.

IRINA. But it turns out actually . . .

CAPTAIN. "Turns out" what?

IRINA. Well, for instance, that Dr. Weiss is here solely for the sake of his wife—went away so as not to interfere with her happiness. And she—out of love for her husband, overcome by his generosity! The Professor is here because of some experiment—he blurted it out to me in his cups one night! Isai and his Anna because of injured self-esteem! Others for material considerations, and so on! Where is the truth to be found? Can it be that everybody—even we—are moved not by lofty ideals but only by personal interests?

CAPTAIN. What monstrous thoughts! Where did all this scepticism come from? And so it turns out, no doubt, that you're the only one here because of some lofty ideal?!

IRINA. . . . that even I am here, the sinner, not so much because of an ideal as because of Dr. Weiss, who was so lonely and pitiful with his wife gone! . .

CAPTAIN. Well, my dear, then I can now confess that even I am here solely because of my beloved daughter, that is, purely out of a desire to preserve her, at her dangerous age, from the attentions of some scoundrel!

IRINA *(inexorably)*. But haven't you been saying how happy you are that Elsa will find a husband not in "the first man that comes along," but among the select, the good, and the honest, as you consider the citizens of our community?

CAPTAIN. But you don't consider them good and honest?

IRINA *(drawing a newspaper out of her briefcase)*. Apparently you haven't been reading the paper lately! *(Hands him the newspaper.)*

CAPTAIN. What's been going on? *(Skims the whole newspaper.)*

IRINA. This article here shows that not only we boarded the ship, but some "uninvited guests" as well . . .

CAPTAIN. That Vitalius?

IRINA. Oh no, worse than that: *our ancestors!* That is, those barbarians with
their primeval, animal instincts, pushed aside only temporarily by civilization, but . . . never completely conquered, lurking in the depths of the Self.

CAPTAIN *(reading).* "So long as we remained in an atmosphere of struggle on
land, the struggle with evil, with nature, and so forth, our spiritual muscles
kept our ancestors in respectful awe! But now, far from the atmosphere of
struggle, we have allowed these barbarians to run around loose, look down
their noses at us and now finally, to bare their teeth . . ."

IRINA. You do understand, Captain, that we have here not a monastery gov-
erned by some abbot and "the fear of God," but an anarchical community
with no reins on our passions and desires.

CAPTAIN. Are you afraid?

IRINA. Anything might happen! In any case, after what I confessed to you, I
don't feel like remaining any longer.

CAPTAIN. Ah, so that's what you're driving at! . . So? All I can do is regret
that you're upset by these articles, which never should have appeared in the
first place.

IRINA. What could we do! We have freedom of the press!

CAPTAIN. Freedom excludes any outside influence! Especially any as corrupt-
ing as that Vitalius! Who were the idiots that allowed him on board?!

IRINA. What could we do? We have the principle of "non-resistance to evil"!

CAPTAIN. Principles are all very well when they are in the service of fundamentals.

IRINA. But suppose the fundamentals are shaken?

CAPTAIN. Then we strengthen them by removing the cause of the shaking!
(Turns sharply.)

IRINA. Where are you going?

CAPTAIN. To do my duty!

IRINA *(restraining him).* On the bridge?! You're not strong enough! . .

CAPTAIN. There's not a moment to be lost.

IRINA. Why so obstinate? . . .

CAPTAIN. "Why so hard?" asked the coal. "Why so soft?" answered the dia-
mond. *(Goes off downstage.)*

IRINA *(alone).* Such satanic pride! . . Oh, if you only knew who your Elsa has
fallen in love with! . . *(Laughs maliciously, then draws a letter from her briefcase
and reads the last lines . . . "Faithfully yours, Bogdan." Unexpectedly falls to her
knees and raises her hands to the sky.)* Oh Lord, art Thou really not in Heaven?!.
Then who will tell me where the truth is in this world and teach me the
way to righteousness?!. *(Meanwhile a group of Anchorite passengers has come on
silently upstage left by the bulwark and can be seen behind Irina, through the smoke.*

Heading the group is Dr. Weiss, supported by Vitalius on one side and Barbara on the other. Dr. Weiss, as much as we can see through the curtain of smoke, is deathly pale and moves with great difficulty. His clothes and shoes are soaked. Vitalius, by contrast, is crimson, bare-chested and barefoot and moves freely. The command "all engines ahead" is heard, startling Irina. She turns and hurries off left. The roar of the ship's steam plant is heard. The curtain of smoke disappears, revealing a mountainous shore on the horizon behind some fast disappearing patches of fog. Dr. Weiss is led into the salon. Dream appears on the roof of the salon half-reclining and looking like some mournful apparition. She leans on her elbows and looks down at what is going on beneath and closely follows everything with a hopeless, feverish look. Elsa leaps onto the platform and passionately addresses those around her.)

ELSA. One man among us, at least, has been found who, without hesitation, was willing to risk his life for his fellow man! I therefore propose we give him an official farewell, as we would an honored guest!

WALKING JOKE *(coming in from the salon, with his right arm in a sling)*. Excuse me! . . They need nurse Irina . . . Where is she?

SEVERAL VOICES. Nurse, where are you? Nurse, they need you!

IRINA *(comes in from left and manages to squeeze to the front of the crowd)*. Here I am! . . What happened? . . What's the matter?

SEVERAL PEOPLE *(one after the other)*. Dr. Weiss wants you . . . Hurry! Hurry! . . He needs help! . . Where've you been? . . He's in the dining room! . . Hurry! . . *(Irina runs off to the salon.)*

ELSA *(to everybody)*. So, do you agree to honor this hero? *(A roar of voices is heard, some approving, some expressing doubts, some arguing with each other.)*

WALKING JOKE. Excuse me! What's going on? What sort of heroics are we talking about? If my hand hadn't been injured by this very "hero," I give you my word of honor I'd have done the same myself! *(Restrained laughter by those present.)* Excuse me, but there's nothing to laugh about here! Especially when a man gives his word of honor! . . *(A new burst of laughter.)* And if one's word of honor is going to be laughed at, then, excuse me, but *I'm* not going to remain in such an uncivilized community! . . Thank God, we're close to shore! *(Points into the distance.)* I see in the distance my native mountains, where I'd rather listen to the laughter of jackals than you laughter, dear friends! *(Demonstratively walks off left.)*

VITALIUS *(dressed in a sailor blouse similar to the one he wore in Act I, comes out of the salon with Barbara)*. Saved! He came to! Finally came all the way to and can't wait to thank all of you for your wonderful help! . . Go ahead, who's first! . . He's already changed! *(Applause and female shouts of "Bravo Vitalius! . . way to go . . . our hero." Several approach to shake his hand. The whole excited throng goes into the salon talking about what has happened. Dream, in unhappy anticipation, moves away from her observation post.)*

BARBARA *(takes Vitalius by the hand).* Oh, thank you again! I thank you with all my heart! . .

VITALIUS. Stop it! For me it was simple.

BARBARA. I'm grateful to you not only for saving my husband but also for the kind, humane way you let me know you didn't love me.

VITALIUS *(amazed).* Well, what do you know! . .

BARBARA. Oh, if you had loved me, you wouldn't have saved your rival! That's obvious.

VITALIUS. Your husband?! . What a thing to say! . .

BARBARA. But that's the way it is! . . But, casting me aside as a woman you have made me a closer friend! Thank you, oh thank you, my dear!

VITALIUS. Enough of these empty phrases! Why wear yourself out "psychologizing"! My God! Life is simpler than it may seem to you. And as for this little event, here's what I have to say: take care of your husband, sweetheart! I just barely got him in time! He didn't fall overboard accidentally! . . Listen when the voice of experience tells you not to leave his side for a moment! I know all too much about these "Drowning Victims"!

MADMAN *(enters right with Dream).* Well? . . Regained consciousness? Everything all right? Come to? Where is he?

BARBARA *(pointing).* Over there!

MADMAN. We're going to anchor here!

VITALIUS. So far from shore?

MADMAN. But where is nurse Irina?

BARBARA. She's with my husband. They're all there.

MADMAN. The Captain told me she's going to desert us! What does it mean? . . *(To Vitalius.)* Are they planning to accompany you ashore? . . I'm against it! Even though I acknowledge your heroic deed. But your presence here has resulted in such complete demoralization that it would be an enormous risk to let anyone go ashore with you! I'm against it.

BARBARA. But you'll certainly let us go, I hope?

MADMAN. Who's "us?"

BARBARA. My husband and me! We're leaving too.

MADMAN. For good?

BARBARA. For good.

MADMAN. The reason?

BARBARA. You know perfectly well!

MADMAN *(to Vitalius).* The fruits of your inspiration? . . Gratitude for the hospitality? *(A group of citizens, who have been off right in the salon for a short while, come in. They are headed by Dr. Weiss, Irina, and Elsa, all dressed in travelling clothes. Dr. Weiss holds the baby in his arms and his breath comes in gasps as he looks at his child. The Madman leaps to the platform and sails into those present with a fiery speech).*

MADMAN. Citizens of Anchorite! Don't succumb to the pernicious influence of that way of life which has intruded here in the form of Vitalius! A way of life brimming over with contradictions and perfidious deceptions, like Vitalius himself! Believe me, once he leaves, the spells he's cast will vanish. There are things that can't be put into words! It wasn't words was it, that brought us all together, but feeling, inexpressible in words! . . Oh, remember the music where I exposed all the sad contradictions of the worldly life! You've forgotten it! You must remember it! *(He rushes into the salon and with inhuman passion plays the indicated piece on the piano. Meanwhile Vitalius has winked at the crowd and then turned on the radio. The radio, to the horror of the weary Dream, instantly drowns out the Madman's music with a merry song. Dream rushes into the salon and interrupts the Madman's playing. He comes rushing out and, like some wild beast, throws himself at the radio, smashes it and flings it overboard with a shout.)*

MADMAN. Drop the anchor! All engines stop! Launch the boats! There's a limit to everything! *(Dream runs off right with a piercing scream "Drop the Anchor." In the distance, apparently on shore, are heard the confused sounds of a bravura march played by some brass band.)*

VITALIUS *(quickly recovering)*. Listen! Hear that music? . . The wind brought it! . . We're here! . . Nobody can drown that out! Nobody, nobody!

BARBARA *(smiling)*. The music of the sirens! . . *(Many of those present repeat after her, like an echo, "the music of the sirens." She takes the child from her husband and presses him to her bosom.)* What is it, Felix? Do you want to be Odysseus? Do you or don't you? *(Excited, she kisses her son.)*

DREAM *(runs up with the Madman to Barbara)*. Leave us your son! We'll raise him far from human sin, struggle, and suffering!

MADMAN. He was born here! He's one of us! He's a citizen of Anchorite!

BARBARA *(moving away from them)*. You're raving mad! . . I'm the mother and I am the one responsible for his future!

DR. WEISS. She's right! . . You don't have a future! . .

MADMAN. Who says?

DR. WEISS. Life itself.

MADMAN *(ironically)*. Vitalius?

BARBARA *(to him, indignantly)*. You madman! *(The noise of the anchor chain interrupts the conversation. At this time a group of four men appear on the platform. Their appearance suggests they are some elegant, solid citizens, foreigners. They wear "diplomat" topcoats, felt hats and caps, gloves, and carry walking canes, travelling bags, cameras and binoculars. On closer look one recognizes the Professor, his moustache and beard clipped short and an elegant pince nez replacing his enormous glasses, two sailors—the red-bearded one and the one in spectacles who had asked Dr. Weiss for an amnesty in Act II—and a third sailor who has appeared earlier. Their arrival provokes perplexed cries among those already on stage. All surround the platform, burning with curiosity.)*

PROFESSOR *(bowing)*. Ladeez and gentlemen! . . *(He manages to remain silent for a moment as the anchor chain roars.)* Ladies and gentlemen! Our part in this little game is over, so we are now leaving. *(Voices are heard: "Why it's the professor! . . He trimmed his beard . . ." and so forth.)* Yes, it's me, a correspondent for *Nature* magazine. And this is *(presenting his fellow passengers one by one)* Professor Lipsky, a sociologist doing research on the bases of the anarchist community, this is Dr. Stein, a psychiatrist studying the phenomena of mass insanity, and this is Marcel Grevier, a playwright in search of a plot for a new social comedy. *(A hum of voices and some nervous giggles by those present.)*

MADMAN. What's this all about? . . You've been perpetrating some hoax on us?

PROFESSOR. Oh, what a way to put it! We've simply been performing *our own* play within *your* play, Maestro! And we played it out to the end quite successfully and wish you the same! *(Voices among those present: "Imagine that! . . Tricky fellows! . . Yeah, I can understand that" and so forth.)*

MADMAN. What was the point of it? . . . This separatism?

PROFESSOR *(didactically, emphasizing each word)*. It was for empirical study of the question "The Artificial Paradise on an Idealistic Base"!

VITALIUS *(to the Professor)*. Well done, damn it! Why the hell did I waste time arguing with you! What a riot! *(Laughs.)*

PROFESSOR *(smiling)*. It was necessary for us to test the psychic infectiousness of the environment and along with it, the resistance of its ideology—your ideology! Here, among other things, you played a part in the hastening of the denouement of this little drama and thus also paid for your illegal passage!

MADMAN *(pointing to two of the Professor's colleagues, the red-bearded one and the one in spectacles)*. Ah! Now I recognize the birds who brought the infection! . . *(They smile in embarrassment.)*

PROFESSOR. Non-resistance to evil! You can't accuse them of anything!

WALKING JOKE *(who has returned by now dressed in a felt cloak and in a tall fur hat)*.

Pardon me! What's going on? *(To the Professor, his colleagues, the Weiss couple, and Irina.)* What's this? You're leaving?

PROFESSOR. We're leaving the game.

WALKING JOKE *(agitated)*. Leaving the game? Now wait a minute please! . . You can't! I was a little hasty myself. We've got to wait.

PROFESSOR. Why?

WALKING JOKE. What do you mean "why"? This ship has been donated to the community!

ELSA *(with unexpected heat)*. Excuse me, it was donated conditionally; on condition the community demonstrate its feasibility.

WALKING JOKE. I know: for a period of two years! And it's almost up!

ELSA. So, what of it? What are you driving at?

WALKING JOKE. That we could stay anchored here for a little, pretend a little that everything on board was going fine, then sell the ship for a little money and split it up among ourselves! *(A loud burst of laughter among those present.)*

ELSA *(addressing all of them with the irony of one "cut to the quick")*. Do you hear that? . . Isn't he something! And he had the nerve to ask me to marry him!

WALKING JOKE. What do you mean? Why "something"? What are you talking about?

ELSA. And he has the nerve to ask! To ask the *daughter* of the very man he proposes to defraud and rob!

WALKING JOKE. What do you mean?

DR. WEISS. You mean, your father . . .

ELSA *(pale with rage)*. Oh, such depravity! He forced me to confess that . . . I didn't want it that way in the first place! I swear to you! But it's beyond my strength! . . Our community . . .

PROFESSOR *(smiling)*. Calm down! It doesn't exist anymore! It disappeared at the first hint of private property! . .

FIRST MAN *(appearing upstage, summons with a yell)*. The boats are lowered! . . Who is going with Vitalius?

SEVERAL OF THOSE PRESENT. All of us! . . Vitalius! . . We're with you! . . *(The girls make a ring around the laughing Vitalius and go off with him up left. The rest follow.)*

BARBARA *(to her husband and Irina)*. Let's go! *(They go off.)*

PROFESSOR *(with a gesture bids his colleagues remain a moment, then leads Elsa downstage)*. I wouldn't want to upset the sick Captain. Tell him farewell for me; I'm returning to London by land for a rest. *(Presses her hand in farewell.)* Goodbye! *(His colleagues raise their hats.)* Also tell him that as of today I consider his charter to have expired.

ELSA. What charter?

PROFESSOR. What! You mean you didn't know that the Anchorite's expedition was organized by the editors of *Nature* magazine with funds left by the philanthropist Stone?

ELSA. First time I've heard anything about it! My father did say something about a subsidy . . .

PROFESSOR. And about the prize?

ELSA. What prize?

PROFESSOR. . . . in case the Community of the Righteous lasted two years?

ELSA. He lost it?! . .

PROFESSOR. A real fortune! . . I feel sorry for the poor man! He had such faith in this enterprise! But, oh dear, it seems I'm spilling the beans! *(With a reproachful grin.)* Following your example . . . Goodbye! *(Bows and with his three colleagues quickly goes off left, where sounds of merriment of those getting into the boats are heard through the sounds of the distant band.)*

ELSA *(distraught).* Goodbye! . . *(Mumbling almost indistinctly to herself.)* So that's it! . . *(Shouts to those who have departed.)* I'll be along in a minute! *(Runs over to the bulwark where the Madman and his lady friend—the only ones left on deck—are watching with gloomy irony as the boats fill up. She forces them to turn to her.)* Tell papa that I've gone for another doctor . . since Dr. Weiss has left. We've got to get somebody! . . I'll be right back. *(Spots the Captain walking in unexpectedly right.)* Ah . . . Papa!. You're up already? . . And I thought . . . *(Runs over to embrace him.)*

CAPTAIN *(kissing her).* Don't worry about a doctor, my dear! . . Your presence here is much more important to my health!

ELSA. I was going to be gone just a little bit and then . . .

CAPTAIN *(good-naturedly).* Oh well, run along then! . . Only hurry back! *(Kisses her again.)* What tired eyes you have! . . And those sparks in your eyes . . . Don't raise your eyebrows like that . . . your mother never once wrinkled her brow! . . *(From left and below is heard Vitalius' excited, enthusiastic voice: "Well, who else? . . Be seated, mates! . . . Shove off!")*

ELSA *(quickly kisses her father and shouts hastily down and left).* Wait! *(She runs off left. The Captain goes over to the bulwark. A pause, during which the merry music from shore is heard exceptionally clearly, mixed with the sound of oars of the boats drawing away from the ship.)*

CAPTAIN *(after a pause).* They shoved off! . . And so many of them! . . Almost all, in fact! But who's left on watch? . .

MADMAN. Nobody . . . See for yourself; they're all leaving! . . All of them! And their suitcases were all packed long ago . . . Clever, wouldn't you say?

CAPTAIN. What nonsense! . . Where do you get these ideas? . .

MADMAN *(with said irony)*. Where? . . You'd do better to explain why you concealed from me the facts as to the Anchorite's true owner!

CAPTAIN. The Anchorite's owner? What a question! . . The ship was assigned to our community . . .

MADMAN. Elsa told us the secret! . .

CAPTAIN. Elsa? I What secret? . .

MADMAN *(sadly)*. The community was already on its last legs. It was finished off with one word—*property,* your *property.* She showed all the greediness of an heiress.

CAPTAIN. Elsa?!! My Elsa?!! My own beloved daughter!! *(He staggers in the direction of the platform, his lips begin to twitch with a grin.)* So that's it? . . Ahh! . . I get it now! Those eyes! . . The raised eyebrows! . . The sparks in the eyes! . . That means he's not dead! . . . He's alive, my father is! . . Alive and laughing at my venture! . . Revenging himself for my rejection of his commercial ideals! . . *(Sinks heavily to the platform floor. Sounds, something like convulsive laughter, come out of his chest.)*

MADMAN *(running over with Dream to him, with sympathetic alarm)*. What's the matter? . . What's the matter? . .

CAPTAIN *(bursting out with desperate, terrible laughter, as if all that laughter he had been accumulating in his breast these many years had burst to the surface all at once, suffocating him in convulsions)*. I was going to conquer nature . . . life . . . ha, ha, ha, ha, ha . . . be above life . . . ha, ha, ha, ha, ha . . . and then, the very one I believed in most! . . Most! Ha, ha, ha, ha, ha . . . my own beloved daughter, for whom I lived! . . A perfect imitation of my wife . . . ha, ha, ha, ha . . . raised her eyebrows, flashed those wicked sparks in her eyes . . . Oh! Ha, ha, ha, ha . . . I can't! . . Isai! . . It's all so goddamn funny! . . You see, Isai, ha, ha, ha, ha . . . you see that this was our ship with the cardboard people . . . Och, I just can't . . . ha, ha, ha, ha . . . The wind blew and . . . ha, ha, ha, ha . . . Ha, ha, ha, ha . . . *(Falls over backwards, his face up, and suddenly lies still, motionless. The Madman exchanges glances with Dream, then falls quickly on the Captain's chest.)*

MADMAN *(after a pause)*. Not a beat . . . not a sound . . . He's dead! . . . Died laughing! . .

DREAM. Dead? . . *(Bends over the Captain's face and looks in his eyes.)* What a derisive look! . . Look at that! . . He's silent but the eyes are still laughing, speaking, going on living! . . *(The music on the shore dies down.)* Yes, yes, go on living! *(Takes off her light blue shawl and covers the deceased's body up to the eyes. To the Madman.)* Go, weigh anchor and let's be off before they have a chance to get back!

MADMAN *(ecstatically)*. You command and I obey . . We don't have to wait for anybody! We don't have to worry about losing anybody! Alone! Alone with you in the vast blue expanses! . . Off for the high seas! . . The wind's just come up again . . . I'll raise the sails! . . *(Runs off right.)*

DREAM *(standing over the dead body with her arms raised skyward)*. Oh, wind! Stormy wind! Oh, breaking waves! . . Take us away from this place! . . No one, no one needs us here! . . Away from land! Away from these people!

CURTAIN.

THE UNMASKED BALL
(THE THEATER OF ETERNAL WAR)

A Play in Three Acts and Four Scenes

CHARACTERS

Director of the Theatrical Institute (Sofya Daryal)

Mary, her daughter

Yu-Gen-Li, a teacher of dramatic arts

Abramson, a furniture manufacturer

Schmidt, a lawyer

Junior Detective, "The Girl in Light Blue" (Tommy Sauce)

Prince Sergius Mashukov

Anatole, a music teacher

Gregoire, a painter

Phillips, a preacher

O'Kay, a retired colonel

Girl in Mourning (Fanny Norman)

Seductive Maiden (Ernestina MacBridle)*

Trompetti, a professor of mime

Senator Creighton

May, a mulatto maid

Baker, a psychology teacher*

Pupils of the Theatrical Institute, guests at the Director's party.

 *Non-speaking roles.

*The action takes place partly in New York City, partly in
a summer house near Atlantic City.*

ACT ONE

Scene One

A living room furnished in the overly theatrical way the Empire style is understood by the prosperous bourgeoisie of the New World. There is something resembling an arch or a two-fold flat at each end of the apron. They serve to create two furnished "corners" or side stages. Of the two the one at stage right is the most intimate, owing to a cozily attractive small sofa and a handsome, semi-lace screen hanging behind it.

Along the sides of this extremely narrow arch and behind it, parts of a massive brocade curtain, drawn in tight folds, hang in splendor. The curtain is golden-rusty-red with some undefined pattern outlined in black silk.

Two portieres of the same color and with the same undefined pattern are seen over the two living room doors left and right. These doors remain wide open during almost the entire act. There is also a door at the center without a portiere. It is a very wide, sliding door with frosted panes resembling a classroom door or an office in a small bank. It remains closed and lighted from behind until the very end of the first act.

There is a piano stage right, by the wall, behind the proscenium opening. It alone does not completely harmonize with the entire style of this living room which displays the ostentatious taste of a regisseur "who knows his own worth," is furnished with gilded, mahogany pieces, bronzed sculpture, and a chandelier and candelabra to match.

Half-length portraits of famous actors and actresses of the 18th and early 19th centuries, skillfully hung on the walls of the garishly elegant interieur, crown—to use the appropriate literary term—its rich decor.

As the curtain rises, some vague emotional sounds reminiscent of Chinese music are heard off right. The music, played by a small, impromptu orchestra, is muffled by the wall.

A group of guests attired in evening dress stand sedately in the doorway stage left and, as if spell-bound, follow some spectacle in the next room, which is apparently jammed with people. Three men stand somewhat apart from the rest of the group, and closer to the footlights. They are the furniture manufacturer Abramson, the lawyer Schmidt, and Colonel O'Kay. The first is a typical businessman, about 50, rather uniquely attractive in the relaxed way he holds himself, with the smooth face of an aging sphinx, adorned with a gray, Assyrian-style beard. The second, the lawyer Schmidt, is still quite a young man, with quite a handsome, even though banal appearance, plainly striving to display poise and confidence, although not always succeeding. The third, Colonel O'Kay, is a good-natured fellow, forty some years old. His sun-tanned face, his elegant gray moustache, his whole military bearing instantly reveal his profession.

ABRAMSON *(after a long pause, not taking his eyes off the spectacle being presented in the room off stage to the left).* What a . . . striking woman!

SCHMIDT. Isn't she though? Don't you like the tricks she does?

ABRAMSON. What's her name?

SCHMIDT. Yu-Gen-Li.

ABRAMSON. Chinese?

O'KAY. Russian mother.

ABRAMSON. And the father?

SCHMIDT. Manchurian—so's her husband!

O'KAY. I hear they're both some kind of witch doctors?

SCHMIDT. Doctors of Tibetan medicine.

O'KAY *(laughing good-naturedly).* Well, it's the same old Chinese stuff—pure hypnosis!

ABRAMSON. Look at that! She threw a rope into the air and it just hangs there on a ring of cigarette smoke.

SCHMIDT. I've already seen that one. Haven't you seen it too, Colonel?

O'KAY. Twice! And I'm spellbound every time.

ABRAMSON. Hey, doves! . . Look at that! . . Look where they went!

O'KAY. And a cat up the rope after them! . . You see that?

ABRAMSON. Fantastic! *(A pause, then a roar of applause in the room offstage left.)* How much does she get for one show?

SCHMIDT *(as if offended).* Yu-Gen-Li, Doctor of Philosophy, Professor of Drama, and sometime physician.

ABRAMSON. Uh huh—so how much then?

SCHMIDT. Playing the role of a buffoon to amuse people is not the same as taking money to *become* one!

O'KAY. Bravo! Well put!

SCHMIDT. Thank you, Colonel!

ABRAMSON *(jokingly, to Schmidt).* How much does this magician pay you for the advertising?

SCHMIDT *(provocatively).* You're always running on about "how much," "how much." Sometimes it might be more appropriate to inquire "what sort of payment" rather than "how much" is paid.

ABRAMSON. Why? . . You mean to say that quality is not, in fact, the same thing as quantity?

SCHMIDT. What's tha-at? Did you hear that, Colonel?

ABRAMSON. The whole question of quality sometimes boils down to one of the quantity of the desired item! I fail to see the big difference!

O'KAY. In your opinion, quality is a kind of mask under which quantity hides?

ABRAMSON. Sort of!

O'KAY. . . . like on the battlefield—let's say—with military camouflage? It would appear that the wind blew down a tree, but it turns out to be camouflage—an artillery screen.

ABRAMSON. An excellent illustration! *(From the left is heard the noise of chairs being pushed back and the hum of voices interspersed with "exotic" music. Those standing in the doorway are directing their attention at something in the hall to the left. Making her way through them is a preoccupied looking and slightly limping girl in a light blue dress. She is wrapped in a cheap, colorful shawl half-covering her chin. She barely reaches the center of the stage before Colonel O'Kay takes after her and seizes her by the hand.)*

O'KAY. Where are you going? . . To the buffet? . .

GIRL IN LIGHT BLUE *(angrily, in a half-whisper)*. Of course not. *(Frees her hand and goes right to the sofa on the apron.)*

O'KAY *(following her)*. Think about the Spartans! *(He sits next to her.)* Don't forget them! Do you hear? Temper your will! Struggle with the pangs of hunger and . . . *(noticing that she makes a face as she removes her shoe)* and leave your shoe alone! Don't screw up your face! Look as if you were in no pain at all! . . Always think of the Spartans!

GIRL IN LIGHT BLUE *(screwing up her face)*. Oh, rest assured, you'd never forget 'em in these shoes!

O'KAY. Tight fit?

GIRL IN LIGHT BLUE. . . . The lucky guys! They used to run around barefoot!

O'KAY. And how they used to be whipped at the altar of their Goddess! Remember that!

GIRL IN LIGHT BLUE. What a thing to remember! . . Thank the Lord we're not pagans!

O'KAY. Ah yes, but it tempered the will! *(Lights a cigarette.)* Remember Leonid and the 300 Spartans.

GIRL IN LIGHT BLUE. They can go straight to hell with training like that! . . Let me have a cigarette . . . To ease the hunger pangs! *(Accepts a cigarette from Colonel O'Kay and lights it.)*

ABRAMSON *(to Schmidt, not taking his eyes off the spectacle in the adjoining room)*. What kind of dance is that?

SCHMIDT. "The Shaman's Exorcism." They dance like that in East Siberia to chase off evil spirits.

ABRAMSON. "Chase off?!" With poses like that she'd be more likely to attract them!

SCHMIDT. Even without the poses Yu-Gen-Li is *attractive* enough!

ABRAMSON. You've gotten to be awfully quick on the draw, my friend! I hadn't noticed that in you before!

SCHMIDT *(smiling)*. Time changes people.

ABRAMSON. . . . and very quickly when the change is desired!

SCHMIDT. What are you hinting at?

ABRAMSON. The way you act as if you were on stage all the time! *(In the hall offstage left the dance music dies down and gives way to a roar of applause. Those standing in the doorway clap their hands and go off left. Colonel O'Kay and the Girl in Light Blue go off hastily after them. Schmidt tries to get Abramson to do the same, but the latter declines politely.)*

SCHMIDT. Don't you want to thank Yu-Gen-Li?

ABRAMSON. I do! But she's too besieged at the moment!

SCHMIDT. What of it?

ABRAMSON. I don't care to be number One Hundred.

SCHMIDT. Do you count everything? . . There's no point in that: in the Lottery of Love number One Hundred enjoys the same odds as number One!

ABRAMSON *(laughing)*. Well, why should an old bachelor like me go on dreaming about the "Lottery of Love"!

SCHMIDT *(with a somewhat contrived grin)*. Look at that! Such resignation to one's fate!

ABRAMSON *(clapping him on the shoulder)*. No, you really are playing a role all the time! That cynical tone! That deliberate "hail fellow well met!" And above all—don't be offended—that wit you seem to have borrowed somewhere! . . Why, I hardly recognize you anymore!

SCHMIDT *(snapping his fingers, seeming to show off)*. But maybe I was only putting on before? . . Pretending?

ABRAMSON. Stop it! I've known you almost since you were a boy! Good-natured, sincere, shy, only a short while ago! And now suddenly! . . Like a different person this past year.

SCHMIDT. But what's better for a lawyer's career—shyness or "hail fellow well met?"

ABRAMSON. Well, that all depends!

SCHMIDT. When you come right down to it, it is a matter of some interest to you too!

ABRAMSON. How so?

SCHMIDT. The fact is, that, serving in the legal department of your furniture business, that is, representing your vital interests to your clients and in court, I . . .

ABRAMSON *(interrupting with a laugh)*. So you're trying to tell me that it's for my sake you've become a different person?! *(Shakes his hand with good-natured irony.)* Well, what do you know! And to think you'd make a sacrifice like that for me!

SCHMIDT *(only slightly affected by the irony).* For you and for me! Our interests coincide! *(From the hall left enters Yu-Gen-Li accompanied by several people among whom are Gregoire, Prince Mashukov, Baker and Trompetti. Snatches of grateful remarks addressed to Yu-Gen-Li are heard, as well as exclamations of amazement, delight, praise, and some questions lost in the general hubbub . . . Yu-Gen-Li gaily dismisses the compliments, not taking the expressions of gratitude seriously, laughs coquettishly, and—a little tired from her dancing—hastily crosses the stage to the right, breathing rather rapidly. She is still a very beautiful, rather dark-skinned young woman, rather more Mongolian than Slavic. She is dressed in a gorgeous silk brocade jacket. She has an exotic necklace weighted down with mysterious amulets around her neck. In her hands is a very black fan with two phosphorouscolored butterflies that quiver as the fan moves. Behind her two pupils from the Theatrical Institute bear a fine, gold cage with snow-white doves and an enormous, wellfed Siberian cat.)*

ABRAMSON. *(approaching her, not so much applauding as making a gesture of applause).* Bravo! Bravo! You have simply conquered me with your art!

YU-GEN-LI."Conquered?" With my dilettantism? Such flattery!

ABRAMSON. You have so much grace, so much skill, so much confidence in your charms! . .

SCHMIDT *(provocatively).* Well, how much then? *(To her.)* He counts everything, a real unusual fellow! Have you noticed? Solves everything on the basis of calculation!

YU-GEN-LI *(meaningfully).* That's not so bad, if you're not afraid of miscalculation!

SCHMIDT *(to Abramson).* You hear that?

YU-GEN-LI *(with a provocative smile).* But someone like him—you may rest assured—will not make the miscalculation!

ABRAMSON. Do you really mean that?

YU-GEN-LI *(evasively).* I suppose so. *(To Schmidt.)* Give me a cigarette! *(Several cases belonging to the admirers surrounding her suddenly appear. She laughs, bows her head to all of them like a Chinese toy, but chooses the cigarette proffered by Schmidt. Then all around several lighters flare up, one by one, and among them—and especially bright—is Abramson's lighter, which Yu-Gen-Li then uses to light her cigarette.)*

ABRAMSON *(to the friendly laughter of those surrounding).* A f-f-fantastic woman! . .

SCHMIDT. I kept telling you! . .

ABRAMSON. . . . one of a kind! *(Yu-Gen-Li waves the sleeve of her brocade jacket and showers him with tiny Chinese paper balloons.)* A sorceress, not a woman!

SCHMIDT. Pure narcotic! And sobering at the same time! You've got to know Yu-Gen-Li.

ABRAMSON *(joking)*. But perhaps it would be better not to? Safer?

YU-GEN-LI. Are you some kind of coward?

ABRAMSON. Hm . . . Some kind of sensible person! *(Meanwhile the cage with the doves and the cat is being carried from behind Yu-Gen-Li to a room offstage right, where part of the group accompanying her is going.)*

YU-GEN-LI *(takes Abramson by the arm and, moving all the way downstage with him, nods in the direction of Schmidt)*. They say the most marvelous things about your summer house on . . .

ABRAMSON. . . . Yellow Beach?

YU-GEN-LI. Is that near Atlantic City?

ABRAMSON *(bowing his head)*. Right on the water.

YU-GEN-LI. They say you're prepared to give it up for the summer for practically nothing *(with a proud gesture points jokingly to herself)* to someone who understands antique furniture!

ABRAMSON. The house is at your disposal, on one condition . . .

YU-GEN-LI. I know what it is. I believe that my sister, just like me, will agree. However, we must talk more about it! *(She turns around, starts to go off right.)* I'll be back in a minute, as soon as I change. *(Glances at the group of pupils and pauses.)* Have you met? Maestro Gregoire—the artist! And this is Mr. Abramson!

SCHMIDT. . . . the famous Richard Abramson, author of *The Evolution of Comfort!* Haven't you read it?

ABRAMSON *(shaking hands with Gregoire in a friendly way)*. I'm just a furniture manufacturer who once gave up a philosophy department for a merchant's counter!

GREGOIRE *(He is a reddish, shaggy-haired small man with a sensitive mouth and nostrils used to smelling. He squints one eye out of an exaggerated sense of self-respect, shifts a portfolio of drawings from under his right arm to his left and, having straightened a pretentious flower in the lapel of his dinner jacket, offers his hand to Abramson.)* So happy to meet you! . . I've heard a lot about you, and about your *factory . . . your antique furniture factory!* Even though I'm mainly interested in contemporary art, just the same . . .

SCHMIDT *(breaks into loud laughter)*. "Antique furniture factory?!" Terrific! That's the way to put words together in this day and time! We could really use an "antique-furniture factory"! *(To Gregoire.)* You're a riot!

GREGOIRE *(somewhat taken aback)*. How's that? I fail to understand . . .

YU-GEN-LI *(impatiently introducing the others to Abramson)*. Fanny Norman! . . Prince Mashukov! . . *(Handshakes, Fanny Norman—the Girl in Mourning—is apparently not actually good-looking, but is aesthetically tolerable thanks to her makeup and to a well-tailored black dress which lends her that air of "noble grief" for which she is so obviously striving. Prince Mashukov, a thoroughly unappealing figure, not quite a provincial shopkeeper, not quite a railroad station porter, is dressed, seemingly through some misunderstanding, in a dinner jacket. Clumsy, blushing, hiding his rough hands behind his back and in his pockets, he absurdly tries to pose in a princely manner and bestow his royal good favor upon the Girl in Mourning.)*

ABRAMSON *(greeting them).* I have the honor . . . Most happy . . .

YU-GEN-LI *(introducing him to the ones remaining).* Mr. Baker, Psychology Instructor in our Theatrical Institute! *(Abramson silently shakes hands with the mummy-like "scholar" of undetermined age.)* And this is our Professor of Mime, Maestro Trompetti!

ABRAMSON *(shakes the well-manicured hand of the affected, stout Italian).* Abramson! So glad to meet you! . . *(He suddenly spots Phillips entering from the left with a barely noticeable limp.)* Bah! . . Look who's here! My old friend Phillips!

PHILLIPS. *(He wears an immaculate dinner jacket with a white boutonniere, and over his eyes are elegant smoky-blue glasses. He is a ruddy little old man trying to appear to be much younger and beams with benevolence. Sooner or later one notices that his left hand plays no part in his constant gesticulation, but always remains stuck in his pocket.)* What a coincidence! . . I'm standing there wondering who that is by the door . . .

ABRAMSON. You've gotten so young! I hardly know you! Tell me honestly now, how old are you?

PHILLIPS *(laughs).* I don't care for counting. That's your vice, not mine!

ABRAMSON. I wouldn't give you a day over forty! That's not the proper thing, my friend, for a "minister of the faith"!

YU-GEN-LI *(to Abramson, gaily).* You have so many friends here that I have no qualms about leaving you! You certainly won't be lonely! *(Runs off right. Two or three seconds later Baker and Trompetti go off right after her. Gregoire settles down by the piano with his portfolio, takes out several nude sketches, goes through them while talking with the Girl in Mourning and Prince Mashukov. All three of them occasionally look in the direction of Abramson, who is occupied with the preacher.)*

PHILLIPS. Fancy meeting you here!

ABRAMSON *(as if to justify himself).* He was the one that dragged me here! *(Claps Schmidt on the shoulder.)* Do you know each other? Hermann Schmidt, assistant to my legal adviser. *(Handshake.)* Stage-struck, so he's even enrolled here at the Institute.

PHILLIPS *(chuckling slyly).* I know! In night school!

ABRAMSON. Who told you? Oh yes! I remember! . . I've even heard that you're "one of the family" here! . .

PHILLIPS. Well, not exactly . . .

ABRAMSON *(interrupting).* What is there in common, now tell me, between you, a minister of the gospel by profession, and . . . a "theatrical institute?" *(Without a pause.)* Ahhh! Now I've guessed it—you teach diction, or declamation, or . . .

PHILLIPS *(interrupts with a false smile of humility).* For pity's sake! Here's someone who should! *(Points to Schmidt)* And not miserable sinners like us!

ABRAMSON *(looking at Schmidt).* Is he really so talented? He kept it so well hidden!

SCHMIDT *(with an ironical bow).* Deeply grateful for the compliment!

ABRAMSON *(putting his hand on Schmidt's shoulder).* But just imagine: a lawyer suddenly taking it into his head to try for an actor's laurels! Can there really be that much money in it?

PHILLIPS. It all depends.

ABRAMSON. How much does a good actor make?

SCHMIDT *(with mock haughtiness).* For playing the part of "The Great Man" Napoleon was awarded an Emperor's crown!

ABRAMSON. For "playing the part?" Not for his sheer genius?

SCHMIDT. If that had been enough, then he wouldn't have studied with Talma the actor!

ABRAMSON. What? Bonaparte studied with an actor? Studied what, if I may ask?

PHILLIPS and SCHMIDT *(together).* The knack of commanding respect!

ABRAMSON. What does that mean?

SCHMIDT. Being *convincing* in the part one plays!

PHILLIPS. Being impressive in the part! *(By this time Trompetti and Baker have returned from the left and have stopped in the middle of the room, after which Prince Mashukov, seemingly at their instigation, leaves the group by the piano and approaches Abramson.)*

PRINCE *(indecisively clasping and unclasping his hands, looking sideways with a stupid expression on his face, and making what seems to be a well-rehearsed speech).* Excuse me! A perfectly idiotic thing has happened to me . . . I live over in Jersey and, no doubt when I changed my clothes, forgot and left my wallet at home . . . I'll have to take a cab back from the station, and I haven't a cent . . . I'll pay you back tomorrow! . . If it won't inconvenience you . . .

ABRAMSON *(coldly, politely).* How much?

PRINCE. Hm . . . three, four dollars.

ABRAMSON *(puts two fingers in his vest pocket).* Oh dear, nothing but a couple of dimes! And my checkbook would hardly be of any help at this late hour! *(To Schmidt and Phillips.)* Perhaps, gentlemen, you can help?

PHILLIPS *(spreading his hands with an air of regret)*. Only my checkbook!

SCHMIDT. Me too.

PRINCE *(to Abramson)*. But maybe with a check like yours I might make a deal at the station with a cab driver?

ABRAMSON. But how are you going to get to the station?

PRINCE. I have a return ticket.

ABRAMSON *(with a piercing, searching stare)*. Don't you keep it in your wallet?

PRINCE. No, in my pocket. Why do you ask?

ABRAMSON. Oh nothing, I just can't figure how you managed to buy the return ticket if you left your wallet at home?

PRINCE *(embarrassed)*. Hm . . . I have a commuter's pass.

ABRAMSON *(seemingly enlightened by these words)*. Ahhh! . . That's something else! Show it to me! I'll look at the agent's signature and give you some practical advice!

PRINCE *(digging in his pockets)*. Where has it disappeared to? . . Hm . . Don't tell me I've gone and lost it!

ABRAMSON *(with an inquisitor's delight)*. You wore a tuxedo on the train?

PRINCE. Hm . . . no! That is, I changed later on the train.

ABRAMSON *(generously opening his claws to release his victim)*. Well then, that's where you must have lost the ticket book!

PRINCE. In all probability! What an idiotic thing to do! *(Shrugs his shoulders, walks away from Abramson in embarrassment, heads over to join Gregoire and the Girl in Mourning, who are both looking through some sketches on the piano.)*

ABRAMSON *(consoling the Prince, ambiguously)*. Awfully idiotic! *(Winks slyly at Schmidt and Phillips, begins to laugh, walks with them downstage and infects them with his good humor. Trompetti and Baker, who have been observing the whole previous scene from the shadows, exchange indistinct remarks and quickly disappear to the left.)*

ABRAMSON *(suddenly stops on the apron and bursts out in laughter, echoed by Phillips and Schmidt.)* I'll be damned! Now I remember! *(Slaps Schmidt on the shoulder.)* You promised us some sort of mystification, supposed to be funnier than hell! Where is it? . . I sense it around here, but I don't seem to be able to find it!

SCHMIDT *(with a musterious smile)*. Everything in its own good time! *(Exchanges whispers with Phillips, who then goes off left.)*

ABRAMSON *(looking at his watch)*. It's high time! And I'm beginning to have apprehensions that not all your promises are serious!

SCHMIDT. For instance?

ABRAMSON. . . . for instance, I still don't see a trace of the very influential Senator Creighton you promised to introduce me to!

SCHMIDT *(with a short bow)*. Not to him, to the hostess here, Madame Daryal—Director of the Theatrical Institute!

ABRAMSON. But you said that he was a relative!

SCHMIDT *(correcting him)*. Of her late husband! Absolutely correct: a distant relative. So?

ABRAMSON. What do you mean, *so?* I would like to meet him, that is if he isn't so distant that he's at some meeting in Washington, when we're here waiting for him in New York!

SCHMIDT *(mocking)*. Conferring on a Sunday? I For the sole purpose of giving you a chance to show off your wit?!

ABRAMSON. Well then, where is he? Are you aware of the position Senator Creighton holds?

SCHMIDT. I am: member of the Customs Committee . . . on matters . . .

ABRAMSON *(correcting him)*. . . . . delivering the Review Board's report on the duties levied on luxuries and antiques! *(Phillips appears at the door left.)* And from this point of view you understand *how much* he interests me?!

SCHMIDT *(chuckling)*. Poor Creighton! What a tragedy when a man is found interesting only from the point of view of "luxuries and antiques!"

PHILLIPS *(approaching them)*. Senator Creighton is here! *(To Abramson.)* Would you like to see him? *(Motions toward the left.)* He's sitting by the window with Madame Daryal! Didn't you notice him?

SCHMIDT *(with a start)*. Really?!

ABRAMSON *(nervously)*. Never saw him before . . .

SCHMIDT. When did he get here?

PHILLIPS. At the beginning of the dove tricks.

SCHMIDT. While Yu-Gen-Li was casting spells over all of us! . . Where is she, by the way? *(Moves a little to the right.)*

PHILLIPS *(to Abramson)*. Let's go, I'll introduce you! *(From the left appear a nervously excited Mary and Anatole, whom she is practically draggin along by sheer force. Mary is a pretty blonde, about twenty, with a rather mature look on her face; Anatole is a handsome, charming young man of the "artistic" type, childishly ridiculous in his way of behaving without any regard for the impression made on socially exacting people.)*

MARY *(still in the doorway)*. Well, play something then! What a stubborn one you are! If you won't do anything in public you'll never be famous! *(Almost collides with Abramson.)* Have you met? *(Playfully.)* My music teacher! Anatole Moravsky! Be a genius any day now! . . Lacks only public recognition! *(Anatole bends his head as he bows and hence fails to notice the hand offered by Abramson. Then raising his head at the same instant Abramson drops his hand, Anatole sticks out his hand nervously, but seeing none offered in exchange, instantly pulls his own back again. Just as Abramson makes a motion of trying the handshake again, Anatole, so as to get out of the whole embarassing situation, turns with a smile to Mary and "as though nothing were the matter," ignores Abramson's hand and runs his own right hand through his tousled hair. Abramson and Phillips fade toward the door to the left with smiles confidently "liquidating" the situation and with exaggerated shuffling of feet.)*

MARY *(turning to the ones leaving, on the verge of taking offense).* Where are you going? . . Listen to a little music first!

PHILLIPS. In one second! As soon as I introduce Mr. Abramson to Senator Creighton!

MARY. Bring him over too!

PHILLIPS. Yes, your majesty! *(Exits left with Abramson.)*

MARY *(seating her music teacher at the piano).* Well now, use your head! This Senator Creighton knows lots of people! If he likes you, you'll soon be giving the most expensive lessons in New York!

ANATOLE. I'm afraid, it's so late! . . Some people are already getting ready to leave.

MARY. You're always so full of excuses!

SCHMIDT *(to Anatole, with light pathos).* How can one decline a request like that—from a super-girl like Mary Daryal?!

MARY *(after a pause).* Do you hear that, maestro, you can't refuse me—I'm a super-girl!

ANATOLE *(good-naturedly).* Wrong.

MARY. How so?

SCHMIDT. You do understand the meaning of "super-girl?"

ANATOLE. Of course! It's a . . . a lady.

SCHMIDT. What do you mean, "lady?"

ANATOLE. What else? As long as a girl's not married, she's a girl. And soon as she's married, she's so to speak, super to all that, that is, a super-girl! *(Schmidt snorts with laughter and then stops immediately.)*

MARY. Right you are! You philosophize beautifully, my dear, but you play even better! Please play for us! *(Anatole picks out several introductory chords and then begins to meditate in music, improvising beautifully and yet with real substance.)*

SCHMIDT *(leading Mary aside).* You're spending the whole evening with him. Is this just to annoy me? Yes? Drive me mad just when I'm taking my examination? Whoever recommended a teacher like that, a person, if I may say so . . .

MARY. You may not say so.

SCHMIDT. You seem to be so fascinated by this simple-minded, or should I say stu . .

MARY *(covering his mouth with her hand)*. . . . don't say it!

SCHMIDT *(taking her hand off his mouth)*. Aha! You're defending him!

MARY. Do you suppose it's possible to offend someone . . . "not of this world?"

SCHMIDT. You have such a kind heart!

MARY. I am proud of it!

SCHMIDT. . . . only not for me!

MARY. Why do you think that?

SCHMIDT. Because you are so . . . so . . . so . . .

MARY *(looking at him, teasing him)*. So . . .?

SCHMIDT. *Strange*—if that's a strong enough word for it!

MARY."Strange?" In what way?

SCHMIDT. In that you . . . you are so unusual in your usualness! . . You know yourself who you really are! But I . . . I can't put it into words. I won't risk it!

MARY *(slyly)*. Words can be committing?

SCHMIDT *(dumbfounded)*. What do you mean?

MARY *(laughs)*. What kind of lawyer are you after that?!.

SCHMIDT *(repeating mechanically)*. "Words can be committing" . . . *(Suddenly bursts out laughing.)* Now I've got it! Now I've got it! Do you know . . . do you know you really are so . . . so . . .

MARY. Mature—is that the word?

SCHMIDT. That's it exactly—extraordinarily mature for your age! *(They both laugh. Mary runs away from him looking preoccupied but very gay.)*

MARY. Now where can Senator Creighton be? He's so fond of music! *(To Anatole.)* Just a minute! . . I'll be right back! *(Swiftly goes off left. Schmidt accompanies Mary to the door, then stops there, as if remembering something, turns, scowls at everyone present and, trying not to attract any special attention, goes off swiftly right. Almost at the same instant the Girl in Light Blue enters left, gives the impression she is shadowing someone and, with a deliberately nonchalant air, disappears right. At this point Gregoire, showing his nude sketches by the piano, addresses Anatole, who has broken off his highly artistic improvisations.)*

GREGOIRE *(seeming to look down from the height of his greatness)*. I do not wish to be in your debt: you have tossed us a small auditory gift; I will reply with a visual one! . . There you are! . . Look and . . . be delighted, if your eye is sufficiently well educated for it!

GIRL IN MOURNING *(to Anatole, langorously, affected, trying very hard to make him take an interest in her)*. How do you like these female bodies? . . Do these lines excite you? . . To me they seem so, so alive, so full of motion . . .

ANATOLE. Very well drawn! Every detail! *(Throwing his head back and staring steadily at the sketches.)* Boy, are they ever nude! As if they'd been undressed twice!

GIRL IN MOURNING. "Undressed twice!" *Touché! (Trompetti and Baker have stopped at the doors left. They look as if they were totally absorbed in a dull, often wordless conversation. Noticing them, the Girl in Mourning affects a coquettish, long-suffering air and puts her hand on her forehead.)* My God, what's the matter with me? . . This weakness and dizziness again!

ANATOLE *(sympathetically).* Don't you feel well?

GIRL IN MOURNING. I've still not fully recovered from all that I went through . . .

ANATOLE. I'm so sorry, I . . . I'm afraid I don't know what it was you went through?

PRINCE *(rather rudely).* Well look—a person in mourning!

ANATOLE. Oh, of course! Who was it that died?

GIRL IN MOURNING *(with an air of long suffering).* Don't ask, I beg you!

ANATOLE. I am sorry!

GREGOIRE *(leafing through his drawings).* In these drawings I tried to show something beyond nudity . . . to do something really significant.

GIRL IN MOURNING *(fanning herself with a white handkerchief with a black border).* And you succeeded! Absolutely. I feel it intuitively! The lines are so alive and full of movement!

ANATOLE. Forgive me, but what does this shameless woman represent?

GREGOIRE. Hm . . . that's one of the sectional sketches for my canvas "Eve"—a theme from the Bible.

ANATOLE *(pointing to the drawing).* Eve? Our ancestor?

GREGOIRE. Yes. *(Draws some tickets out of his pocket and proffers them to Anatole.)* I am donating her in a lottery for charity! Would you like a ticket? Two? Three? . . Two fifty apiece.

ANATOLE *(shaking his head).* No, no . . . that's not Eve! Eve didn't have a navel.

GREGOIRE. Wha-at?

ANATOLE. God created Eve from Adam's rib! . . She wasn't born at all! How could she wind up with a navel? . . *(A pause. General embarrassment. The Girl in Mourning leaves the men, waving her handkerchief as if she hadn't enough air.)*

GREGOIRE *(clears his throat).* I would ask you not to talk about such matters in the presence of ladies!

ANATOLE. I wouldn't have been talking, if you hadn't been exhibiting! *(Takes the sketches from the music stand and puts them away in Gregoire's portfolio.)*

GREGOIRE *(clearing his throat angrily).* I see that you're quite capable of making a scene just to get out of buying a lottery ticket!

ANATOLE. And for whose benefit is this lottery?

GREGOIRE. For the benefit of impoverished artists.

ANATOLE *(sympathetically)*. You are one of them?

GREGOIRE *(flaring up)*. What do you take me for anyway?

ANATOLE. For . . . impoverished, of course! You certainly can't make much with painting like that!

PRINCE *(to Gregoire, who is searching for the proper words to express his outrage)*. Why be upset! Take me, for example, I'm not a bit ashamed of my position! *(To Anatole.)* What an idiotic thing I did! Left my wallet at home, live over in Jersey, have to buy a ticket at the station, take a taxi, pay the porter . . .

ANATOLE *(bursting out in gales of childlike laughter)* . . . You really did it! Beautiful! How can a person be so forgetful! What are you planning to do now?

PRINCE *(embarrassed)*. Me? . . I was planning to ask you for a loan. But . . . if my position is the cause of such merriment . . .

GIRL IN MOURNING *(throwing up her arms, somewhat melodramatically)*. Now this one is offended! . . Isn't it mortifying to be so mistaken about people?! *(Taking Anatole by the hand.)* Why he's a regular child of nature! How could anyone get upset at a child of nature?! *(To Anatole.)* You are good, aren't you? A child of nature? Answer me! . . Kind? Right? Well, tell me, are you good? . . Are you? . .

ANATOLE *(after a moment of hesitation, his eyes downcast)*. Yes! . . I think so! . . How did you notice it right away? . . I am extraordinarily sincere and direct . . . But that's my one fault . . . I don't know of any others.

GIRL IN MOURNING *(presses his hand)*. Oh, I empathized with you instantly! . . Why do you have such warm hands? . . Or is it that mine are so cold? . . Hm . . What's the matter with my heart today? . . dizzy . . everything is whirling around . . . Ach! *(She faints so unexpectedly that Anatole is barely able to catch her by the waist as she falls. Gregoire and the Prince, after a second of confusion, bend over the girl, unbutton the collar of her dress, feel her pulse, etc. Trompetti and Baker close the door left, then the latter dashes off to the room right and disappears with the words "water, water," while the former, dashing around not knowing what to do, takes a small bottle of smelling salts out of his vest pocket and holds it to the nose of the unconscious girl.)*

ANATOLE *(shaken, moved, tugging at the girl, trying to revive her)*. Good Lord, what's the matter with her? . . So young! . . It's terrible! . . Why am I not a doctor? . . It's so horrible to think there are so many unhappy people in this world! Some lack money! Others talent! . . Still others health! *(Suddenly realizing what he has just said, seizes Gregoire by the hand.)* Please don't think I was suggesting . . . I . . .

GREGOIRE *(rudely)*. Shut up! Spare us your verbiage!

ANATOLE *(to him).* Don't be angry, oh please! I feel sorry for you too! *(To the Prince.)* And for you too! . . Don't take me for insensitive! I thought you were joking! I don't have any money with me, either! What an amazing coincidence! That's why I laughed! . . But I'll get some money, I will! I'll run home! Will you be here a little longer? . . . . I live quite close by . . Wait for me below, or we could go together! *(To Gregoire.)* Let's have three tickets for the lottery, please! I'll buy them! All right? *(To the Prince.)* I'll give you enough to get home on! five dollars enough? And medicine for her so she can take it every day! *(During this monologe Baker has entered right with a glass of water, wets the forehead and temples of the unconscious girl, who is gradually coming to. The Girl in Light Blue enters stealthily behind Baker, glances at the Girl in Mourning. Something occurs to the Girl in Light Blue, and she runs over to the door left and draws the curtain tightly across it.)*

GIRL IN MOURNING *(half raising herself up, speaking in a "dying swan" voice).* Thank you! . . I'm better now . . . I was so tired! . . I was too upset . . . *(Stands up.)* I'll go and lie down for a while . . . get some rest . . . *(To Anatole.)* And you're so good! . . . Yes . . . Sweet! . . Kind! . . You're such an exception to this age! *(Goes off right, accompanied by everyone present with the exception of the Girl in Light Blue who runs over to the door left, opens it, parts the curtain with her hand and signals with a nod of her head. In response to her signal Mary appears.)*

GIRL IN LIGHT BLUE *(going up to the wide door center and putting her ear to one of its frosted panes.)* They're still there! . . *(Mary follows her distrustfully, approaches the glass door with some embarrassment.)* Do you hear voices? . . But I can't make out the words . . . must be really secret . . . *(Hitting himself on the forehead.)* Hold it! Now you'll see them! . . *(Rushes over to the light switch and cuts off all the lights in the room. The silhouettes of Yu-Gen-Li and Schmidt are seen clearly on the frosted panes of the center door. They are very close to and facing each other, and are close by the door.*

GIRL IN LIGHT BLUE *(after a short pause, in "conspiratorial" tones).* "Chinese shadows"! . . Just like it? . . "The Chinese Shadow Theater" . . . *(Yu-Gen-Li's shadow is seen caressing Schmidt's chin with her hand. The Girl in Light Blue giggles.)* What a sly old aunt you have! . . Not at all like your mama! Who'd ever think they were blood sisters! *(Notices a new gesture of tenderness by Yu-Gen-Li's silhouette.)* Look, look!

MARY *(interrupting quietly in a breaking voice).* But what's so unusual? They're just friends, that's all!

GIRL IN LIGHT BLUE *(disappointed).* You don't love him any more?!

MARY. Did you suppose I was so jealous?

GIRL IN LIGHT BLUE. In any case . . .

MARY. . . . . you thought you'd help me?

GIRL IN LIGHT BLUE. In any case. . . .

MARY *(her face covered with scorn)*. And what would you like as your reward?

GIRL IN LIGHT BLUE *(hardly pausing to think it over)*. Put in a good word for me with Senator Creighton! . . I asked your aunt, but she . . .

MARY. Aunt Gen doesn't like you.

GIRL IN LIGHT BLUE. . . . she refused!

MARY. . . . because you're too pushy!

GIRL IN LIGHT BLUE. I know.

MARY. So now you've betrayed her in revenge? Right? . . Or just to show off your talents?—as they say "I see all! You can't hide from me!" *(Her speech breaks off at the sight of the two silhouettes on the frosted panes suddenly kissing passionately. A pause.)*

GIRL IN LIGHT BLUE *(with malicious glee)*. Wow, are they ever glued together! . . They managed the job without even using any glue!

MARY *(nervous, enraged)*. Shut up!

GIRL IN LIGHT BLUE *(mimicking Mary)*. But what's so unusual? They're just friends, that's all!

MARY *(laughs loudly and nervously and yells)*. "Words can be committing"! . . Can't they?

GIRL IN LIGHT BLUE *(puzzled)*. What's the matter with you? Tsss . . . Don't shout! *(When Mary shouted the silhouettes on the frosted panes broke apart and a second or two later Yu-Gen-Li runs away from the door, leaving a shadow on the glass growing larger and paler. This is the cue for the light behind the panes to be cut, causing total darkness on the stage, at which moment the Director of the Theatrical Institute (Sofya Daryal), Senator Creighton, Abramson, and Phillips—all invisible in the blackout—enter left from behind the drawn curtain.**

DIRECTOR. Why is it so dark here? . . Who's here?

MARY. Just a minute . . . One minute! . . *(Stumbles around looking for the switch.)*

DIRECTOR. What happened to the lights? Is that you, Mary?

MARY. It's me, Mama, me!

DIRECTOR. What's going on? . . . Who turned off the . . .

MARY *(interrupting)*. It was only a joke! Wait a second! I can't find the light switch . . .

DIRECTOR. You're such a child! *(The stage is flooded with light revealing Mary and the Girl in Light Blue at the switch by the door right. They have collided in the confusion and are almost in each other's arms. A puzzled group at left is revealed, preceded by the Director of the Theatrical Institute in her stiffest "salon" manner, and*

---

*The blackout is aided by the curtain over the half-open door having been drawn previously by the Girl in Light Blue. N. E.)

Senator Creighton. The former—Sofya Daryal—a tall woman of about fifty, almost completely gray, has an extremely severe look on her face, and a gold pince nez lends her a garish, pedantic flavor. The latter is a rather short, stout, fine, comically pleasant-looking old man, instantly suggesting with his bright, expressive features egotism, gluttony, and lechery.)

MARY *(somewhat embarrassed).* There you are! . . . Please excuse me!

DIRECTOR *(shocked).* What will Mr. Creighton think?

SENATOR *(mouths his words a little, the way old men do).* For Christ's sake! Who do you take me for? I don't think anything in such cases.

DIRECTOR. Mr. Creighton is too indulgent!

SENATOR. Nothing of the kind! But all my dignity simply dissolves in the presence of young creatures, searching for the darkness where they may share their girlish secrets! *(As if to confirm these words, Mary at once embraces the Girl in Light Blue around the waist.)*

DIRECTOR *(weighs the situation, motions the Senator to the divan right).* Won't you sit down? *(To Mary.)* We were promised some music, Mary! . . Where is this virtuoso of yours? . . *(To the Senator.)* Her new music teacher! *(To the others.)* Please be seated! *(Mary and the Girl in Light Blue run off right. The Director sits down with the Senator on the divan downstage; all the rest obediently sit down anywhere they can, turned toward the piano, the way people do at a concert.)* I would be interested in your opinion, since this musician would like to teach in our institute! *(Pause.)* Where is he?

SENATOR *(looking at his watch).* I'm afraid I'd better . . .

DIRECTOR. Where are you going? Stay a little longer! We see you so seldom!

SENATOR *(laughing).* I can stay, but will my train to Washington stay? That is the question!

DIRECTOR *(stands up).* No, no! You can't leave before you talk to my sister! Why, poor Gen would be simply crushed! I'll go get her to hurry and the musician too! *(Goes off right, freeing a place for Abramson who immediately comes over.)*

ABRAMSON *(sitting next to Creighton).* Concluding what I was saying about the tariff system and especially the duty on antique furniture . . .

SENATOR. Yes, yes, I recall, you were beginning to talk about . . . about the . . . *(helplessly searches for words in the air with his fingers).*

ABRAMSON. I just wanted to make the observation that it would take a genius to set up a tariff that would suit everyone! *(Colonel O'Kay enters left and walks briskly through the room, Phillips, who has been constantly at Abramson's side, spots Colonel O'Kay, rushes up and mumbles something to him, and the two of them then disappear at the doorway right.)*

SENATOR *(objecting immediately to Abramson's remark)*. And yet it is absolutely necessary that we have one!

ABRAMSON *(moving closer)*. I have heard that you are *not* for raising the duties on furniture imported from Europe and . . . far be it from me to persuade you to change your mind, but, as an old furniture-maker, I would be happy of some assurance that our industry's interests are not going to suffer thereby . . .

SENATOR. Hm . . . That is a ve-ry complex question and . . . I would rather not anticipate the results of the Finance Commission's deliberations!

ABRAMSON. I can appreciate your caution, but . . . *(Gregoire, the Prince, Trompetti, Baker, Colonel O'Kay, and Phillips all come merrily trooping in from the right. Gregoire, egged on by his companions, bravely approaches the Senator and, throwing his hair back, nods to him with undue familiarity.)*

GREGOIRE. I have here the sketches for my canvas "Eve," which is being raffled off! Would you care to have a look? *(Indicates his folder, which he holds securely.)*

SENATOR. Hm . . . All right!

ABRAMSON *(putting on his pince nez)*. . . . . at the price of the tickets first! *(To Gregoire.)* How much are they?

GREGOIRE. Two fifty apiece! . . It's for a worthy cause!

SENATOR *(taking out his wallet and leafing through his money with the air of a man not inclined to part with the smallest portion of it)*. Large bills only! . . How annoying!

ABRAMSON. Don't worry! *(Hands Gregoire a hundred-dollar bill.)* Here's a hundred dollars for two tickets. *(To the Senator.)* One for you. Maybe you'll be the lucky one! *(To Gregoire.)* No change necessary!

SENATOR. One hundred?! Well! . . *(Quickly puts away his wallet.)* It's hard to compete with you . . .

PRINCE *(taking Gregoire's place in front of the Senator)*. An extraordinarily idiotic thing happened to me! I . . .

ABRAMSON *(interrupting)*. I know! They told me: lost two hundred dollars at the station and were left without a penny? *(To the Senator.)* Incredible stupidity! *(Takes out his money and sticks two hundred dollars in the Prince's hand.)* Take these two hundred dollars, I just happen to have found them in the street, and be more careful next time! *(Cuts off the Prince, whose mouth is gaping in amazement.)* Only don't thank me, please! People *must* help one another! That is their sacred duty! *(The Prince seizes Abramson's hand, shakes it vigorously and goes off upstage, putting the money in his pocket.)*

SENATOR *(heartily shaking Abramson's hand)*. You're an unusual man, Dr. Abramson—you have the same kind of heart I do! Seriously! The very same compulsion to be . . . to be extravagantly generous when it comes to one's fellow man! The very same love for these, how would you say it? . . . for our "needy young people"!

ABRAMSON *(confidentially, making a joke out of everything).* . . . especially to young female people? Right?

SENATOR *(giggling with approval).* Hee-hee! And you're a real comedian on top of everything else?

ABRAMSON *(with a very confident, amused smile).* Life is so boring at times!

SENATOR *(enthusiastically).* No, you are one outstanding person, Mr. Abramson! *(Severely.)* Don't protest, please!—I am never mistaken about people!

ABRAMSON *(with a slight bow).* I would be happy if you would give me a chance to prove it! *(Yu-Gen-Li, in a black velvet evening dress with a gold cross around her neck instead of a pendant, and her sister, the Director, enter.)*

YU-GEN-LI *(greeting the Senator).* Please forgive me for being so late!

SENATOR *(kissing her hand).* I did not want to leave without saying goodbye to you!

YU-GEN-LI. Ever since I had the stupid opium habit I get these awful headaches, that just . . .

SENATOR. But in that case . . .

YU-GEN-LI *(interrupting).* Oh no! It's all over now! Please sit down! *(Sits to the right of him with the Director to the left.)*

SENATOR *(standing between them).* Every time I stand between you, dear sisters, I feel like I'm on top of the Urals! *(He laughs.)*

DIRECTOR. We, we can understand *that:* your *high* position in the world . . .

SENATOR. Not that at all! . . The fact is that the Urals *separate* Europe from Asia *(indicating Sofya Daryal, the Director, as he says "Europe," and Yu-Gen-Li as he says "Asia")* and even—one may say—East from West! *(He sits down with the same gesture of placing the sisters in opposition.)*

DIRECTOR *(with a smile).* That's right: I'm from the Volga and was born Russian, while Gen was born a Siberian with Mongolian blood. But I became a regular native of the Far East! . .—spent almost my entire stage career there! Gen and I were reminiscing just the other day how I got her on the stage! She was still a little child when my husband died *(lowering her voice)* your cousin . . .

SENATOR *(with a sigh).* Poor Charlie! Now there was a hell of a character— may he rest in peace! He must have been a real trial, the poor thing! However *(turning to Yu-Gen-Li)* I hear your husband is . . . much the same? . .

YU-GEN-LI. Oh, let's not even talk about it!

SENATOR. Is he still in China? No intentions of coming here?

YU-GEN-LI *(with an appalled smile).* God forbid!

DIRECTOR *(bending toward him and lowering her voice).* My sister and he were recently divorced . . .

SENATOR. Really? . . . Hm . . . well, and . . . what sort of property settlement was there?

YU-GEN-LI. Everything was confiscated on account of his political activity.

SENATOR. You don't say?!

YU-GEN-LI. So without a nickel in the bank I'll just have to go to work!

SENATOR *(absolutely amazed).* You . . . you speak about these unpleasant things as if they didn't concern you at all!

YU-GEN-LI *(melancholy laughter).* That's an actress for you!

SENATOR. I'm overwhelmed by your performance! Although . . I confess I don't know the slightest thing about the theater!

DIRECTOR *(flattering).* You're much too modest!

SENATOR. Honest to God!

DIRECTOR. In any event you must wish us success in my institute—my sister is also involved, as a working shareholder!

SENATOR. Really? . . *(Mary, distraught, enters right. Immediately behind her is Schmidt, looking like a man celebrating an easy conquest.)*

DIRECTOR *(to her daughter).* Well, my dear, where is your virtuoso? . . Why all the delay? *(To the Senator.)* Now don't keep looking at your watch! You'll make it!

SENATOR *(getting up, speaking politely).* I am afraid that I must . . . It's time! *(Many of the guests who arrived on stage after Yu-Gen-Li and the Director's arrival now surround them with the intention of saying goodbye.)*

MARY *(embarrassed).* I can't find him anywhere, Mama! Maybe he left already? Otherwise . . . where could he have disappeared to?

DIRECTOR *(amazed beyond belief).* Left? . . What do you mean "left"? That is impossible!

SENATOR *(pointing to his watch).* I should have left some time ago! *(To Mary.)* Your musician just set an example worthy of emulation! *(A light murmur of approval among the guests getting ready to leave.)*

DIRECTOR. What's this? You too are prepared to go off without taking leave of the hostess?

SENATOR. God Forbid! *(Kisses her hand.)* Absent-mindedness in an artist may be forgiven, but not in the rest of us! *(Light laughter among those present.)*

DIRECTOR. Still, I'm dreadfully sorry! Please forgive me for . . .

SENATOR *(interrupting, affectionately).* You have nothing to apologize for! *(Takes leave of Yu-Gen-Li.)*

DIRECTOR. When will we see each other again?

YU-GEN-LI *(to him).* Come see us at our place in the country! All right? We'll be staying at this—what's it . . .

ABRAMSON *(who has kept his eyes steadily on Yu-Gen-Li and now quickly, masterfully, prompts her).* . . . . at Yellow Beach!

DIRECTOR *(embarrassed).* I'm sorry, but . . .

YU-GEN-LI *(interrupting).* It's near Atlantic City! I'll send you the address!

ABRAMSON *(neither exactly to her nor to the Senator).* No more than three hours from Washington in a fast car!

DIRECTOR *(to the Senator, now that she has recovered from her astonishment).* Bring your wife too, if her health permits!

SENATOR. Thank you! Unfortunately the doctors are shipping her off north! . . But if you're not afraid of being bored with me by myself . . . if the wife's *not there,* then . . .

YU-GEN-LI. Is it really possible to be bored around you? I can't imagine how.

SENATOR. Oh, you are much too kind! Goodbye! . . *(Goes left, accompanied by the Director, her sister and the guests. As they leave the guests are saying goodbye to the hostess, Yu-Gen-Li, the Senator, and the others. On stage, along with Mary, Phillips, Abramson, and Schmidt, remain two groups: one of teachers and the other of pupils of the Theatrical Institute.)*

MARY *(now that the Senator and the others have gone, gives full vent to her annoyance, directing her words partly to Schmidt and partly to the others).* Well, what do you say to that? Eh? Vanished! Disappeared without a trace! . . What a ridiculous thing to happen! *(Breathless.)* I don't even know whether to be angry with him or . . . or . . .

SCHMIDT *(making a big show of looking under the chairs and sofas).* Forgive him! You have to forgive him! After all, can you thrust public performances on timid dilettantes?!. *(Bending over and looking under a sofa.)* Nope, not there either! *(Titters are heard among the Theatrical Institute pupils.)*

MARY *(angrily taking Schmidt by the hand and leading him far downstage).* Your "wit" right now is justified neither by your love for me nor by your jealousy toward him!

SCHMIDT. What makes you think that?!

MARY. I don't believe you any more!

SCHMIDT. Since when, if it's no secret?!!!

MARY. Since half an hour ago, if you're too dumb to figure it out for yourself!

SCHMIDT *(wrinkless his brow, desperately trying to remember).* "Since half an hour ago"? . .

ABRAMSON *(shaking Phillips' hand, with whom he has been standing off to one side and exchanging sotto voce remarks now and then).* You're not going my way? . . No? . . . *(Approaches Mary to take his leave.)*

SCHMIDT *(stopping him)*. Where to? . . Wait a minute! How about the mystification?!. Did you forget?!. *(Mary goes off left.)*

PHILLIPS. Does Mr. Abramson know that . . .

SCHMIDT *(interrupting)*. He'll know everything very shortly! I got special permission for him to stay until the end of the examination!

ABRAMSON. What examination? What are you talking about? *(The Girl in Light Blue, that is, the Junior Detective, runs in from right with a sandwich in one hand and a cigarette in the other. Her boyish manners and masculine voice leave no doubt as to the travesty played by this member of the cast.)*

JUNIOR DETECTIVE *(chewing on his sandwich and taking off his Bubikopf wig)*. God damn, am I tired! . . Beat to hell! Are they all gone?

O'KAY *(and others after him)*. Sh-h! . . . There's an outsider here! . . *(Burst of laughter among the pupils.)* Crazy idiot! *(All are motioning in Abramson's direction with their eyes and gestures. The Junior Detective instantly curls up in great embarrassment, stares at Abramson, backs off from him as if from a veritable apparition and, holding up his dress, rushes off right. First the pupils, who are full of laughter, then the Institute teachers go off after him.)*

DIRECTOR *(enters left with Mary, dolefully finishing up her "maternal admonition")*. . . . . he, my dear, is not a child and ought to understand that even eccentricity has its limits. Otherwise we simply can't have him around in polite society no matter how beautifully he plays the piano!

MARY *(with great sincerity)*. But Mama, I assure you . . .

DIRECTOR. Don't assure me, my friend, your attempts at defending him are starting to provoke me! *(Yu-Gen-Li, strictly business-like, enters left and swiftly goes over to the Director. Right behind her is the maid, carrying a green broadcloth table spread. May (the maid) puts it on one of the chairs and sets about efficiently pushing two tables together, thereby forming at stage left what seems to be one table.)*

YU-GEN-LI. The secretary called and said he hadn't recovered yet and won't be at the examinations!

DIRECTOR. Take his place, Mary! *(To her daughter.)* You aren't too tired?

MARY *(sadly)*. No. *(The maid covers the tables, now perpendicular to the front of the stage, with the green tablecloth and sets several chairs around the table.)*

YU-GEN-LI. Only someone will have to go and see him and get the school journal and the register—he doesn't have anyone to send!

DIRECTOR *(to Schmidt, affectionately)*. May I ask you to do us a favor, Hermann! You've always come to the rescue before!

SCHMIDT. With the greatest pleasure! *(To Abramson.)* I'll be back in ten minutes! *(To the ladies.)* I leave my patron in your care!

DIRECTOR *(smiling)*. You may entrust him to us with confidence! *(Walks off to the center glass door, which has remained closed during the entire act, takes a key from her purse, and sticks it in the key hole.)*

YU-GEN-LI *(almost interrupting her sister).* We won't let him get bored! Hurry! *(Schmidt runs off left. Yu-Gen-Li motions to Abramson to sit down on the sofa downstage right.)* Please sit down until everything is settled. *(To the maid.)* You ought to air the place out and sweep it up! *(having taken hold of the cord to the right of the curtain, to Abramson.)* Don't worry! We'll keep you away from the housework! *(She pulls on the cord; the edges of the curtain slowly draw together, revealing a clear design of black half-masks embroidered on a rusty-gold background, like so many flowers on wallpaper.)* I must get back to the telephone, but . . . Mr. Phillips, I hope, will keep you entertained as befits a real orator! *(When the curtains have almost blocked the view of the living room, the sliding glass door center, unlocked by the Director, slides open, revealing the classroom* interieur *heretofore concealed . . . Yu-Gen-Li coquettishly pokes her head through the part in the curtain and looks with half-closed eyes at Abramson.)* Incidentally, how did you like the examination today?

ABRAMSON. What examination?

YU-GEN-LI. The one our pupils took.

ABRAMSON *(confused).* Excuse me . . . I must have come too late for the performance?

YU-GEN-LI. Not at all! You were part of it from the very start!

ABRAMSON. Me? . . . Whose part did I play?

YU-GEN-LI. The one they tried their talent out on!

ABRAMSON. I don't understand you! What's all this about?

YU-GEN-LI. Ask Mr. Phillips! *(She disappears with a gay toss of the head. Phillips breaks out in merry laughter. Abramson looks at him with poorly diguised amazement.)*

ABRAMSON *(when Phillips stops laughing, after they have been left alone).* What kind of place is this?

PHILLIPS. A military-theatrical institute.

ABRAMSON. What does that mean? What do they study here?

PHILLIPS. The art of camouflage, military camouflage . . .

ABRAMSON. But why should actors learn these things?

PHILLIPS. That which is unnecessary on the boards of the theater is quite necessary on the stage of life.

ABRAMSON. Where?!

PHILLIPS. In the *Theater of Eternal War,* that is to say, our life on this earth. Where everyone struggles for his existence and where man is not so much a wolf to his fellow man as a fox, going on to victory by covering his tracks, by travelling the road of contrivance and pretense!

ABRAMSON *(wiping his hand on his forehead as if it were afire)*. You mean, here they learn—to put it bluntly—how to dissemble while fighting for their interests, and not . . .

PHILLIPS *(getting the drift of Abramson's thinking)* . . . and not put on a cheap show just for the sake of entertaining the audience! You're very clever!

ABRAMSON *(glancing at him)*. This then is the mystification I was promised?

PHILLIPS *(shrugging his shoulders)*. Obviously!

ABRAMSON *(with a grin)*. Well, at last! *(Sits in the corner.)*

PHILLIPS. Would you like to know the whole secret?

ABRAMSON. Of course!

PHILLIPS *(sits next to him and furrows his brow as if collecting his thoughts. A pause.)* Listen!

CURTAIN.

Scene Two

Between Scenes One and Two there is an intermission of no more thar five minutes.
   As the curtain rises, the smaller inner curtain, embroidered with masks, is still drawn. Phillips, standing in the middle of the stage with his back to the audience, is keeping one eye on the crack in the curtain, while Abramson is sprawled on the small sofa right, pensively smoking a cigarette.

PHILLIPS *(turning to Abramson)*. They're getting it all fixed up now! Two or three minutes and everything'll be ready. Do you feel a draft?

ABRAMSON. No.

PHILLIPS. They'll close the windows in a minute! . .

ABRAMSON *(thinking out loud)*. Then that affected Girl in Mourning, and that arrogant artist pretending to be a celebrity, and that idiotic boor posing as a prince and begging for a loan, and that boy dressed up like a little girl, all of them, right up to that sweet attorney Schmidt, everything they did was just part of the role they were playing?

PHILLIPS. That was their examination!

ABRAMSON. And this . . . musician that ran off?

PHILLIPS. Anatole Moravsky?

ABRAMSON. . . . was he too playing today? He too was examined?

PHILLIPS. Alas! . . He merely tried to play, and on the piano at that! *(He laughs.)*

ABRAMSON *(chuckling)*. Why isn't he mastering this "salutary," as you put it, "pretense on the stage of life?"

PHILLIPS. I hear Miss Mary herself is going to teach him this summer!

ABRAMSON. But suppose it's true that "only the grave can cure a hunch-back"?

PHILLIPS. Nonsense! These days *surgery* can straighten out the hunchback bet-ter than any grave and can *transform* our appearance!

ABRAMSON. I realize that—are you judging by your own case?

PHILLIPS. You know, when I wrecked my car, they just about had to pick the pieces off the pavement and stick me together again!

ABRAMSON *(smiling)*. I remember! . . You used to make cracks about sticking you together and then having an arm and a leg come unstuck again!

PHILLIPS. Let's say that was all a little exaggerated! *(Moves one leg slightly and touches his left arm.)* Just the same . . .

ABRAMSON *(continuing)*. . . . and *one* eye, if I'm not mistaken, had to be replaced?

PHILLIPS. No mistake about the number involved! If it had been two I shouldn't have had the pleasure of seeing that sarcastic smile on your face!

ABRAMSON. Now don't get me wrong! I'm not prepared to defend *extremes* in the love for truth! . . Even less so in the presence of a regular *walking commercial* for *surgical masquerade!* However, the other extreme . . .

PHILLIPS *(interrupting, with enthusiasm).* But that's where you're mistaken! Look around. Who conquers in the battle for existence? Not the strongest and the worthiest, not by any means, but rather the shrewdest, the one who adapts better than others, and most of all, the *one most skillful at hypocrisy!*

ABRAMSON *(with a grin).* These stubborn quibblers must annoy you no end?

PHILLIPS *(sugary).* Do I look like it? *(They both laugh.)*

YU-GEN-LI *(parts the curtain slightly and glances at them).* Thank God, you're not bored stiff?

ABRAMSON *(gaily).* Of course not! How could one be bored seeing the truth with its slip-cover off, like a sofa, ready to have the dust of ages beaten out of it!

YU-GEN-LI *(to Phillips).* What are you talking about? *(To Abramson.)* Are you being properly enlightened about everything?

PHILLIPS. About the "theatrical ABC's" of our behavior! I'm convinced it's impossible to tell people in all seriousness "don't lie," "don't pretend," "be modest," "help thy neighbor," when it is *not these things,* but only their appearance which guarantees success in the struggle for their interests!

YU-GEN-LI *(smiling at Abramson).* What do you say to that?

ABRAMSON *(joking).* Me? Not a thing! . . Business is business! . . "No deceit, no sale," as the old saying goes. But what would our learned preacher friend here say about deceiving *morality? (Gives Phillips a friendly pat on the knee.)*

PHILLIPS. In war doesn't one attempt to *mislead* the enemy?

ABRAMSON *(with a grin).* But how can you justify the morality of war? Civil war maybe, but . . .

PHILLIPS. Sending people off to any kind of war without the necessary training in *military deception* is *criminal.* Animals are more honest than we are when it comes to raising their young: they don't deprive them—just to please emasculated truth—of the *art of mimicry,* or of the *art of protective coloring,* or all the instructive *games* in which the young learn to deceive the enemy while fleeing from him or chasing after him!

YU-GEN-LI. Bravo! . . "A" Plus!

PHILLIPS. Glad to do my best, cap'n! *(The Director's voice is heard: "Gen! Gen!")*

YU-GEN-LI. Coming. *(She retires.)*

ABRAMSON *(laughing).* Was that another examination we just had?

PHILLIPS *(smiling guiltily).* Sort of.

ABRAMSON *(laughing).* You're very good at fooling people!

PHILLIPS. Is that . . . a compliment?

ABRAMSON. Hm . . . not terribly flattering in any case! But tell me, where did this whole idea come from?

PHILLIPS. Of the "military theatrical institute?" But . . . all you have to do is recognize that our life is one continuous *war of interests* and along with that one continuous *theater of hypocrisy,* and right away you see the need for an institution where the art and science of the two can be studied!

ABRAMSON. But why hasn't anyone else, other than Madame Daryal . . .

PHILLIPS *(seizing the opportunity).* Because her married life happened to be a failure because of her *excessive frankness.* It conflicted with the conventions of society! A marvelous actress *on the stage,* but she couldn't stand deception *off stage!* And since life never forgives the failure to use the masks it prescribes, and sincerity always *betrays* those devoted to it. Madame Daryal was bound sooner or later to come to the conclusion that it's better to be a failure on the stage than a poor actress in real life, where she had been innocently going around without a mask—for her husband, for her relatives, and for everybody else who then took advantage of her for their own crude, egotistical purposes!

ABRAMSON. Is this how she describes it?

PHILLIPS. Yes, she and her sister. Madame Daryal subsequently re-educated her sister and her daughter in the *theatrical rules of life* . . . The experiment proved successful and . . .

ABRAMSON. I understand: they wanted to share it with others, and so *(in unison with Phillips)* that's how the "military theatrical institute" got its start.

PHILLIPS. Yu-Gen-Li, out of sheer gratitude to her sister, suggested the idea herself!

ABRAMSON. Just as I thought! Only by combining *Western* practicality with *Eastern* cunning could you come up with an idea like that!

PHILLIPS. I call it the road to salvation!

ABRAMSON. You—a minister of the gospel?!

PHILLIPS. If I in my old age came here for an *education,* then . . .

ABRAMSON. You?!. "For an education"?!.

PHILLIPS. Do you suppose that *old people* don't need *education?!.* Wrong! It's even more necessary for us than for young people, who are free of our prejudices and consequently can understand far better than we the *demands* of the *Time!* And since those demands are made mainly by the young people, all we have to do is follow their lead, and learn to imitate them in everything!

MARY *(enters rapidly from behind the inner curtain with a man's coat on her arm and asks Abramson).* Excuse me, is this your coat?

ABRAMSON *(after a moment of confusion)*. No . . . not mine.

PHILLIPS *(carefully examining the sleeves of the coat, which show traces of plaster)*. Tell me! . . Who was it that got here the same time I did, who had such dirty shoulders? Ah-ha! Of course, it's his! He arrived the same time I did!

MARY. Who?

PHILLIPS. Anatole Moravsky.

MARY. *(delighted)*. Really? . . That's right! And that means he's coming back again! *(Runs off gaily.)*

PHILLIPS *(puzzled, watches her as she departs)*. Can it be that it's *not only* his music that's captivating her?

ABRAMSON. Moravsky?

PHILLIPS *(not listening)*. Then her pity for his is *not* insured against excesses?! No foresight at all! . . *(During this last exclamation he glances through the crack in the curtain at precisely the moment the curtain opens, leaving him in the precarious position of a man who has lost his footing. The room which had been hidden behind the inner curtain now turns out to look more like a ball room than a living room. Chairs have been neatly arranged along the walls on both sides of the doors. At the curtain line left downstage is the table composed—with the help of the green broadcloth—of two smaller tables set parallel to the side wall. There are writing materials and sheets of white paper on it. Behind it, to the left, are several armchairs. A piano stands by the right wall. In this act it contrasts sharply with the mechanical playing apparatus attached to it. The room upstage, which had been locked during Scene One is now seen clearly through the wide-open doors. This "classroom" upstage partially suggests a movie studio, partially a psychological laboratory. A blackboard and chalk are visible as are a silver-gray projection screen, several mannequins, mime and plastic posters, photographs, accessories for eurhythmics, and other objects appropriate for an interieur of a "military theatrical institute." As the inner curtain opens a group of students in this "classroom" may be seen following a Behaviorist formula that Baker is writing on the board. Yu-Gen-Li, accompanied by Trompetti and O'Kay, comes out right from the door; all three enter the "classroom" and begin conversing with the Girl in Mourning. Somewhere up left an electric bell is heard ringing. May, the maid, who has just opened the curtain with a cord, goes off quickly left. Mary is standing with the man's raincoat in her arms by her mother. Her mother, the Director, has been sitting at the head of the "Examination Table" in the larger room. Mary stops May, in order to hand her the coat.)*

MARY *(to the maid)*. Hang this up, please!

MAY. Where was it hanging, miss? By the mirror, or . . .

MARY. On the floor! Can't you see the loop is broken?

DIRECTOR *(nervously)*. Hurry up, Mary! That's the second time the bell's rung! *(The maid runs off left.)* It must be Hermann! Be nice to him! It was most kind of him! *(Mary follows the maid out. Abramson and Phillips hesitatingly ease over to the table.)* Please sit down, Mr. Abramson! *She gestures toward a chair downstage left, near the armchairs arranged around the green table.)*

ABRAMSON. I must say I'm a little ill at ease . . . What a formal occasion! . . Am I in the way here?

DIRECTOR *(smiling)*. Of course not! We are most happy to have you! And you're not alone either, a couple of the pupils' relatives are still here! We do all this *just as if* we were right at home!

ABRAMSON. Just the same, knowing that an "examination" is about to begin . . .

DIRECTOR *(laughs)*. Why be afraid of words? *(Pinching the green tablecloth.)* Pay no attention to this official "table mask"! Simply a gesture of politeness toward the pupils!

PHILLIPS *(chuckling and nodding "yes, yes, yes")*. All the same, it's still a final examination! You've got to take that into consideration.

YU-GEN-LI *(goes up to Abramson with the Girl in Mourning)*. I believe you two have met? *(Abramson bows.)* Don't you think she inspires confidence? *(Interrupts herself and turns to her sister.)* Oh yes! Please assure Mr. Abramson how happy we are with his offer, on condition the summer house belong fictitiously not to us, but to her! *(Motions toward the Girl in Mourning.)*

DIRECTOR *(to Abramson)*. That would be the best way, I think! She's not so well known! And besides—don't be upset—I've never had anything to do with business matters!

YU-GEN-LI *(stroking the Girl in Mourning encouragingly on the shoulder)*. And she just happens to be from a business family and so this would be good practice for a "responsible role"!

GIRL IN MOURNING *(in a business-like tone, contrasting sharply to her tone in Scene One)*. What is it? What are you talking about?

YU-GEN-LI. About the summer house near Atlantic City, in Yellow Beach, where a "summer camp" is being planned.

ABRAMSON *(to Phillips)*. What do they mean by that?

PHILLIPS. A summer workshop for our graduates.

YU-GEN-LI *(to the Girl in Mourning)*. Mr. Abramson is offering us a summer house and guest cabins where we can put our institute's entire graduating class, and where, on the occasion of the landlady's imminent departure abroad, the *antique furniture* is being sold! Would you like to play the part of the lady? *(To Abramson.)* Wouldn't grief be appropriate in this role? . . Father dead, husband, mother! A real family drama, after which there naturally comes the desire to go away forever, once all the property can be sold!

ABRAMSON *(to the Girl in Mourning, with great sympathy)*. But—God forbid—didn't such a tragedy just befall you? Or did I get it wrong?

YU-GEN-LI *(laughing together with the others)*. I'm fantasizing! I'm only speaking *hypothetically!* She didn't have anyone die, thank the Lord!

ABRAMSON. You mean, these mourning clothes . . .

YU-GEN-LI. . . . are simply a "costume" . . . She looks too frivolous without them!

DIRECTOR *(to Abramson, interrupting her sister)*. Mourning inspires *confidence.* Don't you agree?

GIRL IN MOURNING. I'm sorry, but I still don't understand what everybody's talking about.

YU-GEN-LI *(with a tone appropriate to a concise summing up of matters)*. Mr. Abramson, wishing a "special sale" of furniture, as he puts it—is using the device of a *fictitious special sale,* supposedly "owner forced to sell, due to . . ."

ABRAMSON *(explaining gently to the Girl in Mourning)*. People are afraid of paying too much in stores, supposing that they can get things cheaper when "owner forced to sell, due to . . ."! And so we'll use this psychology to catch them, we'll rent special quarters for the occasion!

YU-GEN-LI. The furniture salesmen show up masked as "residents" and the selling then becomes a matter of *performing the script* of a special sale. Is that clear now?

GIRL IN MOURNING *(in a tone of approval)*. Well, naturally! . . Was it your invention?

ABRAMSON. No, but . . . no one ever patented it!

YU-GEN-LI *(brightly, provocatively)*. So we are going to take advantage of Mr. Abramson's idea, for which we get the house for the whole summer!

ABRAMSON *(looking ingratiatingly into Yu-Gen-Li's face)*. And if you sell the house, too, then you get a commission on top of everything else! *(Schmidt and Mary enter left shortly before Abramson's last words. They have notebooks and a journal in their hands and give them to the Director.)*

DIRECTOR *(gratefully shakes Schmidt's hand and rings a small bell on the table)*. Let us begin, gentlemen! Please take your places! *(Trompetti, O'Kay, and Baker enter from the "classroom" upstage and take their places at the examination table. Phillips joins the pupils. The pupils, together with some of their relatives who have come to the examination, are spread around, some at the "classroom" doors, some nearby in the living room.)*

SCHMIDT *(to Abramson, going off with him toward the footlights)*. How about that?! Didn't expect such a show? Eh? Now do you know why I brought you here? Are you convinced now that business can borrow from the theater?

ABRAMSON. I'd like to be convinced, my friend, very much! So tell me, *how much* does this old magician get for *educating old people?*

YU-GEN-LI *(unnoticed by Abramson, has come directly behind him).* The fee will depend on the amount of generosity I, as your teacher, manage to inspire in you! *(Abramson laughs in embarrassment and none too smoothly. The Director rings the bell for the second time by which time all the examiners have seated themselves at the table on the side closet to the wall at left. The Director is in the center, to her right is O'Kay, to her left is Baker. At O'Kay's right is Trompetti. On Baker's left, farthest downstage, is Yu-Gen-Li. Mary takes a seat near Trompetti at the narrow end of the table, that is, facing the audience. Mary is handling the secretarial chores during the examination. Not far from Yu-Gen-Li, almost at the footlights, Abramson takes a seat indicated by the Director. He easily and quickly assumes the role of "honored guest.")*

DIRECTOR *(calls upon a pupil on her list).* Mr. Gregoire! *(The painter comes up to the table. Pause. The Director fingers several notebooks lying nearby.)* The subject of your thesis is . . .

GREGOIRE. *On Wit and Aplomb as Auxiliary Means in the Conquest of Fame and Fortune.*

DIRECTOR *(picking out one of the notebooks).* Yes, yes! That's it. *(Leafs through the notebook.)* Well written, very glib. You show that the mere possession of talent by the novice is insufficient for quick recognition, but that superiority in some well-known, popular field is an absolute necessity! *(Looking through the thesis.)* For instance: the art of the "quick retort," the art of "witticism," a gift for "paradoxical ideas," etc.! *(Closing the notebook.)* Quite right! But . . . in practice it doesn't work out so simply for you?

GREGOIRE. You mean I lack aplomb? Or . . .

DIRECTOR *(interrupting).* Oh, you've got aplomb to spare! But as for wit . . . *(snapping her fingers suggesting the lack of something).* What is wit, anyway?

GREGOIRE *(seemingly reciting).* Wit is defined as the ability to find the hidden similarity among dissimilar objects or . . .

DIRECTOR *(interrupting).* Hold it! I am asking you for a *tactical* definition of wit!

GREGOIRE. I have one! Wit means to blind one's competitor with one's artificial intellectual brilliance! Or to repulse him with the poison gas of ridicule! Or to shower him with a deadly hail of cutting witticisms! Or to disarm him on the spot with laughter, which . . .

DIRECTOR *(interrupting).* Yes, yes! That is, in other words, the struggle requires not so much true wit—a gift of God—as its appearance! For instance, at the deciding moment in a conversation in polite society, one requires not a higher education—such as one obtains at a university—but only the *appearance* of a university education!

GREGOIRE. I know that.

DIRECTOR. Knowing isn't enough! You have to know how to do it, demonstrate it, and not hide it from the world! *(Turning to the teaching staff.)* Are there any other questions?

O'KAY *(noisily clears his throat, delivers his question with affected severity).* Who made the greatest contribution to the development of *military camouflage* in the twentieth century?

GREGOIRE. The painter George Solomon, whose idea it was to paint tanks earth colored, ships water colored and cannons tree colored!

O'KAY. Right. *(To the examiners.)* By the way! The Society of Military Science Lovers is planning a fall exhibition of *military camouflage* and invites all of us to participate in the preparation of exhibits!

DIRECTOR *(writing something down).* I had expected this invitation!

O'KAY *(to Gregoire).* And aren't you going to follow that painter's example?

GREGOIRE *(brilliant gasconade).* In painting I prefer pure to applied art, just as in life I prefer the beautiful woman to the practical housewife!

YU-GEN-LI. Now you see how beautifully it all comes out when the reply is prepared *before hand!* Precise, trenchant, *a perfect illusion of the witty retort!* . . Why, for instance, is Schmidt always right on target? Because he follows my advice to the letter: prepare witticisms before hand when a conversation is in the offing! Right, Mr. Schmidt?

SCHMIDT *(rises and bows gaily).* Absolutely! That is the easiest method of passing for a clever man! "Guaranteed."

YU-GEN-LI *(to Gregoire).* I've told you time and again: if a given conversation does not furnish opportunities for wit, then you have to free it up with "leading remarks," inspire questions for which you have the answers already prepared and slip in your clever remarks as if they had just occurred to you!

GREGOIRE. I know that.

YU-GEN-LI. Far better you should not know, but show us you do know, than vice versa!

TROMPETTI *(with an Italian accent).* Is difficult for him, because he has very poor memoty.

GREGOIRE. What makes you think so?

TROMPETTI. You didn't give the money back to Mister Abramson!

GREGOIRE *(suddenly remembers).* Well I'll be damned—slipped my mind completely! *(Takes the $100 from his pocket and returns it to Abramson.)*

ABRAMSON *(to him)*. Oh, for heaven's sake! After all, I bought some lottery tickets! *(Takes them from his vest pocket.)*

YU-GEN-LI *(smiling)*. That was only . . . a "test item!"

ABRAMSON *(giving the tickets back to Gregoire and receiving back his $100)*. What "test item" do you mean?

YU-GEN-LI. Palm off fictitious lottery tickets, take money under false pretenses, find someone to invest in a nonexistent enterprise, and in general exhibit all the *proper conduct* for the "aggressive businessman!"

DIRECTOR *(to Gregoire, who has returned to his place at the examination table)*. As a whole, your concept of the role is correct! A few details . . . But a little extra practice in the summer workshop should take care of that. *(To the examiners.)* I consider he has passed the examination "with conditions!" Are there any objections? *(After a short pause, she extends her hand to him.)* Well! . . Good luck! *(Gregoire shakes her hand and goes from the table back to his seat.)* Next! . . *(Looks through the list.)* Fanny Norman! . . *(The Girl in Mourning approaches the table. Baker leans over to Yu-Gen-Li and says something to her sotto voce relating to the Girl in Mourning.)* Your thesis . . . *(searches for Fanny Norman's notebook)* on the . . .

GIRL IN MOURNING. *The Power of Feminine Weakness.*

DIRECTOR *(finds the right notebook)*. Yes, yes! *The Power of Feminine Weakness.* Very good! Although . . . you might be bolder in analyzing why women can pretend more easily than men!

GIRL IN MOURNING. I argue that it is the direct result of male egotism.

DIRECTOR. And you argue well! Only do so with greater force! After all, if man created law on this earth for his own personal well-being—"might makes right"—completely disregarding the intererests of woman, whom he converts into a slave, then nothing remains for her but constant simulation in those areas where he operates by sheer force!

GIRL IN MOURNING. And hence: a woman piles up so much experience in simulation that it finally becomes "second nature!"

DIRECTOR. Clear as day!

YU-GEN-LI *(turns playfully to Abramson)*. So now you have to learn from the women! *(Laughs.)* You're not bored?

ABRAMSON. Oh, for heaven's sake!

O'KAY *(to the Girl in Mourning)*. Pardon me, but what is the *basic* role you are playing?

GIRL IN MOURNING. "The mysterious woman," intriguing all with the secret of her grief, attracting all with her goodness, helplessness, loneliness.

O'KAY. In short, inspiring sympathy?

DIRECTOR *(interrupting)*. What would you like to ask, Colonel?

O'KAY. I think it would be a good idea to cough every now and then! As if there were something wrong with her chest, tuberculosis, for instance . . .

DIRECTOR. That's going too far! And not very practical either, that is, who would want to marry an invalid?

O'KAY *(defensive)*. I'm not . . . insisting on it! It was just a suggestion.

YU-GEN-LI *(to the Girl in Mourning)*. I agree with my sister and I'd even say you were *too* pale! Unnatural! Remember the words of the great Henri de Regnier! "Use a little rouge or else you'll be so pale people will think you use makeup." As a rule, avoid extremes! Today, for example, you seemed so affected in the "seduction scene" just before you fainted that it came out like a caricature! . . The Professor holds the same opinion! *(Nods in the direction of her neighbor, Baker.)*

GIRL IN MOURNING *(with an ingratiating smile)*. I overdid it, of course! But I wanted to test how effective the most primitive witchcraft would be on a simpleton like Anatole Moravsky.

MARY *(unable to restrain herself)*. He isn't a simpleton at all! I assure you! . .

DIRECTOR *(reproachfully)*. Mary! . . Your secretarial duties do not include taking part in the deliberations! *(General awkward pause.)*

TROMPETTI *(with an Italian accent, to the Girl in Mourning)*. One small comment on the faint! *(Rises and goes over to the Girl in Mourning.)* When you fall unconscious, then, so as to attract a man aesthetically, you shouldn't fall like this! *(Demonstrates a fall to the floor, bending his back as if sitting down.)* That is not plastic! Much better sideways! Like this: stick out your hip, not your fanny! *(Demonstrates, with the inspiration of a ballet dancer something more like a "descent" than a "fall" to the floor.)* More noble and far more effective! And if anyone sympathizes with you at all, then, when you fall like that, he will be so distressed at your misfortune, and your gracefulness will make him lose his head! *(Reacting gaily to the restrained laughter of the others.)* Don't laugh! Someone once said—quite correctly—that even as she falls, the prudent woman rises, a helpless victim in the eyes of the man who is in love with her. *(Sits in his chair amid friendly, approving laughter.)*

DIRECTOR *(to the Girl in Mourning)*. All in all, satisfactory, my dear! From my heart I congratulate you! *(They shake hands.)* Be seated! *(The Girl in Mourning returns to her seat. The Director goes further down the list.)* Ernestina MacBridle! *(The Seductive Maiden approaches the table, apparently playing the role of the social lioness. O'Kay quickly leans over to the Director and asks her about something; she nods her head in assent and quickly turns to the girl.)* Excuse me, I seem to have disturbed you too soon! *(Ernestina MacBridle smiles in reply and returns to her seat.)*

Thomas Sauce! *(Limping noticeably, the Junior Detective approaches the table holding the remains of a sandwich in his hands. His Bubikopf wig, off previously, is now back on and set conquettishly.)* Your thesis . . . *(She reads the title on the notebook the Colonel pushes over to her.) Dramatic Arts in the Service of Public Security* . . .

YU-GEN-LI *(disparagingly)*. Childishly written! But what a gratifying subject!

DIRECTOR *(to the Junior Detective)*. Are you firmly committed to a career as a detective?

JUNIOR DETECTIVE. Yes . . . So?

DIRECTOR. How old are you?

JUNIOR DETECTIVE. Almost twenty.

O'KAY *(aside)*. In two years.

DIRECTOR. You're sure you're not the victim of movies and cheap novels?

JUNIOR DETECTIVE *(still with a mouthful)*. No! Impossible! I am training myself . . . What's the matter? Don't I measure up? *(Chokes on his food.)*

YU-GEN-LI *(hostile)*. What's the matter with him? Didn't the poor boy have any supper?

O'KAY. At my insistence he hasn't eaten for the last two days!

DIRECTOR. Was that to test him?

O'KAY. Yes! To complicate the mission and to temper the character!

DIRECTOR. And why is he limping?

O'KAY. I ordered him to wear tight shoes! So as to make it harder to smile! . .

DIRECTOR. Great! He's passed the examination with distinction!

O'KAY *(as if to explain to those present)*. . . . the detective often finds himself in a very parlous situation and he has got to be prepared for everything before hand!

JUNIOR DETECTIVE *(recovered)*. The Colonel even suggested to me that . . . *(suddenly embarrassed)*.

DIRECTOR. What did he suggest to you?

JUNIOR DETECTIVE. . . . but I refused, I didn't want to be ridiculous like those Spartan nuts! I'm too old to be whipped!

O'KAY *(embarrassed)*. Utter nonsense! . . *(To the Director.)* I swear! He has a sick imagination!

YU-GEN-LI. . . . and the detective's habit of suspecting everybody! *(Trying to get a rise out of him.)* You'll go far, Tommy! Detective work is your true calling! Incidentally, you didn't notice where Anatole Moravsky disappeared to?

JUNIOR DETECTIVE. I wasn't watching him.

YU-GEN-LI. But you know him better than we do! *You* were the one that introduced him as a music teacher to Mary.

JUNIOR DETECTIVE. He must have gone out the back door!

MARY. But his coat is here.

DIRECTOR. Tell us, Tommy, what type of detective do you want to be?

JUNIOR DETECTIVE *(ingenuous)*. They say the most interesting job is the political detective!

DIRECTOR *(frowning)*. "Political?" Why?

JUNIOR DETECTIVE. Because *state criminals* are the most dangerous.

DIRECTOR. And whom do you consider "state criminals?"

JUNIOR DETECTIVE. Anyone who is against the existing system.

DIRECTOR. And do you approve completely of the existing system? *(Pause.)* Suppose, for instance, a bunch of scoundrels turns up at the head of the government. Would you obey them absolutely?

YU-GEN-LI *(entreating ironically)*. My dear! Don't be so rough on him! He's still a child when it comes to ethical problems!

DIRECTOR *(inagratiatingly, didactically, plainly counting on the attention of all present)*. You do remember, of course, Tommy, that we don't accept *just anybody* in the Institute, but only those we find to be *worthy of playing a victorious role on the stage of community life?!*. Our great aim, as you know, is the arming of the unarmed! That is, to give equal odds to *Good* in its fight with *Evil,* and not vice versa! Evil-doers, even without our help, will find the necessary masks to facilitate their evil deeds! *(Looks around significantly at those present.)* I am aware that some people push the right of everyone to hypocrisy too far! But I would like to believe, dear Tommy, that you are not one of them and will justify the faith in your integrity shown by your admission to the Institute!.. *(Tramping down on the orator's pedal at the end of her speech elicits weak applause from several of those present. The Director, with a smile of gratitude, nods to the pupils and extends her hand to Tommy Sauce.)* Be seated, my dear, and relax! As to *technique,* you passed the examination with a mark of outstanding! *(Encouraged by these words the Junior Detective gives the director's hand a loud kiss and, with childish gaiety, returns to his seat. Meanwhile O'Kay begins exchanging whispers with Trompetti and the Director looks through the list of participants, then grandly calls out.)* Prince Sergius Mashukov! *(The clumsy Prince Mashukov steps indecisively up to the table. His face displays the sort of coldness that people have who are unhappy with themselves and with those around them.)*

YU-GEN-LI *(nervously and unkindly)*. A little more life there!.. And what sort of face is that? More softness! More! More! That's the way! Only rich people can allow themselves the luxury of looking so sour! It doesn't cost them a thing! It can cost you plenty!

DIRECTOR *(reads the title on one of the notebooks)*. Your topic was *The Gentleman and his Social Mask?*

PRINCE *(hollowly)*. Yes.

YU-GEN-LI *(to him)*. Why are you wringing your hands? Have you forgotten how to conceal nervousness? How many times have we told you: curl your toes, press down on your big toe! No one will see inside your shoe, and the relief you get from tension is the same as you get from wringing your hands!

DIRECTOR *(to him).* Very odd, that the power of *autosuggestion* helps you so little!

O'KAY *(also to him).* Sorry, I've forgotten, but *who* is it you're trying to portray?

PRINCE. What do you mean "who?"

O'KAY. Well, whom are you trying to depict in real life?

PRINCE. What a question! My own self, of course!

O'KAY. That is, *who?*

PRINCE. A Prince! . . An all-round aristocrat! What of it? *(Restrained laughter all around and whispers back and forth.)*

YU-GEN-LI *(after a short, but heavy pause).* Unconvincing, Prince! . . You ought to pick another role in life; that one doesn't suit you!

PRINCE. But a . . a . . . allow me! I *am* a real prince! My papers are all in perfect order! . . I got them out of Soviet Russia at the risk of life and limb! . .

YU-GEN-LI. Wonderful! In life it is sometimes more important to *seem* than to *be!*

DIRECTOR *(to him).* The feeling of self-worth is very poorly expressed in your case!

PRINCE. What can I do, if they knocked all the "worth" out of me in my ten years in Soviet Russia!

YU-GEN-LI. You've got to learn to act the part again! That's why you enrolled in the theatrical institute!

TROMPETTI *(with his usual Italian accent).* I would also like to say something! *(Rises and goes over to the Prince.)* Listen! I watched how you borrowed the money and here is what I say! If you are very humble when you ask *(extends his hand),* you get very little! And if you are very proud *(raises his head haughtily),* you get nothing except unpleasantness! You have to be both proud and humble, so that the other person will be ashamed to give a small sum! Is that clear? *(While speaking, he demonstrates, to the approving laughter of those around him.)* Plasticity is a great thing, my boy! The way you bear yourself in society can make you a very rich man or a very poor man! *(Again, sympathetic laughter from those present.)* And now, show the faculty how, not sparing strength or health I still managed to teach you how to dance! *(to Mary.)* A foxtrot, if you please! *(Claps his hands three times, while Mary goes over to the piano and sticks the appropriate cylinder in the mechanism.)* Mademoiselle Ernestina MacBridle! Be the partner, if you please! *(The Seductive Maiden, with the appropriate expression on her face for dancing, approaches the Prince. He awaits her in the tense pose of the "escort.")*

YU-GEN-LI *(now brighter, turns to Abramson)*. Isn't the Professor perfectly charming!

ABRAMSON. Inimitable! . . But *(stands up and addresses Trompetti)* excuse me, professor, do you only teach how to borrow money or also how to pay it back?

TROMPETTI. What?! He hasn't paid you back yet?

YU-GEN-LI *(with exaggerated amazement)*. No?!

ABRAMSON. But why waste time discussing such trifles!

YU-GEN-LI *(laughing)*. But you *are* discussing them!

PRINCE *(embarrassed)*. Well I'll be damned! Slipped my mind completely! *(Digs in his pockets.)* And I kept thinking about it . . . What can I have done with it? . . *(Distraught.)* Who would have thought? . . Where can it be? What an idiotic thing . . .

O'KAY. Oh come on, fella, skip the gags! The play is over now!

DIRECTOR. Don't act, prince! Everything in its own time!

YU-GEN-LI *(also to him)*. Unconvincing too! It won't work!

PRINCE *(sincerely)*. So help me God I'm not pretending! I swear . . . *(Suddenly feels the money in the lining of his suit.)* Wait! . . Here's the damned money! *(Gives the money back to Abramson.)* Imagine where the damned stuff disappeared to!

TROMPETTI *(once more clapping his hands three times)*. So! . . Musique! . . *(Mary turns on the mechanism. A foxtrot rings out and the Prince begins dancing with the Seductive Maiden. A few seconds later excited voices are heard coming from the rooms to the right. One hears some sort of altercation and the rapidly approaching sounds of the uncoordinated steps of two people. One can just distinguish the voices of Anatole Moravsky and the maid, May; he wants to get into the living room no matter what, she doesn't want to let him in for anything.)*

ANATOLE *(appears right in the doorway with May, whom he is holding off with a trembling hand)*. Excuse me! I'll only bother you a minute! . . Is there a dance going on? Am I interrupting? *(Mary stops the music. May quickly goes over to the Director, whispers something by way of explanation and runs off left.)*

MARY. What's going on?!. Where have you been?!.

ANATOLE *(taking some money and a bottle of medicine from his pocket)*. I was late on account of a car accident, a child was almost run over! I had to testify, get the boy all calmed down, and . . . *(takes a deep breath)*. Excuse me for "butting in" . . . Here! *(Hurriedly sticks five dollars in the Prince's hand.)* Use it to get home with, for God's sake! Is five enough? I borrowed it from my aunt! Didn't have enough myself! *(Hands the medicine bottle to the Girl in Mourning.)* And this is the prescription from the drug store! For anemia! The pharmacist said your faint was probably due to anemia and says you should take it three times a day. *(The Girl in Mourning, unable to find words, waves her hand, tries to return the bottle.)* Don't worry: it's not bitter! I got them to make it sweet on purpose. *(Turns to Gregoire and offers him money.)* And this is for you! For the lottery tickets! Why don't you take it? Are they all sold? *(Suddenly noticing the session at the examination table.)* What's this?!. A dance and a meeting at the same time?.. Am I interrupting something?.. Yes?.. The *whole* faculty is here! Right? *(Rushes over to the table.)* Listen!.. I applied at the institute here for a permanent position as music teacher... I asked each one of you separately today, and you all said that it depended on the whole faculty. So I ask you, now that you're all here: what will it be, gentlemen? Eh? Can I have a job here?.. It's extremely important for me, since—I can't hide it from you or anybody else any longer—I'm madly in love with Mary Daryal! *(Seizes her hand in a burst of tenderness.)* Yes! Yes! *This* Mary, and I want to propose to her, but I don't dare, I don't dare, because I haven't a regular salary! Forgive me, for God's sake, for being so frank, but, as God is my witness, I fail to see why I should conceal my honest thoughts and plans from everyone!

DIRECTOR. *(She has been several times on the verge of interrupting his monologue addressed to his dumbfounded audience. Now she answers him as she would a madman, with an alarmed, severe, and yet at the same time deliberately tender voice of one afraid of winding up in a ridiculous situation.)* You seem to be rather upset about something and . . .

ANATOLE *(interrupting her with a bitter smile).* You think I'm crazy?

DIRECTOR. No, but . . . you ought to calm down, my dear, if you expect to join us in a fruitful discussion of your "honest thoughts and plans." Furthermore, I rather doubt whether a public meeting of our faculty is the proper place!

ANATOLE *(almost laughing, waves his hand).* I know that it's not *comme il faut!* But can that be any obstacle for one who, like you, is above mere convention?!

DIRECTOR. Quite right, of course, but . . . we are unfortunately busy right now with other matters which cannot be set aside . . . in view of their urgency!

ANATOLE *(letting go Mary's hand).* Ah! That's another matter! In that case, please forgive me. I don't want to interfere! *(Turns to the right with the intention of leaving.)*

MARY. Your coat is in the hall.

ANATOLE *(shakes her hand).* Thank you, darling! See you again soon! *(Bows to all.)* Excuse me, ladies and gentleman! *(Quickly exits left followed by the unblinking stares of all present. Mary, standing still by the piano, looks distraught. Unlike the others she looks after him as if guilty of something, not knowing whether to cry or to laugh. Her mother, nodding to her in the direction of Anatole's departure, rotates a finger by her forehead and shakes her head reproachfully . . The others, finally recovering from their astonishment, look at each other inquisitively and infect each other with giggles. The giggles become louder until they turn into a roar at which point even the Director, unable to restrain herself, joins in. Three or four seconds are filled with unanimous, loud, friendly, self-abandoning, communal laughter. It seems it's going to last forever, but the Director breaks it off by sheer force, getting herself in hand first, and then ringing the bell, so as to bring her colleagues back to being a faculty again.)*

DIRECTOR *(finally producing complete silence with a loud pronouncement).* The examination will continue! *(Mary, robot-like, again starts the mechanism. The interrupted foxtrot of the Prince and the Seductive Maiden resumes.*

CURTAIN.

ACT TWO

A summer house near Atlantic City.

The beautiful facade of a two-story Colonial American style house towers down-stage near the footlights.

A shallow veranda on the first floor occupies the width of the entire stage and has two steps descending to the stage at the footlights. The veranda is bounded by a filigree balustrade.

In the center of the veranda is a door leading to a corridor running between two rows of rooms; on each side of the door there are large curtained windows, of which only one—to the left of the door—has the curtains wide open, allowing one to guess that it is a study.

To the right of the door are an outdoor table and chairs in the Pompei style, as understood by early nineteenth century English carpenters.

On the walls between the windows and the door are large diagonal supports hold-ing vases with flowers twining downward. At left is an easel and canvas facing the porch wall. A palette and brushes lie on a stool next to it.

There are some fancy, exotically painted, frosted lamps on the veranda ceiling.

Above the veranda is a slightly sloping roof. A door with low railings opens onto the center of the veranda roof. On each side of the door are windows. As the curtain rises two people step onto the veranda: a preoccupied Girl in Mourning and some clean-shaven elderly dandy in a duster with a cap on his head and goggles over his eyes.

GIRL IN MOURNING *(takes one of the chairs, lifts it up, turns it in various direc-tions in front of the elderly dandy, runs her hand over the chair back and pats the seat)*. . . . and here's the Pompei suite. You can see for yourself what a nice finish it has! True, the back has a small deviation from the normal line! Just the same it all bespeaks the work of Pierre Clerisseau in the early nineteenth century! . .

ELDERLY DANDY *(quietly, hardly moving his lips, barely restraining a grin)*. Cler-isseau? . . Hm . . . *(Examines the chair carefully.)*

GIRL IN MOURNING. Believe me, if it weren't for the bankruptcy which drove my husband to the grave, I would never let this furniture go . . . *(From right, from the depths of the house, several people are heard to burst into laugh-ter. The Elderly Dandy glances inquisitively at the Girl in Mourning.)* Those are my lodgers eating . . . boarders . . . What can I do, necessity demands! . . *(A new burst of laughter.)* The air here is so intoxicating! . . So is swimming in the ocean . . .

ELDERLY DANDY. How much do you want for this reproduction? *(Takes off his goggles and cap.)*

GIRL IN MOURNING. How much? *(Suddenly stunned.)* What? You? . . My God!

ABRAMSON *(dropping his disguise with a laugh)*. Has Miss Yu-Gen-Li finished her dinner?

GIRL IN MOURNING. I'll call her right now! . . But where is your beard? Shaved it off? So the joke's on me! . . And why didn't I catch on?

ABRAMSON. Overly absorbed in your *own* role! *(Didactically, one finger pointing upwards.)* More attention to the others' roles, if you expect to win in the *theater of war.*

GIRL IN MOURNING *(laughing in turn)*. Bravo! . . You've made terrific progress! . . And you've gotten so young recently that . . . *(A telephone rings in the office.)*

ABRAMSON. That I owe to my tutor! *(Removes his duster.)*

GIRL IN MOURNING. Amazing! . . *(Runs off into the corridor, turns left and appears with a telephone in her hand in the study's open window.)* Hello! . . Who? . . Louder please! . . Who? . . Miss Yu-Gen-Li? . . Just a minute! Hold on! . . And who is this? . . *(From the right, from the depths of the corridor comes the noise of conversation and chairs being pushed back. Yu-Gen-Li, in a summer sports dress, appears and hurries to the telephone.)* Who? . . *(The face of the Girl in Mourning assumes a respectful expression.)* This instant! . . Right away! *(Hands the receiver to the approaching Yu-Gen-Li, smiles conspiratorially at the now silent Abramson, takes his duster and cap and carries them off, disappearing in the depths of the corridor.)*

YU-GEN-LI *(in the window by the telephone, sitting on the back of an easy chair by the desk)*. Hello! . . Senator Creighton? . . You're coming? . . Marvelous! There's a wonderful supper waiting for you! I arranged it myself! . . Car running all right? . . That's the main thing! . . Thirty miles from here? . . Terrific! *(Pause.)* And for those who don't believe in pure goodness of heart, say you're buying the house! . . Yes! . . That explains your trips here! . . Not very frequent ones either! . . People are so nasty! What! . . *(Laughs.)* You're joking! . . *(After a pause spent with raised eyebrows she asks in a tone of "great amazement.")* Buy this house? You like it? Or the furniture? *(Pause.)* Oh, the inhabitants! . . *(Pause. Abramson, after a little hesitation, approaches the window and bows to Yu-Gen-Li, drawing an exclamation of surprise from her.)* Oh! . . My God! I hardly recognize you! *(Points to her chin, extends her hand through the window. Abramson kisses the hand, does not release it until the very end of the telephone conversation. Yu-Gen-Li recovers quickly, puts the receiver to her mouth and laughs politely into it, as if excusing herself.)* I meant to say, "I hardly recognize you" lately! So much *joie de vivre,* so affable! One forgets all his troubles around you! . . Oh yes, I go swimming, every day I go swimming! Only, alas, not in the "ocean of bliss!" *(Pause.)* Of course! . . And tomorrow happens to be the anniversary of my divorce! . . I need support so badly *(looks expressively at Abramson)* from a real friend, kind, solid, competent, like you! . . Of course, I love my sister, but . . . we're so different! . . That's it, just like Europe and Asia! You defined it beautifully! *(Pause.)* I'll be all by myself today! . . My sister is going to bed early on account of her headache, and the rest are going to the movies! . . You're afraid of getting too tired? On the contrary! You'll be all the fresher for the speech tomorrow! I know it's important! . . Thank you, I'll be waiting! *(Hangs up; to Abramson, triumphantly.)* He's coming! *(Comes through the corridor onto the veranda.)*

ABRAMSON *(happy, excited).* What a sorceress you are!

YU-GEN-LI. Only don't breathe a word to my sister! She has personal designs on Senator Creighton!

ABRAMSON. I understand! "Professional jealousy!"

YU-GEN-LI. Now listen to my plan! This Creighton is a terrible glutton!

ABRAMSON. The main thing is that he's a voluptuary, using his position as a member of the family to make up to you!

YU-GEN-LI *(provocatively).* "Professional jealousy" on your part too? *(Laughs.)* Don't worry, I'll set your mind at ease on that this very day!

ABRAMSON. How?

YU-GEN-LI. By offering him some "totally exhausting fare" for dinner.

ABRAMSON. What does that mean?

YU-GEN-LI. Everything very tasty, but . . . not digestible, so that the day after the man "falls out of ranks" . . .

ABRAMSON. Completely?

YU-GEN-LI. That depends . . .

ABRAMSON. Ah! The joke is that Creighton should give his report tomorrow at the Customs Commission, but give it *very poorly!* Right?

YU-GEN-LI. Right: if he's sick in bed the meeting will be postponed until he's well again. But if he's late he'll still be able to present his views!

ABRAMSON. Naturally! Let him oppose the raising of tariffs on foreign furniture tomorrow, but let him do it so badly that at the slightest pressure—that's been taken care of, I can assure you—he'll cave in!

YU-GEN-LI. That's the way it'll be if I serve him lobster with pickles, mushroom soup, fried eel in hot sauce, duck with mushrooms, and red wine jelly!

ABRAMSON. Bravo! It's enough to make your mouth water!

YU-GEN-LI *(flattered)*. Really? Wouldn't you guess right away that all these delicacies are simply a *mask* for a treacherous reception?

ABRAMSON. I pity the victim already!

YU-GEN-LI. À *la guerre comme à la guerre!* And not any victim of mine either, but of his own gluttony!

ABRAMSON. Also try to wear him out, getting him all aroused at being alone with a woman as inaccessible as a fortress, rising like some mirage in the desert!

YU-GEN-LI. I'll try! Only again, don't consider him *my* victim, but . . . the victim of his own lust!

ABRAMSON *(laughs)*. Oh, you're completely innocent! *(Passionately takes her by the hand, looks around, and leads her downstage onto the apron.)* But when are you going to tell me how much you're going to charge as commision on this theatrical deal?

YU-GEN-LI. And when are you going to learn to cover questions like that with the proper mask? . . As your *tutor,* I demand it! Do you hear?

ABRAMSON. But isn't money itself a *mask?* As the Marxists say, capital is nothing but another form of labor! Or do you demand masks on masks in your dealings? But we aren't at war with each other?

YU-GEN-LI. Are you so sure? *(Laughs.)*

ABRAMSON. I hope so! . . And since you're not working on this Creighton for the pure pleasure of it . . .

YU-GEN-LI *(interrupting)*. And how do you know? Making asses out of people is sometimes quite delightful! Don't you enjoy doing it?

ABRAMSON. No.

YU-GEN-LI. This is all something like stalking people in the jungles of our wild civilization! I get a great deal of pleasure trapping stupid wild game with my little schemes! For me it's a sport!

ABRAMSON. Are you really so wicked?

YU-GEN-LI. Not me! But my ancestors, frightful! . . In China we still bring sacrifices to their graves! It's a symbol: *You have to gratify the dead living in your own flesh,* gratify all their desires! *(The Director and the Prince enter.)*

DIRECTOR *(to Abramson)*. We have a favor to ask you!

ABRAMSON. At your service!

DIRECTOR. I've finally succeeded in persuading the Prince to try a different role.

ABRAMSON. Such as? . .

DIRECTOR. He isn't any good at *playing the part of himself,* because he lacks the social wherewithal.

ABRAMSON. What can I do?

DIRECTOR. This: in the process of failing to master the role of "aristocrat," the Prince has almost mastered another role—that of the faithful clerk, and could do very well in one of your furniture warehouses! *(To her sister.)* Isn't that right, Gen?

YU-GEN-LI. Of course! For an antique furniture store, what better person could you find than a representative of antique nobility! The Prince will be a real decoration in your warehouse.

ABRAMSON *(to the Prince).* If I may ask, are you really a Prince? Or is your nobility no more genuine than my furniture?

PRINCE *(offended).* I can show you the documents.

ABRAMSON *(after a short moment of hesitation, slaps him on the shoulder).* Let's go have a talk. *(They walk off.)*

DIRECTOR *(watching them until they disappear).* Well, how is your Abramson?

YU-GEN-LI. Not "mine" yet.

DIRECTOR. Stingy?

YU-GEN-LI. Calculating.

DIRECTOR *(looks around to be sure no one else is listening).* Now listen to the *strategy* I have planned for the home front!

YU-GEN-LI *(with barely noticeable irony).* What kind of strategy?

DIRECTOR. Retreating from Abramson's attacks, which you, of course, provoked, you lure him eventually into a love-ambush and then hold him for ransom!

YU-GEN-LI. He's already been ambushed! *(Imitating Abramson.)* How much and in what form?

DIRECTOR. As much as he can pay and in the form of a subsidy to our Institute!

YU-GEN-LI. Then?

DIRECTOR. Obtain from Senator Creighton . . .

YU-GEN-LI *(interrupting).* Leave us alone together today! I "masked" your absence with a headache!

DIRECTOR. Make him get official government recognition for the Military Theatrical Institute and its whole program.

YU-GEN-LI *(with a smile).* Are you so *ambitious?*

DIRECTOR. It's not me that matters! The happiness of millions depends on the success of our work!

YU-GEN-LI. So does your glory!

DIRECTOR. I don't need it, but an idea—which could save the world—limping along its semilegal existence, does!

YU-GEN-LI *(almost laughing).* Oh! What fancy rhetoric! But why all this high flown eloquence with me? Don't wear yourself out!

DIRECTOR. Many thanks. Oh, speaking of eloquence, Phillips hinted again he'd like a position in the Department of Rhetorical Arts!

YU-GEN-LI. Naturally! Since he's a preacher, he'd be . . .

DIRECTOR *(interrupting)*. I have adopted your plan for a flank movement in the case of Hermann Schmidt. All right?

YU-GEN-LI *(blushes)*. Thank you.

DIRECTOR. . . . however, on the condition that . . . But we'll talk about it later!

YU-GEN-LI *(with a smile)*. Better now! So that I won't suspect you of any "strategies" against me!

DIRECTOR *(raises her eyebrows)*. Aren't we allies in the theater of war? *(Schmidt enters, in elegant riding attire, charming in his high-spirited youth-fulness, air of worldliness, and the masculine beauty of his sun-tanned face and muscular physique.)*

SCHMIDT *(cracking his whip on his boot)*. I'm ready! . . Didn't interrupt you? *(To Yu-Gen-Li.)* Are you going riding?

YU-GEN-LI. I'm afraid . . . I won't make it today! *(Abramson appears in the depths of the corridor.)*

SCHMIDT *(turns around at the sound of Abramson's steps)*. Ah! I understand!

ABRAMSON *(entering)*. The Prince and I have made a deal!

DIRECTOR. You have? Wonderful!

SCHMIDT *(to Abramson, with a grin)*. Back already? . . So soon?!.

DIRECTOR. I was worried that the poor Prince had lost a whole academic year with us for nothing!

YU-GEN-LI. Are we to be held responsible for our pupils' lack of talent?

ABRAMSON. Is that a hint in my direction?

DIRECTOR *(to Yu-Gen-Li)*. You have a cruel heart!

ABRAMSON. I think so too!

SCHMIDT *(teasing)*. And how do you know?

ABRAMSON *(defensive, embarrassed)*. It just . . . seems that way to me!

SCHMIDT *(motioning him to follow him out)*. Hm . . . may I have a couple of words with you?

ABRAMSON. Certainly! What's up? *(They depart. Yu-Gen-Li laughs self-satisfiedly as she watches them leave.)*

DIRECTOR. Are you glad he's jealous? You shouldn't be!

YU-GEN-LI. Why?

DIRECTOR. What would be the point of loving you!

YU-GEN-LI. Who? Hermann?

DIRECTOR. Have you already forgotten that he had good reason to consider himself my Mary's fiancé?

YU-GEN-LI. But she doesn't care for him any more!

DIRECTOR. That can be corrected! You know the reason for it!

YU-GEN-LI. Oh Yes! She met Anatole!

DIRECTOR. You confuse the cause with the result! It was Hermann who, hypnotized by you, was neglecting Mary, and thereby drove her to Anatole!

YU-GEN-LI. So that's it?! Then . . .

DIRECTOR *(interrupting warmly)*. Listen! If this theatrical ignoramus leads her to the altar, he'll compromise not only my daughter, not only me, but my whole life's work!

YU-GEN-LI *(coldly)*. What do you mean?

DIRECTOR. Are you my ally or aren't you?

YU-GEN-LI. What a question!

DIRECTOR. Then here's a strategy for you for our mutual benefit! Break off your relations with Hermann, stop competing with Mary and thus help her to get him back! . . Simultaneously carry on a "position war" with Anatole, wait for an opportunity to hypnotize him and get him away from Mary for good!

YU-GEN-LI. Anatole fears hypnotism more than fire! I've tried already— several times! It's no use! *(May enters and hands the mail to the Director. May has a bandage around her jaw.)*

DIRECTOR *(to her)*. How are your teeth doing?

MAY. Same as ever.

DIRECTOR. You ought to go lie down!

YU-GEN-LI. But what about supper? Who's going to wait on Creighton?

DIRECTOR. I took that into consideration! Tommy will take her place. *(To May.)* Call him!

YU-GEN-LI. Tommy?!. So we can have a real farce?! *(May goes off.)*

DIRECTOR. Don't worry! He's more clever than you think, and Creighton is near-sighted! So! I am waiting to hear whether you go along with my "strategy" or . . .

YU-GEN-LI. But suppose I love Hermann more than you think?!

DIRECTOR *(with one cold snort of laughter)*. You're too smart to put a very high price on illusion! Love is only the halo on sexual attraction!

YU-GEN-LI. But suppose I find it difficult to abandon the illusion?

DIRECTOR. With your powers of auto-suggestion?!.

YU-GEN-LI. But if I'd rather not?

DIRECTOR. That's a different matter! *(Unfriendly, she laughs and looks through the mail.)*

YU-GEN-LI *(after a short pause, smouldering)*. This is no mere passing whim! Do you hear? Such maleable and strong clay for my ideal isn't found everywhere! . . And you know very well how much self-will I inherited! You know that Mongolian blood flows in my veins! . . You know that among my people the woman traditionally trembles before her beloved, like a butterfly before the dragon, and you know what joy it brings me to find such a man!

DIRECTOR *(almost derisively)*. But whatever does that dear, sweet boy Hermann Schmidt have in common with a dragon?

YU-GEN-LI. And do you know *what a man* I have made of him, with my imagination? Do you know what I have created out of him with the power of my love? I have *born him anew,* incarnating in him my most secret dreams!

DIRECTOR. Hold on! . . I can't bear it when you start all this Asiatic rubbish! It's something entirely foreign to me! I never did like your father's slanting eyes!

YU-GEN-LI. Oh, in me, he's invincible! Nothing can weaken the blood of his ancestors!

DIRECTOR. But just the same you *must overcome* this passion!

YU-GEN-LI."Must?!"

DIRECTOR. Must, if you value my taking care of you when you were a poor orphan child! I took pity on the daughter of your terrible father! So you take pity on the daughter of your loving sister!

YU-GEN-LI. You're asking for a sacrifice?

DIRECTOR. A favor, not a sacrifice!

YU-GEN-LI. But . . .

DIRECTOR *(interrupting)*. Didn't you overcome your passion for opium? Didn't you master it?

YU-GEN-LI. I mastered it by exchanging one passion for another! Hermann, Hermann gave a new meaning to my life!

DIRECTOR. Not him; your *atavistic lover,* the role you stuck on him! Set the *real* Hermann free of the spell of your reckless, foolish love! You'll find another to serve as the coat-hanger for your ideal! De-hypnotize Hermann! I know perfectly well how you hypnotized him with the most basic method! *(Music is heard inside the house: Four hands on the piano are playing one of Brahms' merry "Hungarian Dances" with fervor. The two players complement each other nicely and play with real gypsy flair. At the first sounds of music the Director shudders with hostility, frowns, and hastily looks through the mail.)*

YU-GEN-LI *(after a pause)*. Do you hear that? . . Do you hear those four hands play?!. You might think that *one* being was playing: such mutual understanding, such harmony, such passion!

DIRECTOR *(coldly, speaking through her teeth)*. So much the worse if you're right! Loving Anatole Moravsky is just like loving flowers growing on the edge of a precipice! . . And it's your duty to run save my child as soon as she starts to get dizzy!

YU-GEN-LI (unrestrained). Save her?!. With what? Herman's arms? Losing Hermann?! At the price of his love?!.

DIRECTOR. For God's sake, stop the affectation! We're not on the stage, and, as an actress, it only annoys me—I never liked melodrama and absurd idealizing!

YU-GEN-LI. Then why, in that case, do you idealize your pupils?

DIRECTOR. Me? . . I only repay their childish love with maternal love! And that's all!

YU-GEN-LI. I'm afraid you're soon going to be disappointed with them!

DIRECTOR (with a condescending smile). What are you hinting at? At the pupils' party . . . as it's called? An Evening of Bare Truth or . . .

YU-GEN-LI. Bal démasqué!

DIRECTOR. Yes, yes! . . An unmasked ball! Nonsense! Young people simply like to have fun and I don't expect any great "revelations" from it. You and I probably won't be invited anyway—the "old folks" might crimp their style! (Enter Abramson and Schmidt.)

ABRAMSON (happy, excited). Mesdames, can you just imagine? It seems I can still make some people jealous! . . (Laughs loudly.) I seem to have made a mistake when I added up my years, my wrinkles and my gray hair! . . I'm young! Dangerous! I might run off with somebody's woman! Ah? . . What do you say to that? . . And all this wonderful, wonderful feeling in me was brought on by (points to Hermann Schmidt) his jealousy! Fantastic! . . (To him.) How much do I owe you for this surprise? Why, you've made me younger in my own eyes! . . (Laughs loudly, then listens to the music.) Who's playing so brightly over there? (Joins in, humming lightly, "directing" the music with his hand and tapping his foot.)

YU-GEN-LI. It's Mary and her tutor . . .

ABRAMSON. And who? Anatole Moravsky? (Laughs loudly.) Is he here? When did he arrive?

YU-GEN-LI. A long time ago! . .

DIRECTOR (seemingly defending the honor of the home). He has a cottage in the neighborhood! . .

ABRAMSON (laughing). "Chase nature out the door and she flies in the window?"

SCHMIDT (standing between Abramson and Yu-Gen-Li, to the Director). I still fail to understand why you're so afraid of breaking up their friendship.

DIRECTOR. Because obstacles in love only serve to arouse a burning desire to overcome them!

ABRAMSON *(pushing Schmidt aside, stands between him and Yu-Gen-Li).* Now there's a thought! . . I feel like it's the first time I ever heard it!

DIRECTOR *(ironically, to Schmidt).* Do you know—Mary is "re-educating" him these days?

SCHMIDT. Who? Her tutor? . . How sweet!

DIRECTOR. Are you jealous?

ABRAMSON. Is she giving him lessons?

SCHMIDT. Switching roles! . . *(By this time the four-handed playing backstage has stopped and Mary and Anatole, both flushed, appear on the porch.)*

ABRAMSON. Bravo, bravo! . . Was that *you playing?* Marvelous!

MARY. *Merci!* . . Mama, I see you're using the porch? May we work upstairs today?

DIRECTOR *(sourly).* It seems to me you already "worked" this morning?

YU-GEN-LI *(taking Anatole by the arm).* This evening I'm having a dinner tete-à-tete with a certain music-lover! Could I ask you to play a little for us? . . For the proper mood!

ANATOLE. With pleasure!

YU-GEN-LI. We all love your music so much.

DIRECTOR *(with a smile full of significance).* Especially . . . from a distance!

ANATOLE *(flares up).* "From a distance? . ." I understand! . . I don't care for you at close range either!

DIRECTOR *(with a strained smile).* How sweet of you!

ANATOLE *(passionately).* Not sweet at all! Why tell lies? At least I'm sincere!

DIRECTOR. No one could be angry at you!

ANATOLE. I'm too stupid, you suppose? *(Enter May and the Junior Detective.)*

MARY *(to Anatole).* Let's go! We're wasting time! *(They leave.)*

JUNIOR DETECTIVE *(to the Director).* Did you call?

DIRECTOR *(to all).* Excuse us, gentlemen, we have a little confidential matter here, and so . . .

ABRAMSON *(hurriedly).* I'm leaving, I am. I'm not curious! *(He goes off.)*

YU-GEN-LI *(to Schmidt, with businesslike calmness).* I have to tell you something too. *(She takes him off to the study, where they can be seen a little later quite close together, engaged in some intimate, lively conversation in half-whispers.)*

DIRECTOR *(turning to the Junior Detective).* May's teeth are bothering her! . . And now . . .

JUNIOR DETECTIVE. She already told me! . . Fine with me! . . Maybe Senator Creighton will appreciate my talent and recommend me to . . .

DIRECTOR *(waves her hand at him).* Wait a minute, wait a minute! It's not an examination this time. What we need now is some real conspiratorial work! *(To May.)* Lend him your dress!

MAY. Yes m'am! *(She goes off.)*

JUNIOR DETECTIVE *(waits until May leaves, and then quietly).* Who am I supposed to keep an eye on today? Not the Senator himself? He's been here so often!

DIRECTOR *(pretending she hasn't been caught, gamely tries to smile).* You're so unpleasantly shrewd!

JUNIOR DETECTIVE. It won't be a political case?

DIRECTOR. Why should it be?

JUNIOR DETECTIVE. Well, he's in the government!

DIRECTOR. Yes, but . . . this case involves a mission of the highest morality!

JUNIOR DETECTIVE *(as if he didn't quite hear).* A mission of?

DIRECTOR. Look . . . the Senator is a married man!

JUNIOR DETECTIVE. I understand!

DIRECTOR. . . . and since he likes my sister not only as a cousin . . .

JUNIOR DETECTIVE. I understand!

DIRECTOR. . . . she has been too indulgent with him at times . . .

JUNIOR DETECTIVE. I understand!

DIRECTOR. I take a different view of these matters!

JUNIOR DETECTIVE. I understand!

DIRECTOR. . . . especially since Creighton's wife is ill . . .

JUNIOR DETECTIVE. I understand! So there ought to be as little hugging and kissing as possible?

DIRECTOR *(laughing).* What a funny boy you are!

JUNIOR DETECTIVE *(winking).* And if it starts heading in that direction? . .

DIRECTOR. Well . . . walk in with a clean plate or something! In general, don't stay away very long! *(Almost in a whisper.)* You should be sure to keep track of what they're talking about: the things I asked her to, or—she's so forgetful—something else!

JUNIOR DETECTIVE *(puts his finger to his lips as if some deep dark secret were involved).* I un-derstand! . . *(Enter Colonel O'Kay and Gregoire.)*

O'KAY *(to the Director).* We've been waiting for you! . . Did you forget? You wanted to pick out the displays for the "Military Camouflage Exhibition?" *(Clapping Gregoire on the shoulder.)* He really knows how to smear the old paint around! . . Too bad it's peacetime! He'd be sure to get a medal in wartime!

DIRECTOR *(rises, very happy, friendly).* Coming, I'm coming! Suppose you bring a few of them here . . . for a showing! Senator Creighton was very interested in our pupils' work!

GREGOIRE. But where is Miss Yu-Gen-LI?

DIRECTOR *(calls)*. Gen!

GREGOIRE. . . . she promised to pose for me, if I . . .

YU-GEN-LI *(at the window)*. What is it?

GREGOIRE. I finished the background! Remember your promise!

YU-GEN-LI. Ah! Fine! Let me change my clothes first!

DIRECTOR *(to the others)*. Let's go! The displays aren't too heavy?

O'KAY. Tommy can help us! *(Gives him a slap.)* Let's go! . . On the double!!! March! . .

JUNIOR DETECTIVE *(rubbing his back)*. What are you doing, Colonel? I'm not a Spartan, you know! *(Goes off after the Director and Gregoire. O'Kay with a laugh, goes off after them.)*

SCHMIDT *(crudely grabbing Yu-Gen-Li by the hand—she has been standing by the window)*. I don't want you to pose for him with half your clothes off! Do you hear?!

YU-GEN-LI. Let go! That hurts!

SCHMIDT. You don't know when to stop! Like this Abramson, to whom I introduced you purely for business, and not for . . .

YU-GEN-LI *(putting her hand on his mouth)*. Quiet! They can hear us! *(Sits down on the sill, strikes a mournful pose.)* Oh, how sweet is your jealousy at this last moment of parting!

SCHMIDT *(taken aback)*. Parting? With whom?

YU-GEN-LI *(sadly)*. With me!

SCHMIDT *(mocking)*. With my slave? So that I can allow her to whore around on the side?!

YU-GEN-LI *(leaps to the veranda with one jump, as if saving herself from him)*. So as to do my duty!

SCHMIDT. What duty?

YU-GEN-LI. A duty of consience! A duty for family! A duty of gratitude!

SCHMIDT *(with a malicious smile)*. This "inherited ferocity" again?

YU-GEN-LI. I haven't the strength to argue with conscience: it's the voice of my mother!

SCHMIDT *(grabbing his head, sits on the sill)*. Good Lord! "Her father's voice"! All this mysticism is enough to drive a person insane! . . Are you afraid of some puny ghost?

YU-GEN-LI *(approaching him)*. A terrible one! Because he demands sacrifices!

SCHMIDT. But after . . . *(She doesn't let him finish, but with unexpected speed covers his eyes with her hands.)*

YU-GEN-LI. Sleep! . . Sleep! . . You will now awake free from my *hypnotic spell!* . . Do you hear? Completely free! *(Takes her hands from his eyes, which remain closed on his suddenly sunken face.)* But before giving you back your freedom to love whomsoever you please, I want to thank you for the happiness you gave me! *(Kisses his hand.)* Thank you! Thank you, dearest! *(Looks around, then convulsively presses to her his lifeless head and kisses him greedily.)* For the last time! . . Thank you! In what for you was an unfamiliar role, I loved you the way an impulsive actress loves a sensitive partner on stage! *(Painfully.)* Oh, how I wish I knew whether you loved me the tiniest bit! . . But I won't be tempted! No, my dear, no! . . Delusion is so sweet! And the truth so terrible! . . *(Kisses him for the last time.)* Awake now! Awake free, Hermann, and throw off the yoke of my will and the yoke of my love! *(Schmidt obeys her. He regains his consciousness amid some confusion.)* You went and dozed off a little? And they've been waiting for you, my friend!

SCHMIDT *(stretching)*. Where?

YU-GEN-LI. In the studio . . . the Colonel . . . They need to bring the displays in! . .

SCHMIDT *(rising)*. Why didn't he tell me sooner? *(Exits. Yu-Gen-Li remains standing motionless by the window, watching him go off. Then her head sinks to her chest, she covers her face with her hands and shudders, crying silently. Mary and Anatole appear on the upper balcony.)*

ANATOLE *(with a book under his arm)*. Let's go over here! . . Why should we hide? . . It's so nice here: ocean, sky, all stretching off into infinity, and you here with me!

MARY *(sits on the railling)*. Only behave yourself: somebody might see us!

ANATOLE. Are we doing something so shameful?

MARY. I don't want anybody to laugh at you!

ANATOLE. But who cares if people are having a good time?

MARY. I do! . . Because it upsets me to feel so sorry for you!

ANATOLE. But am I . . .

MARY *(interrupting)*. You're too poor to allow other people to enjoy themselves at your expense!

ANATOLE *(sits in a chair)*. Let them! Can't hurt me.

MARY *(frowning)*. Hundreds of people, not nearly so good as you are, inspire respect in others, but you . . .

ANATOLE. I what? . .

MARY *(after a pause)*. You have got to study worldly hypocrisy a little better or you're not going to accomplish anything in this life!

ANATOLE. But I don't need a thing in it other than your love!

MARY *(with a grin)*. Love? Do you suppose it's so easy to love a person that *everybody* laughs at!?

ANATOLE. Who is this "everybody?" Just the fools!

MARY. The fools are in a majority, and the majority rules the world!

ANATOLE. Now, wait a minute! This majority condemns hypocrisy, but you teach it to them here.

MARY *(laughs)*. "Condemns" . . . Ha, ha, ha! . . Well, of course it condemns in the name of that very hypocrisy which is so powerful that it even allows itself to be denied for the sake of a *higher* hypocrisy!

ANATOLE. Very clever! . . The devil himself would break a leg trying to stumble through that one!

MARY *(doctrinairely)*. The condemnation of hypocrisy is nothing more than a survival from the era of Utopian teaching! Simply a polite tribute to religious antiquity!

ANATOLE. That's all?

MARY. You still refuse to see that man was given a tongue not so much to express his thoughts as to conceal them! What is the meaning, for example of *l'arriere pensee,* as the French call it? I explained it in your last lesson!

ANATOLE *(reciting)*. *L'arrière pensée* is that unspoken thought which lies concealed behind the thought expressed.

MARY. Right. And what is the purpose of masking one thought with another?

ANATOLE. It could be almost anything!

MARY. For instance?

ANATOLE. To confuse others as to your true intentions! Or to derail someone you're talking to, direct his thinking in the direction you desire! Or to provoke someone into asking a question revealing the position he secretly holds. Or—catching him off-guard with a question, thereby gaining time to come up with a good answer yourself . . .

MARY. Right. Give me an example of *l'arrière pensée!*

ANATOLE. *(thinks about it for a moment)*. Your eyes are so bright I'm afraid you have a fever!

MARY *(bewildered, raises her shoulders)*. What's the ulterior motive there?

ANATOLE. Simply that I want to feel your . . . pulse!

MARY. What for?

ANATOLE. So as to gain a pretext for touching your hand! *(Takes her by the hand.)*

MARY *(laughs in embarrassment)*. Do you like that? *(In one of the upper windows the Girl in Mourning appears and stealthily, jealously watches Anatole's attentions to Mary.)*

ANATOLE *(with a sigh)*. Yes.

MARY *(stamps her foot)*. Now there you go! This sincerity again! *(Teaching.)* He who wishes to win the heart of his fellow man must pretend to be indifferent to him!

ANATOLE *(shrieks)*. So you want to win my heart?

MARY *(taken aback)*. Me?!

ANATOLE. Of course! You are indifferent to me!

MARY. Yes, but why do you suppose I'm pretending?

ANATOLE *(sadly)*. Oh, so it's "the real thing?"

MARY. And what did you think?

ANATOLE. You said you felt sorry for me?

MARY. Feeling sorry doesn't necessarily mean loving!

ANATOLE *(with unexpected playfulness)*. But I don't believe you!

MARY. Why not?

ANATOLE. That was an *arrière pensée* on your part!

MARY. What do you mean?!

ANATOLE. Your ulterior motive was to *inflame* my passion with pretended indifference! *(The Girl in Mourning bites her lip and disappears.)*

MARY *(with feigned sarcasm)*. My poor friend, cherish your illusions! Remember that the secret of happiness is this: have as few illusions as possible, inspire as many as possible about yourself in others! *(On the first floor Gregoire, Schmidt, and O'Kay carry some models of military camouflage through the corridor into the study. The Director follows them. Under her direction they take the materials they have brought and spread them on the floor, furniture and walls of the study, as if at an art exhibition. Here is a small model of the Trojan Horse, and the* Birnham Woods—*the soldiers covered with branches—which appeared at the walls of Macbeth's castle, and a mannequin of a* modern scout, *dressed in green woods camouflage clothes and a helmet to match, and tanks looking like monsters, camouflaged alike, terrible, and destroyers painted confusing patterns, and gas masks crowning snow-colored protective cloaks, etc. From the window of the study these models spread all around appear as an amusing and sinister reminder of the* basic direction *of the play's action, symbolically underlining with their garish presence the play's* ideological foundation.

ANATOLE *(uninterruptedly continuing the dialogue with Marry, sadly nods his head)*. Now I know why the pupils of your school are having this *bal dèmasqué* day after tomorrow. They're simply exhausted from all this disciplined hypocrisy! . .

MARY *(gaily)*. So you've already heard about the ball? Now there'd be a great place for you!

ANATOLE *(dryly)*. I was already invited.

MARY. Naturally! You're the perfect embodiment of the *bare truth!* How could they get along without you! *(Yu-Gen-Li looks in the study, nods her head approvingly, and goes onto the porch. She is exotically, coquettishly robed as an Indo-Chinese dancer. Gregoire hurries along behind her, carrying a large brocade pillow embroidered with Kanji characters. While Gregoire sets up an easel and canvas sideways to the audience and facing the wall, then sits down to work, Yu-Gen-Li bares her legs and crossing them in Buddha-fashion, sits on the cushion in the pose of a seductive, artistically done piece of sculpture. The stage lighting begins to turn a sunset pink.)*

GIRL IN MOURNING *(appears on the upper balcony with a letter in her hands and turns, quite agitated, to Mary).* Excuse me for butting in! . . Here, read it! . . *(Sticks the letter in Mary's hand.)* Since you're my best friend, I should warn you! *(Mary takes the letter and looks at the signature.)*

MARY. Who's it from?

GIRL IN MOURNING. One of my girl friends . . . You don't know her . . .

ANATOLE. Should I go?

GIRL IN MOURNING *(takes his hand with both of hers and strokes it, as if apologizing, and with a saccharine smile).* Just for a minute! . . Don't be mad at me for interrupting you!

ANATOLE *(freeing his hand).* I'm not mad at all! I'm just very annoyed! *(Goes off. Both girls watch him go out, then look each other in the eye and, neither one able to hold the gaze, look down at the letter. Mary starts to read it attentively.)*

YU-GEN-LI *(to Gregoire).* The sun's going down already! Is there any point in my posing?

GREGOIRE. I could get a little done anyway! . . Smile, please!

YU-GEN-LI *(smiling).* All this smiling today is wearing me out!

GREGOIRE. Day after tomorrow you can get a rest at the party!

YU-GEN-LI. You think they'll invite me to the *bal démasqué?*

GREGOIRE. Of course! Who else is going to hypnotize everybody before the ball starts?

YU-GEN-LI. What on earth for?

GREGOIRE. To make everybody be sincere! We've been theatricalizing so much around here that . . . *(Interrupts himself.)* Move your leg a little! No, not that one! . . *(Dissatisfied with her position, he approaches her and with trembling hands alters the position of her legs.)*

MARY *(returns the letter to the girl, speaks, distraught).* How horrible! Drive somebody you love to suicide!

GIRL IN MOURNING. And all for what? Pure teasing! She was trying to attract him by being indifferent, but instead . . .

MARY. And he chose to take it all for real!

GIRL IN MOURNING. The girl "overplayed her hand a little"! . . Be careful you don't . . .

MARY *(anxiously).* Me?!

GIRL IN MOURNING. You know *who* I'm talking about! *(Mary drops her eyes.)* He's simply a "child of nature" *incapable* of understanding our little tricks!

MARY. But have I really . . .

GIRL IN MOURNING *(interrupting).* It was up to me to warn you, but that's all! *(Turns around to leave.)* Be careful! *(Shakes the letter in front of Mary's eyes.)* Let it be a lesson to you! *(Goes off. Mary sinks unhappily into a chair, "wringing her hands," then wearily stretches them out, leans her elbows on the railing and, with an expression of helpless submission to fate, sits motionless, concentrating her gaze on some steady point.)*

YU-GEN-LI *(to Gregoire, who has returned to his easel with a brush in hand).* How about a few witty remarks? Just to keep in shape!

GREGOIRE *(working swiftly).* Even without them I'm going to be famous soon.

YU-GEN-LI. How?

GREGOIRE. By killing somebody!

YU-GEN-LI. To draw attention to yourself?

GREGOIRE. Naturally! Crime is the shortest road to fame!

YU-GEN-LI. Yes, but the most expensive when the time comes to pay up!

GREGOIRE. It always costs more to go express! But then there are no delays along the way!

YU-GEN-LI. If you don't count the ones in prison!

GREGOIRE. They'll never catch me!

YU-GEN-LI. Are you sure?

GREGOIRE. I'll slay my rival with talent!

YU-GEN-LI. Ah! That's something else!

GREGOIRE. Fragrant, you might say!

YU-GEN-LI. How so?

GREGOIRE. The corpse of the enemy smells good.

YU-GEN-LI *(smiling).* I get it!

GREGOIRE. Was that witty enough?

YU-GEN-LI *(laughing).* Could have been worse! *(Junior Detective enters dressed in May's clothes and made up like a mulatto. He covers the table with an elegant cloth and smooths out the creases in it. Yu-Gen-Li, glancing at this travesty, bursts into laughter for a moment. To Gregoire, who, engrossed in his work, has failed to notice how phony the maid is.)* You've been making great strides lately!

GREGOIRE. Really? My *pictures are getting wittier?*

YU-GEN-LI. I'm talking about your wit!

GREGOIRE. And my *wit* is getting more *picturesque?*

YU-GEN-LI. Bravo! Not bad! . . *(Abramson and Phillips enter left by the footlights. They approach the center of the stage, stop below the porch steps, and then both demonstratively take out their watches.)*

ABRAMSON. Are you giving us a lesson today?

PHILLIPS *(bowing with middle-aged playfulness)*. Your aged pupils thirst for enlightenment!

YU-GEN-LI. I won't make it today! I already warned your classmates!

PHILLIPS. Tob bad! . .

YU-GEN-LI. Well! Both of you have done so well lately . . .

PHILLIPS . . . that it's all right for us to take the day off?

ABRAMSON *(sitting on the steps, to Yu-Gen-Li)*. Rest yourself, my dear! . . *(Significantly.)* You may need your strength today!

PHILLIPS *(sitting not far from Abramson on the steps, turns around, and, looking disgruntled, speaks to Gregoire)*. Were you the one that had the bright idea for everyone to come naked to the party day after tomorrow?

GREGOIRE. Naturally! Otherwise how could it be a *bal démasqué*?

ABRAMSON *(chuckling)*. I was even commissioned to find an appropriate place!

YU-GEN-LI. Meaning?

ABRAMSON. No decorations, no wallpaper, just bare walls! Art lies, you know!

GREGOIRE. Of course! And this must be the evening of *bare truth!* *(Twilight deepens.)*

ABRAMSON. I happen to have a large room ready for renovation in a warehouse in Atlantic City.

PHILLIPS *(to him, almost angrily)*. Are you still going along with this absurd game? Well, just wait! I'll show you day after tomorrow how gorgeous this *truth* is, that our snobs are all so crazy about! You'll see!

YU-GEN-LI *(with a bitter smile)*. Every opium smoker knows what "truth" is when he wakes up in the morning!

PHILLIPS *(to Abramson)*. Do you remember the story about the boy who spoke *nothing but the truth* all day until he had everybody at each others' throats? Like that . . . *(snapping his fingers, as if trying to remember)*.

ABRAMSON. Anatole Moravsky?

PHILLIPS. No, Tommy Sauce. And when he's around God forbid you should speak the truth about anything! He's such an honest detective he'll turn you in on the spot! *(Points to his neck amid growing laughter among the others. Gregoire finally observes the travesty being performed by Tommy Sauce and joins the others in laughter.)* That's what these truth-lovers are! Maids are known to gossip sometimes, but I—honest to God—am less worried about her, than for instance that truth-loving boy!

JUNIOR DETECTIVE *(bowing to him, amid barely restrained laughter by the others)*. Thank you, Mr. Phillips, very kind of you! *(Schmidt enters left by the footlights and stops, puzzled, wondering why the laughter.)*

PHILLIPS *(to the supposed maid).* Not at all, dear! . . . How did your voice get so hoarse? *(Squints his eyes and wipes his glasses rapidly.)* And how are your teeth? You took the bandage off—means it's better? Eh? *(The telephone ringing breaks off the general laughter. The Junior Detective rushes into the study.)*

SCHMIDT *(approaching Abramson).* Where have you been? I've been looking for you! . . What are you laughing about?

ABRAMSON *(gets up from the porch steps).* "A few words" again?

JUNIOR DETECTIVE *(at the telephone).* Hello! . . Right away! . . *(Leaps out the window with the receiver and hands it, with the cord all tangled up, to Yu-Gen-Li, who is still posing.)*

YU-GEN-LI *(into the telephone).* Senator Creighton? . . Two miles from here? Bravo! Oh, don't worry! Drive right up! I'm alone! All alone! . . *(Those present break out laughing at the sight of all the solitude. Gregoire hastily pushes his ease! flat up against the wall and carries the stool with his palette and brushes off left. The Junior Detective runs off into the corridor, looking for someone, at the very moment that a saddened Anatole and the Girl in Mourning, clinging to him, appear at the footlights left. They look as if they'd just come in from a walk. Pause.)* What am I doing? I'm waiting for you and . . . *(having noticed Anatole's arrival)* listening to our neighbor play some music—he's some love-smitten musician! *(The Girl in Mourning, at these words, makes a sign to Anatole to go into the house, hurriedly shakes his hand and quickly retires. Phillips, along with Gregoire, goes off after her.)* Oh, you have feelings like that, too? . . Oh, of course! . . *(Glancing sadly at Schmidt.)* Love is the one thing that can reconcile us with life! *(Pause. Anatole steps onto the porch.)*

SCHMIDT *(takes Abramson left toward the footlights).* I hope you didn't take my little outburst of jealousy seriously?

ABRAMSON. Hm . . you played the role of the jealous lover so convincingly that . . .

YU-GEN-LI. As I said, everybody's gone to the movies . . . *(Anatole disappears deep in the corridor.)*

SCHMIDT *(to Abramson).* But you knew it was only a *game?*

ABRAMSON. I'll try to think so now! *(They head toward the exit left.)*

SCHMIDT. I . . . don't love her!

ABRAMSON. Since when?

SCHMIDT. It was . . . a spell! *(They go off, talking.)*

YU-GEN-LI. That's wonderful! . . Blow your horn twice, I'll be waiting! . . *(By now the Director has appeared at the doorway accompanied by the Junior Detective, who is carrying a fantastically embroidered summer jacket and a vial of perfume with an atomizer. Yu-Gen-Li hands him the telephone receiver, and takes the jacket*

257

and vial from him. As the Junior Detective hangs up, Yu-Gen-Li stands the vial on the table, puts on the jacket with her sister's help and, businesslike, sprays herself with perfume.) He'll be here any minute! . . Tommy, bring the wine!

DIRECTOR *(correcting, with a smile).* May, not Tommy! *(Junior Detective goes off.)*

YU-GEN-LI. Yes, that's right! *(The Director turns on the lights, first on the porch, where the lamps on the ceiling flare up, and then in the study as she enters it, brightly illuminating the military camouflage models.)*

DIRECTOR. All set?

YU-GEN-LI. I guess so . . .

DIRECTOR. Well, I'm leaving! . . *(Meaningfully.)* Do you remember the Creighton strategy?

YU-GEN-LI *(coldly).* Don't worry! . . *(The Director leaves, casting an unfriendly glance at Anatole, who has appeared from the darkness in the corridor.)*

ANATOLE *(with childlike politeness).* When do we start?

YU-GEN-LI *(standing the perfume vial on the sill by the open window).* After you hear the car horn blow twice! *(Reaches through the window and takes a book from the table in the study.)*

ANATOLE. What should I play?

YU-GEN-LI. Something lyric or . . . exciting! *(Sits in an easy chair and begins reading.)*

ANATOLE. Yes ma'am . . . *(Goes out, almost colliding with the Junior Detective, who is bringing in wine, glasses, lobster salad. The Junior Detective then leaves, closing the door behind him. The Director has meanwhile appeared on the balcony above and bends over Mary with some concern.)*

DIRECTOR. What's the matter? . . You seem so upset? . .

MARY. I keep thinking . . .

DIRECTOR. About what?

MARY. . . . what is truth?

DIRECTOR. What kind?

MARY. Any kind. I know what falsehood is: pretense, camouflage, dissimulation, hypocrisy, posing, everything that you've so conscientiously taught me since childhood! But . . . what is *truth,* tell me?

DIRECTOR *(laughing condescendingly).* That which is hidden behind falsehood!

MARY. But there's falsehood everywhere! . . It's in the powder on your apparently calm face! And in the paint on my lying lips! It's in the upholstery of this so-called "antique" furniture! It's in the deception of our whole stay here, in a widow's "own" house, a widow who never had either house or husband!

DIRECTOR. What has made you so upset, tell me?

MARY. That which is called truth!

DIRECTOR. Lots of things are "called"! . . Life teaches you not to believe what things are "called." *(A car horn is heard blowing twice.)* I suffered quite enough in my youth from blind faith in what was called "truth"! . . *(Smiles.)* Speaking of *truth,* nobody really knows the truth! *(Some charming improvisations on the piano by Anatole Moravsky.)* We learn to comprehend "appearances" and not "essences"! We perceive "phenomena," and not the "numena" hidden behind the *mask* of phenomena!

MARY. But then how are we to know what "falsehood" is?! You'd have to know first what "truth" is!

DIRECTOR. We know it *relatively!*

MARY. Ach, "relatively"?! You mean, speaking concretely, that all your criticism of Anatole is only the *relative* truth, not the real truth? Yes?

DIRECTOR. Hm . . if you prefer! In any case . . .

MARY *(interrupting).* Stop! Do you hear him playing? . . Do you hear *what* he is saying with these sounds? *(Nervously presses her mother's hand.)* Is that the *truth* or isn't it? . . Is he lying now or being sincere? . . Do you hear? Do you hear how he's suffering? How he longs for me? How he loves me? . . . *(She cries. Like a good mother, the Director tries to comfort her, but having little success, sinks into meditation, standing behind her like a sentry. By the end of their dialogue the upper part of the house, beginning with the balcony where they are, is illuminated by pale moonlight, which grows brighter each minute.)*

JUNIOR DETECTIVE *(opening the door slightly on the porch, announces).* Senator Creighton!

YU-GEN-LI. Wonderful! *(Junior Detective opens wide the door; Senator Creighton walks on. She meets him halfway and extends both hands, which he, with senile haste, showers with kisses.)* I'm touched and very happy! . . You're a real knight, true to your word! . . Sit down! . . Aren't you tired? Hungry?

SENATOR *(panting).* When I see you I feel like I'm twenty again! . . I assure you—I hardly recognize myself! . . You make people young again, like a sorceress! . . *(Sits down. She fills two glasses with wine.)* But I've taken you away from your book?

YU-GEN-LI. Oh, it's nothing!

SENATOR *(looks at the cover).* What is it?

YU-GEN-LI. Snowdsen's latest play.

SENATOR. Any good?

YU-GEN-LI *(offering him a glass of wine).* Fair. I prefer for the problem to be only *presented* by the playwright, and the *solution* left to the audience!

SENATOR *(accepts the glass, shrugs his shoulders with a smile).* I don't understand the faintest thing about the fine points of the theater! *(Stands up.)* Your health! It's not too strong? *(Waits until the Junior Detective goes out.)* I'm terribly afraid of getting too aggressive around you!

YU-GEN-LI. Don't be afraid! *(They clink their glasses together.)* If we did away with alcohol, people would lose their sincerity altogether!

SENATOR. You're right. Too much temperance can easily lead to being hypocritical with one's self! And that leads to lack of self-respect. *(Drains his glass, then sits at the table next to Yu-Gen-Li.)*

YU-GEN-LI *(presenting the food)*. Would you like a little lobster? I made the mayonnaise myself! *(Puts the food on his plate.)*

SENATOR. I'm flattered! Although at my age . . .

YU-GEN-LI. It's only bad for old people!

SENATOR. Oh really?!. In that case I'll have some! *(Suddenly remembering.)* Yes! Before I forget . . . *(Takes out his wallet.)* Around you a person could forget everything! . . *(Hands her a check.)* There's what I promised!

YU-GEN-LI *(almost shocked)*. What is it?! Ah? . . What is it?

SENATOR *(seemingly timid)*. The price of this house!

YU-GEN-LI *(glances at the check)*. Did you take my little joke seriously? But where did you get the id . . .

SENATOR *(lowering his voice)*. From a secret account.

YU-GEN-LI. I'm asking you where did you get the idea I need it?

SENATOR *(hastily correcting himself)*. From a secret . . . from my wife, don't worry!

YU-GEN-LI. No, no, I won't take it!

SENATOR *(severely)*. Be so kind as to listen to your elders and obey your relatives!

YU-GEN-LI. But really . . . *(Takes the check indecisively.)*

SENATOR. I categorically demand that you be materially provided for! Do you hear? . . . I don't like poor relations! *(The Junior Detective enters with a tureen of soup covered with a plate of spicy, toasted diabli.)*

YU-GEN-LI *(overwhelmed with gratitude, almost throwing herself on the Senator's neck)*. But in that case . . . allow me, as your relation . . .

SENATOR *(making big eyes, indicating the presence of the maid)*. Tsss . . . later!

YU-GEN-LI *(finishing her remark in cool tones)*. . . . . allow me . . . to pour you a little soup!

SENATOR. Please do! *(Coughs, giving a sign to the phony maid to depart. The sounds of the piano have by now become more playful.)*

YU-GEN-LI *(serving him)*. Do you really care for . . . I just adore . . .

SENATOR *(stopping her with a glance)*. Tss . . .

YU-GEN-LI. . . . mushroom soup?

SENATOR. Oh, soup? . . Yes, very much. *(To the Junior Detective, harshly.)*

Bring me some ice water! . . *(The Junior Detective leaves. The Senator watches him depart, then, trembling lightly with lust, turns to Yu–Gen–Li.)* I interrupted you, dearest, forgive me! *(Presses his lips leech-like to her hand. She embraces him tenderly about the neck, then presses against his old lips in imitation of a kiss thirsting for eternity. The Senator forces himself loose and breathes heavily.)* Now I can understand Kaiser Wilhelm!

YU-GEN-LI *(amazed)*. Who? Kaiser Wilhelm?!

SENATOR. Yes! And not only him but all those people who warned us against the "yellow peril."

YU-GEN-LI *(playfully)*. Oh that's it? You mean *against* "Asia"? *(Points to herself.)*

SENATOR *(embracing her)*. I'm against her now! *(Kisses her and whispers something in her ear.)*

JUNIOR DETECTIVE *(appears above, in the doorway leading to the balcony)*. He sent me for some water! . . What should I do?

DIRECTOR. Take him some right away!

JUNIOR DETECTIVE. But it's already on the table!

DIRECTOR *(confused)*. Are you sure? . . What are they talking about?

JUNIOR DETECTIVE. He said he doesn't like poor relations.

DIRECTOR. Well naturally! Who does? . . And what else? . . What did she say about our Institute? About my plans?

JUNIOR DETECTIVE. Nothing yet!

DIRECTOR. Are you sure?

JUNIOR DETECTIVE. Quite. *(The Director, nervously clasping her hands, walks away from Mary. Only then does Mary notice the Junior Detective.)*

MARY. Who is that? . . And where is May? *(Recognizes him.)* Is that you Tommy? *(Laughs nervously.)* But why should I be surprised when everything around here is pure deception! The very air is so full of it, it makes you want to throw up! You can't breathe under your mask! *(Director gives a sign to the Junior Detective to leave.)* Tell me, are those stars up there real or fake? . . Don't you know? . . And that moon—is it really a moon or only an electric light? *(Presses her hands to her breasts.)* Is this a heart beating in me, a real heart, not a windup toy, that hurts me so much? *(Cries. The Junior Detective, looking distraught, goes off with the Director.)*

YU-GEN-LI *(pouring some more for the Senator)*. Drink some, please!

SENATOR. I'm so drunk already from your presence!

YU-GEN-LI *(embarrassed)*. And you're trying to make me drunk with your compliments? *(Calls.)* May! . . Where can she be? *(The Junior Detective enters with a pitcher of water, which he places right under the Senator's nose, and then takes away the dirty dishes.)*

ANATOLE *(unexpectedly appearing on one of the second-story windows)*. Mary! . .
    Why are you crying? Mary!
MARY *(turns around at the sound of his voice)*. Is that you, Anatole? . . . And who's
    that playing downstairs? . .
ANATOLE. Nobody.
MARY. What do you mean?
ANATOLE. It's the pianola.
MARY. What?!
ANATOLE. The pianola . . . the mechanical piano . . .

CURTAIN.

ACT THREE

The scene is one of the rooms being prepared for renovation in a large furniture warehouse. The wallpaper is torn off, the floor is a mess, the plaster on the ceiling is discolored. Ten or twelve lights hang in a perfect row from the ceiling. They have dusty office shades and no more than half of them are turned on. They illuminate mainly the downstage area. Only two walls of the room are visible, they form a corner upstage. In the left wall, which is much longer than the right, there are two doors: a small entrance door by the footlights, and a large one, some distance away, through which one may see a stairway going off up. In the right wall there is a locked door with pieces of paper tacked on it, notices of some kind.

As the curtain rises, two workmen are carrying off the last of the period furniture covered with wrapping paper into the door leading to the stairs. They walk around to the left of the stairs.

The Girl in Mourning walks in from the entrance door with a small package in her hands.

GIRL IN MOURNING. Where is Mr. Abramson? He wanted to be here before nine . . . *(Suddenly recognizes a familiar face in one of the approaching workmen.)* Ah! It's you Prince! . . *(They shake hands.)* How do you like your new job here? Isn't the heat too much?

PRINCE *(smiling).* I'm used to it! . . I used to work in a lumber yard in the USSR, you know!

GIRL IN MOURNING. Really? . . Good for you! *(Fans herself with a handkerchief.)* It's so humid today! . . There'll be a storm!

PRINCE *(almost boastfully).* And on the railroads too! That's harder! Freight trains!

GIRL IN MOURNING. Imagine that! And they say princes are no good for anything!

PRINCE. Pure libel! *(He joins the other workers in carrying out the last pieces of furniture. The room is now bare except for a large, unpainted table left, an unupholstered couch by the right wall, and a half-dozen "Louis XVI" armchairs wrapped in paper.)*

GIRL IN MOURNING. Has everyone arrived by now?

PRINCE. Only Mr. Abramson so far.

GIRL IN MOURNING. Where's he?

PRINCE. Upstairs in his office! *(Another workman brings a broom and sweeps up.)* What's in that package there?

GIRL IN MOURNING. A bathing suit! Today is the "bare truth party" you know, the *bal démasqué*!

PRINCE. I heard! I'd like to come too!

GIRL IN MOURNING. Why not? All you have to do is subject yourself to a little hypnotism first! So as to suppress any false sense of shame!

PRINCE. Hmph! They'd do better to have something to drink first, that would loosen up their tongues!

GIRL IN MOURNING. You're wrong—wine inflames the imagination so much that the drunkard's sincerity is overdone! *(Abramson comes down the stairs.)* Good evening, Mr. Abramson!

ABRAMSON. Good evening to you! Or just the opposite, it's so muggy you can hardly breathe! *(To the workers.)* Well? All set? All cleaned up?

PRINCE. Almost—we can't pack any more in there! *(Points to the room under the stairs.)*

ABRAMSON. Well, that's all right! Let a few pieces stay here. *(Teasing, to the Girl in Mourning.)* Well? . . Do you like the place? Does it predispose one to "truth?"

GIRL IN MOURNING. Absolutely! No wallpaper, no paneling, no decorations of any kind . . . Only we need a little more *light,* so that the bareness of the truth will be even more naked!

ABRAMSON *(approaching the switch and turning on all the lights).* Certainly! How's that?

GIRL IN MOURNING. Marvelous!

ABRAMSON *(to the Prince).* You're not all worn out? . . This *role* isn't too tough for you?

PRINCE *(with a big, stupid grin).* The perfect role for me! Took me years to work out! One might say I broke in this role—excuse me—like an old shoe! *(Takes his reply for wit and unexpectedly bursts into loud laughter. But, seeing no support among the others, sinks into silent embarrassment.)*

ABRAMSON. Oh well, I'm glad to see you like it here so much—I see you're enjoying yourself! *(To the other workman who has finished sweeping up and taken his cap, ready to leave.)* Go ahead, Sam! . . The Prince can handle it himself if need be. *(The workman bows and goes off left.)*

PRINCE *(slightly touched, to Abramson).* You don't have to be formal with me! The title is embarrassing to both of us! . .

ABRAMSON. But you are a *real* Prince, aren't you?

PRINCE. What if I am? Who needs it?

GIRL IN MOURNING *(playing up to him).* Your future wife!

ABRAMSON *(puts his hand on the Prince's shoulder).* Something ought to be *real* in this "antique furniture" warehouse!

PRINCE *(stupidly).* What for?

ABRAMSON. To inspire trust . . . by analogy! *(Laughs tenderly in his face. Enter Yu-Gen-Li left, in an evening gown, with a cross instead of a medalion on her neck and with a large lady's handbag in her hand. Abramson rushes over to meet her, barely restraining his excitement, and kisses her hands passionately. Meanwhile the Girl in Mourning is leading the Prince upstage, toward the door to the stairs, and is arguing about something with him in vigorous half-whispers.)*

ABRAMSON *(not loudly)*. Oh, at last! I've been waiting for you!

YU-GEN-LI. But we just saw each other a little while ago!

ABRAMSON. An eternity! . .

YU-GEN-LI *(leughing)*. Your watch tells funny time!

ABRAMSON. You were the one that changed the gears in it!

YU-GEN-LI. Have you seen the evening news yet? I didn't have time.

ABRAMSON *(joyfully)*. No! But they already telephoned me: everything went "according to plan." *(Turning around.)* Prince, be a good boy and run get us an evening paper. *(The Prince goes off left.)* I am so grateful to you, so obliged . . . *(Interrupting his own words, to the Girl in Mourning.)* Would you like to use my office? *(Points to the stairs.)* My radio is at your service! *(The Girl in Mourning goes off up the stairs; Abramson quickly locks the entrance door and then, with a sudden movement, embraces Yu-Gen-Li and covers her face, neck and bosom with kisses.)*

YU-GEN-LI *(stunned)*. What's the matter with you? Let me go! Are you insane?

ABRAMSON. You're the one that drove me insane!

YU-GEN-LI. Get hold of yourself! . . That's enough! . .

ABRAMSON *(getting hold of himself)*. Forgive me! . . I'm getting the figures mixed up! "Quality" ran off with "quantity" and I'm in your hands! . .

YU-GEN-LI. What on earth are you . . . I don't understand you at all!

ABRAMSON. I don't understand either!

YU-GEN-LI. *(straightening up her rumpled dress)*. What kind of barbarism is that?!. Like some savage!

ABRAMSON. *You* were the one who brought out the savage in me! *You* aroused the barbarian in me!

YU-GEN-LI *(angrily)*. What do you mean?

ABRAMSON *(gasping)*. Have you ever heard of a second youth? You have? There was a *time* of youth, but no *youth* itself! . . And suddenly here it is! "First," "second," "third"—isn't it all the same? It's youth! You gave me real youth and I'll give you everything for it! Only don't take it away from me, because he who hasn't known youth will find his old age unbearable! *(His voice falters, he turns around quickly, puts his handkerchief to his eyes and blows his nose amid his tears.)*

YU-GEN-LI. What's happened to your nerves? I'll call a doctor!

ABRAMSON. Nonsense! I'm all right now! Got over-excited! Or rather, got too much piled up in here . . . *(points to his chest)*. And so . . . it burst.

YU-GEN-LI. It's the humidity . . . It's so hot today! . . There's so much electricity stared up in the air . . .

ABRAMSON. No, no! *Here* is where it's all stored up! Here! *(Takes out his wallet.)*

YU-GEN-LI *(amazed)*. Where? In your wallet or in your chest?

ABRAMSON. Both places! I'm speaking of what I *owe* you! *(Opens his checkbook and starts to write.)*

YU-GEN-LI. Drop it! . . Later! . .

ABRAMSON. Oh no! . . Do you like my house at Yellow Beach? You do? You said that . . .

YU-GEN-LI. Drop it!

ABRAMSON. Fine! I'm ready I Right at your feet!

YU-GEN-LI *(laughing)*. Impossible! The house isn't yours any more! *(Takes a check from her handbag.)*

ABRAMSON How so? . .

YU-GEN-LI. I sold it . . . in accordance with your instructions! *(Hands him the check.)*

ABRAMSON. To who? *(Reads the signature on the check.)* Creighton? . . Give him the check back!

YU-GEN-LI. But the house isn't his anymore!

ABRAMSON. Whose is it then?

YU-GEN-LI. Mine. *(Softly.)* He gave it to me as a present.

ABRAMSON. So that's it?!. Then, in that case, I'll buy it back from you! *(Gives her back the check.)*

YU-GEN-LI *(takes the check)*. All right, but on condition that . . .

ABRAMSON. No conditions! Once it's mine again I'll give it to you!

YU-GEN-LI. What for?!.

ABRAMSON. For Creighton! *(She raises her shoulders in astonishment and looks inquisitively at him.)* For winning the "customs war."

YU-GEN-LI. Ah!

ABRAMSON. I hope we're all even now? *(Kisses her hand.)*

YU-GEN-LI. Not entirely.

ABRAMSON *(startled)*. I made a mistake in the figures?

YU-GEN-LI. You forgot the commission!

ABRAMSON *(striking himself on the forehead)*. That's right! For selling the house! *(Writes out a check. Someone knocks energetically at the door left, which was locked earlier by Abramson.)*

YU-GEN-LI *(bursting into laughter)*. No, I see you're really in love . . .

ABRAMSON. Out of my mind! *(Hands her the check.)*

YU-GEN-LI. . . . if you're getting your figures mixed up. *(She unlocks the door.)*

ABRAMSON *(with agonizing joy)*. Of course! Just what I was saying! *(Enter the Prince and the Seductive Maiden, both with newspapers in hand.)*

PRINCE *(handing Abramson a newspaper)*. Here you are, sir! *(Abramson instantly immerses himself in the newspaper. The Prince ingratiatingly turns to Yu-Gen-Li.)* I too would like to . . . lay it on the old line! I've got so much piled up inside me! . . Could I ask you?

YU-GEN-LI. . . . to hypnotize you? You still don't believe in yourself? Even in this role?

PRINCE. I'm embarrassed . . . I want to do a good job of it, so to say. *(Clarifies his thought with a vague motion of his hand, forming it into a fist.)*

YU-GEN-LI. All right! . . Call Fanny down here and let's begin; before the others get here! It's getting late!

PRINCE. Right away! *(Runs off upstairs, accompanied by the Seductive Maiden.)*

ABRAMSON *(looking as if something very important were on his mind, pointing to the newspaper)*. Paralyzed!

YU-GEN-LI. Who? . Creighton? . .

ABRAMSON *(with a hypocritical sigh)*. You overdid it, my dear!

YU-GEN-LI. Poor old man! . . And did he ever swagger! . . The Don Juan *mask* was more than he could handle!

ABRAMSON. No, he was punished not so much for that, as for his *political mask!*

YU-GEN-LI. "Political"?

ABRAMSON *(whacking his hand on the newspaper, pointing to the article)*. It turns out that he wasn't against raising the tariff on imported furniture at all.

YU-GEN-LI. What do you mean? *(Glances at the newspaper.)*

ABRAMSON. He only *pretended* to be, in order to arouse public opinion!

YU-GEN-LI. You mean I "defanged" him all for nothing, *he* bought me a house all for nothing, and you gave it to me all for nothing?!. *(The Girl in Mourning, the Seductive Maiden, and the Prince come down from the office upstairs.)*

GIRL IN MOURNING *(with newspaper in hand)*. Did you read the article about our Institute? The one about the Military Camouflage Exhibition?

YU-GEN-LI *(to Abramson)*. Oh yes! My sister expected the article today!

GIRL IN MOURNING *(reads with great animation)*. " . . . the displays made by Madame Daryal's Theatrical Institute will undoubtedly be of special inter-est . . ." *(Enter from left a talkative band consisting of Gregoire, Schmidt, Phillips and several male and female pupils of the Military Theatrical Institute. Some of them are in sports jackets; most of them have in their hands small packages, purses, or travelling bags. Having noticed that they are interrupting the reading, the new arrivals stop talking for a moment, listen to its general drift and also look the room over.)* "This institute, as you all know, may be favorably distinguished from others by its *relation* to life, where the struggle for our vital interests develops amid the same *camouflage* as in real *war*. One may boldly predict that sooner or later the enormous national significance for the education of our youth by this kind of Theatrical Institute will be recognized. Even the ancient Greeks understood the advantages in diplomatic matters of appointing *actors as ambassadors*. And this is indeed quite understandable . . ."

GREGOIRE *(having read the newspaper over the Girl in Mourning's shoulder)*. Philosophy marches on! Stop it! It's not worth hearing!

SCHMIDT. I already read the article.

GREGOIRE. The main thing is that there wasn't a word about the actual painting of the displays! I'm not talking about myself, naturally, but about justice!

SCHMIDT. I'm willing to believe you, since this is our "Truth Party."

GIRL IN MOURNING. *(gives up the newspaper to the others and shouts triumphantly)*. The main thing is that the press now *recognizes* us! And with what *sincere* enthusiasm!

ABRAMSON *(taking Yu-Gen-Li aside)*. How much did you have to pay for this "recognition"?

YU-GEN-LI. A quarter per line!

ABRAMSON. Ahh! "Sincerity" is getting pretty steep these days! *(The Junior Detective and Anatole enter left. Their appearance is met by exclamations of "Ah! Anatole!" . . "Maestro Moravsky"! . . "Why so late"? . . "And where's Mary? . ." Meanwhile Abramson leads Yu-Gen-Li to the door right which leads to the hall and opens it, explaining something to her.)*

SCHMIDT *(not without malice)*. Well, ladies and gentlemen, now we can rest easy about the *truth*—even about the most absurd and indecent truth: Anatole Moravsky is now here and that says it all! *(General hearty laughter.)*

YU-GEN-LI *(raises her voice)*. Anyone who would still like to *insure* his truth with *hypnosis*—come over here! *(Points to the door right.)* Who would like to?

PHILLIPS. All of us! . . All . . . *(In gay commotion, nudging each other, the Military Theatrical Institute pupils gradually disappear beyond the door right.)*

YU-GEN-LI *(listens to what one of the female pupils tells her in confidence, then shouts in the direction of those departing)*. Don't be afraid! I won't take away any more of your will power than is necessary for a *bal démasqué!*

ANATOLE *(breaks off from the end of the line of departing pupils and approaches Yu-Gen-Li with great determination)*. I wanted to ask you . . .

YU-GEN-LI (*interrupting*). What? You too? Why *you*? . . Aren't you afraid of my spell anymore?

ANATOLE. I've decided to be "like everyone else." It's all just a joke isn't it? Pure fun?

YU-GEN-LI (*cheerfully intriguing*). Well, it all depends on *what* you call fun!

ANATOLE (*hastily, in confidence*). Mary and her mother are right behind us: hide the newspaper, otherwise Madame Daryal will read about this Creighton business and won't leave Mary here at the party with us!

YU-GEN-LI. What?!. You're asking me to *conceal* the truth?! *You*—the knight of Truth and the incarnation of Sincerity? . . Anatole, I hardly know you!

ANATOLE. Shhh . . that's them! (*Indicates the entrance door, from which a second later Mary and her mother emerge.*)

MARY. We're not late? (*Looks around the room.*) And Anatole is here?

DIRECTOR. Good evening! . . What a day! . . I don't know when it's been so muggy! . . (*Examines the room through her lorgnette as if it were some sort of dive.*)

MARY. Where is everybody? . .

ANATOLE. Over there! (*Motions to the right.*) Why are you so late?

MARY (*quietly putting down the package she brought with her*). Mama wanted to find another costume for me—she thought this one was too frank!

ANATOLE. But that's what we want here! This is, you know, the *bare truth* ball!

DIRECTOR (*with a crooked smile*). This is *your* party, Anatole?

ANATOLE. Not only mine! (*To Mary.*) Let's go over there! (*Takes her by the hand and leads her to the door right.*) They're all there!—Waiting for you!

MARY (*breaks off, runs back to her mother and kisses her*). Goodbye! . . Remember now, you promised to leave me here by myself! Otherwise . . .

DIRECTOR. Don't worry, my friend!

MARY. . . . otherwise you'd inhibit everybody! (*Runs off with Anatole right.*)

DIRECTOR (*looks around the room one more time, stops her sister*). Just where are you going to hide me here?

YU-GEN-LI. You really want to stay?

DIRECTOR. What kind of question is that? You yourself suggested it! . . Guaranteed it at that!

YU-GEN-LI. Hide over there when they come in. (*Indicates the open door leading to the stairs.*) Then I'll hypnotize them into not seeing you! So that you'll be invisible Agreed?

DIRECTOR. All right.

YU-GEN-LI (*nodding her head at her sister and Abramson*). In five minutes I'll be at your service! (*Disappears beyond the door right.*)

DIRECTOR. Where does that door go? *(Indicates the door right.)* Why has everybody disappeared back there?

ABRAMSON. The office. They went back there to change clothes!

DIRECTOR. Or, more precisely, to take them off? . . Don't forget: if the costumes are *too frank* I'm going to take my daughter straight home!

ABRAMSON. How do you define "too frank"?

DIRECTOR *(smiling with condescension)*. The same way you do, no doubt! An unnecessary abundance of the truth insulting to morality!

ABRAMSON. Are you trying to say that an abundance of falsehood is more acceptable?

DIRECTOR. In any case . . .

ABRAMSON *(not allowing her to finish)*. I get it: you're afraid of some sort of excess at this party?

DIRECTOR. "Excess"?!. I have too much confidence in my pupils; especially in this batch.

ABRAMSON. You're proud of them, I noticed, just like I am of a new *batch* of furniture!

DIRECTOR *(with a smile)*. Very clever.

ABRAMSON. Do you think so? *(Takes one of the "Louis XVI" chairs and tears off the wrapping.)* And what would you say, for example, about this actor? Does he really do a poor job of simulating his origin? The true quality of the age of Louis XVI? All the lustre and finery of the eighteenth centory? . . The whole batch is like that and each one's better than the next!

DIRECTOR *(laughing)*. It's only a shame they can't talk!

ABRAMSON. What's the point of talking all the time! . . On the other hand just look *(points to the chair)* how beautifully he beckons you to be embraced by his arms! How eloquently he tempts you to sit in his lap or to lean against his soft back! . . Charming! *(At these last words he sinks into the praised chair with a feeling of enormous satisfaction.)*

DIRECTOR *(laughs)*. So then, according to you, there's no big difference between *your* product and mine?

ABRAMSON. There is! Only not in your favor! My "creations" don't feel anything, while yours . . . *(Draws his hands apart and grows silent.)*

DIRECTOR *(with a frozen smile)*. Go on! . .

ABRAMSON. Do you think it's easy to live all the time in the atmosphere of war, not trusting anyone *completely* and deceiving everyone *beginning* with one's self?

DIRECTOR. Alas! That is the *necessity* that existence imposes upon us!

ABRAMSON. Do you think that it is necessary to *acknowledge every* necessity?

DIRECTOR. Each of your questions is more amazing than the last!

ABRAMSON. "Which foot do you lead off on? Show me!" they said to a centipede one time . . . The centipede thought it over and . . . couldn't budge
from the spot!

DIRECTOR. So, let everyone go his own way and not worry about forward
motion? . . In other words: down with the *elaboration* of our born talents for
mimicry, dissimulation, hypocrisy?!

ABRAMSON. Yes, but what is one's *personal* experience worth in comparison
with our whole *heritage* of experience? For example, my veins flow with
the blood of a people with such enormous experience that it has nothing to
learn from your school!

DIRECTOR *(with a sigh)*. Poor Gen! . .

ABRAMSON. . . . it's even dangerous! You could get all mixed up, like the
poor centipede!

DIRECTOR. But only those who lack a "heritage of experience?" Isn't it true,
that from the *moral* point of view, you don't have to . . .

ABRAMSON *(interrupting)*. Oh, from the moral point of view, it's better to
forget morality altogether in the theater of war! Otherwise excuse me, it's
all too clever—"honest swindling," "truthful lying," and "moral deception"! Less sin!

DIRECTOR *(laughing none too gaily)*. Are you going to advise me to take myself
and my morals off to the desert?

ABRAMSON. What for? You stay here, and send your morals off to the
desert!

YU-GEN-LI *(enters right, and closes the door quickly behind her, turns to her sister)*.
Hide!

DIRECTOR. Already?

ABRAMSON. Not in the desert I hope?

DIRECTOR *(caustically)*. I'm not that righteous! *(To her sister.)* Did you apply
group hypnosis? *(Goes off through the door leading to the stairway and disappears
from sight.)*

YU-GEN-LI. Except for Anatole, naturally . . .

ABRAMSON. Well, what?

YU-GEN-LI. It was rather difficult, but he finally succumbed. Get away from
the door, please: I'm going to bring them in in a minute. *(Abramson walks off
left while Yu-Gen-Li opens wide the door at right, revealing those who have come for
the "bare truth" ball in single file. Most of them are in bathing suits; the Prince has
on only work pants, revealing his torso and bare feet; Phillips has on a coat with all the
buttons buttoned; Gregoire stands out, dressed in black trunks and a skin-colored
jersey, on the front of which is painted a heart, lungs, spleen and intestines, and on the
back of which is a backbone with a kidney on each side and ribs, and headgear consisting*

of a rubber bathing cap with convulutions of the brain drawn on it. Yu-Gen-Li, stepping aside from the door, commands not loudly, but authoritatively.) Come over here and line up! *(The hypnotized throng, with half-closed eyes and expressionless faces, enter the room in single file and halt at the wall right.)* When I clap my hands three times, you will awake, remembering your urge for sincerity and my instructions not to hesitate to express it . . If I raise my hands this way *(shows the appropriate gesture)* it means: freeze where you are, in complete obedience to my commands. Do you hear? . . And now, look over this way: Abramson is here, but he won't inhibit you at all, any more than his friend, whom you must not recognize or take any account of. *(Leads the Director forth by the hand.)* Here she is! . . *(Pause. No reaction on the faces of the hypnotized throng: just as if they were being shown empty space. Yu-Gen-Li raises her voice.)* Attention! . . *(Claps her hands distinctly three times, after which everyone immediately comes to life, vying with each other in exchanging insignificant interjections and filling the stage in a confused mass: some of them sit relaxed at the table, others sprawl on the couch, still others gather around Gregoire, whose costume has attracted great attention.)*

GIRL IN MOURNING. What sort of idiotic costume is that? . . How disgusting!

GREGOIRE. Dope! Can't you see that my costume transcends nakedness?

PRINCE. And what is the cap supposed to depict?

GREGOIRE. A brain with convolutions.

SCHMIDT. Bravo! Now nobody can call you a "brainless idiot."

GREGOIRE. But they can call you one, starting with me. *(Hearty laughter.)*

SCHMIDT. Very funny! I'd transcend your stomach with my fist, but I wouldn't want to soil my hands.

GREGOIRE. Are you afraid to?

PRINCE *(dancing about).* Oh, it's a real pleasure to listen! Pour on the coal! Cuss 'em out! Let's get it off our chests!

JUNIOR DETECTIVE *(to him).* Very interesting! . . You have some reason for cursing, but why should we?

PRINCE. What "reason" do I have? The same one as everybody else, don't I?

JUNIOR DETECTIVE. You're consumed by envy, and we aren't!

PRINCE. Envy?!

JUNIOR DETECTIVE: Of course! You got kicked out of the Institute and turned into a flunky . . . But why should we curse?

PRINCE. Peasant woman's logic!

JUNIOR DETECTIVE *(teasing him).* Would you like me to send you out for some matches! All right? . . Or else for some of last year's snow! I'll give him a tip for it, then take it right back again!

PRINCE. Oh, you wretched creature! . . Peasant woman's logic again, peasant woman's thinking! No wonder you like to wear dresses all the time.
JUNIOR DETECTIVE. You numbskull!
PRINCE. Or maybe you really are a broad? Eh? C'mon now, confess!
JUNIOR DETECTIVE. What's it to you? Want to get married? Forget it, guy! No one would marry an idiot like that!
PRINCE *(to all)*. Hear that, fellows? He admits it himself!
PHILLIPS *(to the Prince)*. And have you read, Prince, about . . . "bisexuality?"
PRINCE *(peasant-like)*. Wha-at?
PHILLIPS. About how each of us has both *male* and *female* in us? Each masked by the other! Haven't you heard?
PRINCE. So? . . Let's find out! Let's take our clothes off, fellas! . . *(Makes an attempt to tear off Junior Detective's costume, for which he receives a resounding slap in the face. The Prince answers with a blow of his fist and the fight is on. Gregoire and the Seductive Maiden also start struggling. The latter, however, falls with a mad shriek on the couch after a few seconds, tearing her leg from the tenacious claws of her adversary. Amid his "bestial" kisses he has been repeating "moor tiu-tiu, moor tiu-tiu, moor tiu-tiu." Yu-Gen-Li, who has been standing the whole time with her sister and Abramson at left near the table in the pose of the silent observer, now runs up to the center of the footlights and raises her hands, making the gesture she demonstrated earlier. Everyone freezes on the spot except Gregoire; he continues his apparently reflex action lisping, "moor tiu-tiu, moor tiu-tiu.")*
YU-GEN-LI *(shouting)*. Stop! . . No violence now, or you'll cripple each other!
GREGOIRE *(tears himself away from the Seductive Maiden's foot with some difficulty, still mumbling "moor tiu-tiu, moor tiu-tiu . . .")*
YU-GEN-LI. Shh! . . What does "Moor tiu-tiu" mean? . .
GREGOIRE. I don't know . . it's what I call the thing about women that arouses me!
YU-GEN-LI. Fine! . . . Call it anything you want, only no raping! *(Claps her hands three times.)* The Unmasked Ball continues . . . *(All return to their former animated condition. The Director says something in Yu-Gen-Li's ear with which the latter readily agrees. Yu-Gen-Li leaps onto one of the chairs by the table and addresses everyone in a loud voice.)* Ladies and gentlemen! So as to avoid all this interference, wouldn't you like to take turns telling each other off? . . Like at an examination? Eh? *(Voices: "Hell with examinations!" "We didn't come here for that!." "Nonsense!" "Trying to force us into something!")* You wouldn't? All right! Only don't expect to make any sense out of a total mess!
ABRAMSON *(loudly and with conviction)*. She's right, my friends! It's in your own interests! *(Voices: "Rubbish!" "Examinations!" etc.)*

SCHMIDT *(outshouting the others).* Why rubbish? Let everybody have a chance to be heard!

JUNIOR DETECTIVE. It's true, you can't hear anything with all the uproar!

PRINCE. And you, pig, you're used to eavesdropping when it's a little quieter? *(Hearty laughter.)*

MARY. My aunt is right, everybody! . . Let's play examination, it could be a lot of fun!

SCHMIDT. Give it a try!

ANATOLE. Give it a try! *(Voices: "Terrific!" "Go ahead, gang!" "We'll try any-thing!" "It's true I don't like to be interrupted!" etc. Meanwhile Yu-Gen-Li, Abramson, and the Director set up a table and chairs left, about the way it was in Act 1, Scene 2, and sit down. Yu-Gen-Li is at the middle of the table, Abramson is to her left and the Director to her right. Phillips struggles up to the table, in spite of the mighty efforts of Schmidt to keep him back.)*

PHILLIPS. I'm going to sit with the examiners! . . Allow me! I was promised the Department of Rhetorical Arts.

SCHMIDT. You? Where? At the Military Theatrical Institute?

PHILLIPS. Yes.

SCHMIDT. By whom?

PHILLIPS. By the Director.

DIRECTOR. When did I "promise" you that?

SCHMIDT *(indignant).* I'm in line for the job!

PHILLIPS. You?!. Milksop?!. And teach eloquence?!

DIRECTOR *(to him).* But when did I . . .

YU-GEN-LI *(to her, interrupting).* He can't hear you! You're not even here as far as he's concerned.

DIRECTOR. Oh, I forgot!

YU-GEN-LI. My sister didn't promise you, she was just considering it!

PHILLIPS. Oh, so that's it?! Tell your sister that in that case she's an old liar, a hypocrite and Balaam's ass!

ABRAMSON. Wait a minute! But you used to speak much better of her?!.

PHILLIPS. It's only now that I see the wicked intrigue and it's all clear now! *(With bitter laughter.)* I'm not good enough for her daughter!

SCHMIDT. But I am! And so I ask you to be more respectful of my future mother-in-law!

PHILLIPS *(fumes and sputters).* You miserable puppy! And you even demand respect? I For whom? Why? For a nasty old idiot! So you'll get your money! . . That's the way youth is growing up! Nothing more to be said: that's who the old folks are supposed to learn from these days.

JUNIOR DETECTIVE *(supported by his comrades).* Don't hold back! . . To hell with this toothless mumbling! . . Old timer, you stink! Down with the garbage!

PHILLIPS *(turns to him, bristles up like a dog).* I'm not garbage, but you are! Because you're the old ones, not me! *(Loud laughter among the young ones present.)* There's nothing to bray at! Do you know what youth is? A young age? An unwrinkled face? Crap! . . You can live so *little,* but experience so *much* that in your face and soul you become a real old man! Youth is noted for high ideals, romanticism, bright hopes for the future, irrational sacrifices! And *what* do you have? Crude materialism, egotism, a sporting attitude toward love and a betting machine attitude to sport, cynicism which allows nothing higher than altitude records by airplanes! And the pitiful careerism of the bureaucrat for whom a political party is just another bureaucratic opportunity, that is, a guarantee of food in your mouth—nothing more! *(He has to really blast out the final phrase, since a roar of indignation and protests has been steadily rising among the young people present.)*

PRINCE. You ugly old monster! What are you driving at, you today! *(Spits acrimoniously.)*

JUNIOR DETECTIVE. "Irrational sacrifices" he wants?! "High ideals?!"

GREGOIRE. So they can start a new war?! The old folks didn't kill off enough young people in the last war?! Not enough?!

PRINCE *(advancing on Phillips).* Oh, you double-dirty scum!

SCHMIDT. We know perfectly well why the older generation starts wars! We know *who* profits from these trashy ideals! We know *who* makes money on the destruction of nations! Who it is that *must* avoid any younger competitors!

PRINCE *(with the support of his comrades).* To hell with this old garbage! . .

YU-GEN-LI *(breaking into the hubbub, in a loud voice).* Not so loud! . . *(Silence for a moment.)* It was decided to play "examination" and here you are playing "meeting," aren't you? . . *(To Schmidt.)* What would you like to say?

SCHMIDT. I maintain that the older generation . . .

YU-GEN-LI *(breaking in).* Talk about *yourself!* That would be more interesting.

SCHMIDT. *(apprehensively).* Why start with *me,* instead of going by the alphabet? My name starts with "S" . . .

YU-GEN-LI. What's the difference? . .

ABRAMSON. That's pedantry for you!

YU-GEN-LI. Speak out! We're all listening.

SCHMIDT. About what?

YU-GEN-LI *(with affected unconcern).* Oh, anything you please . . . Well, suppose . . . do you love me or not?

SCHMIDT. I don't. *(A pause.)* You're not my type! . . And the main thing is, a man has to play the part of some idiot around you. I don't like that at all.

YU-GEN-LI. So-o . . . *(After a moment of hesitation.)* And . . . what do I mean to you?

SCHMIDT. Usually, nothing.

YU-GEN-LI. How so?

SCHMIDT. It's to my *advantage* to be your friend: you're a *clever broad,* who knows how to trade on everything, beginning with your own "exoticism!" On top of that, for a while I thought you were *rich,* until your husband's property in China was all confiscated and it turned out I wouldn't get a nicke! out of you.

DIRECTOR. And do you love Mary? *(Schmidt does not react to the question.)*

YU-GEN-LI. And do you love Mary?

SCHMIDT *(with sincere enthusiasm).* A marvelous girl! Not stupid at all! And such piquant little feet that it's a real pleasure to touch 'em . . . True, her hands are a bit damp! But I suppose that's more from feeling than from T. B. In any case it's a great consolation that her old lady has some dough! So that I can count on a dowry for sure . . .

YU-GEN-LI. Do you want to marry her?

SCHMIDT. Why not?

MARY *(approaching him, mocking).* Doesn't it frighten you that the *erotic side* of marriage gives out, according to statistics, in two or three years?

SCHMIDT. So? We live by *illusion,* not by statistics! . . If you analyze everything you risk leaving the inn hungry! In the "temple of love" it's the same way. Maybe "piquant feet" don't really exist! I mean, there's no question of any "piquant feet" in the morgue or on the operating table!

YU-GEN-LI. What are you driving at?

SCHMIDT *(looking at Mary).* We've got to *believe* in the *eternity* of our love, and not in statistical data! . . We were born into this world thanks to illusion, not calculation. At the time of our creation our parents were inspired by illusion, like "piquant feet" and other extravagances like that!

YU-GEN-LI *(deeply ironic).* You're repeating *my very* words! But now it's *your* truth we're interested in.

SCHMIDT. What more truth do you need?

MARY *(nervously enthusiastic).* The completely bare truth.

GREGOIRE *(hollowly).* Transcending nakedness . . .

SCHMIDT. For instance?

ABRAMSON. For instance, what drove you to acquaint me with Madame Daryal and Senator Creighton and to turn over your mistress to me? *(This question produces a "sensation" among those present, who all quiet down in expectation of some scandal.)*

SCHMIDT *(softly, in the tense silence).* I supposed that you would give me a job as legal adviser, Madame Daryal—the position of teacher in her Institute, and . . .

YU-GEN-LI *(controlling herself with difficulty).* . . . and I what?

SCHMIDT. Freedom. *(Pause.)*

ABRAMSON. M'yesss . . .

DIRECTOR *(with a sigh).* I like his frankness! It all comes out so business-like, logical . . . *(Claps of thunder are heard.)* Oh! There's a storm coming this way.

GREGOIRE *(stands in front of Schmidt, bows rather too freely to the examiners).* Allow me a word or two . . . about those "piquant feet!" As a specialist, so to say!

PRINCE. You scum!

ABRAMSON. We're all listening.

GREGOIRE. Why is it that artists love to paint nudes so much? Aesthetics, you say? Baloney! Don't let anybody kid you! . . It's because the body arouses lust.

PRINCE. He's discovered America!

GREGOIRE. And what is more *real* than lust in this world? That's why we fall for "piquant feet," *we're hanging on to reality.* Now, you wonder—why did I become an artist? *(In proper tone for an answer.)* So as to be around a lot of nudes . . . Why do I want to be famous? *(Same tone.)* So as to conquer the female heart with greater ease, because that's simple for a "celebrity." Why do I practice wit and self-assurance? Because wit and insolence are always very successful with the weaker sex.

ABRAMSON *(somewhat hurt).* You mean, that artistic considerations had nothing to do with the portrait you did . . . of your teacher? *(Indicates Yu-Gen-Li with his eyes and a turn of the head.)*

GREGOIRE. God forbid! What do you take me for? . . . I did it first, so I could contemplate the *piquant décolleté* of the lady in question, and second, so I could foist the painting off on you: I could expect to hit you for a lot, since you're an "admirer" of the model.

PRINCE *(spitting).* Money!

ABRAMSON *(to Gregoire). How much* do you figure?

GREGOIRE. Nothing less than a thousand.

ABRAMSON *(writes out a check).* Two hundred is enough, sight unseen.

GREGOIRE *(laughing).* But wait a minute, I haven't finished the painting yet!

ABRAMSON. *And I'm not going to allow you to finish!* Or else you're likely to finish your life off. *(Hands Gregoire a check, amid general laughter, whereupon the latter walks off upstage.)*

PRINCE *(takes Gregoire's place).* I've been listening to you citizens, and I'm astounded at the deposits of lies hidden in your bourgeois souls! . . I see through this falsehood both as an *aristocrat* by birth and as a *proletarian* by position. And this is what I have to say, from the viewpoint of the two different classes I belong to. Don't dig, damn you, in your shallow souls in search of "absolute truth!" Forget it! *Separate individuals* can't find it. One person's truth is the opposite of somebody else's and the end result is pure subjective self-deception! . . *(Meanwhile Gregoire starts whispering loudly with the Seductive Maiden and others nearby, and starts setting up the dances. The Prince tries to hush him up.)* Shhh! . . Only the collective comprehends the *real* truth, basing it on economic foundations, that is, in other words, the *proletariat,* dedicated to the *baring* of social relations, and not to their *masking.* Understand that?!. And so I say to you: down with the bourgeois lie of rotten capitalism! . . Down with the exploiters in the sheep's clothing of benevolence! . . Long live the *real truth!*

ABRAMSON. Bravo, Prince! . . They turned you into a great record player back in the old country. I congratulate you from the depths of my heart on your *new role. (To the Director.)* And thank you for the recommendation: I just happen to be needing a good agitator at the factory right now.

PRINCE *(showing his teeth in self-satisfaction, softly asks the ones around him).* How about that? Didn't expect that? Really told them that time?

GREGOIRE *(puts on a striped sports jacket and takes off his rubber cap).* Ladies and gentlemen, let's go dance in the office! There's a radio there. *(Takes the Seductive Maiden upstairs. Two other couples also go off with them.)*

GIRL IN MOURNING *(pressing against Anatole, shouts to those around her).* Today is the *bal démasqué,* you know! *(Drags Anatole to the stairs, but he is definitely not giving in to her advances.)*

PHILLIPS *(trips as he gallops over to the Prince. Nervously fingers the buttons on his coat. Can't decide whether to unbutton them or not.)* Do you want the "real truth?" Do you? You're not *afraid* of it?

PRINCE *(spits, with a grin).* I'm no coward.

PHILLIPS. Then realize that the real truth lies in concealing the real truth by any means possible! *(Laughter is heard all around.)* There's nothing to bray at, you jackasses! . . You'd do better to tell me what *truth* gave you *that was worth anything,* besides inventions which made wars all the worse! . . But *illusion* gave you everything, beginning with the blessings of dreams, and ending with the gifts of religion, music, poetry, and art in general!

JUNIOR DETECTIVE *(stretching himself).* Not another "lecture?"

SCHMIDT *(to Phillips)*. Oh, stop it! After all, you didn't get the Eloquence Department!

PHILLIPS *(not paying any attention)*. Magnificent is the actor who acts out a beautiful conception! But despicable is the spy masked in the name of "treacherous truth." Magnificent is the doctor who gives hope to the incurably ill! But horrible is the doctor who kills him with the scientific truth. Magnificent is the preacher who promises us all eternal life! But what do you say about the atheist who takes away that eternal life in the name of some useless, tawdry truth?!. To hell with the truth!!! They should pitchfork it into the hottest fires in hell! . . It should be damned for all eternity!!! With all my being I declare I am against the truth! . . There! . . *(Takes off his glasses, takes out his false eye and puts them on the table.)* There! . . *(Takes the wig off his bare skull disfigured by a crimson scar.)* There! . . *(Takes out his uppers and lowers.)* Just look how beautiful the truth is! Gaze on it! Enjoy it! Get your fill of it! *(With a burst of laughter takes off his coat, revealing his body, barely covered with underwear. He has a large support around his waist and false arms and legs, giving the impression of a cripple made up of artificial pieces. Everyone is horrified and draws away from him, lapsing into silence, broken only by the gay foxtrot which has suddenly sounded out above.)*

YU-GEN-LI *(frowning, gets up, and amid the general confusion, quickly helps Phillips to put his coat on again)*. Don't! . . Why should you be doing this? . . Put your clothes on! *(Picks up the wig from the floor and sticks it on his head.)* Make yourself *presentable!*

PHILLIPS *(putting the eye in and his glasses on)*. Right—"presentable!" "Presentable" in the name of sacred *illusion!* . . *(Puts his teeth in. Those standing by the double doors to the stairway close them, after which the music can hardly be heard.)*

ANATOLE *(to the Girl in Mourning who is cuddling up to him)*. What's the matter with you? Leave me alone!

GIRL IN MOURNING. I'm so afraid! I'm terrified!

ANATOLE. That's no reason to fall all over somebody! Go away!

GIRL IN MOURNING. You're so rude! Here I am looking for protection, while you . . .

ANATOLE. You're looking for an excuse to get closer to me.

GIRL IN MOURNING. And if so! . . Am I so repulsive?

ANATOLE. You are. *(Pause.)*

GIRL IN MOURNING *(amid malicious snickers)*. What an ungrateful beast you are!

SCHMIDT *(mocking)*. A beast "not of this world"!

GIRL IN MOURNING. And I, the idiot, *saved* a first-class bastard like that from suicide?!

SCHMIDT *(jeering)*. "A child of nature!"

MARY *(to the Girl in Mourning)*. When did you ever "save" him?

GIRL IN MOURNING *(breathless, "humiliated and insulted")*. When?! That time when I was worried about your being so cold to him! . . Or rather—about its effect! And I forged a letter as if all this teasing was going to cause a suicide! . . I suppose you've forgotten? I read it to you!

MARY. *Whom* did you "save" him for—you or me?

ANATOLE *(to Mary)*. If you only knew what awful things she said about you!

MARY *(to her)*. You? . . my best friend?!.

GIRL IN MOURNING *(provocatively)*. Who told you I was your friend? . .

MARY *(to her)*. You swore you were!

GIRL IN MOURNING. Idiot! Do you suppose a pretty little wench like you could be a friend of somebody with my looks?!.

MARY. You mean . . . you mean . . .

GIRL IN MOURNING *(mimicking)*. "You mean," you're a fool and that's all!

MARY. So that's it? And a nasty schemer like you tried to rob me of a pure soul like him?! *(She presses against Anatole.)*

GIRL IN MOURNING. But you don't love him!

MARY. I don't?!

GIRL IN MOURNING. Of course not! Otherwise you'd treat him entirely differently! But since you love only yourself, imagining that there isn't anybody better than you . . .

MARY *(interrupting, in a frenzy)*. I don't love Anatole?!. And you dare to say such a thing after all my outpourings, my complaints, my tears?!.

GIRL IN MOURNING. Well, you simply staged that little comedy so you could be touched by your own position! That's all there is to it!

MARY. So, that's it?!!

GIRL IN MOURNING. You don't have to scream!

MARY *(stamps her feet, becoming hysterical)*. Shut up! . . You shut up this instant or I won't be responsible for myself! You know very well *how much I love* Anatole! You wretched creature, you know I love, love, love, love him more than anybody else! *(Through her tears she embraces Anatole about the neck.)* I won't give him up to anybody! Not for anything! Nobody is going to take *advantage of his innocence and idealism!* Nobody in the whole world! I won't allow it! I'd rather die! . . *(Sobs out loud like a little girl.)*

ANATOLE *(pressing her to himself)*. Darling! . . At last I hear what I've been waiting for so long! . . The labor it took to produce this truth! . . But I don't regret it, not one bit! Since I'm getting it all now, with interest! . .

MARY *(astounded, draws away from him, wiping her eyes hurriedly)*. Wait a minute . . . You don't sound like the same person anymore . . . it's not you at all! . . Or does it just seem that way? . . This is the ball of surprises!

ANATOLE *(correcting her)*. "The ball of denouments!" *(Embracing her with great finesse and preparing for the "kissing pose," shouts to someone off in space.)* Eh, cameraman, capture this moment! Get cranking while we're still in the mood! *(Kisses Mary.)*

MARY *(backing off again)*. What are you doing? . . I *hardly recognize* you!

ANATOLE. Really? I'm flattered! . . But I'm still the same person! *(Laughing, he takes a calling card out of his pocket.)*

MARY. What do you mean?

ANATOLE *(holding the card in readiness, speaks with the voice of a gentleman of the world, utterly restrained in any expression of emotion)*. I beg of you, assure your mother as to the "means" of her future son-in-law! . . Here is my card! *(Puts his card on the table.)*

GIRL IN MOURNING *(looks with Abramson at the card)*. "Anatole Billing," on stage and screen—Anatole Moore . . ."

ABRAMSON *(after a brief moment of general bewilderment)*. Son of the famous banker?!. Fifth Avenue, near Forty-Fourth?

ANATOLE *(bowing and clicking his heels politely)*. The very one.

GIRL IN MOURNING. The movie actor?

ANATOLE. Precisely.

ABRAMSON *(to an embarrassed Director and a laughing Yu-Gen-Li)*. How could you and Mary be so deceived?

ANATOLE. That is more a question of my *talent* than their *fault!*

MARY *(almost crying)*. You wretch! You killed "him"! You killed him!

ANATOLE. *Who* are you talking about?

MARY. The one I loved so dearly! *(Covers her face with both hands.)*

PHILLIPS *(reproachfully, walking up to Anatole)*. What did you do that for?

ANATOLE *(self-justifyingly)*. Money won't guarantee *love!* And I fell in love with Mary, practically at first sight.

PHILLIPS. So?

ANATOLE. I didn't want anybody to love me for my money! And so when I met Mary at Tommy's relatives' *(puts his hand on the shoulder of Junior Detective, who seems embarrassed at these words)* I resorted to *falsehood* so as to discover the *truth* later and . . . *(hesitates)*.

ALL *(in a chorus)*. And? . .

ANATOLE. . . . and I asked him to give her the impression I was a failure, making a living giving music lessons.

YU-GEN-LI *(as if to herself)*. So that's it?! *(Stares steadily at the Junior Detective right up to the speech he makes, brought on by the stare.)*

SCHMIDT *(plainly envious)*. A stupid *movie stunt!* What's original about that?

ANATOLE *(parrying the thrust, like a master fencer)*. Its application in real life.

ABRAMSON. May I congratulate you on your success?

ANATOLE. Of course! People in real life are more naive than on the screen!

MARY *(agitated)*. You're certainly sure of yourself! I loved you, taking you for sombebody else!

ANATOLE. I know that. But one can't *conquer* a girl's heart without *putting on a mask.* You taught me that yourself!

JUNIOR DETECTIVE *(his nerves shot, nearly sick, looking like a man who expects the worst)*. Ladies and gentlemen, enough *revelations!* Quite enough, by God! So now it's all clear! It's getting late . . . Everybody wants to dance . . .

YU-GEN-LI *(laughing with disgust)*. Aha! . . "The thief's cap's afire!" As soon as it's his turn, then it's "enough?!"

PHILLIPS. "The cat knows who ate the canary!"

PRINCE *(grabs the Junior Detective by the arm with both hands, with malicious glee)*. Trying to sneak out, you scoundrel?! You won't make it this time! Grab him boys! *(They surround the Junior Detective and amid general jeering laughter shower him with remarks like: "Trapped, eh?" "What have you got to say for yourself, you stoolie?" "Sneaky bastard!" "Spy!" "Sycophant!" "Gossip-monger!" "Stool pigeon!")*

YU-GEN-LI. Shhh! . . *(They all quiet down.)* Tell us, Anatole, after you met Mary, did Tommy render any *other* services to you?

ANATOLE *(with a grin)*. Who would try to slip into an enemy fort without his own *spy!*

JUNIOR DETECTIVE *(breaking loose from the grip the Prince and others have on him)*. Let me go! . . I want to go home, I don't want to stay here with this crummy bunch!

PRINCE. You lie, you carrion! Beat him up! . . We've caught the spy, brothers! Get him!

ALL *(throwing themselves on the Junior Detective.)* Knock him down! Beat hell out of him! Damned spy! Swine! Hurray! . . We trapped the spy! . . *(The Junior Detective is knocked off his feet, thrown to the floor and they begin to beat him up.)*

YU-GEN-LI *(jumps up and shouts, making the special gesture with both arms raised)*. Stop it! . . Get away from him! . . No violence! . . *(The battle ends. The radio offstage stops.)*

JUNIOR DETECTIVE *(his clothes torn to shreds, rubs his bruised and scratched limbs, snapping out through his childish tears, like a mongrel!)*. Scoundrels! . . Arrant knaves! . . When they need to find out something or "slip a knife" into somebody, then they come running to me for help! But now to beat me up?! Right?! Would you like me to name names? . . You were afraid I'd give you away, so you decided to send me on to the next world?

YU-GEN-LI. Who asked you to *spy on anybody?* Aren't you lying to us?

JUNIOR DETECTIVE. *Everybody,* beginning with the Director!

YU-GEN-LI. What?!

JUNIOR DETECTIVE. Here's what—she even got me to spy on you!

DIRECTOR *(leaps up and angrily pounds the table).* You villain! . . Shut up this instant, you traitor! *(A mighty clap of thunder is heard. Pause.)*

YU-GEN-LI *(restrained, softly).* He can't see you or hear you. *(On the threshold of the door leading to the stairs appear a group of pupils, headed by Gregoire, who had gone off to dance.)*

DIRECTOR *(to her sister).* You were *the one who made him* a traitor! You!

GREGOIRE. What's going on? What's all the racket?

DIRECTOR *(peremptorily).* I have too much confidence in Tommy, whom I have always treated like a son! He loves me as much as everyone else does! Consequently . . .

YU-GEN-LI *(interrupting).* Are you so sure the pupils love you?

DIRECTOR. Ask them if you don't know!

YU-GEN-LI *(to all).* Ladies and gentlemen! This is the Ball of Truth! Be honest. Tell me how you like the woman who spares nothing for you, gets you scholarships and . . . *(Cuts herself off, quickly takes a check out of her purse and puts it on the table in front of her sister.)* Incidentally, here's another contribution! I just raised it! *(After a moment of confusion among the pupils.)* So, do you love Madame Daryal? . . Yes or no?

ALL *(as one).* No!

DIRECTOR *(takes firm grip of herself, laughs dryly, turns to her sister).* It's just amazing how hypnotism can be misused! Ai-yai-yai, where are your ethics?! But this time you and your indiscriminate hypnotism have made a big mistake: the evidence is my own daughter's vote against me.

YU-GEN-LI. I assure you that . . .

DIRECTOR *(interrupting, with a sarcastic grin).* Don't make empty assurances! Everyone knows how much my daughter loves me!

ABRAMSON *(loudly, distinctly, with a polite smile).* Tell us, Miss Mary, do you love your mama *very much?*

MARY. No.

DIRECTOR. What?!!

MARY. I'm bound together with her *by blood,* that's true, but . . . you're not really asking about that love, are you? And she taught me such a mistrust of people, of the world, of love itself, that . . . Now I don't trust either her or her system of education . . .

DIRECTOR. What's she talking about? . .

MARY. You can't force people to spend their whole lives hiding in the "trenches"! Youth is drawn to valor, risk, self-sacrifice!

DIRECTOR. What is it you want?

MARY *(doesn't hear the question).* When I fell in love with Anatole I began more and more to dream that Mama died, leaving behind a legacy immune to criticism, that I would go to her grave every day with flowers and cry, cry endlessly at my being a poor orphan . . . *(Presses her handkerchief to her eyes? Anatole consoles her.)*

DIRECTOR *(barely restraining her furious anger).* So that's it?! Enough! There's a limit to everything! *(To her sister.)* This hypnosis will cost you! I don't allow anyone to come between me and my daughter!

YU-GEN-LI *(to her pupils, authoritatively, hypnotically).* Shut your eyes and ears! Be perfectly indifferent to everything! There! . . *(The pupils comply with her demand, remain where they are perfectly motionless, with eyes closed and with their hands over their ears. Yu-Gen-Li turns sharply to her sister.)* You don't believe me?! No?! You don't believe that that's their *own truth,* and not my suggestion?! All right then! Look! *(Puts the cross around her neck to her lips.)* I swear to you by this!

DIRECTOR. What are you swearing by?! *(Tears the cross away from her. Another deafening clap of thunder is heard.)* I'm not going to let you hide behind that mask!!!

YU-GEN-LI. Get hold of yourself! . . You're mad! I swore by a *symbol,* not a mask.

DIRECTOR. Don't lie! You've turned the symbol into a mask. There are enough frauds hiding behind it without you! . .

YU-GEN-LI. But listen . . .

DIRECTOR *(choking with anger).* What do you want to prove today?!. What?!. What do I need your *truth* for—one-side, subject to doubt, is that *human* truth or the result of the *swine* living in man?!! Can it be that I have actually wasted my efforts on some egotistical, puny rabble *(pointing to those hypnotized)* among whom a mother can't even trust her own daughter! If that's the real truth, then God damn every last one of them, right here and now!!! May God's lightning strike them dead on the spot!!! *(A terrible clap of thunder is heard.)*

ABRAMSON *(rises and anxiously goes over to the Director).* Calm down, for God's sake! . . Would you like me to bring you some water?

DIRECTOR *(cools down and, a little shocked, raises her eyes upward).* This is too much! . . Almost *on purpose!*

ABRAMSON. A terrible storm!

DIRECTOR. This stupid thunder! No sense of measure! Like some shabby *theater,* some *melodrama* . . . Too much of a coincidence! . . *(Blows her nose and wipes her eyes.)* I got all *carried away* because of the storm! An actress' temperament! . . *(Offers her hand to Yu-Gen-Li.)* Forgive me! . . It's stupid to pay any attention to tasteless theatrical effects . . . I took the whole *game* for truth! . . If it had all been *serious,* then they'd have had such an orgy, such a slaughter, that . . . The instinct for hypocrisy saved them . . . Maybe we've just had the real examination *today?* . . Eh? . . In any case I became even more convinced today in the great importance of an *education in the theatrical rules of life!* . . *Sincerity* is fine for angels! But for the swine, with their bestial inheritance, it's simply dangerous and detestable! Brrr . . . Well, I'm going now! I don't wish to inhibit the young people.

ABRAMSON. Aren't you afraid of the rain?

DIRECTOR *(laughing).* No, of the thunder, and only when it gets this theatrical! *(Hands the cross to her sister.)* Don't be angry at my nerves!

YU-GEN-LI *(pushing the check toward her which has been lying on the table).* Don't forget the money! *(Puts the cross in her purse.)*

DIRECTOR *(kisses her sister and takes the money).* Now the only thing left is the Creighton strategy and . . . we'll be all even! . . They say he's more influential than ever! *(To Abramson.)* Goodbye! . . *(Nodding in the direction of those hypnotized, to Yu-Gen-Li.)* I trust you'll hypnotize them into *completely forgetting* . . . what has happened?

YU-GEN-LI. Well, of course! *(The Director goes off left, accompanied to the door by Abramson and Yu-Gen-Li. When the door has closed behind her they both wearily and anxiously exchange glances of mutual understanding and quickly return to the group of those hypnotized. From a distance are heard the last claps of thunder of the passing storm.)*

ABRAMSON *(seizes Yu-Gen-Li's arm, stops her and points toward those hypnotized).* How *terrible* it is, just the same!

YU-GEN-LI. What? . . Hypnosis? . .

ABRAMSON. Like robots!

YU-GEN-LI *(grinning).* Do you think most of us are very *different* from them? . . Alas! . . Every one of us, with only a few exceptions, is under the *hypnotic spell* of newspapers, advertisements, learned authorities, religious superstition, gossip, and such trash.

ABRAMSON. But in that case it would be so easy to change life for the better!

YU-GEN-LI. Of course! All we have to do is get all the hypnotists to agree with one another.

ABRAMSON. You mean—all the social theorists?

YU-GEN-LI. I mean all those for whom a mass like that *(points to those hypno-tized)* is merely an *invitation to conquest!* Merely the *Theater of Eternal War!* *(She hands her purse to Abramson and walks around the hypnotized people, one at a time, tenderly pulling their hands away from their ears.)*

ABRAMSON. What a heavy purse you have! What in the world's in it?

YU-GEN-LI. The skeleton keys to paradise.

ABRAMSON. "Skeleton keys?"

YU-GEN-LI *(sighing with sad irony)*. The real keys aren't given to poor sinners.

ABRAMSON. May I look?

YU-GEN-LI. Go ahead. *(He sits on the couch, opens the purse and draws out in amazement some opium pipes, a tiny alcohol lamp, long needles, and so forth. Mean-while Yu-Gen-Li stands in front of the hypnotized ones and commands them.)* Attention! . . *(A pause.)* Before you return to your usual roles, forget the revelations about each other you *dreamed about!* . . Do you hear? . . *(Claps her hands thrice.)* Awake! . . *(Sits on the couch, tries to conceal from the eyes of her pupils the smoking instruments which have been taken from her purse. The hypno-tized ones open their eyes, come to, stretch a little, and ask one another: "Well, what now?" "What time is it?" Everybody here?" "This is taking a long time! . . "Was there a storm?" "Who said the dance was starting?" "What's going on?")*

GREGOIRE. Let's go upstairs! Enough of this! Everybody dance! This is the Unmasked Ball.

ALL. Let's go! Let's go! *(The noisy bunch heads for the stairs. The first couple to go is Gregoire and the Seductive Maiden, the second is the Prince and the Girl in Mourn-ing, the rest rush off behind them. Last to leave are Hermann Schmidt, Mary, and Anatole Moravsky.)*

ANATOLE *(takes Mary familiar by the arm and whispers something in her ear, then laughs)*. I tell you: don't believe in just any truth!

MARY. You've really changed today!

SCHMIDT *(to her)*. Let's dance!

ANATOLE *(too familiarly, defiantly)*. I asked her first!

SCHMIDT. So that's it?! *(They disappear, arguing. Yu-Gen-Li takes a soft piece of opium from her purse and rolls it into a small ball, to be put on a needle.)*

ABRAMSON *(following the departing ones with his eyes)*. Which of the two will she prefer? What do you think?

YU-GEN-LI. Isn't it all the same! *(Takes one of the pipes in hand, sets the alcohol lamp on a nearby chair and lies on the couch.)* Please turn off some of those annoying lights! *(Points to the ceiling.)*

ABRAMSON *(turns off almost all the lights except for the one over the couch)*. You're not jealous of *him* any more?

YU-GEN-LI *(smiling wanly, lights the alcohol lamp)*. He doesn't really exist, you know! *(Above, a radio is heard—jazz—not too loud, tender, and voluptuously exciting.)*

ABRAMSON *(politely)*. Am I disturbing you? . . Should I go?

YU-GEN-LI. On the contrary! You can help me. *(Offers him the needle with the ball of opium on the tip.)*

ABRAMSON *(growing somber, unsure what to do)*. You don't really want me to . . .

YU-GEN-LI *(interrupting)*. Don't argue! *(Gives him the needle.)* And when I fall asleep, take me home!

ABRAMSON *(none too confidently)*. But what good is it to conquer others when you have no control over yourself? . .

YU-GEN-LI *(with crooked, mocking lips)*. Our *internal theater of military operations* is more complicated than you might think.

ABRAMSON. Can the passion for drugs be so powerful, that . . .

YU-GEN-LI. Winning for the sake of winning is nonsense, when it's giving in that promises happiness! *(Suddenly loses control of herself, convulsively turns and lies face down, buries her face in the back of the couch and cries silently.)*

ABRAMSON *(alarmed)*. What's the matter?

YU-GEN-LI *(wipes her eyes, raises herself on one elbow and sniffs)*. Oh, nothing . . . Just nerves! . . It makes me mad that *he* pretends so much *here*! . . Like some stranger . . . I know perfectly well how *much* he loves me over *there*. *(Draws Abramson to her, and, with his help, begins smoking.)*

ABRAMSON. Where is "over there?"

YU-GEN-LI *(calming down)*. Over there . . . far from the roar of our *eternal war*! . . far from this endless war of the sexes, with its betrayals, victims, and endless grief! . . Over there, where sweet butterflies flutter around the dragon's jaw! . . in the world of long desired and *certain* truth. *(Puffs greedily. Her lips gradually relax into a beatific smile.)*

CURTAIN.

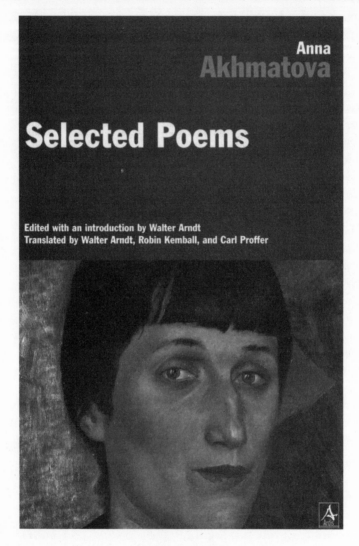

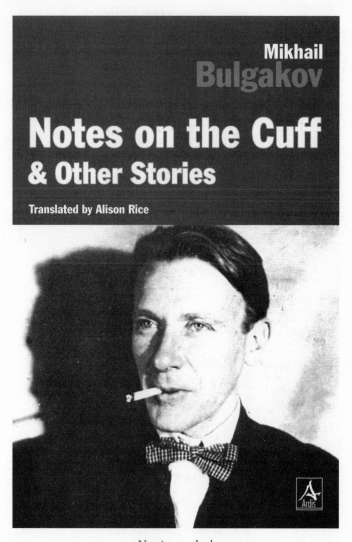

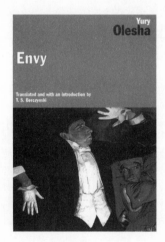

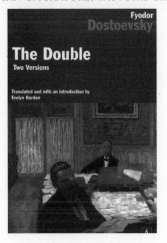

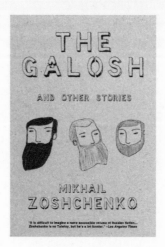

THE GALOSH
Mikhail Zoschenko
Translated by Jeremy Hicks
978-1-59020-211-1 • PB • $14.95

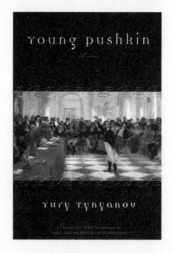

YOUNG PUSHKIN
Yury Tynyanov
Translated by Anna and Christopher Rush
978-1-58567-962-1• HC • $35.00

THE OVERLOOK PRESS
New York, NY
www.overlookpress.com
www.ardisbooks.com